Trapped in the Middle?

THE INITIATIVE FOR POLICY DIALOGUE SERIES

The Initiative for Policy Dialogue (IPD) brings together the top voices in development to address some of the most pressing and controversial debates in economic policy today. The IPD book series approaches topics such as capital market liberalization, macroeconomics, environmental economics, and trade policy from a balanced perspective, presenting alternatives, and analyzing their consequences on the basis of the best available research. Written in a language accessible to policymakers and civil society, this series will rekindle the debate on economic policy and facilitate a more democratic discussion of development around the world.

OTHER TITLES PUBLISHED BY OXFORD UNIVERSITY PRESS IN THIS SERIES

Economic Development and Environmental Sustainability
Edited by Ramón López and Michael A. Toman

Stability with Growth
Joseph E. Stiglitz, José Antonio Ocampo, Shari Spiegel, Ricardo Ffrench-Davis, and Deepak Nayyar

The Washington Consensus Reconsidered
Edited by Narcís Serra and Joseph E. Stiglitz

Capital Market Liberalization and Development
Edited by José Antonio Ocampo and Joseph E. Stiglitz

Industrial Policy and Development
Edited by Mario Cimoli, Giovanni Dosi, and Joseph E. Stiglitz

Time for a Visible Hand
Edited by Stephany Griffith-Jones, José Antonio Ocampo, and Joseph E. Stiglitz

Debates on the Measurement of Global Poverty
Edited by Sudhir Anand, Paul Segal, and Joseph E. Stiglitz

Overcoming Developing Country Debt Crises
Edited by Barry Herman, José Antonio Ocampo, and Shari Spiegel

Good Growth and Governance in Africa
Edited by Akbar Noman, Kwesi Botchwey, Howard Stein, and Joseph E. Stiglitz

The Economic Development of Latin America since Independence
Luis Bértola and José Antonio Ocampo

Law and Economics with Chinese Characteristics
Edited by David Kennedy and Joseph E. Stiglitz

Intellectual Property Rights
Edited by Mario Cimoli, Giovanni Dosi, Keith E. Maskus, Ruth L. Okediji, Jerome H. Reichman, and Joseph E. Stiglitz

Global Governance and Development
Edited by José Antonio Ocampo

The World Economy through the Lens of the United Nations
Edited by José Antonio Ocampo, Anis Chowdhury, and Diana Alarcón

The Future of National Development Banks
Edited by Stephany Griffith-Jones and José Antonio Ocampo

Trapped in the Middle?

Developmental Challenges for Middle-Income Countries

Edited by

JOSÉ ANTONIO ALONSO
JOSÉ ANTONIO OCAMPO

OXFORD
UNIVERSITY PRESS

OXFORD
UNIVERSITY PRESS

Great Clarendon Street, Oxford, OX2 6DP,
United Kingdom

Oxford University Press is a department of the University of Oxford.
It furthers the University's objective of excellence in research, scholarship,
and education by publishing worldwide. Oxford is a registered trade mark of
Oxford University Press in the UK and in certain other countries

First Edition published in 2020
Impression: 1

Published in the United States of America by Oxford University Press
198 Madison Avenue, New York, NY 10016, United States of America

British Library Cataloguing in Publication Data
Data available

Library of Congress Control Number: 2020939199

ISBN 978-0-19-885277-3

DOI: 10.1093/oso/9780198852773.001.0001

Printed and bound in Great Britain by
Clays Ltd, Elcograf S.p.A.

Contents

List of Figures

List of Tables

List of Acronyms

ADB	Asian Development Bank
AEC	ASEAN Economic Community
AFAS	ASEAN Framework Agreement on Services
AfDB	African Development Bank
AFTA	ASEAN Free Trade Area
AIA	ASEAN Investment Area
AIIF	Asian Infrastructure Investment Bank
ARTC	Automotive Research and Testing Center
ASEAN	Association of South East Asian Nations
ATRI	Automotive Testing and Research Institute
BANCOLDEX	Banco de Comercio Exterior de Colombia
BEPS	Base Erosion and Profit Shifting
BIO	Belgian Investment Company for Developing Countries
BNDES	Banco Nacional do Desenvolvimento
BRICS	Brazil, Russia, India, China, and South Africa
CABEI	Central American Bank of Economic Integration
CACM	Central America Common Market
CAF	Development Bank of Latin America (Corporación Andina de Fomento)
CAR	Capital Account Regulation
CARICON	Caribbean Community and Common Market
CATARC	China Automotive Technology and Research Center
CDB	Caribbean Development Bank
CDC	Commonwealth Development Corporation
CIS	Commonwealth of Independent States
COFIDES	Compañía Española de Financiación del Desarollo
CORFO	Corporación de Fomento de la Producción
CRIATEC	Brazilian Seed Capital Fund
DAC	Development Assistance Committee (OECD)
DBSA	Development Bank of Southern Africa
DCF	Development Cooperation Forum
DEG	Deutsche Investitions—und Entwicklungsgesellschaft
DFI	Development Financial Institutions
DPL	Development Policy Lending
DVA	Domestic Value Added
DVC	Domestic Value Chain
EAP	East Asia and Pacific
EBRD	European Bank for Reconstruction and Development

ECLAC	UN Economic Commission of Latin American and the Caribbean
ECOSOC	UN Economic and Social Council
ECOWAS	Economic Community of West African States
EECA	East Europe and Central Asia
EEU	Eurasian Economic Union
EFSI	European Fund for Strategic Investment
EFTA	European Free Trade Association
EIB	European Investment Bank
EIBG	European Investment Bank Group
EU	European Union
FCL	Flexible Credit Line
FDI	Foreign Direct Investment
FDN	Financiera de Desarrollo Nacional
FINAGRO	Financiamiento del Sector Agropecuario
FINDETER	Financiera de Desarrollo Territorial SA
FINNFUND	Finnish Fund for Industrial Cooperation
FMO	Nederlandse Financierings-Maatschappij voor Ontwikkelingslanden
FSAP	Financial Sector Assessment Programs
FUNTEC	Scientific and Technical Development Fund
FVA	Foreign Value Added
GDP	Gross Domestic Product
GNI	Gross National Income
GPEDC	Global Partnership for Effective Development Cooperation
GVC	Global Value Chain
GVCR	Global Value Chains Report
HDI	Human Development Index
HICs	High-Income Countries
HIPCI	Highly Indebted Poor Countries Initiative
IADB	Inter-American Development Bank
IBRD	International Bank for Reconstruction and Development
ICRG	International Country Risk Guide
ICT	Information and Communication Technologies
IDA	International Development Agency
IFF	Illicit Financial Flow
IFU	Investment Fund for Developing Countries
IMF	International Monetary Fund
IPCC	International Panel on Climate Change
IPEA	Institute of Applied Economic Research
IPG	International Public Goods
IPR	Intellectual Property Rights
IsDB	Islamic Development Bank
ISO	Infrastructure Standard Organization
KATECH	Korea Automotive Technology Institute
KATRI	Korea Automotive Testing and Research Institute
KfW	Kreditanstalt für Wiederaufbank

LAC	Latin America and the Caribbean
LAIA	Latin American Integration Association
LARF	Latin American Reserve Fund (FLAR in Spanish)
LDCs	Least Developed Countries
LGFV	Local Government Financial Vehicle
LICs	Low-Income Countries
LMICs	Lower Middle-Income Countries
M&A	Merger and Acquisition
MAI	Malaysian Automotive Institute
MARGMA	Malaysian Rubber Glove Manufacturers' Association
MARPMA	Malaysian Rubber Products Manufacturers' Association
MDB	Multilateral Development Banks
MDGs	Millennium Development Goals
MDRI	Multilateral Debt Relief Initiative
MENA	Middle East and North Africa
MICs	Middle-Income Countries
MIT	Middle-Income Trap
MNC	Multinational Company
MSMEs	Micro, Small, and Medium Enterprises
MTR	Marginal Tax Rates
NAFINSA	Nacional Financiera SA
NAFTA	North America Free Trade Agreement
NAM	North America
NBER	National Bureau of Economic Research
NDB	New Development Bank
NDBs	National Development Banks
NIS	National Innovation System
NORFUND	Norwegian Investment Fund for Developing Countries
ODA	Official Development Assistance
OECD	Organisation for Economic Co-operation and Development
OeEB	Oesterreichische Entwicklungsbank
OEM	own equipment manufacturing
OPIC	Overseas Private Investment Corporation
PCL	Precautionary Credit Line
PERs	Public Expenditure Reviews
PPP	Purchasing Power Parity
PROPARCO	Promotion et Participation pour la Coopération Économique
PTA	Preferential Trade Agreement
PTR	Public Testing and Research
QI	Quality of Infrastructure
R&D	Research and Development
RPG	Regional Producer Goods
RPIC	Rubber Products Industry Club
SA	Southern Asia
SACU	South African Customs Union

SBI	State Bank of India
SDGs	Sustainable Development Goals
SDR	Special Drawing Rights
SDRM	Sovereign Debt Restructuring Mechanism
SEGIB	Secretaría General Iberoamericana
SEWDFUND	Swedish Development Finance Institution
SIFEM	Swiss Investment Fund for Emerging Markets
SIMEST	Società Italiana per le Imprese allËstero
SMEs	Small and Medium-Sized Companies
SOFID	Sociedade para o Financiamento do Desenvolvimento
SPF	Social Protection Floor
SSA	Sub-Saharan Africa
TAI	Thailand Automotive Institute
TFP	Total Factor Productivity
TIWB	Tax Inspectors Without Borders
TOSSD	Total Official Support for Sustainable Development
TVE	Technical and Vocational Education
UAE	United Arab Emirates
UDEAC	Economic Union of Central Africa
UMICs	Upper Middle-Income Countries
UNCED	United Nations Conference on Environment and Development
UNCTAD	United Nations Conference on Trade and Development
UNDP	United Nations Development Programme
UNIDO	United Nations Industrial Development Organization
UNU-WIDER	United Nations University-World Institute for Development Economics Research
VAT	Value Added Tax
WEO	World Economic Outlook
WHO	World Health Organization
WTO	World Trade Organization

List of Editors and Contributors

Editors

José Antonio Alonso is professor of Applied Economics at the Universidad Complutense de Madrid. Previously, he was Adjunct Professor at the Columbia University (SIPA), General Director of Economic Cooperation at the Instituto de Cooperación Iberoamericana, vice-chancellor at Universidad Internacional Menendez Pelayo and director of the Instituto Complutense de Estudios Internacionales (ICEI). He was member of the High-Level Group of Wise Persons on the European Financial Architecture for Development (2019), member of the Committee for Development Policy (UN ECOSOC) from 2007 to 2018 and member of the European Advisory Group of the Bill and Melinda Gates Foundation from 2012 to 2014. Currently he is a member of the Consejo de Cooperación para el Desarrollo (Spain). His main research areas focus on growth and development, international economic relations, and financing for development, with several books and many articles published in academic and specialized journals.

José Antonio Ocampo is professor at the School of International and Public Affairs, Member of the Committee on Global Thought and co-President of the Initiative for Policy Dialogue at Columbia University. He is also the Chair of the Committee for Development Policy, an expert committee of the United Nations Economic and Social Council (ECOSOC). Previously, Ocampo served in a number of positions in the United Nations and the Government of Colombia, most notably as United Nations Under-Secretary General for Economic and Social Affairs; Executive Secretary of the Economic Commission for Latin America and the Caribbean (ECLAC); Minister of Finance and Public Credit; Director of the National Planning Department; Minister of Agriculture and Rural Development; and member of the Board of Banco del República (Central Bank of Colombia). Ocampo has published extensively on macroeconomic theory and policy, international financial issues, economic and social development, international trade, and Colombian and Latin American economic history.

Contributors

Renato Baumann is DPhil in Economics, Oxford University, technical staff at IPEA since 1975, Director, UN/ECLAC Brasilia Office (1995–2010), Director, IPEA International Division (1988–1989; 2012–2014), Advisor to vice-president, World Bank (2010), Deputy Secretary of International Affairs, Ministry of Planning (2016–2018), Undersecretary of Foreign Investment, Ministry of Economy (February 2019–March 2020), Professor, Department of Economics, Universidade de Brasília (1983–2019), 1st Prize, MA dissertation (BNDES Prize, 1978), 1st Prize, Doctoral Thesis (National Association of Graduate Courses in Economics, 1983). He has authored, co-authored and edited fourteen books and tens of articles.

Otaviano Canuto is a senior fellow at the Policy Center for the New South, a nonresident senior fellow at Brookings Institution, and principal of the Center for Macroeconomics and Development. He is a former vice-president and a former executive director at the World Bank, a former executive director at the International Monetary Fund and a former vice-president at the Inter-American Development Bank. He is also a former deputy minister for international affairs at Brazil's Ministry of Finance and a former professor of economics at University of São Paulo and University of Campinas, Brazil. He has authored and co-edited six books and over 160 book chapters and academic articles, and is a frequent contributor to numerous blogs and periodicals.

Matheus Cavallari works as Senior Advisor for the Executive Director at the World Bank. He served as Alternate Executive Director at the IMF and as Deputy Secretary for Economic Policy at the Brazilian Ministry of Finance with focus on capital markets. Matheus was a member of the Board of Auditors at the Bank of Brazil—Investment Bank (BB-BI) and of the Board of Directors at the Funding Authority for Studies and Projects (FINEP). Previously, he worked for the Vice-President of the Poverty Reduction and Economic Management Network at the World Bank. Between 2004 and 2011, he was a partner of one of the pioneer hedge funds in Brazil, where he worked as chief-economist, macro-strategist, and portfolio manager. In 2008, he was member of the Portfolio Management Subcommittee at the Brazilian Financial and Capital Markets Association (ANBIMA).

Richard Doner is Goodrich C. White Professor (Emeritus), at Emory University. Professor Doner's scholarship focuses on the political economy of development, especially in Southeast Asia. His books include *The Politics of Uneven Development: Thailand's Economic Growth in Comparative Perspective* (Cambridge University Press, 2009); *From Silicon Valley to Singapore: Location and Competitive Advantage in the Disk Drive Industry* (with David McKendrick and Stephan Haggard, Stanford University Press, 2000); *Driving a Bargain: Automobile Industrialization and Japanese Firms in Southeast Asia* (Univ. California Universty Press, 1991). Edited volumes include *Explaining Institutional Innovation: Case Studies from Latin America and East Asia* (SSRC 2010); and *Economic Governance and the Challenge of Flexibility in East Asia* (with Frederick Deyo and Eric Hershberg, Rowman and Littlefield 2001). His work on the political origins of institutions and innovation has appeared in many specialized journals.

Indermit Gill is a non-resident senior fellow in the Global Economy and Development program at the Brookings Institution. He is also a professor of the practice of public policy at Duke University, where he was previously director of the Duke Center for International Development. Gill worked at the World Bank from 1993 to 2016, where he held a number of leadership positions including director for development policy in the Office of the Chief Economist, chief economist for Europe and Central Asia, and staff director for the 2009 World Development Report on Economic Geography. Before that, he was economic adviser in the East Asia and Pacific Region office and lead economist for human development in Latin America and the Caribbean.

Jonathan Glennie is a writer, researcher and consultant on sustainable development, human rights and international cooperation, looking in particular at the changing nature of development cooperation as global paradigms and relationships evolve. He has held senior positions in several international organizations (including Ipsos, Save the Children, ODI, Christian Aid). He has published two books on aid (*The Trouble with Aid: Why Less Could Mean More for Africa* and *Aid, Growth and Poverty* with Andy Sumner) and has been a regular columnist for The Guardian's Global Development website. As a consultant, he has worked with governments, international agencies, foundations, and civil society organizations as they renew their strategies for a new era. His next book, *The Future of Aid: Global Public Investment*, will be published in November 2020.

Stephany Griffith-Jones is Financial Markets Director at the Initiative for Policy Dialogue, Columbia University; Emeritus Professorial Fellow at the Institute of Development Studies, Sussex University; Senior Research Associate Overseas Development Institute; and non-resident fellow at the Center for Global Development. She is an economist researching and providing policy advice on reform of international financial architecture from a development perspective, and national and regional development banks. Griffith-Jones led several major international research projects with networks of senior academics, policymakers and bankers from developed and developing countries. Published widely, having written or edited twenty-five books (her latest co-edited with José Antonio Ocampo is entitled *The Future of National Development Banks*) as well as numerous journal and other articles. She has advised many international organizations (the European Commission, the World Bank, various UN agencies, IADB and several governments and central banks, including for the UK, Chile, Sweden, Tanzania, Brazil, and the Czech Republic).

Christopher Hoy is a Research and Policy Fellow (the equivalent of an Assistant Professor) at the Crawford School of Public Policy. He completed his Masters in International and Development Economics at Yale University and his PhD in Economics at the Australian National University (with examiners). Christopher has published numerous academic articles and policy papers and has pioneered the use of randomized control trials in Papua New Guinea and the Pacific. He has also worked as an economist for a range of organizations including the World Bank, Asian Development Bank, UNICEF, the Overseas Development Institute (ODI), Innovations for Poverty Action (IPA), and the Australian Government.

Homi Kharas is a Senior Fellow at the Brookings Institution. In that capacity, he studies policies and trends influencing developing countries, including aid to poor countries, the emergence of the middle class, and global governance and the G-20. He has served as the lead author and executive secretary of the secretariat supporting the High Level Panel, co-chaired by President Sirleaf, President Yudhoyono, and Prime Minister Cameron, advising the UN Secretary General on the post-2015 development agenda (2012–2013). He has been a member of the High Level Panel on the future of the OECD DAC. He ended his 27-year career at the World Bank as Chief Economist of the East Asia and Pacific region. He has published articles, book chapters, and opinion pieces on global development policy, global trends, the global food crisis, international organizations, the G20, the DAC, and private philanthropy.

Keun Lee is a Professor of Economics at the Seoul National University, and the founding director of the Center for Economic Catch-up. He is the winner of the 2014 Schumpeter Prize for his monograph on *Schumpeterian Analysis of Economic Catch-up* (Cambridge

University Press, 2013), as well as the 2019 Kapp Prize from the EAEPE, for his article on national innovation systems. He is also a Fellow of the CIFAR program on Innovation, Equity and Prosperity, an editor of *Research Policy*, and an associate editor of Industrial and Corporate Change. He served as the President of the International Schumpeter Society (2016–2018), and was a member of the Committee for Development Policy of UN (2014–2018) and a council member of the World Economic Forum (2016–2019). He obtained his PhD in economics from the University of California, Berkeley. One of his most cited articles is a paper on Korea's Technological Catch-up published in Research Policy, with 1,200 citations (Google Scholar). His H-index is 40, with approximately 105 papers with more than 10 citations. He most recent book is *The Art of Economic Catch-up: Barriers, Detours, and Leapfrogging* (Cambridge University Press, 2019).

Juliana Martínez Franzoni is Full Professor at the University of Costa Rica. She conducts comparative research on social policy in Latin America. She has been a Fulbright scholar and a visiting fellow at the Kellogg Institute for International Studies (USA), DesiguALdades-net (Germany), CIEPP (Argentina), and the University of Austin (USA). Her most recent articles were published in *Social Politics* (2017) *Latin American Research Review* (2014) and *ECLAC Review* (2014). Her most recent book, written with Diego Sánchez-Ancochea, is *The Quest for Universal Social Policy in the South: Actors, Ideas and Architectures* (Cambridge University Press, 2016). She is editor of *Social Politics* and undertakes regular consultancies with different international institutions such as UNDP and UN-Woman.

Emilio Padilla Rosa is Full Professor in Applied Economics at the Autonomous University of Barcelona (UAB). He is currently the director of the Department of Applied Economics at UAB. Previously, he was the coordinator of the PhD program in Applied Economics at UAB from 2014 to 2019. His research focuses on environmental and resource economics and ecological economics. Some of his main research interests are the economics of climate change, environmental taxation, the relationship between economic growth and environmental degradation, and distribution issues and the environment. He has participated in several national and international projects and also contracts with different institutions (such as UNIDO, UN Environment, and The World Bank). He has published many articles in specialized peer-reviewed journals, and several books and book chapters.

Mario Pezzini is Director of the OECD Development Centre, since 2010. Within this position, he also served as Acting Director of the OECD Development Co-operation Directorate in 2015, and has been nominated, since then, as Special Advisor to the OECD Secretary-General on Development. Before joining the Development Centre, Mario Pezzini held several senior management positions in the OECD, where he has been working since 1995. Prior to joining the OECD, he was Professor in Industrial Economics at the *Ecole Nationale Supérieure des Mines* de Paris as well as in US and Italian Universities. Moreover, Mario Pezzini served as an Advisor in the field of economic development, industrial organization, and regional economics in international organizations and think tanks (e.g. ILO, UNIDO, European Commission, and Nomisma in Italy). He started his career in the Government office of the Emilia-Romagna Region.

Tiago Ribeiro dos Santos is an advisor to the Executive Director for Brazil, Colombia, Dominican Republic, Ecuador, Haiti, Panama, Philippines, Suriname, and Trinidad and

Tobago at the World Bank since 2018. A career diplomat in the Brazilian Ministry of Foreign Affairs, he has worked at the Brazilian Embassy in Washington DC, and has taken positions at the United Nations Division and the Financial Policy Division in the Brazilian MFA headquarters. He holds a master's degree in public policy from the Harris School at the University of Chicago.

Diego Sánchez-Ancochea is the Head of the Oxford Department of International Development and Professor of the Political Economy of Development at the University of Oxford. He was previously director of the Latin American Centre in the same university. His research focuses on the determinants of income inequality and the role of social policy in reducing it. He has published extensively on these topics and others related to Latin American political economy in diverse international journals. He is also the co-editor of four books and the co-author of two books with Juliana Martínez Franzoni: *Good Jobs and Social Services: How Costa Rica Achieved the Elusive Double Incorporation* (Palgrave Macmillan) and *The Quest for Universal Social Policy in the South: Actors, Ideas and Architectures* (Cambridge University Press). He is Region Head of Oxford Analytica and has done regular consultancies for the ILO, UNDP, and other international organizations.

Ben Ross Schneider is the Ford International Professor of Political Science and director of the MIT Brazil program. Prior to joining the department in 2008, Schneider taught at Princeton University and Northwestern University. Schneider's teaching and research interests fall within the general fields of comparative politics, political economy, and Latin American politics. His books include *Reinventing Leviathan: The Politics of Administrative Reform in Developing Countries* (2003); *Business Politics and the State in 20th Century Latin America* (2004); *Hierarchical Capitalism in Latin America: Business, Labor, and the Challenges of Equitable Development* (Cambridge University Press, 2013); *Designing Industrial Policy in Latin America: Business-Government Relations and the New Developmentalism* (2015); and *New Order and Progress: Democracy and Development in Brazil* (Oxford University Press, 2016). He also has published on topics such as democratization, technocracy, education politics, the developmental state, business groups, industrial policy, and comparative bureaucracy.

Andy Sumner is a Professor of International Development in the Department of International Development at King's College London. He is also Director of the Economic and Social Research Council (ESRC) Global Challenges Strategic Research Network on Global Poverty and Inequality Dynamics. He has twenty years' international research experience using both qualitative and quantitative methods and has published extensively, including more than ten books and fifty journal papers and book chapters. His most recent books include *Global Poverty* (Oxford University Press, 2016) and *Development and Distribution* (Oxford University Press, 2018). He was appointed at King's in 2012 and was a founding Co-Director of the King's International Development Institute, which later became the Department of International Development. He holds associate positions at Oxford University; the Center for Global Development, Washington DC; the United Nations University, WIDER, Helsinki; and the Centre for Economics and Development Studies, Padjadjaran University, Indonesia.

Rolph van der Hoeven, PhD is, since 2007, Professor of Employment and Development Economics at the International Institute of Social Studies in the Hague (ISS) at Erasmus University (EUR) in the Hague (as of 2015 emeritus). He worked from 1974 to 2008 in Zambia, Ethiopia, Geneva, and New York in different functions for the United Nations, amongst others as Chief Economist for UNICEF, Director for Policy Coherence at the ILO and as Manager of the World Commission on the Social Dimension of Globalization. His current memberships include that of the Advisory Council of International Affairs (AIV) and of the Knowledge platform INCLUDE of the Dutch Government; the UN Committee for Development Policy (UNCDP); and the board of Trustees of the KNCV Tuberculosis Fund. He has authored or edited more than a dozen books, and numerous articles and book chapters on various aspects of economic reform, employment, inequality, and of social development in general. His latest (co-edited) volume is *Sustainable Development Goals and Income Inequality*.

1

Economic Traps and Progress in Middle-Income Countries

An Introduction

José Antonio Alonso and José Antonio Ocampo

1.1 Convergence and Divergence in the International System

Economic convergence between countries is at the very core of modern theory of economic growth. Countries with similar basic parameters are expected to have similar steady-state per capita incomes over the long term, as suggested by Robert Solow's canonical model. Moreover, because capital has diminishing marginal returns in this model, the speed of convergence will be higher the farther the country is from its respective steady-state. Thus, the growth rate of lagging countries should be faster on average than that of the rich countries, a necessary (but not sufficient) condition for convergence.

Historical reality, however, has shown that these predictions are very poor. When data are examined corresponding to a wide range of cases and over a sufficiently long period of time, it is found that economic convergence has been limited to a small group of countries; moreover, economic divergence has proven to be the most widespread and persistent condition.

Indeed, two trends have dominated the evolution of global inequality, beyond any nuances imposed by the statistical sources used in any given case (Milanovic, 2005; Piketty, 2014). In the first place, the level of inequality within countries was persistently high during the whole nineteenth century and the beginning of the twentieth century, experiencing a significant downward correction after the 1930s, and more clearly after World War II. This positive change was maintained until the beginning of the 1980s, and was followed by rising domestic inequalities, broadly affecting most countries regardless of their level of development and region. The recent resurgence in inequality has been conditioned by both contextual factors (such as the impact of globalization and technologies on employment and wages) and policy choices (such as market deregulation and the decline in fiscal progressivity).

José Antonio Alonso and José Antonio Ocampo, *Economic Traps and Progress in Middle-Income Countries: An Introduction* In: *Trapped in the Middle? Developmental Challenges for Middle-Income Countries.* Edited by: José Antonio Alonso and José Antonio Ocampo, Oxford University Press (2020). © OUP. DOI: 10.1093/oso/9780198852773.003.0001

Another major trend has affected the distribution of income between countries, where (with very slight interruptions) inequality experienced a continuing upward trend until the final decades of the twentieth century—a trend that was particularly sharp during the nineteenth and the first half of the twentieth century. This means that the consolidation of global capitalism came hand-in-hand with an unprecedented expansion of income inequalities between countries. However, this trend appears to have experienced a certain downward correction in the past two/three decades, which has now been interrupted and was more pronounced when GDP per capita is weighted by country size. Behind this process is the intense growth enjoyed by a group of emerging market economies, generally Asian, some of them with very large populations (notably China and, to a lesser extent, India). This convergence, however, cannot be generalized to the rest of lagging countries, despite the fact that, over the past two decades, the average growth rate of the developing world exceeded that of the developed one.

So far, these rough trends, well-founded in the data, have aroused a wide consensus among analysts. However, that agreement is weakened when it comes to the identification of both the causes of the recent increase in inequality and whether current trends can be expected to continue. However, both aspects are crucial for defining the future of the middle-income countries (MICs). In an effort to simplify a very complex landscape, two major interpretive trends could be mentioned.

The most optimistic analyses suggest that we stand at the dawn of a new stage of progressive economic convergence, thereby ending earlier periods characterized by an accentuation of international inequalities. Although this positive process has so far affected only a small group of countries (the thirteen success stories identified by Spence, 2011), its effects are foreseen as spreading widely throughout much of the developing world. At the basis of this process are the intertwined effects of globalization and the revolution in information and communication technologies (ICTs), which are redefining patterns of organization of productive processes on a global scale.

Perhaps the most eloquent defender of this position is Baldwin (2016), who suggests that we are now at the beginning of a new stage of the globalization process. In the prior phase, economies took advantage of the increasing returns that the industrial revolution promoted, encouraging the concentration of production, and the consequent expansion of international trade (*Globalizing Local Economies*). During that phase, "productivity surged in the North, and this sparked a cycle of industrialization, agglomeration, and innovation that yielded a huge North–South knowledge gap" (Baldwin, 2016: 16). But, we find ourselves at the beginning of a new phase (*Globalizing Factories*) in which the revolution in ICT has relaxed the constraints that underpinned prior imbalances in the global dissemination of knowledge, facilitating the distribution of productive processes worldwide and promoting both deindustrialization in the North and industrialization in diverse regions of the South. As a consequence, "the ICT revolution unleashed an historic transformation that might be called the Great Convergence" (Baldwin, 2016: 16).

Although in a less-well articulated, this same idea of progressive convergence seems to guide a wide range of authors who have drawn attention to the emergence of the Global South (among them Ridley, 2010; Kenny, 2012; UNDP, 2013; Radelet, 2015). In all these cases, it is presumed that the successful behavior of a group of countries with emerging markets (including China) prefigure what may happen in the immediate future with a broad variety of developing countries.

Countering this optimistic vision are skeptical authors who see current trends in the global economy as involving simultaneous processes of convergence and exclusion. According to this line of thought, the economic success of developing countries is not impossible, but it remains for the moment a minority experience. While there are undoubtedly forces that can facilitate the dissemination of progress through competition, international trade and investment, and technological learning and diffusion, many other forces operate in the opposite direction, instead facilitating economic concentration and income disparities between countries as a result of asymmetries that characterize global markets. We should add that the COVID-19 pandemics has generated new uncertainties in international trade, especially regarding the future of global value chains, which were the main engine of growth of trade over the past four decades or so.

Development theory has devoted effort to understand the factors that generate economic asymmetries at the international level. Exploration led theorists to assume the presence of discontinuities in the development process, as well as the potential existence of multiple equilibria for an economy. Thus, they built the concept of the "poverty trap," understood as a low-level equilibrium into which economies can be plunged as a consequence of the mutually reinforcing effects of certain retarding factors. In essence, such a trap involves a system of self-enforcing mechanisms driven by market failures (including problems of coordination) that inhibits progress toward higher levels of development (Azariadis and Drazen, 1990; Bowles et al., 2006). Normally, this concept is used to characterize the situation of the poorest countries (as in Nelson, 1956). Within this vision was the implicit idea that, once the poverty trap has been overcome, a country could follow a path of sustained growth that would bring it closer to the high-level equilibrium characteristic of a developed country.

Unfortunately, historical experience has apparently failed to lend credibility to this simplified view. Although it is true that certain economies remain mired at a level of high vulnerability and low dynamism, as the poverty trap diagnosis suggests (as in some sub-Saharan African nations) (Guillaumont, 2009), other countries have managed to experience episodes of intense growth, even repeatedly, allowing them to advance their levels of development and to move toward higher incomes (Hausmann et al., 2005).

In other words, the poverty trap does not represent a mandatory or universal restriction preventing the growth of low-income countries. Moreover, the same evidence reveals that exceeding the low-income level and reaching the middle-income level is not enough to assume that a country will continue the process of convergence toward high-income status. In fact, few countries have successfully completed that transit; and many seem to have gotten stuck in the middle-income group—which has led some authors to transfer the concept of a "trap" to MICs. This would describe the case of discontinuities in the convergence process that derive not so much from absolute deficiencies (as in the poverty trap) as from restrictions and bottlenecks occurring in the complex transformation required to move toward higher levels of development.

It must be admitted that the concept of a "middle-income trap" (MIT) has been presented in the literature with a deficit of theoretical foundation. Some authors (such as Agenor and Canuto, 2012) have sought to give analytical support to this idea, but empirical works often employ the concept with diverse interpretations. Thus, in some cases the trap is associated with the long period that a country has spent within the middle-income group (Gill and Kharas, 2007; Felipe et al., 2012); in other cases, the trap is associated with the recurrence of slowdowns that interrupt intense growth in MICs (Eichengreen et al., 2012 and 2013; Aiyar et al., 2013). Some authors use this concept to refer to the difficulties that countries experience in trying to change their growth regime, from one based on the accumulation of factors to another oriented toward the continuous improvement of productivity (Gill and Kharas, 2007 and 2015); finally, still other authors associate this trap with the difficulties experienced by MICs in pursuing a process of successful convergence toward the leaders (Im and Rosenblatt, 2013; Robertson and Ye, 2013).

Alternatively, other authors consider that the main developmental constraints suffered by MICs, rather than being endogenous (as MIT would suggest), are mainly caused by the asymmetries of global markets, which would tend to reproduce international inequalities. Ocampo (2013), for example, identify three essential asymmetries of the international system (see also Ocampo and Martin, 2003). The first is a high concentration of research and development, and therefore technical progress, in the developed countries. This may be associated with large or even prohibitive entry costs into the more dynamic technological activities and explain why such activities are dominated by developed countries and multinational enterprises from these countries. The second asymmetry is the greater vulnerability of developing countries to external shocks, both those associated with terms of trade fluctuations—which affect many developing countries—and also with the volatility of private external financing, which particularly affects middle-income countries—the so called "emerging markets." The third is asymmetry in the international mobility of factors of production: capital and highly skilled labor are highly mobile, but low-skilled labor is not, a fact that generates distributive effects in favor of the more mobile factors and, therefore, the countries that are abundant in those factors.

So, the question arises: do middle-income traps (MITs) really exist? If yes, how do these pitfalls manifest, what are their causes, and what economic policy measures are required to escape from them? This volume, which brings together diverse views on this important matter, is dedicated to answering such questions. Nevertheless, it is not the purpose of the book to offer apodictic responses, or to close a debate wherein many indeterminacies persist. Rather, the priority is to provide new evidence and perspectives of analysis, to enrich the debate on the challenges that a large number of countries face, and under which over three-fourths of the global population lives.

Before embarking on an examination of the reality of the data, however, it is convenient to present certain conceptual clarifications that will support the interpretation of the subject.

1.2 Two Preliminary Conceptual Precisions

1.2.1 Middle-Income: Absolute or Relative?

According to a wide array of authors, the MIT affects countries when they reach a certain absolute level of income (Spence, 2011; Felipe et al., 2012; Eichengreen et al., 2013). For example, when Spence (2011) refers to problems related to middle-income transitions (he does not use the term “trap”), he is referring to countries with a per capita income of between $5,000 and $10,000, an interval relatively close to thresholds defined for upper middle-income by the World Bank.[1] On the other hand, Eichengreen et al. (2013) study the economic setbacks suffered by MICs and identify two breakpoints: one between $10,000 and $11,000, and another between $15,000 and $16,000. While the first of these intervals coincides with the World Bank definition of the upper middle-income group, the second falls within the scope of high-income countries. Finally, Aiyar et al. (2013) also examine episodes of slowdowns suffered by countries—in this case in relation to Solow model’s predictions—and observe that the middle-income group experiences such episodes more frequently, due to causes distinct from those of other country groups. These authors identify MICs as those with per capita income between $1,000 and $12,000.

Countering these assessments are those who consider the MIT to be associated not so much with access by countries to an absolute level of income, but with the difficulties facing countries located on the intermediate rungs of the international income ladder in sustaining a process of convergence toward upper positions.

[1] In 2019 the World Bank thresholds of GNI per capita for different country groups were: under $1,025 for low-income countries; between $1,026 and $3,995 for lower middle-income countries; between $3,996 to $12,375 for upper middle-income countries; and above $12,376 for high-income countries.

Here, middle-income is defined by the country's relative income level as compared to a leading economy (usually the United States) (Im and Rosenblatt, 2013; Agenor and Canuto, 2012; Robertson and Ye, 2013).

Differences between these approaches go beyond classification criteria. In both cases, it is presumed that middle-income traps (MITs) appear to be associated with development difficulties faced by countries that have already reached a certain level of productive and institutional complexity. The first group assumes that the causes of such a trap are exclusively endogenous, and manifested upon reaching a certain level of development, while the second group sees the causes as referring to a combination of domestic and international factors, expressed when a country tries to shorten the distance vis-à-vis the leader.

Settling the contention between these approaches is not easy, as both make sense, but it should be recognized that, if MITs are understood to be associated with the difficult competitive position of MICs, "squeezed between the low-wage poor-country competitors that dominate in mature industries and the rich-country innovators that dominate in industries undergoing rapid technological change" (Gill and Kharas, 2007), then the most appropriate analytical option for defining middle-income should be a *relative* one. At the same time, MITs should be understood as prolonged interruptions in a process of convergence by these countries toward the leading countries.

1.2.2 The Nature of MITs

Whatever the assumed meaning, in order to be consistent with historical experience, the concept of the MIT must be accompanied by three additional observations.

The first refers to the *contingent nature* of the MITs: not all countries are obliged to suffer such traps, and those that do may well overcome them. This is in accordance with evidence that several of today's developed countries were MICs in the past. Thus, MITs are neither inevitable nor universal; rather, they should be seen as one possibility, deriving from multiple restrictions that countries encounter when seeking to achieve higher income levels. The path from medium to high income may be a narrow corridor, but it exists.

Second, MITs must relate to *new or specific factors* faced by countries when accessing middle-income status; they cannot refer to obstacles or restrictions affecting all developing countries, regardless of income level. Even if the problem is shared by different kind of countries, it should entail stronger constraints for countries' progress when they reach middle-income status—developing technological capacities is an important example.

Finally, the concept of a trap refers to a failure deriving from the presence of a set of *mutually reinforcing restrictions*, thus indicating problems of coordination and requiring complementary responses in various fields. Isolated difficulties, however severe they may be, are not sufficient here; rather, the difficulties must interact and reinforce one another and affect economic growth. Nevertheless, the specialized literature has sometimes identified as traps what may be mere obstacles to development faced by MICs, while in several cases failing to explain the system of interactions underlying such obstacles.

1.3 Empirical Evidence

1.3.1 Transit between Groups

Some authors have related the concept of the MIT to prolonged permanence by a country within a middle-income stratum. One can check the extent to which this is empirically valid by analyzing changes to the composition of groups of countries by income levels, as offered by the World Bank. Since the late 1980s, the World Bank has classified countries into four groups (low-income, lower middle-income, upper middle-income, and high-income), according to their respective GNI per capita. Each of these groups is defined based on income thresholds expressed in dollars, and those thresholds have been updated based on the evolution of international inflation.[2]

When this classification is used, a notable change is perceived in the conformation of the international system over the past three decades. In 1990,[3] the middle-income group consisted of 76 countries, with 48 countries in the low-income group and a similar number (41) in the high-income group. As of 2019, only 31 countries were situated in the low-income group; the high-income group had increased to 80, while the middle-income group had expanded to 107 countries (around half of those registered) (Table 1.1). As a consequence of these changes, the bulk of the global population (about 75 percent of the total) is today living in a MIC, which together contribute 36 percent of global GDP (in PPP terms). In other words, most of the existing countries are now located in a group that is defined by a double criterion of exclusion: those that are no longer poor in the strictest sense, but still far from being considered rich.

These changes—the thinning of the low-income group and the widening of the middle- and high-income groups—are not merely the result of economic growth at international level. Additionally, a spurious statistical effect is present, as many

[2] The World Bank set the original per capita income thresholds for these groups taking into account not only the GNI, but additional measures of well-being. Later, it adopted the GNI as a synthetic indicator of all these measures in order to operationalize country groupings. The World Bank updates the original thresholds by adjusting them for the inflation rates of Japan, the UK, the USA, and the Eurozone; as a consequence, the thresholds remain constant in real terms over time (http://data.world bank.org/about/country-classifications/a-short-history).

[3] The World Bank classifications have only been available since 1987; the 1990 classification is based on data from 1988.

Table 1.1 Changes in country groupings (number of countries, 1990 and 2019)

Year		2019				
		LICs	LMICs	UMICs	HICs	Total
1990	LICs	25	18	5	—	48
	LMICs	2	20	24	2	48
	UMICs	—	—	11	17	28
	HICs	—	—	1	40	41
	Non-classified	4	9	19	21	53
	Total	31	47	60	80	218

Notes: LICs (low-income countries); LMICs (lower middle-income countries); UMICs (upper middle-income countries); HICs (high-income countries).

Source: Authors' estimates, based on World Bank data.

countries that entered the middle- and high-income groups over the period were either not independent (formerly composing parts of other countries) or were not classified by the World Bank in 1990. If the analysis were limited to countries that persisted and were recorded over the entire period, the number of transitions between groups would be lower. Thus, in the three decades considered, 23 countries (48 percent of the total) moved from low-income countries (LICs) to MIC status, and 19 countries (25 percent) went from MIC to high-income countries (HICs) status. Judging by the success rates indicated, overcoming a low-income condition may seem to be easier than rising above middle-income, but such a perception is frankly inaccurate. The MIC group is very heterogeneous and usually divided into two strata; when that division is taken into account, we can see that 24 countries out of 48 (50 percent) rose from lower middle- to upper middle-income, and 17 countries of 28 (60 percent) went from upper- -middle- to high-income during the period. Thus, the data do not seem to indicate the presence of insurmountable obstacles for countries to move between groups.

However, this optimistic assessment is corrected when the types of countries that effectively transitioned from middle- to high-income is taken into account. In this respect, four groups can be identified: (i) those European countries that have long benefited from redistributive European policies and the institutional modernization involved in European Union (EU) integration (Greece, Portugal, Malta, Hungary, Poland); (ii) numerous small island states whose GNI relies on service activities (Antigua and Barbuda, Barbados, Guam, New Caledonia, Seychelles, Saint Kitts and Neves, Palau, Trinidad and Tobago); (iii) two oil producing countries (Oman and Saudi Arabia);[4] and (iv) a small group of countries that experienced continuous economic growth and transformation (Chile, Republic of Korea, Panama, and Uruguay). Of these groups, it is the fourth

[4] Saudi Arabia was initially in the high-income group but fell to middle-income in the early 1990s.

(perhaps with the exception of Panama) that appears to correspond more faithfully to what is considered an endogenous process of convergence: a very small group on which to reject the potential existence of MITs.

This conclusion is further consistent with that reached by Spence (2011) in identifying cases of recent successful growth. Looking at a broader time range, beginning in the 1960s, he identifies just 13 countries that have shown a growth rate greater than or equal to 7 percent across twenty-five years.[5] Among these are the cases of Japan, where growth was combined with post-war reconstruction, city-states like Singapore and Hong Kong, oil producer Oman, and the small European island of Malta. The remaining eight countries are proper developing economies that managed to maintain a path of intense growth. The author's laconic conclusion is clear: "it's not a very long list, since there are about 180 countries in the developing world" (Spence, 2011).

Felipe et al. (2012) reach a similar conclusion in their study of mobility between income groups over a long historical period (1820–2010). More precisely, in the period after 1950, only nine countries managed to move from lower middle- to upper middle-income (requiring 28 years as a median period to do so); and 23 countries made the transit from upper middle- to high-income (requiring a median period of 14 years). This is not a very broad showing, given that a historical period of six decades is being considered. As a consequence, the authors point out that, as of 2010, 35 out of 52 countries showed characteristics associated with sinking into a MIT,[6] and of these 30 were lower middle-income and five were upper middle-income (although nine countries in the first group and two in the second were recognized as likely to escape from the MIT).

The evidence here collected suggests that, although the transit from middle to high income is not impossible, it has been successfully completed by only a limited group of countries. Not much has been achieved, especially if one takes into account that global GDP grew over the period, which has necessarily led countries to a shift toward higher-income strata when thresholds are defined as absolute levels of income.

1.3.2 Relative Convergence

An alternative approach that avoids the aggregate effect of growth is to refer country groupings not to absolute thresholds of income level, but rather to relative levels vis-à-vis the income of the leading economy (generally, the United

[5] These successful cases are Botswana, Brazil, China, Hong Kong, Indonesia, Japan, Korea, Malaysia, Malta, Oman, Singapore, Taiwan, and Thailand.

[6] Felipe et al. (2012) consider a country to be in a middle-income trap when it has persisted in the MIC group beyond the median number of years spent before advancing to the high-income group.

States). This approach places the transition of middle-income countries within the broadest and best-founded framework of economic convergence (Barro, 2012).

To undertake a simple approximation of this approach, here the middle-income thresholds are defined by levels equivalent to 15 percent and 40 percent of the PPP GDP per capita of the United States;[7] additionally, it will be understood that economic convergence occurs when that ratio rises, revealing a shortening of the relative distance from the leader. The analysis considers only those countries that at the beginning of the period (1990–2018) were situated in the middle- and low-income strata (Figure 1.1).[8]

In 1990, 75 of 126 countries were LICs, while the other 51 fell into the MIC group. There were three regions which were mainly composed of MICs: Eastern Europe and Central Asia (20 of 28 developing countries in the region), Latin America and the Caribbean (15 of 23 countries), and the Middle East and North Africa (MENA) (7 of 9 countries). The other three regions were mainly formed by LICs: Southern Asia (6 of 6 countries), Eastern Asia (14 of 18), and Sub-Saharan countries (38 of 42). Three decades later two-thirds of countries (86) reduced their relative distance to the leader which allowed them to climb up in income ladder. As a consequence, the groups of LICs and MICs have shrunk: in 2018, they contained 66 and 45 countries, respectively, while the group of HICs grew with 16 new countries. More precisely, 11 countries moved from LICs to MICs and 16 went from MICs to HICs, while two countries fell from MICs to LICs.

Three regions accounted for most of these changes. More precisely, *Eastern Europe and Central Asia* was the region with more mobility. Four LICs (Albania, Armenia, Bosnia Herzegovina, and Kosovo) moved to MICs; and eleven more, former MICs, achieved high-income status, eight of these (Croatia, Estonia, Hungary, Latvia, Lithuania, Poland, Romania, Slovak Republic) being new members of the EU and three (Kazakhstan, Russia, Turkey) outside the EU. In the opposite direction, Ukraine moved from MIC to LIC. In the case of *Latin America and the Caribbean* two countries (Dominican Republic and Peru) moved from LICs to MICs and three other countries (Trinidad and Tobago, Chile, and Panama) from MIC to HICs. In the opposite direction, Jamaica fell from MICs to LICs. Finally, in *Eastern Asia* three countries moved from LICs to MICs (China, Indonesia, and Mongolia) and two others from MICs to HICs (Malaysia and Republic of Korea).

The other three developing regions experienced only minor changes. In fact, in *MENA* no country changed its income status in the period. In *Southern Asia* only two countries moved from LICs to MICs (Bhutan and Sri Lanka). And, finally, in

[7] These thresholds have been chosen because they lead to a classification very similar to that offered by the World Bank with absolute income thresholds. Robertson and Ye (2013) offer a list of MICs defined as the middle 40 percent of countries ranked by GDP. The resulting thresholds are lower but not so different from those suggested here: from 8 percent to 36 percent of the US per capita GDP.

[8] Countries (or territories) with less than 500,000 inhabitants have been excluded.

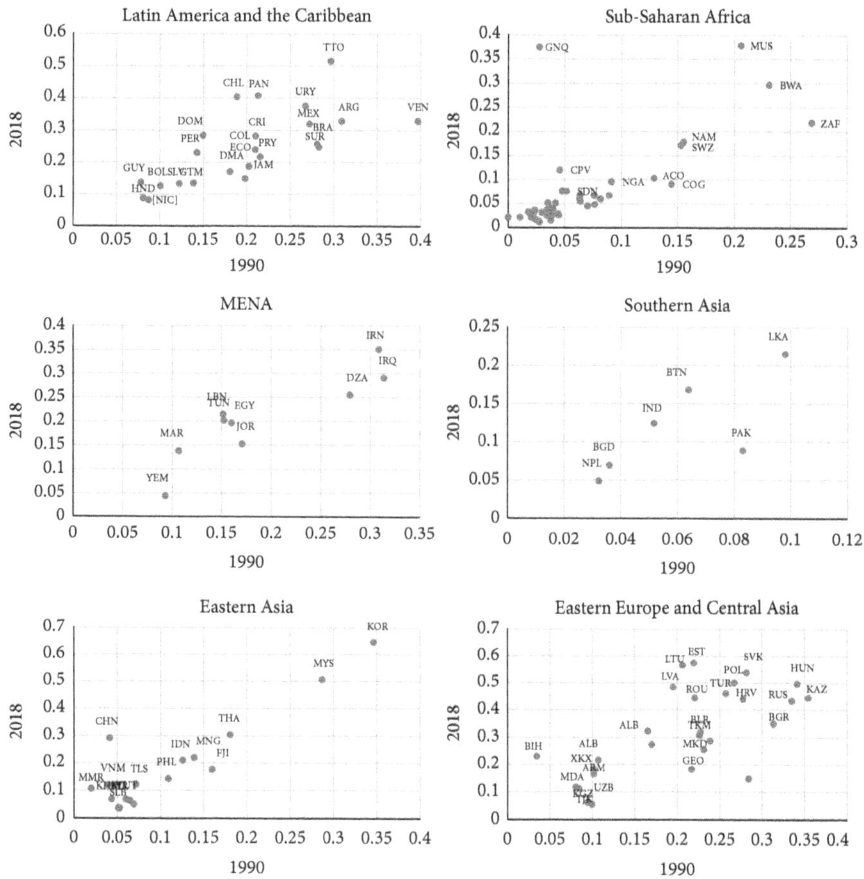

Figure 1.1 Per capita GDP (in PPP) in terms relative to that of the USA

Sub-Saharan Africa only one country moved from LIC to MIC (Equatorial Guinea), while another country (Gabon) found itself on the opposite route and lost its status as a HIC, falling into the middle-income group.

In sum, when the categories of countries are defined according to convergence toward the leader, the cases of success in overcoming middle-income status are very limited. If those countries incorporated into the EU are excluded, only eight successful cases of transition have been confirmed internationally over the past three decades: Chile, Panama, Trinidad and Tobago, Republic of Korea, Malaysia, Kazakhstan, Russia, and Turkey.

These bodies of evidence, although confirming the difficulties inherent in economic convergence, are not sufficient to prove the existence of MITs. Economic convergence has revealed itself as a more complicated, laborious, and lengthy process than most simplified versions of the Solow model tend to suggest. In fact, in the same period (1990–2019), only three developed countries (Ireland, Norway, and Luxembourg) have managed to significantly reduce their distance relative to the USA. Thus, convergence toward the leader seems to be an elusive goal for almost all countries.

Moreover, as the contrasting tone of two careful explorations show, empirical evidence, by itself, has not so far been able to clearly settle the existence of a MIT. On the one hand, Im and Rosenblatt (2014), based on building transition matrices in the distribution of international income in the period 1950–2008, suggest that "MICs do not really look that different in terms of transitions across the inter-country distribution of income"; and their complementary study of the growth dynamics of MICs "does not confirm one clear pattern that can be easily characterized as a trap" (Im and Rosenblatt, 2014: 25). In contrast, Robertson and Ye (2013), based on a time series analysis of long-term convergence for the period 1950–2010, find that 19 of 46 countries satisfy their definition of a MIT.[9] Definitively, the existence of a MIT seems to be an issue that requires analytical and empirical exploration.

1.4 In Search of Explanations

If the empirical account is far from conclusive, no greater clarity emerges from theoretical explanations of the potential causes of MITs, where indeterminacies abound.

Thus, some authors have associated MITs with the recurring slowdowns suffered by countries that had enjoyed remarkable economic dynamism in prior periods. Such stagnations (or regressions) predominantly occur in the middle-income strata (Aiyar et al., 2013; Eichengreen et al., 2013).[10] The most central cause identified with such episodes is the depletion of labor surplus transfers from the agricultural sector to the manufacturing sector (or, more generally, from sectors of low productivity to sectors of higher productivity).

Beyond the existence of such episodes, their conceptualization as traps is debatable. Moreover, Pritchett and Summer (2014) question whether such episodes of slowdown require a specific explanation: in their view, they can be considered as the consequence of a basic statistical law of "regression to the average." Since episodes of intense growth cannot be expected to be sustained over time, they will frequently be punctuated by discontinuous drop-offs. As they remark, regression to the mean is "far more robust in the data than, say, the much-discussed middle-income trap" (Pritchett and Summer, 2014: 1).

[9] They define a MIT as a situation in which a country's per capita income over the long-run is: (i) stationary, and (ii) located in the middle-income band (defined in terms of the PPP GDP per capita relative to that of the USA).

[10] Eichengreen et al. (2013) define such slowdowns as a decline of at least 2 percentage points relative to a 7-year moving average.

Another group of authors refer MITs to the difficulties that countries experience in moving from a productive specialization based on unskilled labor to a situation where innovation, technological capabilities, and job qualifications play a greater role (Gill and Kharas, 2007 and 2015; Ohno, 2009; Eichengreen et al., 2013; Lee, 2013 and 2019). As countries progress, they lose some portion of their cost advantages and are forced to look to innovation and labor qualification as new ways to improve productivity. If such a transition does not occur, it may be that those countries are unable to compete against both the low-wage countries that dominate mature industries, and the high-income countries that dominate innovative, high-technology industries.

Making this productive transition is not easy, as simultaneous processes are required in many distinct areas: educational achievements, the improvement of infrastructures and institutions, the development of technological capabilities, and the strengthening of domestic financial markets, among other factors. All this suggests that the production transition is difficult to complete, as countries often get stuck in the middle of the process. However, to characterize these situations as traps would require a better foundation of the dynamic interactions of the retarding factors.

This is what Agenor and Canuto (2012) attempted, through a model with a knowledge externality that affects the creation of new productive activities. Their model leads to multiple equilibria, including the possibility of a low-productivity growth trap for MICs. While this is an interesting approach, it is too specific in terms of the factors considered to serve as a general framework for explaining MITs.

Without diminishing the relevance of the productive transformations, a number of authors have considered that some of the problems faced by MICs derive from the inability of such countries to pair growth with a parallel process of institutional change (Paus, 2014; Alonso, 2016; Doner and Schneider, 2016). The causes of that dissonance usually refer to factors associated with social fragmentation and the complex arithmetic of power group interests. Marked social inequality, the segmentation of markets caused by informality, institutional capture by elites, or the fragmentation of economic groups may frustrate the building of social coalitions to support a continuing process of institutional reform. The consequences include states with low fiscal strength, a limited capacity for the provision of public goods, and, at times, a notorious credibility deficit that challenges the construction of socially supported development strategies. The diagnoses advanced by these authors are supported by the recurrent institutional crises suffered by MICs. However, their explanation is affected by a lack of a convincing theory on the process of institutional change.

Finally, other authors consider that the causes of MITs can be located in the interaction between domestic weaknesses and an increasingly demanding international environment (Paus, 2014 and 2019). MICs today operate in more open and competitive markets, where the potential to transition between specializations based on cost advantages and those based on knowledge has narrowed down over time. This is a consequence of the evolution of global value chains and the implementation by some emerging countries of strong strategies to increase manufacturing exports (as in the case of China). In this case, MITs would develop not only from endogenous factors, but from conditions imposed by the changing structure of international markets. This approach is taken to the extreme by Bresser-Pereira et al. (2020), as they suggest that growth slow-downs are caused by a "liberalization trap," rather than a middle-income trap (MIT). Many MICs were forced—or chose—to open their economies in the 1980s, making it more difficult for countries to preserve macroeconomic stability, driving them to situations with chronic overvaluation of exchange rates, premature deindustrialization, and low growth.

1.5 Policy Responses

The route followed thus far leads to an ambiguous conclusion. On the one hand, there is insufficient clarity or consensus around the existence and characterization of MITs; but, at the same time, it is generally admitted that MICs face severe challenges in sustaining a continuous path of progress. This second conclusion indicates that, even if more analytical work is required, the debate around MITs has made a positive contribution to the development agenda by revitalizing reflection on the active policies required to promote the transformation and growth of countries that have risen above the poverty line.

In fact, many authors have associated MITs with the inability of some countries to adapt their policy responses to specific problems that emerge as they move ahead in their transformation process (Gill and Kharas, 2015; Agenor et al., 2012). As growth based on the accumulation of factors declines, countries need to find new sources of growth to provide continued progress in productivity; and in order to activate these sources, new and different policies are required that are not necessarily the same as those used for rising above low-income levels. Therefore, even if the "middle-income trap is myth, it provides impetus for policymakers to reassess their strategies once the traditional sources of economic growth have diminished" (Larson et al., 2016: 1).

In order to inform policy responses, some authors attempted to identify those factors that had allowed successful countries to avoid MITs. For example, Aiyar et al. (2013) find an ample group of MIT determinants by means of probit regressions, although their results do not admit an easy interpretation in policy terms. On the other hand, Melguizo et al. (2017) looked for attributes that countries which avoided the MIT had decades before their transitions, in order to identify key drivers for countries to escape from MIT; their results should equally be considered as tentative.

Even if more work is needed in this area, the degree of agreement around policy responses is much broader, with the following seven issues emerging as central areas of attention according to the contributions to this volume:

a) *Strong macroeconomic policies*: Macroeconomic stability is a necessary (but not sufficient) condition to facilitate a convergence process. Achievement of this objective entails the maintenance of consistent macroeconomic policies that favor domestic savings and investment, avoid excess external indebtedness, and preserve basic equilibria. However, MICs particularly suffer the consequences of the cyclical behavior of international capital markets, due to their recurring need for financing, the weakness of their currencies, the narrowness of their domestic financial markets, and in some cases the fragility of the institutions in charge of financial regulation and supervision. Therefore, it is important to ensure the adequate regulation of financial markets, in order to avoid the accumulation of risks by national agents, and also to strengthen domestic financial institutions, to encourage the mobilization of domestic resources (see chapters 6, 11, and 12). Additionally, it is important to widen the opportunity to implement countercyclical policies through macroprudential measures, such as those associated with the regulation of capital accounts (see chapters 11 and 15).
b) *Industrial policy and technological upgrading*: Progress by the MICs requires a continuous process of production sector development and the improvement of technological capabilities. Historical experience reveals that such processes are not a spontaneous result of changes in a country's cost conditions. Rather, it is necessary to implement industrial policies with a long-term perspective that allow new productive capacities to be deployed, to improve the climate for competition in markets, and to strengthen the national science and technology systems. Identification of the most appropriate paths for such processes remains subject to discussion (see chapters 2, 6, and 9) and perhaps lagging countries should avoid just transplanting the routes followed by the leaders (see chapter 3).
c) *International competitiveness*: It is not possible to sustain a process of continuous growth if countries are unable to present a diversified and competitive offer that international markets will find compelling. The development of export capacities in sectors of high dynamism and high added value is one necessary approach to overcoming perceived MITs. However, this objective will not be met merely by opening markets: it is further necessary that countries implement active policies aimed at deploying competitive capabilities and supporting national companies to penetrate international markets, including through a favorable insertion in global value chains (see chapters 3 and 14).

d) *Investment in education*: Advancing the processes of industrial and technological change is difficult if no parallel effort is made to improve the educational levels of the population. In the MICs, the objective is not necessarily to expand access to primary education (already virtually universal in many of these countries) but to strengthen secondary, vocational, and university education, better connecting the availability of training with labor needs and improving the quality of the education system as a whole (see chapter 9). In addition to improvements in levels of productivity entailed by such efforts, educational investment will contribute to encouraging citizen demands on public sector policies and institutions, thereby improving the conditions of governance (see chapters 4 and 5).

e) *Improvement of infrastructures*: Infrastructure development is a strategic objective to facilitate productive change, to promote environmental sustainability, to improve distributive parameters (both socially and geographically), and to strengthen local financial markets. Despite its strategic function, the deficiencies that MICs suffer in the area of infrastructure are multiple (see chapters 10 and 11). Overcoming these shortcomings requires an investment effort, which in turn needs not only domestic resources, but appropriate financial mechanisms in the international arena. It is important that both the Multilateral and National Development Banks adapt their instruments and business models to the needs of the MICs in this vital dimension (see chapters 11 and 12).

f) *Institutional improvement*: Development is a complex process that requires economic change accompanied by reform of those institutions that structure social interaction. However, the latter do not always respond with a dynamism consistent with economic change. This problem is especially pronounced in the case of MICs, leading to fragile institutions and limited foundations of the social fabric. Informality is but one exponent of this dissonance. Nevertheless, in order to advance their development, countries require institutions with the capacity to design and implement public policies, the credibility to manage distributive conflicts, and the capability to deal with external shocks (see chapters 4, 5, and 6).

g) *Fighting inequality and social exclusion*: To consolidate development achievements, improve the quality of institutions, and promote social stability, it is necessary to combat the conditions of marked inequality that characterize a large number of MICs. Strengthening of the education system should be aimed precisely at promoting equal opportunities; but it is likewise necessary to strengthen the fiscal capacity of the State to design an adequate path toward the universalization of basic social services (see chapters 7, 8, and 9).

To overcome development obstacles, MICs will need not only appropriate national responses, but also some changes in the rules at the international level.

The international system has managed to define those support mechanisms required by the poorest countries to emerge from their vulnerable situation, but no similar effort has been developed to identify the support mechanisms and instruments required to encourage the convergence process of MICs. Thus, it is necessary to correct this lack of reform in the multilateral sphere, in the fields of trade (see chapter 14), development financing (see chapters 11, 12, and 13), and international monetary institutions (see chapter 15).

1.6 Structure of the Book

Gill and Kharas (2015: 4) recognize that their proposals on MITs have been motivated by "the absence of a satisfactory growth theory that could inform development policy in middle-income economies," and insist "it was a trap of ignorance about the nature of economic growth in middle-income countries" (Gill and Kharas, 2015: 4). This volume aims precisely to reduce that ignorance, calling on a large body of leading specialists to reflect on the development challenges that MICs face (whether or not they are termed "traps"), as well as the most appropriate policies for overcoming them.

The book is structured into three main sections: the first examines development challenges; the second concerns domestic policies; and the third considers international relations. The first section opens with chapter 2, by Homi Kharas and Indermit Gill, on *growth strategies to avoid MITs*. These authors begin by recognizing the limited capacity that growth theory has shown in explaining the drivers that promote the growth of MICs. The Solow model can explain the growth of low-income countries, and the Romer and Lucas models can be useful in explaining the growth of developed countries, but a gap persists in our understanding of the sources of growth of MICs. To cover that gap, these authors propose that Schumpeterian growth models can offer new and useful ideas.

Chapter 3, by Keun Lee, focuses on problems related to the *development of technological capabilities and productive upgrading* as a way to avoid MITs. Lee's message is clear: in order to advance a catch-up process, countries should avoid revisiting paths previously followed by leading countries. The new route will not be simple, and Lee suggests three significant detours. The first is to promote imitative innovations in the form of petit patents and trademarks, as opposed to pursuing a high level of Intellectual Property Right (IPR) protection. The second detour is to favor promotion of domestic value-added and to reduce a country's reliance on global value chains before its economy is fully coupled with them. The third detour is to specialize in short-cycle technology-based sectors, instead of seeking to enter directly into long-cycle technology-based sectors and segments that are hallmarks of advanced economies.

Chapter 4, by José Antonio Alonso, analyzes problems related to *institutional change*. The author discusses the criteria that define institutional quality, and he examines the various ways in which institutional change occurs. When institutional change is empirically analyzed, two anomalous behaviors can be found in two middle-income regions: an excessive fluidity of institutions in one case (Latin America) and, in contrast, an excessive stickiness of institutions in the other (MENA). Based on prior work, Alonso explores the determinants of institutional quality; his results suggest that per capita income, tax revenue, redistribution (rather than just inequality), education, and international openness all appear to be strong determinants of institutional quality.

Chapter 5, by Richard Doner and Ben Schneider, examines the difficulties that MICs experience in *implementing the policies* needed for economic convergence. These policies require institutions that are capable of effective consultation, monitoring, and credible enforcement. However, such institutions are difficult to construct in MICs because of the existence of social groups that obstruct the building of coalitions needed for institutional upgrading. While coalition-building is decisive, bureaucratic resistance and the fragmentation of political institutions can pose additional obstacles to effective policy and institution-building. Finally, the authors suggest that such demand-side disarticulation is often mirrored and intensified by supply-side factors—namely, by weakly institutionalized party systems.

Chapter 6, by Mario Pezzini, is oriented to the need for MICs to *build national strategies* to mobilize domestic resources and improve quality of spending. Those strategies should be designed and implemented in ways that engage citizens in institutionalized democratic deliberation processes that provide spaces for local experimentation. In order to put all these efforts in place, strengthening the right capacities of MICs governments is essential. To this purpose MICs should make full use of the benefits of international cooperation, in particular on strategy building and on the mobilization of domestic resources.

The second section opens with Chapter 7, by Chris Hoy and Andy Sumner, and is dedicated to analysis of the *potential fiscal space of MICs for tackling poverty*, even if that fiscal space is effectively locked by the domestic political economy. The chapter offers estimates of the capacity for national redistribution in the form of new taxes, or the reallocation of public spending toward cash transfers to the poor. They find that up to three-fourths of global poverty at the $1.90 per day poverty line—and even three-fourths of global poverty at $5 per day—could be eliminated through nationally funded redistribution in the form of a reallocation of public finances and/or new taxes.

Chapter 8, by Juliana Martínez Franzoni and Diego Sánchez-Ancochea, looks at ways through which the *universalization of social policies in MICs* can be achieved. Much of the social science literature defines universal social policies as a set of tax-funded programs that provide everyone with equally generous services and transfers. However, many MICs face abundant obstacles in meeting this objective. Building on previous work, the authors separate universal outputs from strategies to achieve them—both short- and long-term—and they introduce the concepts of policy architectures and trajectories to achieve this end. A second contribution of this chapter is to link discussions around instruments and politics.

Chapter 9, by Rolph van der Hoeven, is dedicated to examining the *labor market regimes* based on the experiences of those MICs that have fared better in terms of virtuous growth. In this author's view, the key factor is the development of domestic innovation capabilities to move up the value chain and to generate sustained productivity growth. To restore a balance in society, development policies need to be strengthened by good labor market policies that not only reduce income inequalities in general, but that reverse the declining labor share in national income and support workers against inevitable economic transformations (in terms of introducing or strengthening unemployment insurance and basic social protections, independent of job status).

Chapter 10, by Emilio Padilla, discusses the need for MICs to implement effective *policies for environmental sustainability*. Some environmental policies are affordable and may even provide welfare enhancement and economic and social gains for MICs. However, environmental and green industrial policies require good governance as well as good quality institutions in order to avoid rent-seeking and political capture. The international context of environmental awareness and the stringency of policies in rich nations and international agreements play an important role in the potential gains to be made by promoting green transformations in MICs.

This part concludes with Chapter 11, by Stephany Grifith-Jones, on *the role of national development banks* (NDBs). In her vision, national development finance is crucial for funding sufficient investment, a pre-condition to allow MICs to grow in a macroeconomically and environmentally sustainable way. The chapter stresses NDBs' contribution to supporting innovative sectors, as well as sustainable infrastructure. The support of innovation with long-term financing is complementary to the other functions of these institutions, including supporting the provision of public goods (such as fighting climate change) and financial inclusion. In all cases, NDBs should not supplant private financing but should rather complement and leverage additional private funds for innovative activities and for counter-cyclical financing at the national level.

The third part refers to the responsibilities that international actors must assume regarding the problems and challenges faced by MICs. This section opens with chapter 12, by Otaviano Canuto and colleagues, aimed at analyzing how *Multilateral Development Banks (MDBs) address the policy needs of MICs*. Policy responses should be deployed in areas such as human capital accumulation, the development of high cognitive skills, the fostering of entrepreneurship, the availability of advanced infrastructure, and macroeconomic stability. In all these areas

MDBs have defined instruments and policies for supporting national efforts. Accordingly, there seems to be a convergence between overcoming growth traps and the activity of MDBs en route to countries' graduation.

Chapter 13, by José Antonio Alonso and Jonathan Glennie, is dedicated to analyzing how the *development cooperation system* should change in order to be effective in the context of the highly ambitious 2030 Agenda. The emergence of MICs in the development cooperation policy is partially pushing these changes. First, development cooperation must modernize the way it measures impact, focusing not just on what is financed directly, but also on the kinds of incentives for change that it can promote. Second, cooperation should be better able to manage the developing world's increasing diversity: it should operate with differentiated agendas, and with a mixture of different modalities and instruments. And, third, the development cooperation system must embrace all countries and actors, building international collective action in favor of sustainable development.

Chapter 14, by Renato Baumann, seeks to discuss the effectiveness of signing preferential trade agreements and participating in value chains as two ways for MICs to overcome MITs. In terms of integration into value chains, the requirements are diversified and comprise favorable conditions at both the micro and the macro levels. As to the question of whether preferential trade agreements increase the chances of belonging to a value chain, evidence suggests that a number of customs unions fail to manifest significant value-added production, while some of the most successful examples do not adopt common tariffs. Thus, belonging to a regional group is not a sufficient condition for participating in value chains.

Finally, chapter 15, by José Antonio Ocampo, focuses on the problems that MICs have in relation to the *international monetary and financial system*. MICs maintain a status of dependence in the global reserve system and face significant volatility of external financing, which in turn generates risks of both macroeconomic and financial crises and constrains domestic macroeconomic policy. Such risks can contribute to the generation of a MIT, and the instruments put in place to manage those risks, both domestically and internationally, remain far from complete. Finally, the author discusses the inadequate representation that MICs have in the governance of the system.

1.7 Acknowledgments

Like all collective projects, this volume has benefited from numerous forms of personal and institutional support. We first extend our gratitude to the collaborating scholars, who have contributed their specialized knowledge on the subject and have shown generous flexibility in adapting their contributions to the project's conditions. Most of the chapters were presented in a first version at an International Workshop held in Madrid on June 10 and 11, 2019. The Ramón Areces Foundation provided its comfortable facilities and the assistance necessary to facilitate development of the Workshop, which also benefited from economic support from the Spanish Cooperation (General Direction of Sustainable Development Policies at the Spanish Ministry of Foreign Affairs, European Union and Cooperation). All of the book's chapters have been enriched by discussions held during those two days. Finally, we thank Oxford University Press for its willingness to feature this volume among its publications and are particularly grateful to its editorial team for their understanding and support. As usual, any mistake is our exclusive responsibility. The book will have fulfilled its purpose if it contributes to better identifying and exploring the development challenges that affect MICs and if it is able to revitalize discussions about the appropriate national and international responses to them.

References

Agenor, Pierre-Richard and Canuto, Otaviano (2012): "Middle income traps", Policy Research Working Paper 6210, Washington, DC: The World Bank.

Agenor, Pierre-Richard, Canuto, Otaviano, and Jelenic, Michael (2012): "Avoiding middle-income growth traps", Economic Premise no. 98, November, Washington, DC: The World Bank.

Aiyar, Shekhar, Duval, Romain, Puy, Damien, Wu, Yiqun, and Zhang, Longmei (2013): "Growth slowdowns and the Middle-Income Trap", IMF Working Paper 13/71, Washington, DC: IMF.

Alonso, José Antonio (2016): "Beyond aid: reshaping the development cooperation system", in J. A. Ocampo (ed.), *Global Governance and Development*, Oxford: Oxford University Press.

Azariadis, C. and Drazen, A. (1990): "Threshold externalities in economic development", *Quarterly Journal of Economics* 105: 521–6.

Baldwin, Richard (2016): *The Great Convergence. Information Technology and the New Globalization*, New York, Cambridge MA, Harvard University Press.

Barro, Robert (2012): "Convergence and modernization revisited", *NBER Working Paper* 18295, https://www.nber.org/papers/w18295.

Bowles, Samuel, Durlauf, Steven N., and Hoff, Karla (2006): *Poverty Traps*, Princeton, NJ: Princeton University Press.

Bresser-Pereira, Luiz, Araújo, Eliane Cristina, and Costa Peres, Samuel (2020): "An alternative to the middle-income trap", *Structural Change and Economic Dynamics* 52: 294–312.

Doner, Richard and Schneider, Ben Ross (2016): "The middle-income trap. more politics than economics," *World Politics*, 68, no. 4: 608–44.

Eichengreen, Barry, Park, Donghyun, and Shin, Kwanho (2012): "When fast growing economies slow down: International evidence and implication for China", *Asian Economic Papers*, 11: 42–87.

Eichengreen, Barry, Park, Donghyun, and Shin, Kwanho (2013): "Growth Slowdowns redux: New evidence on the middle-income trap", NBER Working Paper 18673, Cambridge, MA: NBER.

Felipe, Jesus, Abdon, Arnelyn, and Kumar, Utsav (2012): "Tracking the middle-income trap: What is it, who is in it, and why?" Levy Economics Institute, Working Paper 715 Bard College.

Gill, Indermit S. and Kharas, Homi (2007): *An East Asian Renaissance: Ideas for Economic Growth*, Washington, DC: The World Bank.

Gill, Indermit S. and Kharas, Homi (2015): "The middle-income trap turns ten", Policy Research Working Paper 7403, Washington, DC: The World Bank.

Guillaumont, Patrick (2009): *Caught in a Trap. Identifying the Least Developed Countries*, París, Economica.

Hausmann, Ricardo, Pritchett, Lant, and Rodrik, Dani (2005): "Growth accelerations", *Journal of Economic Growth*, 10 (4): 303–29.

Im, Fernando Gabriel and Rosenblatt, David (2013): "Middle-income traps: A conceptual and empirical survey", Policy Research Working Paper 6594, Washington, DC: The World Bank.

Kenny, Charles (2012): *Getting Better: Why Global Development is SUCCEEDING, and How We Can Improve the World Even More?*, New York: Basic Books.

Larson, Greg; Loayza, Norman, and Woolcock, Michael (2016): "The middle-income traps: Myth or Reality?", *Research Policy Brief* no 1, March, The World Bank.

Lee, Keun (2013): *Schumpeterian Analysis of Economic Catch-up: Knowledge, Path-Creation, and the Middle-Income Trap*, Cambridge: Cambridge University Press.

Lee, Keun (2019): *The Art of Economic Catch-up: Barriers, Detours and Leapfrogging*, Cambridge: Cambridge University Press.

MelguizoMelguizo, Angel, Nieto-Parra, Sebastian, Perea, José Ramón, and Ariel Perez, Jaime (2017): "No sympathy for the devil! Policy priorities to overcome the middle-income trap in Latin America," OECD Development Centre Working Papers 340.

Milanovic, Branko (2005): *Worlds Apart: Measuring International and Global Inequality*, Princeton, NJ: Princeton University Press.

Nelson, Richard R. (1956): "A Theory of the Low-Level Equilibrium Trap in Underdeveloped Economies". *The American Economic Review* 46 (5): 894–908.

Ocampo, José Antonio (2013): "Rethinking Global Economic and Social Governance", in Joseph E. Stiglitz and Mary Kaldor (eds.), *The Quest for Security: Protection without Protectionism and the Challenge of Global Governance*, New York: Columbia University Press, pp. 313–42.

Ocampo, José Antonio and Juan Martin (2003): *Globalization and Development: A Latin American and Caribbean Perspective*. Palo Alto, CA: Stanford University Press, ECLAC and World Bank.

Ohno, Kenichi (2009): "Avoiding the middle-income trap: renovating industrial policy formulation in Vietnam", *ASEAN Economic Bulletin* 26 (1): 25–43.

Paus, Eva (2014): *Latin America's Middle Income Trap*, Financing for Development Series no 250, ECLAC.

Paus, Eva (2019): "Innovation strategies matter: Latin America's middle-income trap meets China and globalisation," *The Journal of Development Studies*, 56 (4): 657–79.

Piketty, Thomas (2014): *Capital in the Twenty-First Century*, Cambridge, MA: Harvard University Press.

Pritchett, Lant and Summers, Lawrence H. (2014): "Asiaphoria meets regression to the mean", NBER Working Paper No 20573, Washington.

Radelet, Steven (2015): *The Great Surge. The Ascent of the Developing World*, New York: Simon and Schuster.

Ridley, Matt (2010): *The Rational Optimist: How Prosperity Evolves*, New York: Harper Collins.

Robertson, Peter E. and Ye Longfeng (2013): "On the existence of a middle income trap", The University of Western Australia Discussion Paper 13.12, The University of Wester Australia.

Spence, Michael (2011): *The Next Convergence. The Future of Economic Growth in a Multispeed World*, New York: Farrar, Straus and Giroux.

UNDP (2013): *The Rise of the South: Human Progress in a Diverse World*, New York: Human Development Report.

2

Growth Strategies to Avoid the Middle-Income Trap

Homi Kharas and Indermit Gill

2.1 Introduction

The World Bank currently classifies 107 countries as middle-income. They have a combined GDP of $31 trillion and a population of 5.7 billion people. The country are so different that it is not surprising that the question of what drives middle-income growth has no easy answers. In fact, it would be quite fortuitous if there were a unifying idea that applied to all middle-income countries. Yet there does seem to be something special about middle-income countries that distinguish them from low-income or high-income countries. Despite the diversity of contexts, there appear to be guideposts and a framework to which middle-income country policymakers should pay close attention. This framework and its implications for development policy is the subject of this chapter.

The motivation for policymakers is to avoid what has come to be known as "the middle-income trap" (MIT, Gill, Kharas et al., 2007). Since we coined the term in 2006, the MIT has been the subject of scores of investigations.[1] The investigators have generally tried to answer one of two questions: Is there evidence to support the existence of the trap, and what can middle-income countries do to spring free of it? The evidence in support of its existence has been mixed, and the policy discussions have—to put it bluntly—been largely unhelpful. Our objective in this chapter is to reflect on what makes middle-income countries different and to provide some generalizations about policymaking in middle-income countries.

Our original MIT proposition was that of the possibility of a trap, not its inevitability. We used MIT as a device to highlight a concern with our limited understanding of middle-income country growth drivers and with the absence of a functional theory to guide policy advice to middle-income country governments. Solow–Swan models that stressed capital accumulation and exogenous technological change did well to explain growth in low-income countries. Lucas–Romer models emphasizing learning and endogenous technical change identified the

[1] See "An East Asian Renaissance," published by the World Bank in 2007.

Homi Kharas and Indermit Gill, *Growth Strategies to Avoid the Middle-Income Trap* In: *Trapped in the Middle? Developmental Challenges for Middle-Income Countries*. Edited by: José Antonio Alonso and José Antonio Ocampo, Oxford University Press (2020). © OUP. DOI: 10.1093/oso/9780198852773.003.0002

main drivers of growth in advanced economies and explained why capital and know-how did not easily flow to poorer economies. But neither class of models has, to our knowledge, satisfactorily explained successful transitions from one type of growth to the other, so the ability to advise middle-income countries, that are essentially in this transition mode, has been constrained. Using the empirical findings about how to sustain growth based on either model did not seem useful for interpreting and understanding the growth challenges in middle-income countries.

In this chapter, we start with a brief overview of recent empirical work on the MIT. Then, we present three facts that suggest that middle-income country growth processes are different from those in other countries, and so do need to be understood as distinctive. We suggest that Schumpeterian models, as formalized by Aghion, Howitt, and others, that stress the importance of effective competition regimes, adroit management of economic crises, and mechanisms to maintain social mobility provide a good starting point for a policy discussion on middle-income country growth.

2.2 The Middle-Income Trap: A Brief Review of Empirical Evidence

Much has been written about what makes for a successful development strategy in a middle-income country—both before and after we first introduced the notion of a middle-income trap more than a decade ago. A few years ago, in Gill and Kharas (2015), we tried to summarize the state of the debate. Since then, scores of new articles have appeared. A search of "middle income trap" in Google Scholar yields about 242,000 results. Here, we will not try to catalog or classify the newest contributions. We reflect instead on how best to distill what has been learned.

The extensiveness of the MIT literature highlights one of the key features of the middle-income trap: it is not a phenomenon that is easily defined—indeed, many papers postulate different definitions—but it is quite obvious when you see it. If Argentina and South Africa record per capita growth rates of 0.5 percent and 0.3 percent per year on average, between 1980–2019, then surely they can be described as being in a "trap."[2] If Mexico, with all the advantages of proximity and integration with the United States, only grows by 0.8 percent over this same period while Poland, similarly placed geographically next to high income, high performing economies like Germany, grows by 2.5 percent, then again there is something important to say about their comparative growth rates. It seems legitimate to claim Mexico is in a MIT, while Poland is not. Cumulatively, of course,

[2] Data from the IMF World Economic Outlook April 2019 database. All growth rates evaluated from 2011 purchasing power parity (PPP) estimates of GDP per capita.

these per capita differences in growth can generate huge changes in the welfare of citizens. In the early 1980s, after the oil price shock, Mexicans were 50 percent richer than Poles. Today, Poles are 50 percent richer than Mexicans.

These two examples suggest at least two core ideas behind the middle-income trap concept. One is the idea of low absolute growth, stretching into the future, in select middle-income countries—a band of middle-income doldrums, so to speak, that countries cannot easily sail through. The second is the idea that low growth in middle-income countries is not inevitable, again suggesting that policy and institutional design in middle-income countries can determine if long-run incomes stall within the middle-income range or if growth can be sustained to transition through to high-income levels.

Among the large number of papers that try to establish empirical relationships between initial income levels and subsequent growth, we refer the reader to Eichengreen et al. (2013). They identify two ranges of growth slowdowns, defined as a decline of at least 2 percentage points per year compared to a seven-year moving average; one, between $10,000 and $11,000 and the other between $15,000 and $16,000. Others looking at growth slowdowns include Aiyar et al. (2013) who find that middle-income countries have a greater frequency of slowdowns than low-income or high-income countries. Spence (2011) finds countries clustering in a narrow band of income between $5,000 and $10,000, while Felipe et al. (2012) look at the number of years that countries have stayed within given middle-income bands and finds examples of countries spending decades with the same country classification. Pritchett and Summers (2014) propose that "regression to the mean" explains why growth rates often do not persist in the medium- and long-term, and why, consequently, we might see a drop-off in middle-income country growth.

A variant of the approach of looking at all countries' growth experience and teasing out middle-income slowdowns is to try to identify "club convergence" (Agenor and Canuto (2012); Im and Rosenblatt (2013)). Robertson and Ye (2013) develop this idea rigorously and consistently. They focus on long-run income levels to which countries are converging. They define a middle-income trap as being a situation where this long-run, steady-state income level is middle-income. The benefit of this approach is that it avoids potential misinterpretations of structural breaks, slow convergence, or stochastic fluctuations that can appear in recorded growth episodes, especially when these are measured in years rather than decades. They find evidence of a substantial number of countries (around half their sample of forty-six middle-income countries) satisfying their statistical criteria for a MIT.

In addition to low absolute growth or convergence to a middle-income level, the second core idea of the MIT is that middle-income countries may need to develop specific policy and institutional underpinnings to achieve high-income levels. In spirit, this work builds on the growth diagnostics literature initiated by Hausmann at al. (2006) that tries to identify which of a number of policies are the critical obstacles to growth. They consider finance, human, and physical capital; domestic savings; and government effectiveness and/or failure. The value of this strand of analysis is that it focuses directly on the policy issues with which middle-income policymakers are most concerned, rather than the more abstract notion of whether or not a country is in a trap. Doner and Schneider (2016) take this one step further, shifting the emphasis from the nature of the policies and institutions to an emphasis on building political support and stakeholder coalitions to coordinate broad-based innovation over the long-term.

A good recent example of this work is by Melguizo et al. (2017). They look at the policy attributes of today's high-income countries at a time one decade before these countries passed the threshold between upper middle-income status and high-income status. They then compared these policy attributes with those existing in a number of upper middle-income countries in Latin America and identified the largest discrepancies. Based on this, they conclude that the key policy reforms needed in Latin America are: better rule of law, improved secondary and tertiary education, higher tax revenues, political stability, higher investment levels, better technological diffusion, and improved stock markets and credit markets.

In a similar vein, political scientists have also taken an interest in the role played by domestic and external institutions. A special issue of the *Journal of Development Studies* edited by Kang and Paus (2019) brings attention to this work. In particular, political scientists argue that external conditions interact with domestic conditions, around the specifics of globalization, technology diffusion and value chains. Paus (2019) stresses the new global context created by China's size and extraordinary performance across a number of industries ranging from low-tech to high-tech. She claims that China has generated a "Red Queen" effect, meaning that countries have to upgrade faster and faster just to retain their competitive positions, and argues that weaknesses in funding small and medium-sized enterprises as well as new entrepreneurs hobble the efforts of many middle-income country governments today.

Raj-Reichert (2019) looks at Malaysia's efforts to move up the value chain in electronics, where it has a strong industrial production base. She feels domestic production became too oriented to low value-added segments and blames inadequate skills formation and the liberalization of domestic content regulations. However, she does not discuss Malaysia's efforts at skills upgrading, including through the establishment of the first government agency anywhere in the world to explicitly provide programs to attract, nurture, and retain talent in the country. TalentCorp was established in January 2011 and has successfully helped over 5,000 experts to return to Malaysia. She also does not discuss the skills training programs offered by Penang's universities. In fact, Rasiah (2002) had earlier extolled successful government–business coordination in Penang to develop the SME subcontracting industry, efforts that included public training programs.

The debate on what policies matter in middle-income countries has been taken up by economists in cross-section regressions to understand growth dynamics. There have been too many efforts at doing this to list here, but all face significant methodological challenges. Feng et al. (2019) discuss the estimation problems caused by parameter heterogeneity and cross-sectional error dependence, as well as the more famous issues of variable selection made famous by Sala-i-Martin's (1997) "I Just Ran Four Million Regressions" paper. They point to the finding by Durlauf et al. (2001) that linear growth models applying equally to all countries are flawed, with evidence strongly suggesting varying coefficients across countries depending on their level of development. Feng et al. do find that the traditional negative correlation of initial income on subsequent growth holds for most of the time, but with an important exception when it reverses sign between $2,554 and $14,510 (2014 dollars). In this range, it is hard to catch up because those who start with higher incomes achieve faster growth. Like others before, Feng et al. find that parameter coefficients vary considerably by stage of development.

The growing sophistication of the econometrics on the MIT is perhaps at odds with the quality of the data to which it is applied, and the difficulties in generating solid conclusions from datasets that typically contain less than a hundred countries (eighty-nine countries in the case of Feng et al. 2019).

Perhaps the most salient conclusion to draw from the literature on MITs is that the impact of policies and institutions seems to be very context specific, so cross-country analysis can only be indicative to guide the analyst towards potential variables of significance. There are few clear results. As we emphasized before:

> We came across many cases where policy makers who had observed the growing diversification of the economy as it transitioned from low- to middle-income status sought to continue that process by artificially encouraging new industries (most commonly IT industries) with no economic foundation. The important lesson of Imbs and Wacziarg (2003) that more advanced countries tend to specialize was ignored. These [middle-income] countries became trapped when they failed to identify alternative sources of demand to replace exports [that were losing price competitiveness to low-income suppliers].
>
> At the other end, we also saw countries trying to leapfrog prematurely into "knowledge economies", with none of the institutional infrastructure in place to accomplish this. Poor quality universities, low levels of human capital, limited venture capital, regulatory barriers and incomplete rule of law present significant barriers to becoming an innovation-driven economy. Middle-income countries that invest heavily and prematurely in trying to become "knowledge economies" can find low returns to such investments. The combination of

wasted fiscal spending and a faulty growth diagnostic can lead to substandard performance—another example of the middle-income trap."[3]

The inherent difficulty with empirical analysis of the MIT, then, is that only around eighty countries have actually passed through Eichengreen's upper threshold. Of this number, twenty are small islands, and another dozen are city-states or oil-exporting enclaves, so the universe of 'normal' countries that have successfully transitioned is very small indeed. Add to this the fact that changes in globalization and technology may also change the transition parameters, and one quickly narrows down even further reliable historical comparisons of countries that escaped the MIT. It is this empirical problem that encourages us to approach the question from a new angle.

2.3 Three Facts about why Middle-Income Countries Are Different

In this section, we highlight three empirical observations that make us believe that middle-income countries are different from other countries. The observations are about the lack of worldwide, or even club, convergence; the heterogeneity of parameters in growth regressions, and the characteristics of countries transitioning across income categories.

2.3.1 Convergence

In *The Handbook of Macroeconomics*, Jones (2016) breaks down differences in GDP per capita across countries into differences in the capital–output ratio, differences in human capital per worker, and an unexplained residual of total factor productivity (TFP) growth. Using data from the Penn World tables, he then argues that there is very little difference in capital–output ratios across the full income spectrum of countries, some difference in human capital that could explain why rich countries have at least twice the income levels of poor countries, and a very large difference in total factor productivity that explains all the rest. In general, and somewhat counter-intuitively, the share of TFP in explaining the difference in income levels across countries is larger the poorer the country.

One way of visualizing these findings is to plot country growth rates against their initial income level. In the Solow model, countries with lower income levels have less capital per worker. Growth is a process of capital deepening. With less capital per worker and diminishing returns to capital in a Cobb–Douglas

[3] See *The Middle Income Trap Turns Ten*, published by the World Bank in 2015.

production function, the return on capital is higher in poor countries, so they should grow faster. To test this, we follow Jones' methods but with updated data (see Feenstra et al. (2015)) and plot GDP growth for the thirty-year period 1987–2017 against a country's initial level of income, standardized against that of the United States. In Figure 2.1, the plot is shown for countries classified by the World Bank in 1987 as "low income," "middle-income," or "high income." We also show the plot of all countries. In each case, a linear regression line is shown. We start the analysis at 1987 because this is the first year for which the World Bank provides country classifications. It also allows for substantial country coverage; starting earlier risks losing countries because of data gaps; starting later reduces the time frame of analysis. Note that the x-axis in the bottom right panel of Figure 2.1 uses a logarithmic scale.

The main feature of Figure 2.1 is the wide disparity of growth rates regardless of initial income level. In the top left panel, looking only at low-income countries,

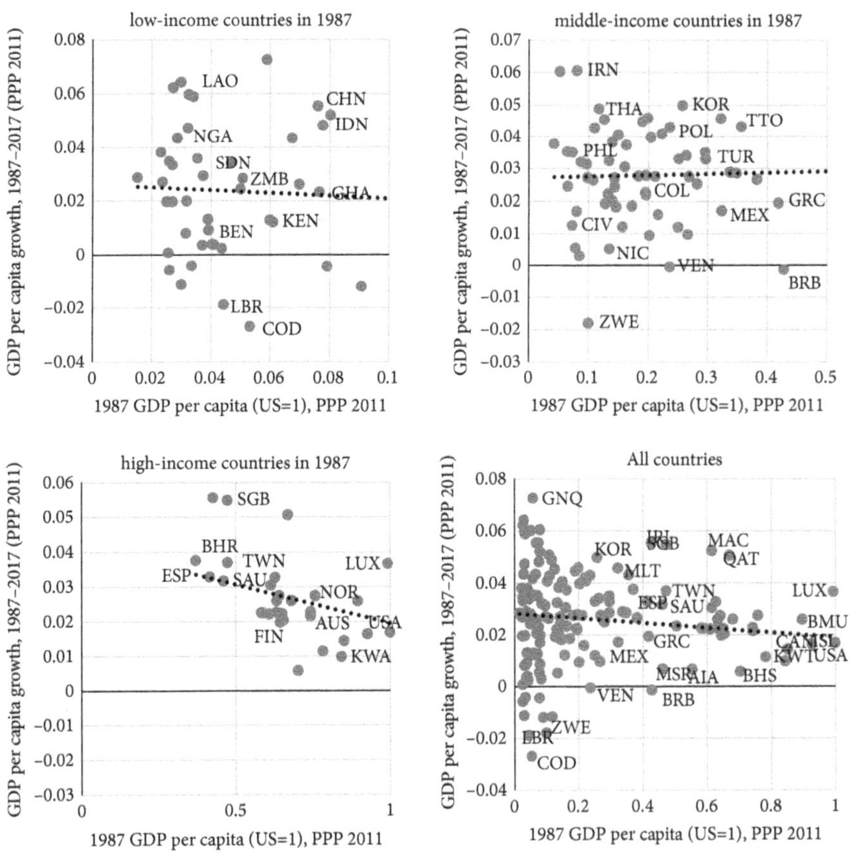

Figure 2.1 Convergence, 1987–2017, by country income group

Sources: GDP data come from Penn World Table version 9.1 (see Feenstra et al. (2015)). Income classifications are based on historical World Bank classifications.

there is some suggestion that poorer countries grow more rapidly, but the relationship is weak. Many countries have had negative growth rates over this period. For middle-income countries, the relationship between growth and initial income levels appears to reverse itself, but the relationship is weak and the variance of growth outcomes is high. High-income countries display the familiar pattern of convergence that many others have found. At a minimum, the data suggest that explaining growth remains difficult for all countries, including those in middle-income.

2.3.2 Parameter Heterogeneity

One of the obstacles in undertaking empirical analysis of growth is the limited number of country observations compared to the number of potential explanatory variables. A common technique employed to mitigate this problem is to impose an identical aggregate production function across all countries (eg, Mankiw et al. 1992). But this has its own limitations, so Durlauf et al. (2001) and Feng et al. (2019) have introduced ways of allowing the parameters estimated in the growth regressions to vary according to selected country characteristics. These exercises suggest that parameter heterogeneity is indeed widespread. For example, Durlauf et al. (2001) conclude that "evidence of parameter heterogeneity is strongest for the poorest countries in the sample." Eichengreen et al. (2017) conducted a similar analysis aimed at identifying whether economic factors associated with growth appear to differ across income groups. They find that the efficiency of a country's financial system matters less for growth as one moves up the income scale. Similarly, as income grows, demographic variables such as the gender ratio become less important. Instead, other variables like government debt ratio, capital inflow dependence, and currency crisis status take precedence.

Another approach is to expand the data set by using growth in sub-national regions, along the lines of Barro and Sala-i-Martin (1990). Until recently, such analysis was restricted to advanced economies because sub-national growth data did not exist in developing countries. A new literature, however, has established a close correlation between night-time luminosity data collected using satellites, and GDP growth (Hu and Yao (2019) provide a recent overview). Using this data, sub-national growth can be computed for all countries in the world and is readily available to researchers (Ghosh et al. (2010)).

Based on this, Cohen et al. (2019) utilize a database of over 3,000 subnational regional growth rates. Their paper divides the data using the national income classifications for 2003 provided by the World Bank into low-income, middle-income, and high-income.[4] Each classification has sufficient degrees of freedom to estimate a growth regression.

[4] Data are from the sources described in Cohen et al. (2019), except for the distance to the nearest port that are from the National Geospatial-Intelligence Agency (2019).

Table 2.1 Parameter heterogeneity according to level of development: Determinants of sub-national growth, 2003–2013

	(1)	(2)	(3)	(4)
	All	**Low income**	**Middle income**	**High income**
GDP per capita (Ln, 2006)	−0.009***	0.004	−0.012***	0.001
	(0.001)	(0.004)	(0.002)	(0.002)
Rule of law (2000)	−0.007***	0.019	0.005*	0.096***
	(0.002)	(0.013)	(0.002)	(0.019)
Rule of law2 (2000)	0.002	0.020**	0.002	−0.040***
	(0.001)	(0.008)	(0.003)	(0.008)
Normalized difference vegetation index (Ln)	0.010***	0.015*	0.010***	0.012***
	(0.002)	(0.007)	(0.003)	(0.003)
Distance to roads, (m, Ln)	−0.003	−0.013*	−0.003	0.006***
	(0.001)	(0.005)	(0.002)	(0.001)
Travel time to cities (min., Ln)	0.009***	0.025***	0.005**	0.005***
	(0.001)	(0.005)	(0.001)	(0.001)
Travel time to capital (min., Ln)	−0.002***	−0.005***	0.000	−0.001
	(0.000)	(0.001)	(0.000)	(0.000)
Drought exposure (Ln)	−0.001	−0.006	−0.001	0.002
	(0.002)	(0.006)	(0.002)	(0.002)
Distance to the nearest port (m, Ln)	0.005***	0.007*	0.006***	−0.001
	(0.001)	(0.003)	(0.001)	(0.001)
Malaria suitability (Ln)	−0.002***	0.002	−0.003***	−0.002***
	(0.001)	(0.003)	(0.001)	(0.001)
Conflict deaths 1989–2000 (per 100,000, Ln)	0.002**	0.001	0.002*	−0.003
	(0.001)	(0.002)	(0.001)	(0.002)
Constant	−0.089**	−0.226*	−0.049	−0.257***
	(0.028)	(0.089)	(0.031)	(0.035)
Observations	3,131	885	1,637	540
Adjusted R^2	0.1375	0.0801	0.0841	0.2362

Notes: Dependent variable is log-difference in night-time luminosity per capita between 2003 and 2013 in annual terms. Estimation is by ordinary least squares (OLS) with standard errors. World Bank national income classifications are for 2003. Middle-income category combines lower middle-income and upper middle-income countries.

*** $p < 0.01$, ** $p < 0.05$, * $p < 0.1$

The results are re-created in Table 2.1. Here, we are not interested in issues of variable choice and model selection but focus on the differences in the parameter estimates for different country classifications. For example, the first row shows that while there is significant conditional convergence in middle-income countries, this does not hold for low-income or high-income countries. On the other hand, the rule of law appears to be more important in high-income countries compared with middle-income countries. Similarly, travel time to the capital is more important in low-income countries than middle-income countries. For some variables, the parameter signs reverse. All of this suggests that reliance on empirically estimated growth models is unlikely to be a robust guide for providing policy advice to middle-income countries because the sample of such countries is small compared to the range of plausible policy and institutional variables and their interactions.

2.3.3 Transition Dynamics: The Dominance of Total Factor Productivity

A third empirical observation is that the main factor differentiating countries that cross from one income category to another is total factor productivity growth. A study by Kim and Park (2017), from the Asian Development Bank, divides countries into five initial income categories: lower-low, upper-low, lower-middle, upper-middle, and high. They assign each category a number and look at the growth performance of countries that stayed in the same group between 1975 and 2014 (11, 22, 33, 44, and 55) compared with those that transitioned up by one category (12, 23, 34, and 45). Their results are reproduced in Figure 2.2.

Figure 2.2 shows, by construction, that growth is higher in upward transitioning countries than in countries that remain in the same category. But the difference in growth rates is not large; only 1 to 2 percentage points per year. Cumulatively, over a 40-year period, these add up to significant changes in relative income level. The most striking feature of Figure 2.2, however, is that the contribution of capital

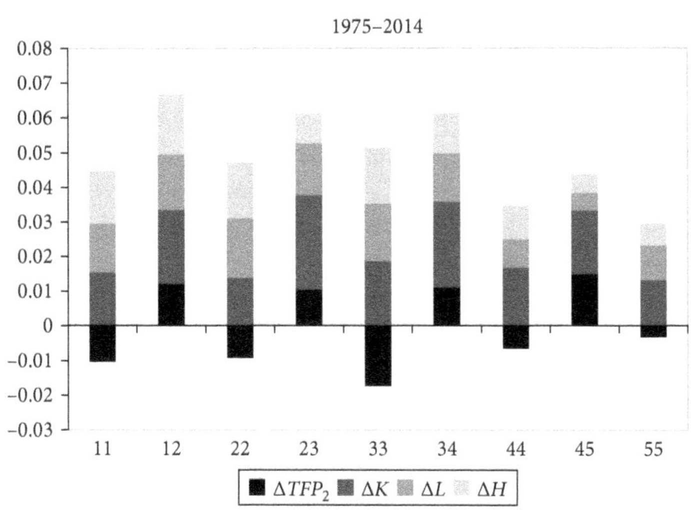

Figure 2.2 Contribution of factors to economic growth, by income and transition country groups

Source: Kim and Park (2017).

accumulation, labor force growth, and human capital development is more or less the same in countries that stay in their income category and those that transition upwards. The major difference lies in the relative contribution of total factor productivity growth. In every case, countries that stayed in their same income category have displayed negative TFP growth, while those that were able to transition out show TFP adding at least one percentage point to annual growth over the period.

These findings parallel those of Eichengreen et al. (2017) who find evidence that those countries successfully advancing from middle- to high-income status succeed in recording higher TFP growth rates, despite having similar investment rates, as compared to a control group of countries that remain middle-income over long periods of time.

2.4 A Short Guide to Successful Middle-Income Transitions

What do we make of these observations? In general, one has to agree with Barro (2012), who writes: "My view is that one has to accept the idea that pinpointing precisely which X variables matter for growth is impossible."

As noted above, Jones (2016) and Kim and Park (2017) find that middle-income growth is all about TFP. Jones breaks this into two components: the stock of ideas and everything else, that is, misallocation. He writes, "When resources are allocated optimally, the economy will operate on its production possibilities frontier [but] when resources are misallocated... TFP will be lower." Jones presents numerous examples of misallocations that can affect growth, including knowledge spillovers, geography, and discrimination. The key, then, is optimizing the allocation of resources; be they human, capital, or anything in between.

Accepting the view that empirical analysis is of limited use, and that the problem is all about differences in TFP, is disturbing. It implies that giving policy advice on raising TFP, which is almost defined as the "black box" of growth accounting that measures what we do not know, is likely to be very complicated. For this reason, we revert back to theory, and to drawing lessons from practitioners.

2.4.1 A Theory of Middle-income Country Growth

If middle-income country growth depends both on accumulation and innovation—as it intuitively does—the problem can be categorized as follows. Middle-income country growth involves: (1) putting in place the mechanisms for increasing investment in both physical and human capital (ie, accumulation), (2) creating the incentives for innovation, and (3) creating the institutions to ensure that they affect timely transitions from accumulation to innovation, that is, they don't end up being stuck with structures that they don't have much use for any more. This three-pronged strategy compares with a single pronged growth strategy in low-income countries (which primarily have to focus on accumulation), or high-income countries (which primarily have to focus on innovation, albeit embodied sometimes in capital accumulation).

Policymakers dealing with complex problems need good conceptual guides—this is where theories such as Aghion and Howitt's (1992) formalization of the Schumpeterian model of creative destruction prove useful. Such models help explain, in plain English rather than in mathematical abstractions, what determines outlays on human capital accumulation, investments in infrastructure, and efforts to speed up innovation. They may also help in timing institutional adjustments so that the structural changes needed for economies to thrive are not stymied. We think this class of theoretical models is especially useful—perhaps even indispensable—for understanding how countries grow through middle income, the difficult stage of development between per capita output levels roughly between $1,000 and $12,000. The key insights are related to how we should think about competition policy, social mobility, and economic crises. By itself, each one is not novel. But, taken together, they may well give us the framework to guide policymakers concerned with boosting middle-income country growth and avoiding the middle-income trap.

It should be noted that competition policy, social mobility, and economic crises are interrelated; put another way, there are complementarities and tradeoffs among them that countries must exploit or manage. Additionally, their effects on investment, innovation, and growth are non-linear; that is, the dose of each measure—competition, mobility, and crises—must be calibrated. Given these complexities, there are bound to be difficulties in implementing an approach involving both creation and destruction, both accumulation and innovation. This is perhaps what makes economic growth in middle-income countries especially difficult.

2.4.1.1 Competition Policy and Investment

The classical view on competition is that perfect competition in an industry incentivizes firms to compete and to invest so as to gain market share as a way of maximizing profits. Thus, the standard neoclassical prescription for middle-income countries has been to liberalize markets. Schumpeter argued the opposite—that investment is higher when large firms either dominate markets and can command monopoly profits which provide them cash to invest, or when they see market domination, with super-normal profits, as a potential future if they successfully invest in a new technology. A simple summary of the effects of competition on investment by firms is that it can be either positive or negative.

But we can say more. A survey of the evidence by Mathis and Sand-Zantman (2014) points to the impact of competition on investment as depending on the competition policy measure, the type of investment, and the state of capital markets. Privatization of public enterprises, for example, can ease entry by new firms and hence increase investment. But because the incentives of the previous managers may be more political and less profit-driven, privatization may reduce investment. The effects of competition on investment also depend on how much firms have to depend on retained earnings or extra-normal profits for financing investment. Mathis and Sand-Zantman explain why functioning of capital markets can make all the difference.

> How market structure impacts investment has also to be tackled with respect to financial constraints. One of the Schumpeter arguments in defense of monopoly was that investment requires cash-in-advance spending and that only monopoly had access to large financial reserve. A counter argument would be to claim that, if the product market is profitable, any firm could go on the financial market and borrow the necessary amount. In fact, it is here necessary to specify both the potential financial imperfections and the impact of the market structure on these imperfections. (Mathis and Sand-Zantman 2014: 4–5)

Now, if we consider innovation as somewhat different from investment, the channels through which competition affects growth are different. The standard reference on this question is Aghion et al. (2005), which proposes a distinction between the incentives facing firms that are in neck-and-neck competition and those that are lagging far behind the industry leaders. For the former, innovation is a way to pull ahead of its competition and earn higher profits. For the latter, there are few incentives to innovate because the returns will be low—a lagging firm will not be able to climb the technology ladder to an extent that would allow it to have above-normal margins to recuperate the expenses incurred by innovating. This characterization leads to industrial structures that result in a non-linear or "inverted-U" relationship between competition and innovation formalized by Aghion and Howitt (1992) in their Schumpeterian Model: greater competition leads initially to more innovation, but only up to a point. When competition is already high, there is typically a technological gap between leaders and followers, and even greater competition will induce the latter to simply give up and reduce innovation still further.

An interesting case study of how East Asian economies caught up to the West is provided by Keun Lee (2014). Lee gives special emphasis to the speed of technological change. Unlike others who make general arguments for the advantages of backwardness or the benefits of being a first-mover, Lee notes that incumbency can best be challenged by a newcomer when technology is changing rapidly and affords opportunities for leapfrogging. He uses this insight to suggest that middle-income countries should specialize in those sectors where technology is moving most rapidly. In these sectors, Lee emphasizes the role of utility models or "petite patents": institutional rules that require a somewhat lower level of innovation in return for shorter protection periods of only 10 years, but that can be registered faster and at lower cost.

For an example of a scenario in which competition could fuel growth consider Latin America, a region that continues to struggle to accelerate growth. Between 2000 and 2016, growth averaged just 2.8 percent per year, well below the 4.8 percent average rate in fifty-six other emerging economies. Latin America faces a critical competition gap, which determines the growth patterns that have persisted for years. Although the region is home to some highly productive global companies, it lacks the backbone of midsize firms that drive innovation and competition—and create productive, well-paying jobs—in more vibrant economies (McKinsey Global institute (2019)). Compounding the problem, many Latin American economies have a long tail of small, often informal companies that collectively employ millions, but that hold back growth because of their low productivity. Domestic competition is not strong enough to either push these firms to innovate, or to force them into bankruptcy and release the resources they employ into more productive uses.

The McKinsey report argues that in order for midsized firms to thrive, policy-makers across Latin America must create a competitive business environment in which digital technologies can thrive, innovation is rewarded, and opportunities are created for all. The rise of competitive, midsized firms would boost productivity, advance skills and wages, and spur innovation. A policy conundrum emerges from the Aghion–Howitt theory. In low-income countries, domestic markets are small, competition is soft, and economic rents are ubiquitous, so the returns to innovation are small and firms do not invest too much. Greater competition (for example, because of import liberalization) can encourage domestic firms to innovate to preserve their market power. Similarly, in rich economies, where competition is strong and firms have frontier technologies, there are large incentives to invest and innovate to escape from the low margins generated by competition, so firms invest heavily in R&D to try and gain a competitive edge. But in middle-income economies, the situation is far less clear, and the impact of greater competition on investment and innovation could be positive or negative depending on the technological characteristics of the industry, on financial markets and other structural features. Decision-makers must carefully consider their environment before drafting policy that will impact competition.

2.4.1.2 Crisis Management and Institutional Change

Next, let us consider the role that crises, destruction, and institutional change play in determining a country's growth, particularly for middle-income countries.

Schumpeter, writing during the Great Depression, saw downturns not as times of crisis but of cleansing.

> They are but temporary. They are the means to reconstruct each time the economic system on a more efficient plan. But they inflict losses while they last, drive firms into the bankruptcy court, throw people out of employment, before the ground is clear and the way paved for new achievement of the kind which has created modern civilization and made the greatness of this country.
>
> (Schumpeter 1934: 113)

Caballero and Hammour (1994) have formalized this notion of cleansing during recessions in a manner consistent with the empirical regularities that recessions tend to be shorter and sharper than expansions, that crises are periods of concentrated job destruction but little or no job creation, and countries with fewer labor and capital market imperfections tend to shift sooner from economic destruction to creation.

For low-income countries, since economic crises and recessions mostly involve destruction with little that is creative, they tend to be periods of social suffering with a limited upside in terms of accumulation. The lesson for these countries is to avoid crises at all costs, and much of the growth literature points to the costs of crises, especially those that are long and serious. Jones and Olken (2005), for example, document the fact that most variation of growth is within countries, over time, rather than between countries. They show that most countries have some decades where they converge to the United States, and other decades where they diverge. In the latter case, featuring episodes of economic crises, physical capital accumulation tends to collapse. The most rapidly growing countries over very long periods of time are those that have the fewest years of low or negative growth, rather than those that have a few years of very rapid growth.

In middle-income countries, however, the Schumpeterian insight is both novel and helpful: crises during the middle-income period could be beneficial or they might be the source of a trap; it all depends on how they are managed. Robinson (2009) argues that the most important consequence of a crisis is not the direct effect of lost jobs and incomes, but the indirect effect on how crises affect the reform of institutions. Following Paul Romer's line of "a crisis is a terrible thing to waste," Robinson argues that periods of crisis have the potential to change institutions and policies in far-reaching ways by disrupting reactionary coalitions and allowing for the emergence of new cross-cutting political coalitions that have a vested interest in good economic policies over decades. His optimistic view is that during crises, outdated arrangements—jobs, contracts, policies, and institutions—can be reformed in a way that has broad-based appeal.

The Commission on Growth and Development (2008) similarly commented on the role of crises, acknowledging that they provide an opening to implement major reforms that otherwise would have been blocked. However, their report also cautions that crises simply provoke change, not necessarily change in the right direction. Strong leadership and competent and influential technocrats are needed in order not to waste a crisis. This is echoed by Robinson who concludes that crises, such as the collapse in commodity prices that accompanied the Great Depression, could well explain aspects of the middle-income trap in Latin America, rather than providing a way to escape the trap. In fact, Robinson concludes on a pessimistic note that much of the time crises will be too small to affect real change in the political equilibrium or, if they are large enough, could as readily lead to problematic change as to positive reforms.

At the risk of simplification, we can conclude that in low-income countries crises and/or recessions are problematic as they almost always lead to collapses in accumulation. In high-income countries, crises can often be positive, as they accelerate reallocation of resources towards more productive use, and can propel changes in institutions and political coalitions to support stronger economic performance. But in middle-income countries the history of crisis management is decidedly mixed, sometimes serving to reinforce a MIT, but occasionally also offering a political pathway out. The subject needs to be studied a lot more.

2.4.1.3 Social Mobility, Entrepreneurship, and Innovation

As more and more of an economy shifts from accumulation to innovation, a third central feature of Schumpeterian growth models becomes important: the social nature of entrepreneurs, and the implications of successful innovation or income distribution and the notion of a "fair" economy.

Since the book on *Redistribution with Growth* by Chenery et al. (1974), development economists have treated improved income distribution as an important corollary of growth and espoused the virtues of inclusive growth, or growth with equity. In a more recent empirical overview, Berg et al. (2018) find that lower inequality is robustly correlated with faster and more durable growth, with the main channels operating through human capital accumulation and reduced fertility, investment-reducing political and social instability, and greater difficulties in adapting to economic shocks.

But how should middle-income countries think about inequality? The main implication of Schumpeterian growth models of creative destruction is that innovation could increase income inequality but, when accompanied by policies to prevent barriers to new business creation, also generates greater social mobility as successful entrepreneurs move into the ranks of the economic elite. Readers should note the linkage with competition policy in product markets. The question then is whether the problem, from a growth point of view, is one of inequality or of social mobility. Aghion et al. (2015) are less concerned about inequality because "overall, [the] findings vindicate the Schumpeterian view whereby the rise in top income shares is partly related to innovation-led growth, where innovation itself fosters social mobility at the top through creative destruction."

The linkage between innovation, on the one hand, and both higher income shares for the top 1 percent and higher upward social mobility, on the other hand, suggests that the dangers for policymaking lie with lobbying and incumbency rather than with inequality itself. In fact, the degree of social tolerance for inequality is often linked with perceptions of future mobility. When the latter is high, then tolerance for inequality is also high and vice-versa.[5]

The policy implications of these two theories are quite different. Traditional development economists have been more concerned with inequality and emphasize greater redistribution, most typically through publicly funded transfers and safety nets. On the other hand, Schumpeterian economists talk about the policies of growth and institutions to support growth (Aghion, 2017). They emphasize property rights (Acemoglu and Johnson, 2005) and an enabling environment to encourage entrepreneurship. The central point is that the source of wealth matters for people's perceptions of inequality. If wealth is derived from innovation and growth (from which others in society also benefit), it is viewed positively, but if it is derived from economic rents it is resented. The policy implication is that tax regimes should differ depending on the source of income, not just its level.

Rodrik (2015) provides a reason why social mobility in middle-income countries may be falling. Manufacturing employment has traditionally been viewed as a vehicle for social mobility—seen as the way that people in today's high-income economies pulled themselves into the middle class—but may be a shrinking option for today's middle-income countries. In Germany, for example, manufacturing employment peaked close to 40 percent in or around 1970, declining noticeably since then. In the Republic of Korea, manufacturing's share of employment peaked at 28 percent in 1990. In today's middle-income economies, industrialization has been slowing and has peaked at even lower levels, so that deindustrialization has started sooner. In the USA, the UK, Sweden, and Germany, deindustrialization set in after the countries had almost reached high income; in China and India, peak manufacturing employment happened during lower-middle income levels. In principle, higher value-added services could serve as the "escalator sector" in middle-income countries. But if Rodrik is correct about manufacturing employment becoming slower and lower, the potential for falling into the MIT is going up, not down.

The World Bank has also looked at social mobility in developing countries (see Narayan et al. (2018)). It finds that greater economic mobility across generations leads to faster growth. Unfortunately, income mobility also appears to be lower in developing countries compared to high-income countries. In most developing

[5] See Carol Graham's (2013) "Pursuing Happiness: Social Mobility and Well-Being."

economies, there is significant persistence in relative income immobility, that is, in the impact of a parent's educational level on the educational attainment of their son or daughter. Partly, this results from low levels of public spending on education: on average, developing countries spend less than 3 percent of GDP on education when their per capita income is $500 or less, rising to over 4 percent at about $2,000, but then stagnating (or even declining somewhat) until $9,000. At that stage, public spending resumes an upward climb, reaching 5.5 percent of GDP in high-income countries.

The World Bank identifies a few ways to equalize economic opportunity: decent maternal care and early child development; accessible quality education for all; and efficient labor markets. Each is amenable to public policy through investments, regulations, and incentives.

2.4.2 The Practitioner's Perspective

An alternative way of thinking about how to avoid the MIT is by explicitly focusing on the criteria used by international institutions like the World Bank to graduate countries from middle-income to high-income status. If countries graduate, then by definition they have escaped the MIT, so a focus on graduation criteria may shed light on the necessary policy reforms.

The World Bank policy seeks to graduate middle-income countries from IBRD lending when they are able to sustain long-term development without further recourse to Bank financing and when they have reached a sufficiently advanced level of development. This deliberately vague definition includes three concepts: (i) a relatively high level of income; (ii) an ability to access private capital markets on reasonable terms; and (iii) the establishment of institutions that are strong enough to sustain economic and social development in the long-term.

Heckelman et al. (2011) from the World Bank have empirically analyzed the conditions under which countries were graduated and "degraduated" (returned to borrowing status). Since 1970 there have been twenty-five instances of graduation and six reversals. The World Bank authors find the probability of a country graduating depends on income levels (above the graduation threshold), various dimensions of institutional quality such as political freedoms and civil rights, quality of public bureaucracy, rule of law and corruption, and indicators of volatility or vulnerability, including country size, export concentration, and recent episodes of financial crisis.

But moving from these results to policy advice is not straightforward. The difficulty is that variables like income level and access to private capital markets are endogenous and so beg the question of what can be done to get high scores in these domains. An associated problem is that the institutional variables may be correlated with other variables that are excluded. For example, none of the three core concepts of Schumpeterian growth considered above—competition policy, crisis management or social mobility—are incorporated into the analysis.

2.5 Concluding Thoughts

Empirical evidence supports the idea that there are many things that are special about middle-income economies. They seem to have a different mix of growth drivers than low-income countries as well as advanced economies, and different growth dynamics. There is a growing body of empirical evidence to suggest that the structural and policy variables in a growth regression have different values (and sometimes different signs) for middle-income countries compared to other countries.

Several analyses use findings of this type to identify key areas that middle-income countries should focus on if they desire to sustain growth. The implication is that without such a switch in focus, middle-income countries will lose growth momentum and stall, that is, fall into a MIT.

The difficulty is that there are many econometric problems that bedevil such regressions, including potentially spurious significance given the very large number of models that are being estimated. Coupled with the limited number of actual transitions from middle-income to high-income levels, empirical assessments seem to have limits in what they offer to policymakers. Where results are robust, they tend to be fairly general (open economies grow faster). Where the empirics are more specific (secondary education is a key for middle-income country growth), they are less robust (maybe tertiary education is of equal or greater importance).

These issues lead us to rely more heavily on theory, and especially to search for theories with transitions and dynamics as central tenets, as we have come to think of middle-income countries as being in a complex transition phase between accumulation and innovation-based economies. Schumpeterian growth processes, formalized by Aghion and others, seem to offer fresh and useful ideas, as compared with Solow or Romer growth models. We found a number of case studies based on these ideas that illustrate how one can move towards quite specific policy recommendations for middle-income countries, for example on targeting sectors with short technology cycles.

We are also intrigued by the insights generated by political scientists thinking about the institutional arrangements that need to be put in place and sustained to avoid a MIT. Their thinking about how hyper-globalization and technological change alter the context for and prospects for avoiding the MIT has opened up a whole new line of exciting research.

One of the complexities of policymaking in middle-income countries, in particular, is that they have diverse technology, industrial organizational, and political economy structures. The lesson of Schumpeterian economics is that the impact of policies will be different, sometimes dramatically so, depending on these structures, so generic prescriptions ("liberalize, privatize, stabilize") may not always be valid. Accepting this view is not an open invitation to heterodoxy, but rather a suggestion that due care and diligence is needed to understand specific contexts before providing policy prescriptions. We have concluded that a serious look at the competitive environment, the vulnerability to and management of crises, and social mobility should be high on the agenda of countries seeking to avoid the MIT.

With this perspective, it is hard not to conclude that the challenges faced by middle-income countries are daunting. Most of these economies have a large tail of underperforming firms, suggesting that the short-run costs of opening up to stronger competition would be high. Many, including a large number of small island economies, are vulnerable to financial shocks and natural disasters. Social mobility is still far lower in developing countries than in advanced economies, suggesting that education systems and the environment for entrepreneurship and innovation remain weak. These seem to us to be the core challenges that make the MIT a real and serious problem for many countries.

One implication of this diagnostic of the MIT is that simple policy and institutional criteria should not be the sole guide to the graduation of countries from eligibility to borrow from international financial institutions. Given the relatively high fraction of graduation "mistakes," with six out of twenty-five cases needing to be reversed, we doubt that reviewing existing graduation policies as a guide to avoiding the MIT provides useful insights for policymakers in middle-income countries. Quite the reverse: our sense is that perhaps it is the graduation criteria themselves that need to be reviewed to capture the features of countries successfully avoiding the MIT—for example by adding national innovation strategies, metrics of social mobility, and an ability to withstand and benefit from global competition to the list of criteria to be considered.

2.6 Acknowledgment

We would like to thank Helena Hlavaty for her assistance with preparation of this paper.

References

Acemoglu, Daron and Johnson, Simon (2005): "Unbundling Institutions," *Journal of Political Economy* 113, no. 5: 949–95. https://economics.mit.edu/files/4467.

Agenor, Pierre-Richard, Canuto, Otaviano, and Jelenic, Michael (2012): "Avoiding middle-income growth traps," *Economic Premise*, no. 98. Washington, DC: World

Bank. http://documents.worldbank.org/curated/en/422121468155111398/Avoiding-middle-income-growth-traps.

Aghion, Philippe (2017): "Entrepreneurship and Growth: Lessons from an Intellectual Journey," *Small Business Economics* 48, no. 1: 9–24. https://doi.org/10.1007/s11187-016-9812-z.

Aghion, Philippe and Howitt, Peter (1992): "A Model of Growth Through Creative Destruction," *Econometrica* 60, no. 2: 323–51. DOI: 10.2307/2951599.

Aghion, Philippe, Bloom, Nick, Blundell, Richard, Griffith, Rachel, and Howitt, Peter (2005): "Competition and innovation: An inverted-U relationship," *The Quarterly Journal of Economics* 120, no. 2: 701–28. https://www.ucl.ac.uk/~uctp39a/ABBGH_QJE_2005.pdf.

Aghion, Philippe, Akcigit, Ufuk, Bergeaud, Antonin, Blundell, Richard, and Hémous, David (2015): "Innovation and Top Income Inequality," ***NBER Working Papers*** 21247. https://www.nber.org/papers/w21247.

Aiyar, Shekha, Duval, Romain, Puy, Damien, Wu, Yiqun, and Zhang, Longmei (2013): "Growth Slowdowns and the Middle-Income Trap," IMF Working Paper No. WP/13/71.

Barro, Robert (2012): "Convergence and Modernization Revisited," *NB*ER Working Papers 18295. https://www.nber.org/papers/w18295.

Barro, Robert J. and Sala-i-Martin, Xavier (1990): "Economic Growth and Convergence across The United States," NBER Working Papers 3419, National Bureau of Economic Research, Inc.

Berg, Andrew, Ostry, Jonathan, Tsangarides, Charalambos, and Yakhshilikov, Yorbol (2018): "Redistribution, inequality, and growth: new evidence," *Journal of Economic Growth* 23, no. 3: 259–305. DOI: 10.1007/s10887-017-9150-2.

Caballero, Ricardo J. and Hammour, Mohamad L. (1994): "The Cleansing Effect of Recessions," *The American Economic Review* 84, no. 5: 1350–68. https://economics.mit.edu/files/12632.

Chenery, H., Ahluwalia, Montek S., Bell, C. L. G., Duloy, John H., and Jolly, Richard (1974): *Redistribution with Growth; Policies to Improve Income Distribution in Developing Countries in the Context of Economic Growth*, Oxford: Oxford University Press.

Clemence, Richard V. (ed.) (2017): *Essays on Entrepreneurs, Innovations, Business Cycles and the Evolution of Capitalism: Joseph A. Schumpeter*. Abingdon: Routledge, 113.

Cohen, Jennifer L., Desai, Raj M., and Kharas, Homi (2019): "Spatial Targeting of Poverty Hotspots," in Homi Kharas, John W. McArthur, and Izumi Ohno (eds.), *Leave No One Behind*, Washington, DC: Brookings Institution Press, pp. 209–37.

Commission on Growth and Development (2008): *The Growth Report: Strategies for Sustained Growth and Inclusive Development*, Washington, DC: The World Bank. https://openknowledge.worldbank.org/handle/10986/6507.

Doner, Richard F. and Schneider, Ben Ross (2016): "The middle-income trap: more politics than economics," *World Politics* 68, no. 4: 608–44. DOI: https://doi.org/10.1017/S0043887116000095.

Durlauf, Steven, Kourtellos, Andros, and Minkin, Artur (2001): "The local Solow growth model," *European Economic Review* 45: 928–40. https://bit.ly/2KU9Gud.

Eichengreen, Barry, Park, Donghyun, and Shin, Kwanho(2013): "Growth Slowdowns Redux: New Evidence on the Middle-Income Trap," NBER Working Papers 18673. https://ideas.repec.org/p/nbr/nberwo/18673.html.

Eichengreen, Barry, Park, Donghyun, and Shin, Kwanho (2017): "The Landscape of Economic Growth: Do Middle-Income Countries Differ?" Asian Development Bank Economics Working Paper Series 517, August. https://www.adb.org/sites/default/files/publication/350021/ewp-517.pdf.

Feenstra, Robert C., Inklaar, Robert, and Timmer, Marcel P. (2015): "The Next Generation of the Penn World Table," *American Economic Review* 105 no. 10: 3150–82. www.ggdc.net/pwt.

Felipe, Jesus, Abdon, Arnelyn, and Kumar, Utsav (2012): "Tracking the middle-income trap: What is it, who is in it, and why?" Levy Economics Institute, Working Paper 715.

Feng, Guohua and Gao, Jiti, and Peng, Bin (2019): "An Integrated Panel Data Approach to Modelling Economic Growth," available at SSRN: https://ssrn.com/abstract=3348229 or http://dx.doi.org/10.2139/ssrn.3348229

Ghosh, T., Powell, R. L., Elvidge, C. D., Baugh, K. E., Sutton, P. C., and Anderson, S. (2010): "Shedding light on the global distribution of economic activity," *The Open Geography Journal* 3, no. 1: 148–61. https://www.aiddata.org/geoquery-datasets/gdp-grid.

Gill, Indermit S. and Kharas, Homi (2015): "The middle-income trap turns ten," *The* World Bank Group: Policy Research Working Papers 7403. http://documents.worldbank.org/curated/en/291521468179640202/The-middle-income-trap-turns-ten.

Gill, Indermit S., Kharas, Homi, and others (2007): "An East Asian Renaissance: Ideas for Economic Growth," The World Bank. https://openknowledge.worldbank.org/bitstream/handle/10986/6798/399860REPLACEM1601OFFICAL0USE0ONLY1.pdf?sequence=1&isAllowed=y.

Graham, Carol. (2013): "Pursuing Happiness: Social Mobility and Well-Being." The Brookings Institution. https://www.brookings.edu/blog/social-mobility-memos/2013/10/24/pursuing-happiness-social-mobility-and-well-being/.

Hausmann, Ricardo, Rodrik, Dani and Velasco, Andrés (2006): "Getting the diagnosis right," *Finance and Development* 43, no. 1: 12.

Heckelman, Jac C., Knack, Stephen, and Rogers, F. Halsey (2011): "Crossing the threshold: an analysis of IBRD graduation policy," World Bank Policy Research Working Paper no. 5531. https://bit.ly/34lopWG.

Hu, Yingyao and Yao, Jiaxiong (2019): "Illuminating Economic Growth," IMF Working Paper 19/77. https://www.imf.org/en/Publications/WP/Issues/2019/04/09/Illuminating-Economic-Growth-46670.

Im, Fernando Gabriel and Rosenblatt, David (2013): "Middle-income traps: a conceptual and empirical survey," The World Bank Group: Policy Research Working Papers 6594.

International Monetary Fund (2019): *World Economic Outlook Database* (April). https://www.imf.org/external/pubs/ft/weo/2019/01/weodata/index.aspx.

Jones, Benjamin and Olken, Benjamin (2005): "The Anatomy of Start-Stop Growth," NBER Working Papers 11528. https://www.nber.org/papers/w11528.pdf.

Jones, Charles I. (2016): "The Facts of Economic Growth," in John B. Taylor and Harald Uhliq (eds.), *Handbook of Macroeconomics*, volume 2, 3–69. Amsterdam: Elsevier.

Kang, Nahee and Paus, Eva (eds.), (2019): "The Political Economy of the Middle Income Trap: The Challenges of Advancing Innovation Capabilities in Latin America, Asia and Beyond," *The Journal of Development Studies*. DOI: 10.1080/00220388.2019.1595601.

Kim, Jungsuk and Park, Jungsoo.. (2017): "The Role of Total Factor Productivity Growth in Middle Income Countries", Asian Development Bank Economics Working Paper Series 527, November. https://www.adb.org/sites/default/files/publication/383176/ewp-527.pdf.

Lee, Keun (2014): *Schumpeterian Analysis of Economic Catch-Up: knowledge, path creation, and the middle-income trap*. Cambridge: Cambridge University Press. DOI: https://doi.org/10.1017/CBO9781107337244.

Mankiw, N. Gregory, Romer, David, and Weil, David (1992): "A contribution to the empirics of economic growth," *The Quarterly Journal of Economics* 107, no. 2: 407–37. https://eml.berkeley.edu/~dromer/papers/MRW_QJE1992.pdf.

Mathis, Jérôme, and Sand-Zantman, Wilfried (2014): "Competition and Investment: What do we know from the literature?" Institute D'Economie Industrielle, March. http://idei.fr/sites/default/files/medias/doc/by/sand_zantman/Competition_and_Investment.pdf.

McKinsey Global Institute (2019): "Latin America's missing middle: Rebooting inclusive growth," https://mck.co/2Dh8Ljq.

Melguizo, Angel, Nieto-Parra, Sebastian, Perea, Jose Ramon, and Perez, Jaime Ariel (2017): "No sympathy for the devil! Policy priorities to overcome the middle-income trap in Latin America," OECD Development Centre Working Papers 340. Paris: OECD Publishing. https://doi.org/10.1787/26b78724-en.

Narayan, Ambar, Van der Weide, Roy, Cojocaru, Alexandru, Lakner, Christoph, Redaelli, Silvia, Mahler, Daniel Gerszon, Gupta, Rakesh, Ramasubbaiah, N., and Thewissen, Stefan (2018): *Fair Progress? Economic Mobility across Generations around the World*, Washington, DC: World Bank.

National Geospatial-Intelligence Agency (2019): "World Port Index, Pub. 150, 27th Edition," https://msi.nga.mil/Publications/WPI (accessed September 12, 2019).

Paus, Eva (2019): "Innovation Strategies Matter: Latin America's Middle-Income Trap Meets China and Globalisation," *The Journal of Development Studies* 56, no. 4: 657–79. DOI: 10.1080/00220388.2019.1595600.

Pritchett, Lant and Summers, Lawrence H. (2014): "Asiaphoria meets regression to the mean," NBER Working Papers 20573.

Raj-Reichert, Gale (2019): "Global Value Chains, Contract Manufacturers, and the Middle-Income Trap: The Electronics Industry in Malaysia," *The Journal of Development Studies* 56, no. 4: 698–716. DOI: 10.1080/00220388.2019.1595599.

Rasiah, Rajah. (2002): "Government-business coordination and small business performance in the machine tools sector in Malaysia," *Small Business Economics* 18: 177–95.

Robertson, Peter E. and Ye, Longfeng (2013): "On the Existence of a Middle Income Trap," The University of Western Australia: Discussion Paper 13.12. https://bit.ly/2OCttiY.

Robinson, James A. (2009): "Good Crises? Implications for Developing Countries," World Bank Paper. https://scholar.harvard.edu/files/jrobinson/files/jr_wb_goodcrises.pdf.

Rodrik, Dani. (2015): Premature Deindustrialization. NBER Working Paper 20935. http://www.nber.org/papers/w20935.

Sala-i-Martin, Xavier X. (1997): "I Just Ran Four Million Regressions," NBER Working Papers 6252. DOI: 10.3386/w6252.

Schumpeter, J. A. (1934): "Depressions" in Douglass V. Brown et al. (eds.), *The Economics of the Recovery Program*. New York: Whittlesey House.

Schumpeter, J. A. (2017): *Essays: On Entrepreneurs, Innovations, Business Cycles and the Evolution of Capitalism*. Abingdon: Routledge.

Spence, Michael (2011): *The Next Convergence: The Future of Economic Growth in a Multispeed World*. New York: Farrar, Straus and Giroux.

3

Innovation and the Three Detours for Economic Growth beyond the Middle-Income Stage

Keun Lee

3.1 Introduction

Lee (2019) argues that the advanced economies and latecomer economies have different economic growth mechanisms and that a very "narrow passage" exists between these countries. The narrowness of this passage has been discussed in that book in terms of the presence of one failure (capability failures) and one barrier (intellectual property rights (IPR) protection by the incumbent North). Then the first step must be to correct capability failure by providing latecomers with learning opportunities in order for them to enhance their innovation capabilities, and thereby cultivate their innovation capabilities, as well explained in Lee (2013c, 2019: ch. 3.2).

An essential requirement for a latecomer firm to build innovation capabilities is to establish its own in-house research and development (R&D) center. Independent R&D efforts are required because foreign firms become increasingly reluctant to grant technology licenses to the rising latecomer firms, especially when the latter attempts to enter the higher value-added or profitability markets that are dominated by advanced countries. Thus, investing in R&D is required not only for the further absorption of advanced technologies but also for the development of the latecomers' technological capabilities. Developing in-house R&D capabilities is crucial for a firm to engage in product differentiation, produce high-end goods, and afford the higher wage rates that prevail at the upper middle-income stage; meanwhile, the continuous production of low-end goods alone cannot sustain the price competitiveness of a firm, thereby placing this firm in a MIT (middle-income trap).

By establishing in-house R&D laboratories, firms may explore diverse channels of learning and access foreign knowledge beyond simple licensing. Accessing foreign knowledge and trying new modes of learning are crucial because isolated

Keun Lee, *Innovation and the Three Detours for Economic Growth beyond the Middle-Income Stage* In: *Trapped in the Middle? Developmental Challenges for Middle-Income Countries*. Edited by: José Antonio Alonso and José Antonio Ocampo, Oxford University Press (2020). © OUP. DOI: 10.1093/oso/9780198852773.003.0003

in-house R&D efforts are often insufficient in building indigenous R&D capabilities. A diverse set of alternative modes of learning is available, including co-development contracts with foreign R&D specialist firms and/or public R&D institutes, mastering the existing literature, establishing overseas R&D outposts, and initiating international mergers and acquisitions (M&As). For example, since the early 1990s, a small number of Korean firms began to establish overseas R&D posts to obtain easy and fast access to foreign technologies that cannot be easily acquired through licensing.

In the meantime, the 'one barrier' refers to the barriers associated with the negative impacts of strong IPR protection in the advanced economies on exports from the emerging economies, which often show up in IPR disputes between the late entrants and incumbent firms. Actually, a recent empirical study has verified that strong IPR protection in the forerunning economies, for instance in the USA, often acted as a barrier to exports from the catching-up countries, for example by the Republic of Korea or China (Shin et al., 2015). Furthermore, as has been discussed extensively in Lee (2019: ch. 2), there are number of cases of latecomer firms involved in IPR litigation raised by incumbent firms.

The existence of such a "one failure and one barrier," which makes the transition rare and difficult, necessitates finding a detour and a new path to build innovation capabilities, avoiding futile effort to replicate or emulate the practices in the advanced economies. In other words, while the consolidation of technological capabilities at the firm level has long been suggested as vital for economic catch-up, our distinction is that capability building should be carefully designed and implemented within a broad framework called the NIS (national innovation systems). This was proposed by Schumpeterians, such as Nelson (1993) and Lundvall (1992), as elements and relationships which interact in the production, diffusion, and use of new and economically useful knowledge. Otherwise, the process of capability building would be derailed and delayed. For instance, capability building would be less effective if a latecomer economy adhered to an NIS providing a very high level of IPR protection even at an early stage of development. In sum, differences in innovation systems at the firm, sector, and national level lead to differences in learning and innovation performance and, consequently, to differences in economic performance, in particular at the middle-income stage, which is our concern here.

When there is a mismatch among the components of the NIS, capability-building becomes a more time-consuming and costly activity that may even result in failure. Therefore, firms must consider a diverse level of innovation capabilities, such as imitation, adaptation, or minor innovations (often represented by petit patents) versus creative or radical innovations (often represented by regular patents). Given that not all technologies and related sectors are the same in terms of their potential for learning and catching-up, strategic thinking is also required when setting priorities and sequencing over diverse technologies and sectors.

The same can be said with regard to the degrees and modes of participation in global value chains (GVCs).

Considering the above arguments, this chapter discusses the three detours that can help latecomers effectively and promptly build their innovation capabilities as well as catch up with their forerunners. The first detour involves promoting imitative innovations and diffusion in the form of petit patents and trademarks under loose IPR regimes instead of providing a higher level of IPR protection. The second detour involves promoting domestic value-added (DVA) and reducing the reliance of economies on GVCs instead of merely trying to increase the level of their GVC participation. The third detour involves specializing in short-cycle technology-based sectors/segments (with low entry barriers) instead of long-cycle ones (with high entry barriers) that serve as hallmarks of advanced economies. These detours are necessary because technological catch-up (closing the technological gap) involves not only learning and building capabilities but also finding niches and room for specialization along strategic priorities and sequences (Lee and Malerba, 2018). The goals of effectively specializing and seeking niches are consistent with those of technological diversification because repeated entries into new technological areas will result in diversification. In other words, no diversification can be achieved without a series of successful specializations in a few sectors.

The above view and strategy of technological diversification can be contrasted with the idea of trade-based diversification using the concept of the product space. A group of scholars involving Hausman and Hidalgo introduced the product space concept to measure the sophistication of the trade structure of a country.[1] They divided the specialization pattern of a country into core versus peripheries based on the sophistication of its products. They proposed that a country can achieve gradual sophistication (and diversification) in its trade structure by moving into neighboring spaces or capturing low-hanging fruits. Therefore, the export structure of a country must be diversified into highly sophisticated products to achieve sustained export performance and economic growth. However, such an idea has some limitations from the perspective of developing countries.

These scholars considered the proximity among product spaces as an important variable in determining the feasibility of diversification. However, their criterion did not disclose much information about the "directions" of diversification among numerous neighboring spaces. In other words, they focused on the "distance" rather than on the "directions" of diversification. The distance-based argument of diversification fails to determine which sectors in latecomer economies must be diversified first among the—possibly several—potential spaces with the

[1] See Hausman et al. (2007) and Hidalgo et al. (2007).

same distance. These scholars also used income level as a weighing factor to calculate the degree of sophistication of a product; in other words, those countries that produce the goods that are currently being exported by high-income countries are considered highly sophisticated. This method makes such a measure somewhat tautological, that is, a country can become rich by producing goods that are currently being produced by wealthier countries. Specifically, this strategy informs latecomer countries that they must try to produce those products that are being produced by the incumbents, but do not inform them how they can compete with incumbents in the same or similar sectors.

We propose that while trying to avoid any direct collision with incumbent countries, latecomer countries must find a niche for themselves in order to survive and compete effectively in a different market. In sum, these scholars did not propose an effective way for middle-income countries to reach the core structure. They merely argued that countries can reach the core only by traversing "empirically infrequent" (meaning long) distances or by making a long jump, which is very difficult to achieve. In addition, they did not discuss how these countries could traverse that long distance to the core space, a problem that resembles leapfrogging in our terminology. In our framework, realizing a diversified entry into new sectors by leapfrogging is a critical part of the overall catch-up strategy which is discussed in Lee (2019: ch. 5).

In what follows, this chapter discusses the three detours in sequence. Then, the final section concludes.

3.2 Detour One: From Imitative to Innovation

A large volume of literature on the relationship between IPR protection and economic growth tends to represent the former using the degree of protection of patent rights. From the catch-up perspective, this practice entails two problems. The first problem is whether or not patents are the most appropriate measures of innovation for latecomer developing economies, where the capability of firms is too weak to generate innovations, and thus firms often tend to produce minor, adaptive, or non-patentable innovations. The second problem is whether or not the provision of stronger IPR protection (including patent protection) can lead to more innovation, especially in developing economies where firms usually do not have pre-existing innovation capabilities, which is referred to as a capability failure in this chapter. This section discusses the detour of providing a lower level of IPR protection to encourage minor innovations in the form of petit patents during the transition stages. This is done because higher IPR protection cannot stimulate innovation under the condition of capability failure. The nature of this detour is that one must learn and build capabilities before receiving monetary incentives for correcting market failures.

Given the two problems raised above, previous studies have generated divided findings on the direct impact of patent rights on output growth in developing countries, with some researchers finding significant effects while others do not. Most of these studies do not examine alternative means of protecting IPRs and their possibly different impacts on countries at different stages. The effectiveness of patents for appropriating returns to innovation in developing countries also warrants further research.

In developing countries, utility models (often called petit patents) may serve as useful alternative outlets for emerging innovation. Both patents and utility models are exclusive rights granted for an invention that allow the rights holder to prevent others from commercially using the protected invention without authorization for a limited period. However, utility models and patents protect different types of innovations for various durations.

Patents protect innovations of relatively high inventiveness, while utility models protect those of relatively low inventiveness. Patents are granted for inventions that are novel, non-obvious, and have industrial applicability. They are typically effective for 20 years beginning from the date of application, cover several products and processes, undergo substantive examination, and are costly to obtain (filing fees, attorney costs, and translation fees where applicable). By contrast, utility models offer second-tier protection for minor inventions exhibiting a practical or functional advantage over existing ones. The processes or methods of production are typically excluded from these models, the protection of which typically lasts for 6–10 years. Applying for utility models is generally less expensive than applying for patents and does not require substantive examination (for novelty, non-obviousness, and industrial applicability). The inventiveness threshold of utility models is much lower than that of patents, and utility models are thus usually sought for small, marginal innovations that may not meet the patentability criteria.

Not all countries that provide patent rights, especially those with an Anglo-Saxon legal tradition such as the United States and the United Kingdom, also provide utility models. The developed countries that protect utility models include Germany and some European countries following the tradition of a continental legal system. This observation is not surprising because utility models originated in Germany, a former latecomer economy that attempted to catch up with the United Kingdom. Given their origin, utility models have been sought as a device for catch-up, and Japan quickly adopted this system by trying to learn from and catch up with Germany. Thus, the countries being protected by utility models are mostly former or current developing economies, such as Korea, Taiwan, China, and Malaysia; India, following the British legal tradition, did not adopt the utility model system. Utility models were thus the dominant form of IPRs in these countries in certain years (eg, the 1970s and the 1980s in Korea and from 1990 to the early 2000s in China).

Korea is among those developing countries that intensively exploited utility models (Lee and Kim, 2010). In 1961, the Korean government revised its intellectual property laws and established its first autonomous IPR system, which protects both conventional and minor innovations. Given that the technological capabilities of Korean firms lagged during the 1960s and 1970s, they relied heavily on imported technologies and reverse engineering, and then adapted these technologies to satisfy local needs. This practice enabled these firms to learn from foreign technologies. Accordingly, Korean inventors actively filed for utility model protection for their incremental innovations; the number of utility model applications exceeded that of invention patents until the early 1990s. Consequentially, the ratio of utility models to patents reached nearly 2.5 in 1975, and 1.8 in 1985. Since then, this ratio has continued to decline to reach 0.4 in 2000. Although patent and utility model applications continue to increase, their composition has shifted radically.

Since the mid-1980s, Korea has had its own valuable patentable assets to protect, while foreign companies have such assets that they want to protect within Korea. Major IPR reforms were legislated in the mid-1980s, and both the strength and scope of patent protection within Korea has increased since 1987. Substance patents for pharmaceutical and chemical materials and products were introduced along with protection for computer software and materials. The term of patent protection was also extended from 12 years to 15 years. By 1995, the number of patent applications exceeded that of utility model applications. These trends correspond to the transformation of Korea from a nation doing imitations to one doing innovations.

The above case of Korea is consistent with the view that different forms of IPRs have varying effects on different stages of economic development. More importantly, it shows that petit patents can serve as a transition variable for latecomers to increase their innovation capabilities during the intermediate stage and to generate higher-level patentable innovations at the later stage. This process creates a "detour" in the sense that the latecomer economies do not directly replicate the practices of advanced economies but take a different road before heading toward the same direction. Therefore, patent protection matters to industrial activities only after these countries reach a threshold level of indigenous innovative capacity as well as an extensive science and technology infrastructure.

Some researchers argue that utility models helped eventually to initiate a patenting and innovation culture in East Asia, and a World Bank study also reports that utility models allowed domestic producers in Brazil to adapt foreign innovations to their local needs and conditions.[2] Thailand also witnessed a surge in its petit patent applications after introducing this system in 1999. A study of

[2] See World Bank (2002).

Japan reveals that, on balance, the adoption and promotion of utility models positively affected the increase in Japan's total factor productivity (Maskus and McDaniel, 1999). A study using world data shows that patent protection contributes to innovation and economic growth in developed countries but not in developing ones, while utility model protection allows developing economies to build up their indigenous innovative capacities (Kim et al.,2012). In our firm-level analysis of Korean firms, we find that when firms are technologically lagging, utility models (or minor inventions) contribute to the growth of firms and to their capacity to produce (future) patentable inventions. After firms become technologically advanced, their performance is driven less by utility model innovations and more by patentable innovations. These results indicate that specific types of IPRs are more appropriate for countries at different stages of their economic development.

3.3 Detour Two: More, Less, and More GVC again

The need to take a detour to realize an upward transition and a successful economic catch-up can also be discussed in relation to the dynamic patterns of an economy's participation in GVCs. The value chain refers to a series of value-creating activities that transform raw or intermediate materials into finished products. Supply chains have become global in scope, and more intermediate goods are being traded across borders. Thus, the GVC concept has become highly relevant in understanding emerging economic relations by helping to establish a framework for understanding how international supply chains link economic activities within specific industries at the global, regional, national, and local levels (Gereffi, 2014).

Baldwin (2016) proposed that joining a GVC will help in the industrialization of a latecomer economy instead of building entire value chains in that economy. In other words, industrialization has become a radically less complex and faster process because the supply chain industry is less lumpy and less interconnected domestically. Baldwin attributed this idea to the fact that off-shored production brings elements (such as economy of scale) that took Korea and Taiwan several decades to develop domestically. His main point is that building an entire value chain in a latecomer economy (such as was done by Korea) is very difficult and risky, and this sort of activity will not provide sufficient economy of scale to achieve cost competitiveness in each value chain due to the limited market size (as in the case of Proton in Malaysia). He observed that unlike the failed "build strategy" in Malaysia, a successful case is the "join strategy" of the automobile sector in Thailand, where the Thai factories established by Japanese firms (eg, Toyota) only focused on assembly and the promotion of Thai component suppliers under a local contents requirements clause. According to Baldwin, one of the key points for such success was the firms' focus on a particular market segment (eg, light pickup trucks and vans) instead of trying to produce a whole range of models. This allowed it to achieve a sufficient scale economy at minimum cost for international competitiveness.

The contrast between variety and scale is not new; such difference was initially discussed in a new trade theory proposed by Krugman (1991), who pointed out the gains from trade in terms of the scale economy associated with specializing within a sector across different countries. However, a more important issue is whether a narrow specialization in a specific value segment is powerful enough to free a country from MIT. In fact, Thailand has not escaped MIT if the World Bank criterion of 20–40 percent of the level of the USA is applied. Thailand's GDP per capita reached 20 percent of that of the US in the early 1990s but it has since remained around the 30 percent level. The same can be said for Mexico, which has a very high level of participation in GVCs. The country's GDP per capita was 35 percent of that of the USA in the early 1990s or around the time of NAFTA, but has continued to decline steadily since then. Specifically, Mexico's GDP per capita stood at below 33 percent in 2015.

Baldwin's idea of the gains from GVCs has two problems. First, this idea focuses on the gains from cost savings rather than on rents associated with product differentiation or innovations. Second, the idea shows that latecomer firms forever remain as dependent suppliers to leading firms from high-income countries rather than becoming independent suppliers to multiple clients, thereby enjoying a better bargaining power in price negotiation or a bigger share in global profits. Regardless of the presence or absence of bargaining power, latecomer supplier firms under foreign-dominated GVCs are always subject to multinational companies (MNCs) shopping for lower costs, either from low wages or from the devaluation of currencies. The mutual competition among latecomer firms and economies that trade the same or similar goods and services presents another problem. This is called the adding-up problem. The GVC clusters in emerging economies may present another enclave without much spillover or linkage to create domestic value-added in wider segments of the national economy and society of the relevant country; Baldwin himself recognized the possible limitation of GVC participation in the subsection in his book on the "expansion and sustainable question." This is an aspect for which he does not have an acceptable answer.

Taiwan is one of the few emerging economies (with a certain size) that used to have a high degree of GVC participation but has moved beyond middle-income status to join the ranks of high-income economies. Taiwan's income per capita has already reached more than 80 percent of that of the USA. How did Taiwan move beyond middle-income status? Taiwan is a unique case that can be understood by referring to its innovation capabilities, shown by the fact that its number of registered US patents exceeded 10,000 in early 2010 and outnumbered that of the UK and France. Thus, Taiwan ranks fourth in the world after Japan, Germany, and Korea in terms of the number of registered US patents. In comparison, Thailand or Mexico each had less than 200 US patents in the 2010s. Although Baldwin mentioned Foxconn as an example of a company that grows within GVCs, this firm continues to prosper not on its scale-based cost advantages but on its innovation capabilities. Furthermore, Foxconn acts as an independent supplier to multiple global firms, including Apple (which is in direct competition with Samsung), and has even acquired Panasonic, a former symbol of Japan's economic prowess. But, Thailand and Mexico have failed to generate firms such as Foxconn. In contrast, Taiwan has generated a large number of locally owned or controlled firms that used to be foreign direct investment (FDI) firms or subsidiaries of MNCs.[3]

Merely joining GVCs does not guarantee an entry into higher value-added segments and a transition to high-income status because an economy may remain stuck in performing low value-added activities without value upgrading. However, we note that latecomers 'must' join GVCs at their early stage of development to facilitate their learning and capability-building. While joining GVCs is necessary for learning, the joining economies are still at risk of being stuck in low value-added activities with no opportunty to move toward the higher tiers in the value chain, consequently placing them in the MIT. In other words, determining who captures and how to capture the "bigger share" of the value in GVCs is very important, and a battle for this position may occur among the key involved parties. Their experiences indicate that Taiwan, Korea, and China have been able to create more domestic value-added after learning through their participation in GVCs.

The degree of participation in GVCs can be measured by the FVA (the share of foreign value-added in gross exports), which indicates what percentage of a country's gross exports consists of inputs that are produced and imported from other countries. In other words, a higher (lower) value of FVA indicates further (or less) integration with the global economy through GVCs. This index can represent the degree of an economy's participation in GVCs (or backward linkages) as shown in Figure 3.1[4]

Figure 3.1 shows the FVA estimation results for Korea and China. Since the 1960s and 1970s the FVA in Korea continued to increase following the country's participation in GVCs through OEM-based (own equipment manufacturing-based) exports, starting from labor-intensive goods, until reaching a peak in the early 1980s. Since then the FVA in Korea started to decline until the mid-1990s and rose again after the country joined the OECD. Specifically, Korea's FVA peaked over 36 percent in 1980 and dropped to 28 percent in 1993, the year Korea became an OECD member. Actually, Korea experienced a rapid catch-up between

[3] This observation on Taiwan was made by Amsden and Chu (2003).
[4] The figures and related discussion rely on Lee et al. (2017).

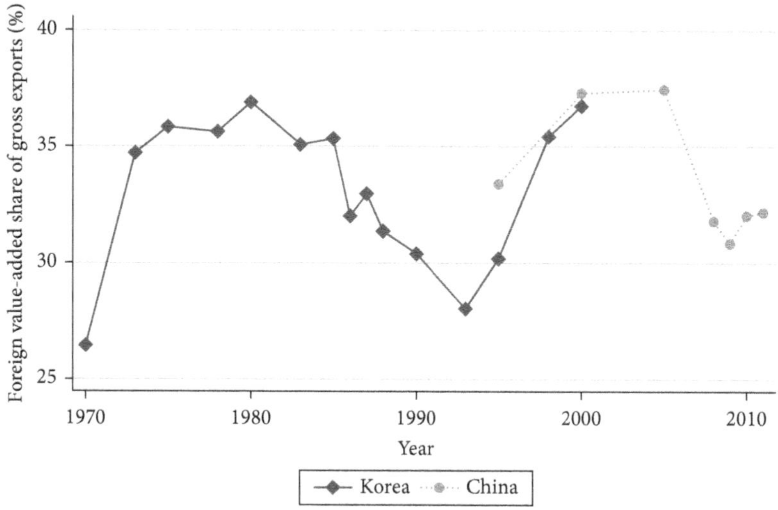

Figure 3.1 Trend of the GVC participation degree (FVA): Korea and China
Source: Author's estimation (Korea), OECD TiVA (China).

the mid-1980s and the mid-1990s, but was facing the possibility of falling into the MIT from the early to mid-1980s because of its rising wage rates and low value-added export structure. This pattern of more GVC, less GVC, and then more GVC again suggests that Korea has escaped from the MIT by increasing the share of local value-added in its exports since the mid-1980s. Although not shown here, the trend of FVA in Taiwan is similar to that in Korea, and its FVA decreased in the 1980s and has increased again since the 1990s. Figure 3.1 also shows the case of China since 1995. China's FVA peaked at 37 percent in the early 2000s and declined to 31 percent in the late 2000s. This trend implies that as a successful catch-up economy, China is replicating the pattern of Korea and Taiwan but with some lags (approximately 15–20 years).

These successful catch-up economies experienced a decade-long decline in their FVA, which decreased by over 5 percentage points or from approximately 35 percent to 30 percent or lower. Accordingly, if we check whether a similar pattern has occurred in other Southeast Asian or Latin American economies, we find no such case. After the launch of NAFTA, Mexico showed the highest degree of integration with GVCs but experienced no period of decline in its FVA to create local value chains.

With regard to the determinants of the degree of FVA in gross exports, Korea and Taiwan experienced an increase in their local value-added (or a decrease in their FVA) as shown in Figure 3.1 from the mid-1980s to the mid-1990s or after they improved their NIS. This was achieved by rapidly increasing their degree of local creation and diffusion of knowledge, which can be measured by the national-level self-citation of a country or the share of country-owned patents in the total citations made by all patents owned by a country.[5] Knowledge localization is a key NIS variable that is related to the source of knowledge acquisition. This variable reflects the dependence of the created knowledge on domestic knowledge bases. In other words, knowledge localization measures how much knowledge is created domestically in terms of citing the patents owned by assignees of the same nationality.

This variable of knowledge localization or the degree of intra-national knowledge creation and diffusion by Korea and Taiwan reached 5 percent (similar to the average of middle-income countries) in the mid-1980s and increased to more than 10 percent (the average of high-income countries) by the late 1990s. The correspondence between knowledge localization and decreasing FVA (or increasing local value-added) implies that increasing local value-added has been supported or made possible by the increasing degree of local knowledge creation and diffusion by indigenous actors. By contrast, the knowledge creation and diffusion of other middle-income countries, such as Brazil and Argentina, remained below 5 percent throughout the entire period.

We can also examine the role of GVCs in the transition from low- and middle-income to high-income status using the more–less–more again hypothesis, which posits that further participation in GVCs is desirable at the initial stage of growth to allow economies to learn from the outside, and that the upgrading and transition at the middle-income stage requires some effort or stages of seeking separation and independence from foreign-dominated GVCs. At the final stage, latecomer firms and economies may have to seek for an opening to integrate themselves back into GVCs after building up their own local value chains. However, gaining independence is a difficult and risky process. The key to overcoming these difficulties is to command a certain level of in-house capabilities in both marketing and technological innovation. Avoiding the road toward independence may be a short-term option, but such an option cannot be sustained in the long run because the leading MNCs in the existing GVCs are always looking for locations with cheap wages and contract firms. This is neatly illustrated by the cases of firms in the Brazilian footwear sector.

In a sense, this chapter sees both the perils and potentials of GVCs. The perils emerge because GVCs may simply aim for a global profit maximization that is led by MNCs and driven by waves of global financialization, squeezing profits from the lower tier of GVCs. Such an attempt is not designed to create more local value-added or employment opportunities. Some potential might also emerge because GVCs may offer initial learning channels. However, an eventual separation or independence from these chains must also be considered; otherwise, an economy may lose in its competition with other sites and firms in other

[5] This idea goes back to the Lee (2013a: 49; fig. 3.1).

lower-wage economies. As such, these economies must aim for a transition from their participation in GVCs to the creation of local value chains and innovation systems. According to the experiences of Korea's, Brazil's, and India's plush toy, footwear, and information technology sectors, respectively (discussed in Lee (2019: ch. 4.4), such a transition becomes possible if economies have the "decision and will" to achieve eventual independence based on the indigenous ownership of their firms.

3.4 Detour Three: From Short-Cycle to Long-Cycle Technologies

The fact that all sectors differ from one another in terms of their innovation patterns and market structure is one of the key ideas in Schumpeterian economics, as exemplified by the concept of sectoral innovation systems. This concept implies that the patterns and possibility of technological catch-up by latecomers may also differ across sectors. This observation introduces the sectoral choice or specialization of latecomers as another important question in our search for the transition path from poor to rich nations. Sector choices are important because not all sectors are the same in terms of their entry possibility, and latecomers are "late entrants" in the already-established international division of labor must seek suitable entry points. Therefore, catch-up must be considered as a matter of learning and building capabilities as well as of finding niches and sectoral specialization for latecomers. Therefore, as firms build more or new capabilities over time, they may enter new and different sectors.

Given that many developing countries initially face labor (natural resource) abundance, they are advised to specialize in labor (resource)-intensive sectors at an early stage of development; thus, the capital–labor ratio is a key variable in sectoral specialization. For economies that are far behind the frontiers of technological know-how and skills, that have an abundant supply of labor, and that have a scarce amount of capital, market forces and traditions generally support labor-intensive sectors and do not require high levels of technological or business sophistication to be effective. However, successful economic development beyond the low-income level requires the development of the competences of firms and the institutions that support them.

Historical experience shows that as these capabilities continue to develop, the next stages of economic development occur as resources continue to flow into those sectors with high capital intensity. Historical experience also shows that latecomers first choose those sectors in which technologies are relatively constant and mature, thereby allowing a high degree of technology transfer at a low cost. For developing countries that have built up a reasonably strong capability for training labor and that have at least a cadre of reasonably sophisticated business leaders, the competitive capability of their sectors is within reach and has low entry barriers despite requiring a considerable amount of learning time and effort. Paying lower wages can also help build the competitive capability of certain countries. The fact that the technologies in such sectors are usually mature or do not change rapidly indicates that upon achieving competitive competence, the problems in keeping up with technological advances can be managed. Entering these industries can help those countries behind the frontiers to climb the economic ladder.

Higher value-added sectors then become the next targets for middle-income countries that have built up relatively high levels of capabilities. Korea and Taiwan reached this stage by the mid-1980s. However, indigenous firms directly compete with firms in countries that are at the technological frontiers and that have a much greater amount of experience in the field. The lower wage rates alone do not generate a competitive advantage in these sectors, and continuing competitiveness is strongly tied to the ability of firms to keep up with others even as their technologies change rapidly. Thus, finding a niche in many high value-added sectors/segments presents a challenge for catch-up economies at the upper middle-income stage. The cycle time of technologies can be an effective criterion to choose among the many high value-added or capital intensive sectors, because the sectors and activities associated with short cycle time of technologies tend to be of low entry barriers and high growth prospects.

The cycle time of technologies is about how fast technologies change or become obsolete over time; specifically, cycle time can be calculated as the time difference between the application year of the citing patent and that of the cited patents.[6] Therefore, this variable reflects one important attribute of knowledge that becomes obsolete over time. In this regard, some knowledge becomes obsolete quickly, while other pieces of knowledge take a longer period to become obsolete. The speed of obsolescence is expected to affect the chances of catch-up. If knowledge has a long-life expectancy, then mastering the knowledge and technology in that field requires more time. However, if knowledge is short lived, then catch-up countries are not required to master old technologies, which is consistent with the low entry barriers from the latecomers' point of view. Thus, specializing in short-cycle technology-based sectors/segments represents both low entry and better growth prospects, which in turn are associated with few collisions with the technologies of advanced countries (less IPR disputes), less royalty payments, first- or fast-mover advantages, or product differentiation; for example, information technologies have a shorter cycle than pharmaceuticals in the sense that the new innovations in information technology tend to rely less on the existing stock of knowledge.

[6] See Jaffe and Trajtenberg (2002). If a patent applied to the USPTO in 2000 cites a patent applied in 1995, the cycle time in this specific case is 5 years.

The advantage of specializing in short-cycle technologies is consistent with the leapfrogging concept, in which the emerging generations of technologies allow catch-up countries to have a head start. In the competition within a new techno-economic paradigm, both incumbents and latecomers start from the same starting line, and incumbents often stick to their existing technologies from which they derive their supremacy. Leapfrogging is similar to the "long jumps" mentioned by Hidalgo, who argued that economies should shift to product spaces that are located far away from their current position in order to achieve a structural transformation.[7]

The technological development of Korea over the last three decades reflects the increasing specialization of the country in short-cycle, less tacit, and high modularity technologies during its catch-up phase.[8] Korea began to specialize in labor-intensive (low value-added) industries, such as the apparel or shoe industries, in the 1960s. The economy then moved to the shorter- or medium-cycle sectors of low-end consumer electronics and automobile assembly in the 1970s and 1980s, to the shorter-cycle telecommunications equipment (telephone switches) sector in the late 1980s, and to memory chips, cell phones, and digital televisions in the 1990s. In sum, Korean industries kept moving to shorter-cycle technologies to achieve technological diversification.

We can discuss the actual trends in the cycle time of technologies as calculated from the US patents held by selected economies, such as Korea, Taiwan, and China. For example, a value of eight as the average cycle time indicates that the average cycle time of patents is 8 years (ie, the patents held by Korea and Taiwan tend to cite 8-year-old patents on average) and that the related technologies are considered outdated or useless after eight years. Since the mid-1980s, Korea and Taiwan have shifted to technologies with increasingly short cycles. Therefore, the average cycle time of those patents held by Korea and Taiwan was shortened from eight to six or seven years by the late 1990s. This duration is two to three years shorter than the average cycle time of patents held by European G5 countries, patents which have cycle times of 9–10 years since the late 1980s because of their strong performance in high value-added long-cycle sectors, such as pharmaceuticals and machine tools. Consequently, the patent portfolios of Korea and Taiwan completely differ from those of advanced countries. We consider the mid-1980s as an important turning point during which Korea and Taiwan achieved a sustained catch-up beyond the middle-income stage. Both economies reached the upper middle-income level during this period, and the GDP per capita of Korea reached 25 percent of that of the USA. Since then, Korea and Taiwan continued to increase their R&D expenditures, and their R&D/GDP ratio surpassed the 1 percent level. Along with upgrading their technological capabilities, these economies

[7] See Hidalgo et al. (2007). [8] See Lee (2013a: ch. 7) for more details.

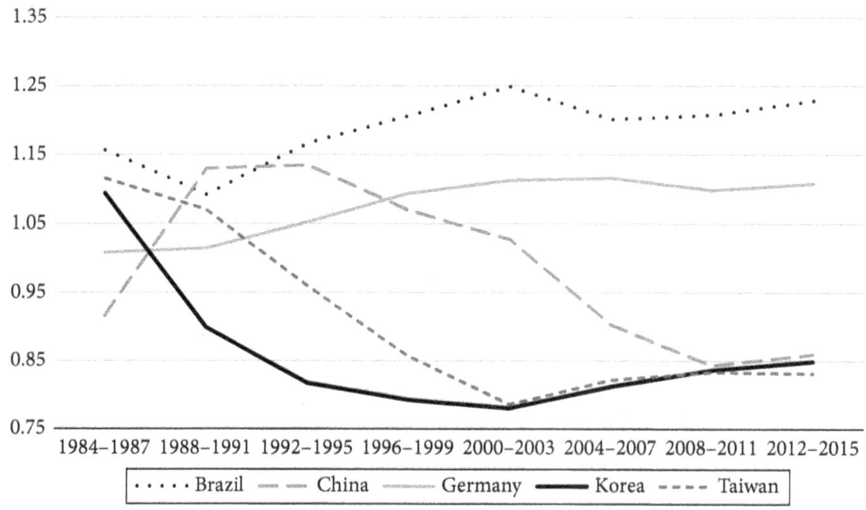

Figure 3.2 Period of the average cycle time of technologies in selected economies

Note: The absolute values of the cycle time of technologies are normalized by dividing by the world average so that the value of 1 may be the average of the cycle time.

Source: Lee (2019: fig. 3-1); Calculations using the raw data downloaded from the USPTO Patent Grant Red Book (Full Text, 1976–2016, http://patents.reedtech.com/pgrbft.php) after the data mining and cleaning.

shifted to short-cycle technology-based sectors, such as information technology products.

After achieving technological catch-up, the specialization of Korea and Taiwan needs to reach maturity or turn to long cycle technologies. Figure 3.2 shows the trend of the normalized values of the average cycle time of technologies calculated from patents registered in the USA. It is shown that after both economies reached their lowest level in the early 2000s, their technologies turned toward long cycles, such as biological or science-based technologies. China is following a similar path with about a 10-year lag. Such a strategy can be considered a "detour" because latecomer countries do not directly and immediately replicate the path and industries of advanced economies that specialize in long-cycle technologies, such as Germany which tend to boast a much longer cycle time for its technologies. Instead, those countries that successfully caught up initially moved toward sectors with short-cycle technologies and then moved toward sectors with long-cycle technologies after reaching maturity. If you specialize in long cycle technologies from the beginning, as does Brazil in Figure 3.2, the economy would find it difficult to achieve commercial success given the high entry barriers and greater level of competition with the advanced economies.

Hausman et al. (2007) suggest that a developing country should become similar to a rich country. However, we propose that the transition strategy of a developing country must not involve trying to become similar at an early stage but trying to be different by entering sectors that are based on short-cycle technologies instead of those that are based on long-cycle technologies and are dominated by rich countries. However, as economies reach technological maturity and develop a high level of capabilities (as Korea did in the early 2000s), they become driven to adopt long-cycle technologies, such as bio-medical or pharmaceutical industries, which is what Samsung has been trying to achieve recently.

Therefore, the prospects for a country moving beyond the middle-income stage can be judged by whether this country is experiencing a "technological turning point" to enter sectors based on short-cycle technologies along the curve of the cycle time of technologies. Figure 3.2 shows that China passed such a turning point from the mid- to the late 1990s or approximately 10–15 years later than Korea. The weighted average cycle time of Chinese technologies from 2000 to 2005 was 8.07 years, which was closer to the Korean/Taiwanese average of 7.69 years from 1980 to 1995 than to the Brazilian/Argentinean average of 9.26 years in the same period (note that Brazil and Argentina are more engaged in long-cycle technologies than in short-cycle ones).[9]

Overall, in contrast to the comparative advantages in trade (trade-based specialization) as initially determined by endowment conditions, we suggest that the dynamic comparative advantages in technology (technological specialization) are determined not by natural resource endowments but by the R&D and design capabilities that are accumulated by humans over time. This technology-based specialization complements trade-based specialization along the latent comparative advantages at the low- or lower-level middle-income stage as suggested by Lin (2012). The latter focuses on low- or lower-level middle-income countries (eg, China in the early 1980s) that are choosing between the right latent comparative advantage sectors and the wrong comparative advantage sectors, while the former focuses on upper-level middle-income countries (eg, China today) that are choosing between short- (low originality) and long (high originality)-cycle technologies. In a sense, short-cycle technologies provide latecomers with a niche and ensure a high rate of profitability as revealed in the firm-level analysis in my book (Lee, 2013a: ch. 5).

Increasing the specialization in short-cycle technologies results in technological diversification. As shown in their cycle time curves, Korea and Taiwan gradually shortened their cycle times since the mid-1980s. However, this gradual shortening does not indicate that these economies have specialized in a few sectors; rather, they continued to enter progressively newer sectors with shorter cycle times, which is essentially a process of industrial diversification into new or unrelated fields at times of paradigm shifts or low entry barriers.

[9] See Table 8.4 in Lee (2013a).

Technological diversification can be measured by the number of technological fields in which countries have registered patents from out of the 417 three-digit fields in the US patent classification system. High-income countries have registered patents in about 40 percent of the 417 classes in the US patent system.[10] Korea and Taiwan demonstrated an impressive catching-up performance compared with other middle-income countries; that is, they began from the same base and eventually surpassed the average level of high-income countries by the early 1990s. This achievement is very important because many scholars consider the diversification of export structure to be a necessary condition for sustained export performance and economic growth as well as an important challenge being faced by developing countries. Developing countries can diversify themselves by moving into short-cycle technology-based sectors. Our criterion is dynamic because we do not suggest that catch-up economies must target a specific or fixed list of short-cycle technologies. Instead, these economies must keep moving into shorter-cycle technologies to achieve technological diversification.

The results of the country-panel growth equation in Lee (2013a) show that for four Asian economies, economic growth (per capita income growth) has a negative and significant correlation with the cycle time of technologies, and the opposite holds for typical middle-income countries.[11] This fact holds the secret for a successful transition. Fast-growing Asian economies, such as Korea and Taiwan, have caught up with high-income countries by specializing in short-cycle sectors since the mid-1980s.

By contrast, a wrong transition strategy would be to specialize in long-cycle sectors, which can be regarded as an attempt to directly replicate the knowledge base of high-income countries by specializing in high-quality and highly original technologies. Several advanced Latin American countries, such as Brazil and Argentina, have tried to traverse this path because of their advanced level of scientific research. Actually, the average cycle time of technologies shown by the US patents filed by Latin American economies shows very long periods (longer than 10 years), which correspond to getting into sectors such as pharmaceuticals. These sectors require a longer time to absorb knowledge and to make commercial success, which means high entry barriers for latecomers and greater difficulty in increasing the degree of knowledge localization and diversification. This may lead to a continuous reliance on advanced countries, thereby decreasing the chances for a country to consolidate indigenous knowledge bases. These issues are one aspect of the middle-income trap.

[10] See Figure 9.1 in Lee (2013), drawn by the author and based on NBER patent data.
[11] Lee (2013: ch. 3).

3.5 Summary and Concluding Remarks

This chapter began by acknowledging the differences in the economic growth mechanisms employed by advanced economies and latecomer economies at middle- or lower-income stages and by highlighting a very "narrow passage" between these countries. In this case, how to achieve a transition from low- and middle-income status to high-income status warrants a thorough examination. Taking various detours is necessary to achieving such a transition because of two failures (capability and size failures) and one barrier (IPR protection in the North). This chapter explains the nature of the narrow passage in terms of three detours. The first detour is promoting imitative innovations in the form of petit patents and trademarks instead of trying to promote a high level of IPR protection, including patent rights. The second detour is first prioritizing domestic value-added and reducing a country's reliance on GVCs before an economy is fully coupled with GVCs. The third detour is specializing in short-cycle technology-based sectors instead of trying to directly enter long-cycle technology-based sectors or segments that are the hallmarks of advanced economies.

One remaining and interesting issue would be the question of whether there exists any proper sequence among the three detours proposed in this chapter. The actual courses of the three detours are somewhat complicated and intertwined thus it is not easy to pin down exact timings for the beginning and duration of the detours. In other words, we have to first discuss when the beginning of each detour stage is, for example, the stage of imitation, less GVC (or more DVC), and short-cycle technology, respectively, and then to discuss when the end of each detour stage will be and thus when the switch to the final stage will be made, such as the switch to innovation, more GVC, and long-cycle technologies. What follows is a short reflection of the three detours in terms of this issue.

Regarding the detour from imitation to innovation, an obvious indicator of switching to innovation is whether firms set up their own in-house R&D centers, whereas they used to rely on licensing during the imitation stage. An effort to establish in-house R&D began in the early to mid-1980s in Korea (Lee, 2013b). While this phenomenon is one of the signs for a switch to innovation-led growth, what matters is how much progress has been made after this initial switch. One indicator of such progress would be the relative number of utility models (so-called petite patents) vs. regular invention patents. It was only in the early 1990s (or 1993) when the number of regular patents became larger than that of utility models (Lee and Kim, 2010). In this sense, we can say that a transition from imitation to innovation started in the mid-1980s and was properly made in the early to mid-1990s, within a period of 10 years or so.

Regarding the detour from more GVC, less GVC, to more GVC again, the period of less GVC started in the early 1980s and building up the domestic value chain continued for more than 10 years or until the early 1990s in Korea (see Figure 3.1). Next, according to Figure 3.2, the period of specializing in short-cycle technologies extended from the mid-1980s to the early 2000s, or 2001 to 2003.

Then, based on the above discussion, we can say the following. Note first that the stage of imitation is considered to be the period since the early 1970s when Korean firms actively imported foreign technology in the form of licensing, as elaborated in Chung and Lee (2015) and it lasted until the early 1990s, which is when there was a proper switch to innovation-led growth. This means that in terms of the starting period, the imitation stage began first in the 1970s, followed by the stage of building domestic value chains beginning in the early 1980s (or 1980), and finally the specialization into short-cycle technologies came last or the mid-1980s.

This sequence of imitation first and then building domestic value chains (the localization of imported capital goods) and finally specializing into short-cycle technologies seems to make sense. The sequence was also kept in terms of the ending period of each detour. In other words, the switch to innovation happened first in the early 1990s, followed by the switch to more GVC taking place in the mid-1990s, and finally the switch to long-cycle technologies happened in the early 2000s. Put together, this sequence means that the latecomer economies first learn by imitation, then try to build their own value chains while localizing some of the capital goods they used to import, and finally find their niche in short-cycle technology areas as they get closer to the frontier of the MIT.

While the consolidation of technological capabilities has long been suggested as a vital requirement for economic catch-up, this chapter shows that such consolidation must be carefully designed and implemented with the equally vital strategic idea of the three detours. Otherwise, the process of capability-building becomes derailed and delayed. For the first detour, capability-building becomes less effective if a latecomer economy provides a very high level of IPR protection and only recognizes regular patents instead of petit patents. The selection of technologies becomes derailed if a latecomer attempts to enter those sectors or segments with long cycle times or high entry barriers. Latecomer economies may also participate in GVCs because they must be open to learning from the outside at the initial stage but the final goal of learning is for these economies to stand alone with their own learning and innovation mechanisms; it is like a child who learns to walk is to eventually walk alone. Thus, independence is the end point of learning. Likewise, participating in GVCs must be accompanied by an effort to build a local knowledge base and to increase domestic value-added at the intermediate stage.

Short cycles provide middle income countries with opportunities to catch up with those economies that command a certain degree of technological capability. However, frequent changes in technologies may create an additional barrier against catching up because these changes interfere with learning and lead to the truncation of the learning process. Thus, traversing the path of short-cycle technologies may not always be smooth and easy. Selecting the road of short-cycle technologies thus requires a certain threshold level of technological capability by the firm- and national-level institutions and policies. Such a level of capabilities is only available to some upper middle-income countries. Inheriting mature industries from countries with high income levels may help build such capabilities, and this finding complements Lin's idea of latent comparative advantage. However, refusing to take risks may keep a country in the MIT, while taking risks does not guarantee success. The transitional path is a necessary yet insufficient condition for eventual upgrading.

In the meantime, a less risky road might be attempting to upgrading into a higher-end segment in the resource-based sectors, particularly for some countries, such as Chile and Malaysia, as discussed in Lebdioui et al. (2020). Combining innovation with resource-based activities, they can become higher value-added. In addition, they tend to be in sectors with low-entry barriers associated with each country's natural endowments. Given that some agricultural products are now regarded as very promising high-tech sectors, specialization into such sectors is not inconsistent with the idea of a short cycle time, given that it is advisable to seek sectors with low entry barriers but high growth prospects.

3.6 Acknowledgments

This chapter draws on Lee (2019: ch. 3). The original texts are substantially reduced and edited, reflecting the comments from the Workshop for this book project held in June 2019, Madrid. I thank the two editors of this volume, José Antonio Ocampo and José Antonio Alonso Rodriguez, for useful comments.

References

Amsden, A., and Chu, W. (2003): *Beyond Late Development: Taiwan's Upgrading Policies*, Cambridge, MA: MIT Press Books.

Baldwin, R. E. (2016): *The Great Convergence*. Cambridge, MA: Harvard University Press.

Chung, Moon Young, and Lee, K. (2015): "How Absorptive Capacity is Formed in a Latecomer Economy," *World Development* 66: 678–94.

Gereffi, Gary (2014): "Global value chains in a post-Washington Consensus world," *Review of International Political Economy* 21(1): 9–37.

Hausmann, R., Hwang, J., and Rodrik, D. (2007): "What you export matters," *Journal of Economic Growth* 12: 1–25.

Hidalgo, C. A., Klinger, B., Barabási, A. L., and Hausmann, R. (2007): "The product space conditions the development of nations.,". *Science* 317(5837): 482–7.

Jaffe, Adam B. and Trajtenberg, M. (2002): *Patents, Citations and Innovations*, Cambridge, MA: MIT Press.

Kim, Y. K., Lee, K., Park, W. G., and Choo, K. (2012): "Appropriate intellectual property protection and economic growth in countries at different levels of development," *Research Policy* 41(2): 358–75.

Krugman, Paul (1991): *Geography and Trade*, Cambridge, MA: MIT Press.

Lebdioui, A., Lee, K., and Pietrobelli, C. (2020): "Local-Foreign Technology Interface, Resource-based Development, and Industrial Policy: How Chile and Malaysia are escaping the Middle-Income Trap," Journal of Technology Transfer. DOI: https://doi.org/10.1007/s10961-020-09808-3

Lee, Keun (2013a): *Schumpeterian Analysis of Economic Catch-up: Knowledge, Path-creation, and the Middle-income Trap*, Cambridge: Cambridge University Press.

Lee, Keun (2013b): "How Can Korea be a Role Model for Catch-up Development?," in Augustin K. Fosu (ed.), *Achieving Development Success*, Oxford: Oxford University Press (for WIDER).

Lee, Keun (2013c): "Capability Failure and Industrial Policy to Move Beyond the Middle-Income Trap," in J. E. Stiglitz and J. L. Yifu (eds.), *The Industrial Policy Revolution I*, Basingstoke, UK: Palgrave Macmillan, pp. 244–72.

Lee, Keun (2019): *The Art of Economic Catch-up: Barriers, Detours and Leapfrogging in Innovation Systems*, Cambridge: Cambridge University Press.

Lee, K. and Kim, Y. K. (2010): "IPR and technological catch-up in Korea," in: H. Odagiri, A. Goto, A. Sunami, R. Nelson, (eds.), *Intellectual Property Rights, Development and Catch-up*, London: Oxford University Press.

Lee, K., and Malerba F. (2018): "Economic Catchup as an Evolutionary Process," in R. Nelson, et al., *Modern Evolutionary Economics: An Overview*, Cambridge: Cambridge University Press.

Lee, K., Szapiro, M., and Mao, Z. (2017): "From Global Value Chains (GVC) to Innovation Systems for Local Value Chains and Knowledge Creation," *The European Journal of Development Research* 30(3): 424–41.

Lin, J. Y. (2012): *The Quest for Prosperity: How Developing Economies Can Take Off*, Princeton, NJ: Princeton University Press.

Lundvall, Bengt-Åke (1992): *National Systems of Innovation*, London: Frances Pinter Publishers.

Maskus, K., and McDaniel, C. (1999): "Impacts of the Japanese patent system on productivity growth," *Japan and the World Economy* 11: 557–74.

Nelson, Richard R. (1993): *National Innovation Systems: A Comparative Analysis*, New York: Oxford University Press.

Shin, W., Lee, K., and Park, W. G. (2015): "When an Importer's Protection of IPR Interacts with an Exporter's Level of Technology," *The World Economy* 39(6): 772–802.

World Bank. (2002): *Global Economic Prospects and Developing Countries*, New York: Oxford University Press.

4

Is There an Institutional Trap in MICs?

José Antonio Alonso

4.1 Introduction

It is assumed that as countries progress, they require more complex institutions to manage the problems of social coordination that emerge in more extended markets, and to respond to the governance conditions of a more demanding society. In other words, the development process requires a path of institutional change. However, economic and institutional processes frequently do not evolve at the same pace, as institutions are subject to greater inertia. As a consequence, either institutions fall increasingly behind social demands or, alternatively, changes in formal institutions are apparent, not properly rooted in social behavior.

These problems are particularly relevant in middle-income countries (MICs), as such countries tend to experience frequent episodes of intense economic growth and social change that put their institutional frameworks under pressure. Transforming these episodes into a sustained process of economic convergence towards high-income countries (HICs) would require a successful process of continuous institutional improvement. However, it is difficult to synchronize these two processes.

In fact, we might identify two frequent "pathologies" in the evolution of MICs. In some cases, the institutional framework seems to be resistant to change, and countries maintain outdated institutions, increasingly unsuited to the new social reality. As a consequence, there will be an increasing social disregard for the inherited institutions, particularly among more dynamic social sectors. In other cases, countries are involved in a process of recurrent changes (sometimes cosmetic ones) in formal institutions, making it difficult for the new rules to settle in society. In this case, the level of institutional instability is high and the capacity for institutions to effectively shape social behavior is low. These two processes weaken the institutional framework, because they damage the levels of predictability, legitimacy, and capacity for enforcement of the rules.

On the one hand, hierarchical societies with authoritarian regimes, low levels of education, as well as a strong presence of traditional values tend to have institutions that are highly stable and inertial, but over time increasingly unadapted to social reality. On the other hand, when the recognition of political rights is

José Antonio Alonso, *Is There an Institutional Trap in MICs?* In: *Trapped in the Middle? Developmental Challenges for Middle-Income Countries*. Edited by: José Antonio Alonso and José Antonio Ocampo, Oxford University Press (2020).
© OUP. DOI: 10.1093/oso/9780198852773.003.0004

accompanied with high and chronic social inequalities, formal institutions tend to be built on weak foundations, being subject to a process of recurrent changes. Because institutions are either unsuitable or unstable, they are not internalized in social behavior, weakening the credibility and capacity of enforcement rules.

Both pathologies could lead countries into a vicious circle: as people do not trust public institutions they do not support the process of reinforcing the state (weak taxation being an exponent of that); and given its limited capacity and resources, the state is unable to provide the public goods that the society demands, which reinforces people's distrust in the sate. Thus, it is important to know if there are any causal relationships among these three elements: weak institutions, rigid social hierarchies and inequalities, and fragile "fiscal covenants." At the same time, as these factors are common in many MICs, we should explore whether this reinforcing system operates actively in these kinds of countries. In other words, it is important to know if there is any discontinuity in the process of institutional improvement that could be characterized as an "institutional trap" connected with MIC status.

Specialized works have tended to associate the "MIC trap" with obstacles that hinder the productive and technological changes required to move countries towards more dynamic and knowledge-based economies. Therefore, in this approach, problems would be located in the "hardware" of the economy. If there were an institutional problem, it would mainly refer to the weakness of those economic institutions oriented to encouraging human capital and technological capacities.

Persuasive as it is, this interpretation does not capture all factors that cause the recurrent slowdowns suffered by MICs. Some of these factors are located in the "software" (rather in the "hardware") of society, as they remit to the difficulties that countries face in responding to the greater demand for good governance that derive from the process of economic growth.

The recent experience of many MICs can usefully illustrate this last idea. During the last decade, an ample group of MICs suffered severe political crises that were expressed as a combination of population unrest, massive protests, and generalized questioning of the existing institutional framework in the involved countries. These crises affected an ample group of MICs located in both the Middle East and North Africa (eg, Egypt, Tunisia, Algeria, Jordan, Lebanon, or Morocco) and in Latin America (eg, Nicaragua, Ecuador, Colombia, or Chile). Although each case shows specificities, there are also common elements among them: characteristically, in all cases social movements demand changes in governance, claiming for more open, credible, and inclusive institutions.

We have limited knowledge about which institutions matter the most for countries to make a successful transition from MICs to HICs. Empirical research in this field is scarce, but tentative results suggest that: (i) first, demand for better institutions change in accordance with the countries' levels of income; and

(ii) second, if institutions attempt to protect property rights and create markets that seem to be particularly relevant for promoting growth in low-income countries (LICs), institutions oriented to manage distributive conflicts become increasingly relevant as countries climb up the income ladder (Das and Quirck, 2016). Chile could be seen as a good example, as social protests emerged in 2019 which were not necessarily related to a decline in the economic conditions of population, but rather to a demand of more transparent and inclusive institutions.

In short, we need to explore in more depth the obstacles that MICs suffer in the process of improving their institutional framework. In order to do this, it is important to explore the determinants of the quality of institutions. More precisely, using our prior works, we underline the relevance that a group of macro-variables have in the process of improving institutions (Alonso and Garcimartín, 2013; Alonso et al., 2020). Broadly speaking, our results show that the level of income per capita, the soundness of the "fiscal covenant," income redistribution (rather than mere inequality), the level of education, and international openness are strong determinants of institutional quality.

Two interesting implications arise from these results. First, in contrast to other studies, institutional quality is here referred to variables that can be potentially modulated by public policies, rather than by immutable historical or geographical factors (eg,, latitude, colonial ties, or legal origin); and secondly, as MICs present weaknesses in many of the identified determinants of institutional quality, this could help to explain why institutions are sometimes so fragile in MICs.

The remainder of the chapter is organized into four sections. Section 4.2 presents some elements of the theoretical frame in which institutional change can be understood. Section 4.3 is oriented to empirically explore whether MICs have recognizable patterns in their processes of institutional change. Section 4.4 presents some of the results of our exploration into determinants of institutional quality, using different econometric procedures. Finally, our main conclusions are presented in Section 4.5.

4.2 Reforming Institutions: An Eclectic Approach

4.2.1 Criteria for Defining the Quality of Institutions

It should be acknowledged that there is no unified theoretical framework that persuasively explains institutional change (Kingston and Caballero, 2009), and moreover, no agreement has been reached around what should be considered as a "good" institution (Malito et al., 2018).[1] Rodrik (2007: 51) identifies high-quality

[1] Part of this section is drawn from Alonso et al. (2020).

institutions as "those that induce socially desirable behaviour on the part of economic agents," but this statement is too abstract and difficult to transfer to empirical terms.

Moreover, measuring institutional quality poses plenty of dilemmas. Some analysts consider that institutions should be measured by what a given institution produces (its outputs and outcomes) (Andrews, 2014; Rotberg, 2014). However, such an option is debatable, because empirical experience reveals that most outcomes that might be considered for measuring the quality of institutions are the result of a complex and poorly understood array of economic and social factors, rather than the direct and exclusive consequence of institutions.

Others analysts argue that institutions must be assessed in view of how they operate. For example, regarding the state (a central part of any national institutional framework), Fukuyama (2013) suggests considering its *capacity and autonomy*, while Rothstein (2011) defends consideration of its *impartiality*. Moreover, Fukuyama (2013) holds that the operative functioning of institutions should be separated from the normative ends that they are meant to serve.[2] However, this approach is difficult to accept, as the way in which normative mandates are fulfilled by institutions should necessarily be part of any institutional assessment (Rothstein, 2011).

Finally, certain researchers operate by collecting disaggregated information focused on just one outcome, in one field, in order to measure institutional activity (Andrews, 2014). They assume that good and not so good institutions coexist within a country. Even if this observation could be true, the approach conflicts with the idea that the institutional framework is not a juxtaposition of autonomous institutions, but a *connected structure of institutions* that operate at different levels. As a consequence, a functionalist approach based on an assessment of singular institutional arrangements can be inappropriate, with a more "macro-systemic" approach to measuring the quality of institutions being required (Rolland, 2004).

It is very difficult to settle among these opposing positions. A reasonable departure point should be to identify the general functions (or attributes) that institutions must fulfil (rather than their specific outputs and outcomes) as criteria of institutional quality. As two canonical definitions suggest, institutions "are the humanly devised constraints that structure political, economic and social interactions" (North, 1991: 97); or more precisely, "a system of rules, beliefs, norms, and organizations that together generate a regularity of (social) behaviour" (Greif, 2006: 30). Both definitions underline that institutions operate like a social "software" that shapes social expectations and provides some stability and predictability to human conduct. However, in spite of the

[2] Fukuyama (2013: 13) defines governance as "government's ability to make and enforce rules, and to deliver services, regardless of whether that government is democratic or not."

centrality of these definitions, the debate over the conception of institutions remains active (see, eg, Hodgson, 2006).

Beyond other discrepancies, two general conceptions on institutions seem to underlie this debate. On the one hand, some authors tend to conceive of institutions as rules that are the result of human actions and define exogenous incentives and constraints on agents' behavior (the *rule-based* conception). Institutional purpose is to reduce transaction costs and provide predictability to social interaction. In this approach, enforcement of rules is considered a separate issue from the formation and content of rules (eg, North, 1990). This approach tends to implicitly identify the *efficiency and predictability* of the given rules as the main factors in assessing the quality of an institution.

Elsewhere, other authors consider institutions as mainly endogenous and self-enforcing equilibria (*equilibrium-based* conception). In this case, enforcement is mainly endogenized, and institutions are conceived as equilibria in a sequence of repeated games (eg, Aoki, 2001; Greif, 2006). Agents create the structure that provides the motivation to act in accordance with the behavior predicted by institutions, thereby perpetuating their structure. In this vision, it is important to study the incentives framework created by institutions, as well as the reasons why agents operate according to that framework: that is, the *credibility and legitimacy* of institutions are also important factors of institutional quality (Greif and Kingston, 2011).

In spite of their differences, these two approaches are not necessarily incompatible (Greif and Kingston, 2011; Hindriks and Guala, 2015). Therefore, in an eclectic approach and in order to evaluate institutions, it would be important to know: (i) whether they are able to reduce uncertainty by providing regularities (*predictability*) to social interactions; (ii) whether rules and expectations are generating correct incentives (*static and dynamic efficiency*) for reducing costs of transactions and for addressing coordination failures: here it is important to distinguish static efficiency from dynamic efficiency, the former related to the capacity to promote efficient equilibria, the latter linked to the capacity to anticipate social changes (*adaptability*) (North, 2005); and (iii) finally whether individuals have the motivation to obey those rules (*credibility and legitimacy*), which is related to the distributional effects of institutions (Knight, 1992; Fukuyama, 2011). These four dimensions (predictability, static and dynamic efficiency, and legitimacy) should be considered as criteria of a good institutional framework.

4.2.2 Models of Institutional Change

Even if desirable criteria of quality were defined, many obstacles conspire against the creation of better institutional arrangements. First, there is a need to overcome the strong inertia that characterizes institutions: as Veblen had emphasized, many institutional arrangements persist long after their primary causes have changed (it is the "archaism" of inherited institutions). The stickiness of existing institutions is the consequence of various factors: (i) the generalized dynamic returns that characterize institutions;[3] (ii) the rooted commitments and social networks that are the base of any institution; and (iii) the objectification that an institution promotes in norms, beliefs, and values, as shared understanding of social interactions.

Secondly, changing institutions implies the modification of the way in which roles, resources, and pay-offs are distributed among social agents. Any institutional change necessarily creates winners and losers, and the latter will try to block the change (which remits to the political economy of the reforms).

Finally, if rules are to be effective, they (and beliefs, values, and norms that accompany them) have to be internalized in social conduct. Therefore, a huge effort should be made in the dissemination of the new rules and the establishment of mechanisms for their enforcement.

Given their powerful inertia, analysts have tended to conceive institutional change as a "punctuated" process in which long periods of stability coexist with episodes of abrupt changes. Overcoming institutional inertia is easier when society falls into an episode of disruption or in an extremely demanding situation (critical junctures). When major events dislocate the existing political and economic balance in a society, it is more likely that people call their prior expectations and beliefs into question, in this way facilitating the search for new institutional arrangements.

However, most institutional changes cannot be properly associated with abrupt and discontinuous transformations, but instead with a sequence of gradual modifications over time. Mahoney and Thelen (2009) explore these kinds of changes. They accept that institutions are relatively enduring features of social life but consider that the inextinguishable ambiguity of rules (even formal ones) creates room for gradual and continuous changes in the enactment, interpretation, or enforcement of rules. In the context of an uncertain and changeable stetting, "compliance is inherently complicated by the fact that rules can never be precise enough to cover the complexity of all possible real-world situations" (Mahoney and Thelen 2009: 11).

Additionally, the limited cognitive capacity of social actors contributes towards reinforcing the presence of important gaps between the established rules and their interpretation and enforcement. These gaps open the window to a process of gradual institutional change that can follow three modal types:[4] (i) layering, when new rules are introduced on top of or alongside existing ones; (ii) drift, when rules are reinterpreted due to shifts in the environment;

[3] Formal institutions have high fixed costs in order to set up, but very low marginal costs when they operate.

[4] Mahoney and Thelen (2009) consider a fourth type, displacement, in which the existing rules are replaced by new ones, but this type is not necessarily "gradual."

Table 4.1 Models of institutional change

		Timing	
		Frequency	**Punctuated**
Nature of changes	Radical	Serial replacement (Levitsky and Murillo, 2013)	Critical junctures (Acemoglu and Robinson, 2012)
	Gradual	Gradualism (Mahoney and Thelen, 2009)	Stickiness of institutions

Source: Author based on Levitsky and Murillo (2013).

and (iii) conversion, when the enactment of existing rules is changed due to their strategic redeployment.

On the other hand, based on the experience of some Latin American countries, Levitsky and Murillo (2013) draw attention towards those cases in which institutions are built on very fragile foundations and without being rooted within society. As a consequence, they lack the stability and regular enforcement that are normally conferred upon institutions. In these cases, institutions can change broadly, in terms of the content, durability, and enforcement of rules: what Levitsky and Murillo (2013) coined as "serial replacement." As a result, actors cannot reliably use formal rules to guide their expectations and institutions lose one of their basic functions, which is to provide reasonable levels of predictability to social behavior.

Finally, there can be a fourth possible option in which institutions reveal high levels of resistance to any change, even if society is subject to a slow and continuous trend of transformations. In that case, institutions seem relatively immovable (which could be called "institutional stickiness"), as only minor and gradual changes in the institutional framework are occasionally adopted. This option is more frequent in societies that are highly stratified and have authoritarian regimes, in which social movements are weak and rather disorganized.

In sum, the way in which institutions change depends on both contextual factors that affect society (eg, crises or episodes of social disruption) and internal factors, related to the levels to which rules are socially enrooted, and their level of compliance and enforcement (Table 4.1).

4.3 An Empirical Characterization

4.3.1 Is There any Empirical Singularity in MICs?

Empirical evidence reveals that factors that ignite economic growth are not necessarily the same as those that sustain it in the long-run (Rodrik, 2007).

The presence of some favorable factors, either at the national level (eg, a change in the political environment or in social expectations) or in the international realm (eg, a surge in commodity prices) can cause an episode of intense growth in a developing country. However, maintaining a sustained process of growth over time is a harder challenge that requires a continuous process of productive transformation and institutional change. Many MICs have enjoyed (in some cases repeatedly) episodes of very intense growth, but only a few countries (mostly from Asia) were able to sustain a process of successful growth and economic convergence with the level of income of developed countries (Hausmann et al., 2005).

As Rodrik (2007) underlined, in the long run, the main thing that ensures convergence with the living standards of advanced countries is the acquisition of high-quality institutions. Actually, it is difficult to preserve a continuous dynamic of economic growth without endowing society with a sound institutional underpinning that properly maintains dynamism, manages distributive tensions, and generates resilience to external shocks.

In accordance with this assumption, we want to explore if MICs show any particularity in their process of improving institutions. Such a purpose has to deal with the deficient information on institutional quality that currently exists. Indicators based on more carefully theoretical foundations (such as the Bertelsmann Transformation Index or the Institutional Profile) cover only a very short timeframe, while most of those available for longer periods are affected by different flaws, in terms of validity, reliability, precision, that affect intertemporal and international comparisons (Arndt, 2009). As a compromise, we have opted for the International Country Risk Guide (ICRG) as it is the best database with a longer timeframe, with its components most clearly linked to the institutional framework.[5]

As expected, the data confirm that a significant relation exists between institutional quality (ICRG) and the GDP per capita at the international level (Figure 4.1). Additionally, with data covering a longer period (1990–2013), a process of institutional convergence seems to be operating. The lower the level of institutional quality of a country in 1990, the higher the increase of its ICRG in the period (Figure 4.2). There are potential reasons for convergence, as a process of institutional diffusion and learning can operate effectively among countries. The equation of absolute convergence confirms this result, with a β parameter of −0.509 (Table 4.2).

In order to explore if convergence is conditional on a country's characteristics, we included some dummies that referred to country groupings. If these dummies

[5] We mainly used the sum of many components of the political risk index of the ICRG. It refers to some important components linked to institutional features (such as government stability, internal and external conflict, corruption, the military in politics, law and order, democratic accountability, and quality of the bureaucracy).

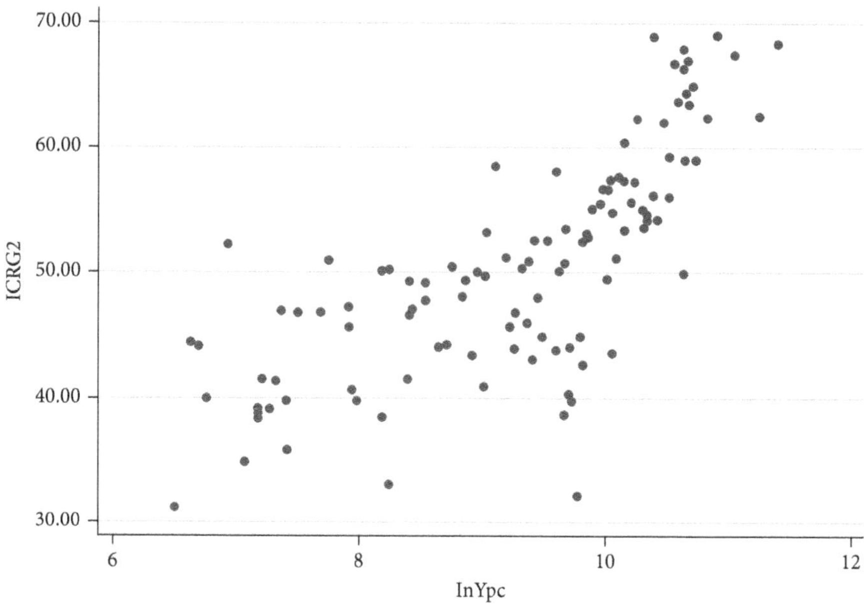

Figure 4.1 Institutional quality and GDP per capita (PPP) by countries

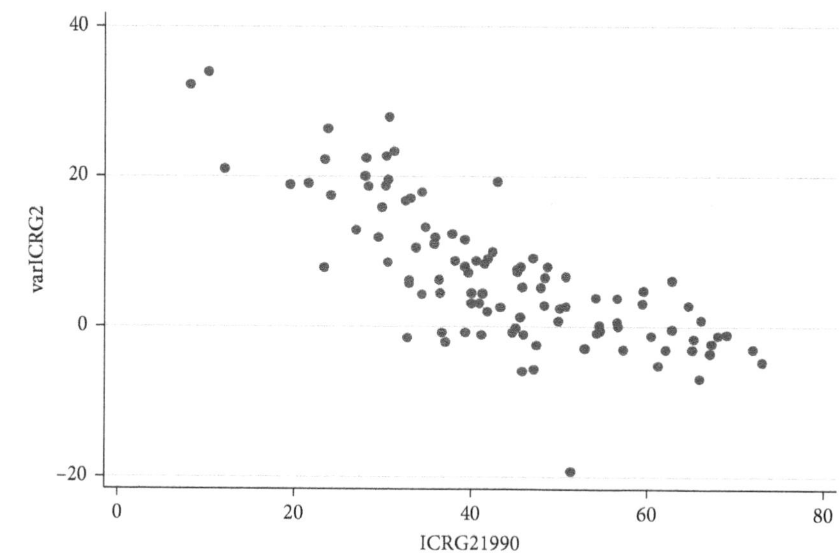

Figure 4.2 Absolute convergence in the level of institutional quality (1990–2013)
Source: Author's estimates based on the World Bank and ICRG.

Table 4.2 Institutional convergence (1990–2013)

	Absolute convergence	Conditioned convergence
Institutional index 1990	−0.5099***	−0.6513***
	(0.0423)	(0.0624)
EAP		−0.3782
		(2.2740)
NAM		3.4815
		(4.2866)
EECA		−5.3162
		(3.7572)
LAC		−4.2607
		(2.1333)
MENA		−5.7359
		(2.6210)
SA		−3.1636
		(3.8062)
SSA		−6.8646
		(2.2076)
Number of observations	102	102
F(1, 100)	144.8	21.26
Prob>F	0.0000	0.0000
Adj. R squared	0.5875	0.6161

Source: Author's estimates.

are referred to income groups, only the coefficient attributed to LICs is significant and negative. That is, the process of institutional convergence does not seem to present any particularity in MICs, which can be in accordance with the heterogeneous composition of this group of countries. However, if the same procedure is applied to regions, three dummies are significant and negative: Sub-Saharan Africa, Latin America, and the Middle East and North Africa (MENA) (Table 4.2). As Latin America and MENA are regions mainly formed by MICs, the results could indicate that some groups of MICs suffer visible obstacles in their process of convergence. In other words, institutional change could be an important challenge to MICs' development, even if the evidence is not sufficient to conceptualize the existence of an "institutional trap."[6]

Another simple way to confirm if MICs suffer particular problems in the process of improving their institutions is to explore the relation between the index of institutional quality and a country's level of income. As mentioned earlier in this section, a positive relation exists: the higher the GDP per capita, the higher the level of institutional quality. But if a dummy is introduced to capture the group of developed countries, the slope of the relationship for this group is clearly steeper

[6] It is difficult to conceptualize these obstacles as an MIC trap for two reasons: (i) because they cannot be generalized to all MICs; and (ii) because similar problems are suffered by sub-Saharan Africa, which is a low-income region.

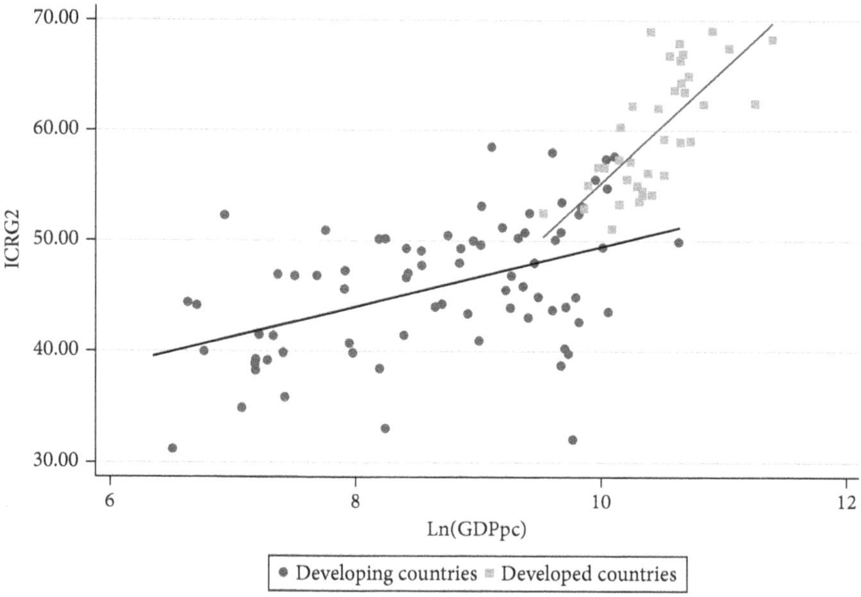

Figure 4.3 Institutional quality and GDP per capita
Source: Author's estimates based on ICRG.

than that for developing countries (including MICs) (Figure 4.3). This is not due to the use of a particular indicator (the ICRG), as the same pattern is found when other indicators of institutional quality are employed.[7] Therefore, empirical exploration suggests that MICs should make a leap in the quality of their institutions if they want to better adjust the sequence of institutional change with the process of economic growth.

In sum, empirical exploration confirms that there is a significant group of MICs belonging to two regions (Latin America and MENA) that suffer particular problems in the process of institutional improvement.

4.3.2 Institutional Change in MICs: Stickiness and Fluidity

As mentioned, in order to be sustainable, the process of economic development requires that it is accompanied by a sequence of institutional changes. The potential dissonance between these two processes is limited in HICs, because they have relatively stable economies with sounder institutions; they are usually also open societies with consolidated democracies, demanding populations and competitive markets, which facilitates the process of institutional change. In the case of

[7] Similar results are obtained when the Worldwide Governance Index is employed.

MICs, however, the potential dissonance between the processes of economic and institutional change gains greater relevance, as these countries experience episodes of intense growth and social change accompanied by high levels of economic and political instability.

Even so, there are some MICs that have maintained a successful process of economic and institutional transformation that allowed them to progressively converge toward the living conditions of developed countries (Republic of Korea, Taiwan, Spain, and Ireland are examples). But this is not a universal experience: an ample group of MICs have had limited success in accompanying their social and economic transformation with an equivalent process of reforming institutions. Among these countries we could identify two different pathologies that affect two regions mainly formed by MICs: that is, the excessive institutional stiffness (Arab countries), in one case, and too much institutional fluidity (Latin America), in the other.

First, one group of countries (mainly located in the Middle East and North Africa) have shown enormous resistance to undergoing a process of institutional change that keeps pace with their social and economic transformation. The presence of a hierarchical society, with strong traditional values, low levels of education, and limited democracy has severely hindered the process of institutional change. In fact, during the last three decades, the institutional frameworks of these countries have shown a powerful inertia, which contrasts with the visible changes that have occurred in the social and economic realms.

In the early 1990s, the region was comprised of very traditional societies (Lebanon being an exception) whose economies were based on the exportation of primary products, such as oil, minerals, and agricultural products. Ruled by authoritarian regimes, in most of these countries the levels of recognition for political liberties and civil rights were very low (with countries classified as "partly free" or "not free" by Freedom House). Populations were mainly located in rural areas, with levels of education significantly lower than those of other MIC regions (such as Latin America) (Figures 4.4).

Over the last 25 years, these societies have experienced a gradual process of change. In average terms, the GDP per capita PPP in constant dollars has maintained an annual growth rate of 2.2 percent, which means that the level of income per capita multiplied by 1.8 during this period. There has been an important generational change, as massive cohorts of people born in the 1970s and 1980s reached legal age. At the same time, there was an important process of urbanization and an improvement in the levels of people's education (the years of education moved from 3.4 in 1990 to 6.2 in 2010). These two processes were accompanied by a change in social values, particularly among young people: greater segments of society have been increasingly exposed to Western influences through both their access to new communication technology (mainly mobile phones and the Internet) and the modernizing effect that migrants can have (by their visits and return) on their home communities.

However, these social changes occurred within a rigid framework of formal institutions that have hardly changed during the period: the consequence was a progressive estrangement between society (particularly its younger sectors) and formal institutions. As a consequence, the legitimacy of formal institutions was silently questioned, as they were increasingly maladapted to the new social reality, and capacity for enforcing rules was equally weakened. The Arab Spring that emerged in 2011 was a clear expression of the conflict caused by this dissonance between formal institutions and society.

Social mobilization was, in these cases, a spontaneous expression of resentment at the traditional Arab dictatorships, the corruption in political life, and the deterioration of countries' economic conditions (with high levels of unemployment and inflation). Protesters in traditional monarchies (such as Jordan and Morocco) demanded more political and civil rights, as well as promoting a transition towards constitutional monarchies. At the same time, protesters in Republican regimes (such as Egypt and Tunisia) wanted an overhaul of political leaders and free elections. Thus, there was a common and vague demand for institutional change, even if there was no consensus among protesters about the alternative political and economic model to be implemented.

The result of these movements was clearly unbalanced and frustrating. Egypt, Tunisia, Yemen, and Algeria entered an uncertain transitional period, Morocco adopted minor reforms, Syria and Libya sank into civil conflict, while the monarchies in the Persian Gulf remained unshaken by events. Unsatisfactory as it was, this episode seems to be a first step in a longer and inevitable process of questioning and reforming a very rigid institutional framework.

The other pathology shows the opposite feature: an excessive fluidity of institutions. When formal institutions are weak and not properly embedded in society, they can be subject to a recurrent process of change, limiting the capacity for rules to be rooted in society. This pathology is more frequent when there is an acute conflict between political and economic democracy: that is, when democracy (and formal rights) are based on a fragmented society which has deep and chronic social inequalities. Strong inequality leads to socio-political instability, facilitates institutions that are captured by powerful groups, and reduces people's disposition toward cooperative action. At the same time, in the context of fragmented societies, it is more difficult to build stable social coalitions, therefore dominant groups try to combine authoritarianism and populism to maintain their hold on power. As a consequence, political life will become very unstable, motivating frequent (and sometimes cosmetic) changes in the institutional framework.

The example of this pathology is a group of Latin American countries. In most of these countries, populations are mainly located in urban areas and enjoy

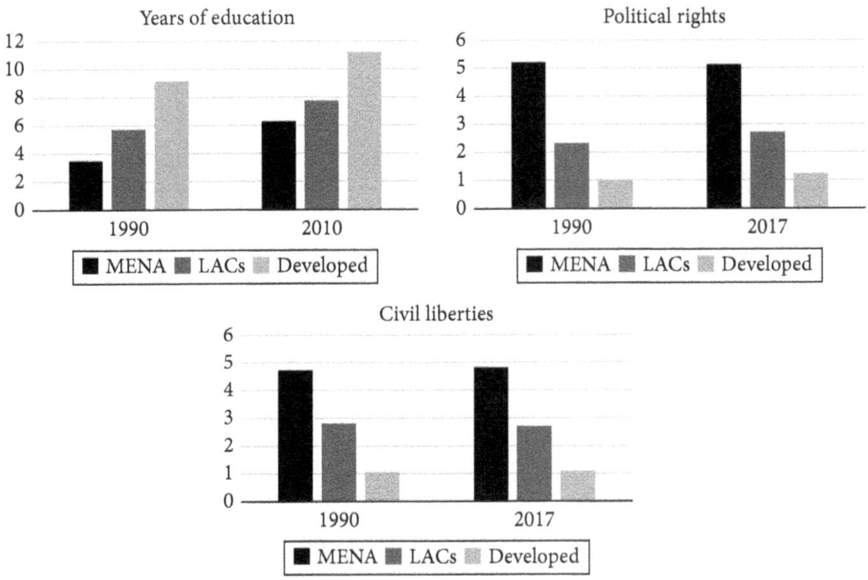

Figure 4.4 Education and democracy in MENA and LACs

Sources: Barro and Lee (2016); Freedom House.

MENA: Algeria, Egypt, Iran, Lebanon, Morocco, Syria ,and Tunisia; LACs: Argentina, Bolivia, Brazil, Chile, Colombia, Costa Rica, Dominican R., Ecuador, El Salvador, Guatemala, Honduras, México, Nicaragua, Panama, Paraguay, Peru, Uruguay, and Venezuela; Developed: Australia, Austria, Belgium, Canada, Denmark, Finland, France, Germany, Greece, Ireland, Italy, Japan, Luxemburg, The Netherlands, New Zealand, Norway, Portugal, Spain, Sweden, Switzerland, the UK, and the USA.

Political rights and Civil liberties are measured with 1 being the most free and 7 the least free ratings.

acceptable levels of education and (differently from MENA) their political regimes can be considered to be free or partly free democracies (Figure 4.4). However, levels of inequality are higher than in MENA and the capacity of the State to reduce inequality (measured through "redistribution") is very low (Figure 4.5).

In their historical experience, institutional change, rather than being infrequent (punctuated equilibrium models) or ongoing and gradual (gradualist models), is frequent and sometimes radical (Levitsky and Murillo, 2013). Some of these changes are motivated by the rulers' aspirations to preserve the support of a particular social group or to obtain positive value for an international audience but with limited impact and enforcement (eg, some laws against gender violence or for the protection of indigenous people in Latin America). As a consequence, institutional fluidity hinders the capacity to enforce rules and reduces levels of stability of the institutional framework. This relationship may be self-reinforcing: as institutions are stable, individuals adapt their strategies to them, reinforcing the rules; on the contrary, if rules are continuously changing individuals do not invest in consolidating those rules.

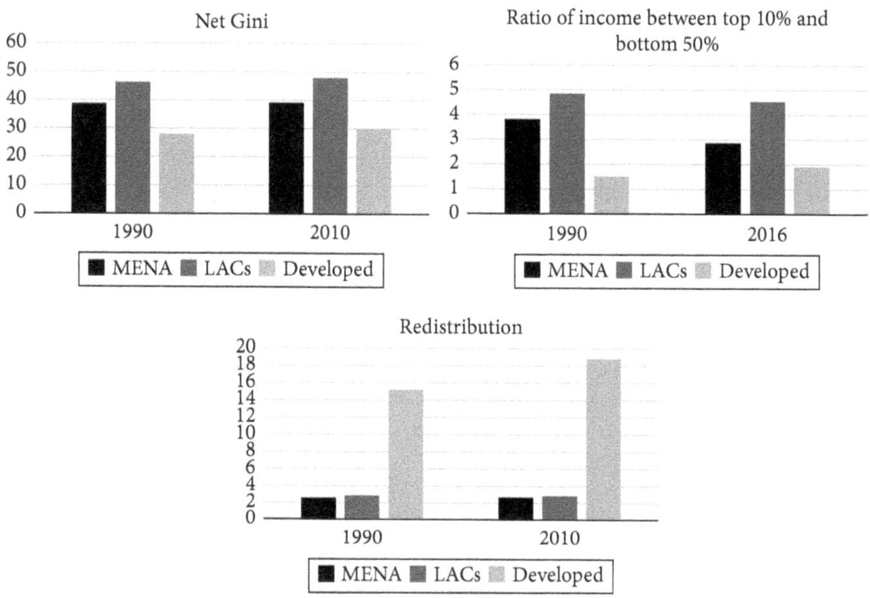

Figure 4.5 Inequality in MENA and LACs

Sources: Solt (2016); World Inequality Database.

MENA: Algeria, Egypt, Iran, Lebanon, Morocco, Syria, and Tunisia; LACs: Argentina, Bolivia, Brazil, Chile, Colombia, Costa Rica, Dominican R., Ecuador, El Salvador, Guatemala, Honduras, México, Nicaragua, Panama, Paraguay, Peru, Uruguay, and Venezuela; Developed: Australia, Austria, Belgium, Canada, Denmark, Finland, France, Germany, Greece, Ireland, Italy, Japan, Luxemburg, the Netherlands, New Zealand, Norway, Portugal, Spain, Sweden, Switzerland, the UK, and the USA.

Redistribution is the difference between market Gini minus net Gini.

Many examples illustrate the fluidity of institutions in Latin America. This process has even affected the main meta-institution in a country: its constitution. In Bolivia, Dominican Republic, Ecuador, Peru, and Venezuela constitutions were replaced at least ten times during the first century of their independence (Levitsky and Murillo, 2013). Moreover, many countries with relatively new constitutions (such as Bolivia or Venezuela) have changed or reinterpreted the regulation related to the Presidency's re-election in the last two decades.

A good exponent of the institutional fluidity in many Latin American countries is the dissolution of the system of traditional parties, which occurred during the last two decades. Political parties are structures of intermediation that provide stability to the process of social participation in the political process. However, in the last two decades only a small group of parties in the region have shown stability over time, while new parties have emerged and vanished as occasional responses to political demands, basically linked to the personalist leadership of some candidate. On the other hand, recurrent instability opens up the space for populist options, as ample social sectors look for redeemers or "caudillos" (rather than reformers) to lead the government, which in turn reinforces the weaknesses of institutions.

Therefore, two groups of MICs present specific problems that affect their processes of institutional change: excessive institutional stickiness in one case and excessive institutional fluidity in the other. These problems seem to be linked with some general features of these countries, particularly related to the level of education, the level and durability of social inequality and the way in which the institutional framework is rooted in societies. In Section 4.4, we will explore these determinants of institutional quality in more depth.

4.4 Macro Determinants of Institutional Quality

4.4.1 Macro Determinants of Institutional Improvements

Since institutions are subject to great inertia by nature, many researchers have tended to investigate as determinants of institutional quality variables that are relatively constant over time, such as those related to the geographical or historical features of countries: latitude, colonial ties, legal tradition, dominant religion or ethnic fragmentation appear among the explanatory variables used (Gallup et al., 1998, La Porta et al., 1999, Chong and Zanforlin, 2000, Acemoglu et al., 2001, Glaeser and Shleifer, 2002, Easterly and Levine, 2003, among others). Needless to say, were these factors the main determinants of institutional quality, there would be little room for improving the institutional framework. Fortunately, empirical estimates do not seem to unequivocally support these hypotheses. Even if some of these variables appear to be significant, most of these relations are either weakly robust or vanish altogether once the estimations are controlled for per capita income (Islam and Montenegro, 2002; Alesina et al., 2003).

Alternatively, we want to search for general determinants of institutional quality that can be potentially modulated by collective action and by public policies. For this purpose, we can turn our attention to some theoretical proposals that have tried to explain how economic, political, and institutional forces mutually interact and evolve. For example, Besley and Persson (2011) build a model where state capacity, political violence, and income are jointly determined in an integrated formal framework. In their approach, higher income reduces the likelihood of repression and civil war by raising the opportunity cost of investing in violence; while the reduction of violence contributes to economic and social progress. More generally, there are two-way forces acting between income and state capacity. On the one hand, higher income strengthens the incentives for incumbents to invest in fiscal and legal capacity, so long as the cohesiveness of institutions and political stability are not a problem. On the other hand, higher fiscal capacity can raise incomes by reducing the incentives for incumbents to earn rents through inefficient or predatory procedures. Moreover, a higher legal capacity reduces frictions and raises income by promoting the efficient functioning of markets.

Along similar lines, Gradstein (2003 and 2008) builds a model in which a bidirectional relation between economic development and institutional quality is considered. More precisely, he assumes that a fraction of investment is devoted to rent-seeking activities. This fraction is endogenously determined by the extension of property rights enforcement. Since this enforcement is a public good that needs to be financed, a certain level of tax revenue (and national income) is required. Better enforcement enhances economic growth, which in turn (by increasing the overall tax base) facilitates the protection of property rights. Although in principle a low taxation level fosters consumption and growth, steady state income can be lower, since low taxes also limit the enforcement of property rights; and conversely, higher taxes reduce current consumption but increase the steady state income by improving property rights protection. Thus, two alternative steady states can emerge: one with high levels of property rights enforcement (good institutions) and high income, and another with minimal protection of property rights (bad institutions) and low income.

Finally, North et al. (2009) distinguish two different types of social organizations that emerged to deal with violence: the "natural state order" (or limited access order), based mainly on personal boundaries and restrictions on individual freedom; and the "open access order," based on impersonal relationships, political competition, and constraints on the Executive. Political management of violence and provision of social stability is based on the manipulation of economic privileges in the former case, and on rules and organizations in the latter. Therefore, the stability of the open access order rests on its ability to provide *credible commitments*, but since the masses participate in this order, *some form of distribution is inevitable*, by way of sharing the gains of long-term economic growth.

It is worth mentioning that beyond their differences, all these studies identify variables that seem to be associated with the quality of institutions. Among them, the country's level of income, political stability (and legal capacity of the state), a manageable level of inequality (or acceptable level of social cohesiveness), and sufficient fiscal capacity must be underlined.

4.4.2 An Empirical Model

In accordance with our theoretical exploration, in Alonso and Garcimartín (2013) and Alonso et al. (2020) we consider five potential determinants that are directly or indirectly linked with those criteria that determine the quality of institutions (static and dynamic efficiency, predictability, and legitimacy) (Table 4.3). Three of these variables emerged in our theoretical review: development level, income distribution, and tax revenue. The remaining two, openness and education, although not present in those theoretical approaches, are well connected with the criteria mentioned above, as both are likely to impact the dynamic efficiency of institutions.

The first study (Alonso and Garcimartín, 2013), through an IV 2TSLS[8] estimate, confirmed that institutional quality was positively affected by a country's development level, the soundness of the "implicit fiscal covenant" between state and citizens (measured by taxes over GDP), and (relatively weakly) by the average level of education. At the same time, institutional quality was found to be negatively conditioned by inequality (Table 4.3). As in other works (ie, Rodrik et al., 2004), Alonso and Garcimartín (2013) did not find a significant relation between trade openness and institutional quality. This was, however, a counter-intuitive result, because it is expected that openness encourages (and demands) a sounder institutional framework.

Additionally, although previous studies had highlighted historical and geographical features as determinants of institutional quality (country location, colonial origin, legal system tradition, ethno-linguistic fragmentation, natural resources endowment, etc.), in Alonso and Garcimartín (2013) we found that, once the estimations have been controlled for per capita income, these variables either play no role in shaping institutional quality or only an indirect role, by way of conditioning the aforementioned variables.

Due to non-availability of data, estimates by Alonso and Garcimartín (2013) were affected by an important limitation: only static econometric techniques were employed. Since institutional quality exhibits high inertia, and because there are clear problems of reverse causality, the use of dynamic techniques would seem a more adequate approach. In a new study Alonso et al. (2020) offered new estimates based on dynamic econometric tools,[9] as well as a more careful procedure for dealing with collinearity between explicative variables. In spite of the differences between the econometric approaches, the two studies concurred in their results.

Thus, the new estimate showed that institutional quality is positively affected, first, by country's development level: a higher level of development leads to higher institutional quality, but as the latter also promotes economic development, this implies that the two variables can interact and create a virtuous circle. This two-way relation between institutions and a country's level of income is consistent with the theoretical models of Besley and Persson (2011) and Gradstein (2003); and empirically, this relation between institutional quality and level of income

[8] That is, two stages least squares with instrumental variables.

[9] More precisely, they employ the generalized method of moments (GMM) or, more specifically, the system GMM of Arellano and Bover (1995) and Blundell and Bond (1998), as an extended version of the first difference-based approach originated in Arellano and Bond (1991).

Table 4.3 Determinants of quality of institutions IV TSLS

Variable	Coeff. (T ratio) Education exogenous	Coeff (T Ratio) Education endogenous
Intercept	−2.63 (1.70)	−2.64 (1.76)
GDP pc PPP	0.26 (2.12)	0.27 (1.96)
Gini Index	−0.75 (2.40)	0.76 (2.47)
Taxes	0.73 (2.76)	0.72 (2.83)
Education	0.33 (2.03)	0.32 (1.70)
Openness	0.12 (1.04)	0.12 (1.04)
MENA	−0.59 (2.49)	−0.59 (2.49)
EE and CA	−0.69 (4.81)	−0.69 (4.73)
Adjusted R^2	0.80	0.80
N of observations	78	78
Infra-identification test: Kleibergen–Paap (χ2 6)	14.88 (12.59)	14.00 (12.59)
Statistical J (valor de χ2 (5))	10.89 (11.07)	10.89 (11.07)
Endogenous	GDP pc PPP 2004, Gini index, taxes, and international openness	GDP pc PPP 2004, Gini index, taxes, education and international openness
Instruments	GDP pc 1990, squared GDP pc 1990, fuel, ethnic fragmentation, population, and regional dummies	GDP pc 1990, squared GDP pc 1990, fuel, education 1990, ethnic fragmentation, population, and regional dummies

Source: Alonso and Garcimartín (2013).

was confirmed by Chong and Zanforlin (2000), Islam and Montenegro (2002), and Rigobon and Rodrik (2004).

Second, institutional quality is linked to the soundness of the "implicit fiscal covenant" between state and citizens. Basically, this literature considers taxation as part of a broader State-building agenda: that is, taxation can transform the State to become both stronger and more responsive to its citizenry (among others, Levi, 1988; Bräutigam et al. 2008; and Moore, 2004). This idea had also been developed by different theoretical models in which taxes not only reduce the need for seigniorage, but also diminish the risk of social polarization and instability (Cukierman et al., 1992), and, in a context of less polarized public finance, facilitate a better provision of public goods (Alesina et al., 1999). In empirical terms Baskaran and Bigsten (2013) show that a higher fiscal capacity leads to higher-quality institutional frameworks. On the other hand, with data from sub-Saharan countries, Broms (2015) showed that taxation spurs citizens to monitor and take a more active interest in politics.

Third, the average level of education equally affects the quality of institutions: a better educated population tends to be more demanding about the quality of the institutional framework, while at the same time education is required to build better institutions. Both factors connect with the proposal by Glaeser et al. (2007) regarding the role that education plays as a driver of democratic institutions in fostering non-violent conflict resolution. And this relationship has been confirmed by other researchers such as Evans and Rauch (2000).

Fourth, institutional quality was found to be negatively conditioned by inequality: strong inequality leads to conflict, socio-political instability, and insecurity; it reduces people's disposition toward cooperative action; and it facilitates the capture of institutions by powerful groups who are orientated to particular interests rather than to the common good (Alesina and Rodrik, 1993; Alesina and Perotti, 1996; Easterly, 2001; and Keefer and Knack, 2002; and in historical terms, Engerman and Sokoloff, 2002 or Acemoglu and Robinson, 2011).

Finally, in contrast with prior works, in this new estimate a strong and positive relation between institutional quality and international openness is found. It is confirmed therefore that fostering a more dynamic, competitive, and demanding environment will fuel greater demand for good institutions, reduce rent-seeking activities, and facilitate learning processes and the imitation of international good practices.

Estimates in Alonso et al. (2020) additionally present two interesting results. First, given the relatively moderate performance of the distribution variable of net income in the basic model, they replaced income distribution with income redistribution, since this better reflects the active role played by the State.[10] This variable presents a stronger relation with institutional quality. Second, the model has also been estimated by defining the variables in terms of distances from the leader, instead of using the (original) levels of variables (Table 4.4).[11] This aims to test whether institutional quality is better explained by the relative position ("laggardness") of a country. The theoretical foundation of this approach rests on the idea that there are both "learning and institutional convergence across societies over time" (Fukuyama, 2011: 437). Additionally, this approach introduces non-trivial non-linearity and interactions between countries. Results confirm this approach.

[10] Probably, social mobility could be considered as an alternative way to measure this aspect, but there are not reliable data about this variable at international level. Therefore, we measured redistribution as Gross (market) Gini index minus net Gini index.

[11] Namely, the value of each explanatory variable for each country/year is computed as the difference between the maximum value of each period and each country's value (except for income distribution, where the leader is defined as the country with the minimum value), taking the logarithm of the evaluated distance afterwards.

Table 4.4 Determinants of institutional quality, estimation using "distance to the leader"

Variables	(1)	(2)	(3)	(4)
Lag 1 of depend.	0.976***	0.884***	0.953***	0.923***
	(0.126)	(0.133)	(0.129)	(0.136)
Lag 2 of depend.	-0.217**	-0.135	-0.208**	-0.176*
	(0.103)	(0.106)	(0.102)	(0.103)
Per capita GDP	-0.0638**	-0.0586**	-0.0638**	-0.0596**
	(0.0270)	(0.0276)	(0.0266)	(0.0271)
Income redistribution	-0.0145*	-0.0208**		
	(0.00756)	(0.0104)		
Openness	-0.0301**	-0.0305**	-0.0310**	-0.0301**
	(0.0139)	(0.0138)	(0.0138)	(0.0138)
Education	-0.0119*	-0.00908	-0.0117*	-0.00724
	(0.00696)	(0.00701)	(0.00664)	(0.00732)
Taxes		0.000290		
		(0.00591)		
PC1 (Taxes + Redistrib.)			-0.00864**	
			(0.00409)	
PC1 (Taxes + Distrib. + Redistrib.)				-0.00937**
				(0.00434)
Observations	1,611	1,559	1,559	1,551
Number of countries	102	101	101	101
p-val.(Sargan)	0.705	0.571	0.437	0.413
p-val.(Hansen)	0.517	0.622	0.632	0.478
p-val.(AR1)	0.000875	0.00348	0.00103	0.00255
p-val.(AR2)	0.425	0.354	0.687	0.516
Number of instrum.	70	70	70	70

Robust standard errors in parentheses. *** $p < 0.01$, ** $p < 0.05$, * $p < 0.1$.

4.5 Conclusions

Reforming institutions is a challenging task for MICs. As empirical evidence shows, two regions comprised of MICs, Latin America and MENA, seem to suffer particular problems in the process of institutional convergence at an international level. A more detailed analysis suggests that, with some exceptions, countries in these two regions suffer two pathologies in the process of institutional change: an excessive institutional stickiness, in the case of MENA, and an excessive institutional fluidity, in the case of Latin America. These two problems affect the level of stability, effectiveness, and credibility of institutions. Some macro determinants can condition the process of overcoming these deficiencies: particularly, the level of education, social inequality, and taxation emerge as important explanatory variables, although with different weights in each region.

The relevance of these variables as determinants of institutional quality has been raised in prior research. Broadly speaking, the results of a new estimate confirm that income per capita and tax revenue appear to be sound determinants of institutional quality; additionally, redistribution (rather than simply inequality) and education also positively impact institutional quality, this last variable in a weaker way. Finally, it must also be stated that, contrary to other studies, in our estimates international openness does indeed seem to be a strong determinant of institutional quality.

Therefore, in order to improve institutions, countries could operate on one or several of these factors, although the final outcome could also depend on the level of achievements at the international level (as suggested by the "distance to the leader" estimation). In our view, these findings carry remarkable implications: they suggest that (while not an easy task) MICs have room for policies that could encourage the improvement of institutions, thus impacting one of the potential causes of an MIC trap.

References

Acemoglu, D. and Robinson, J. (2001): "A Theory of Political Transition," *American Economic Review* 91: 938–63.

Acemoglu, D. and Robinson, J. (2006): *Economic Origins of Dictatorship and Democracy*, Cambridge: Cambridge University Press.

Acemoglu, D. and Robinson, J. (2012): *Why Nations Fail. The Origins of Power, Prosperity and Poverty*, New York: Random House.

Acemoglu, D., Johnson, S., and Robinson, J. A. (2001): "The colonial origins of comparative development: An empirical investigation," *American Economic Review* 91, no. 5: 1369–401.

Alesina, A. and Perotti, R. (1996): "Income distribution, political instability and investment," *European Economic Review* 40, no. 6: 1203–28.

Alesina, A. and Rodrik, D. (1993): "Income distribution and economic growth: A simple theory and some empirical evidence," in A. Cukierman, Z. Hercovitz, and L. Leiderman (eds.), *The Political Economy of Business Cycles and Growth*, Cambridge, MA: MIT Press.

Alesina, A., Baqir, R., and Easterly, W. (1999): "Public goods and ethnic divisions," *Quarterly Journal of Economics* 114: 1243–84.

Alesina, A., Devleeschauwer, A., Easterly, W., and Kurlat, S. (2003): "Fractionalization," *Journal of Economic Growth* 8, no. 2, pp. 155–94.

Alonso, J. A. and Garcimartín, C. (2013): "The Determinants of Institutional Quality. More on the Debate," *Journal of International Development* 25, no. 2: 206–26.

Alonso, J. A., Garcimartín, C., and Kvaras, V. (2020): "Determinant of Institutional Quality: An Empirical Exploration," *Journal of Economic Policy Reform* 23 (2): 229–47.

Andrews, M. (2014): "An ends-means approach to looking at governance," Center for International Development Working Paper 281, Harvard University.

Aoki, M. (2001): *Towards a Comparative Institutional Analysis*, Cambridge, MA: MIT Press.

Arellano, M. and Bond, S. (1991): "Some tests of specification for panel data: Monte Carlo evidence and an application to employment equations," *Review of Economic Studies* 58: 277–97.

Arellano, M. and Bover, O. (1995): "Another look at the instrumental variable estimation of error-components models," *Journal of Econometrics* 68: 29–51.

Arndt, Christiane Elisabeth (2009): *Governance Indicators*. Maastricht: Boekenplan.

Barro, Robert and Jong-Wha Lee (2013): "A new data set of educational attainment in the world, 1950–2010," *Journal of Development Economics*, 104: 184–98.

Baskaran, T. and Bigsten, A. (2013): "Fiscal capacity and the quality of government in Sub-Saharan Africa," *World Development* 45: 92–107.

Besley, T. and Persson, T. (2011): *Pillars of Prosperity. The Political Economics of Development Clusters*, Princeton, NJ: Princeton University Press.

Blundell, R. and Bond, S. (1998): "Initial conditions and moment restrictions in dynamic panel data models," *Journal of Econometrics* 87: 115–43.

Bräutigam, D., Fjeldstad, O. H., and Moore, M. (2008): *Taxation and State-Building in Developing Countries*, Cambridge: Cambridge University Press.

Broms, R. (2015): "Putting up or shutting up: On the individual-level relationship between taxpaying and political interest in a developing context," *Journal of Development Studies* 51, no. 1: 93–109

Chong, A. and Zanforlin, L. (2000): "Law Tradition and Institutional Quality: Some Empirical Evidence," *Journal of International Development* 12, no. 8: 1057–68.

Cukierman, A., Sebastian, E., and Tabellini, G. (1992): "Seignorage and Political Instability," *American Economic Review* 82: 537–55.

Das, K. and Quirk, Th. (2016): "Which Institutions Promote Growth? Revisiting Evidence," *Economic Papers* 35, no. 1: 37–58.

Easterly, W. (2001): "The Middle Class Consensus and Economic Development," *Journal of Economic Growth* 6, no. 4: 317–35.

Easterly, W. and Levine, R. (2003): "Tropics, germs and crops: how endowments influence economic development," *Journal of Monetary Economics* 50, no. 1: 3–39.

Engerman, S. K. and Sokoloff, K. L. (2002): "Factor Endowments, Inequality and Paths of Development among New World Economies," *NBER Working Paper*, No. 9259, Cambridge, MA: National Bureau of Economic Research.

Evans, P. and Rauch, P. (2000): "Bureaucratic Structure and Bureaucratic Performance in Less Developed Countries," *Journal of Public Economics* 75: 49–71.

Fukuyama, F. (2011): *The Origins of the Political Order: From prehuman times to the French revolution*, New York: Farrar, Straus and Giroux.

Fukuyama, F. (2013): "What is governance?," Washington, Centre for Global Development Working Paper, 314.

Fukuyama, F. (2014): *Political Order and Political Decay: From the industrial revolution to the globalization of democracy*, New York: Farrar, Straus and Giroux.

Gallup, J. L., Sachs, J., and Mellinger, A. (1998): "Geography and Economic Development," NBER Working Paper, No. 6849, Cambridge, MA: National Bureau of Economic Research.

Glaeser, E. L.and Shleifer, A. (2002): "Legal Origin," *Quarterly Journal of Economics* 117: 1193–229.

Glaeser, E. L., Ponzetto, G. A., Shleifer, A. (2007): "Why democracy needs education," *Journal of Economic Growth* 12: 77–99.

Gradstein, M. (2003): "Governance and Economic Growth," Policy Research Working Papers 3098, Washington, DC: Word Bank.

Gradstein, M. (2008): "Institutional Traps and Economic Growth," *International Economic Review* 49: 1043–66.

Greif, A. (2006): *Institutions and the Path to Modern Economy. Lessons from Medieval Trade*, Cambridge: Cambridge University Press.

Greif, A. and Kingston, C. (2011): "Institutions: Rules or Equilibria?," in N. Schofield, and G. Caballero (eds.), *Political Economy of Institutions, Democracy and Voting*, Heidelberg: Springer-Verlag.

Hausmann, R., Pritchett, L., and Rodrik, D. (2005): "Growth Accelerations," *Journal of Economic Growth* 10: 303–29.

Hindriks, F. and Guala, F. (2015): "Institutions, rules, and equilibria: a unified theory," *Journal of Institutional Economics* 11, no. 3: 459–80.

Hodgson, G. M. (2006): "What are Institutions?," *Journal of Economics Issues* 40, no. 1: 1–25.

Islam, R. and Montenegro, C. (2002): "What Determines the Quality of Institutions?" Policy Research Working Paper, No. 2764. Washington, DC: World Bank.

Keefer, P. and Knack, S. (2002): "Polarization Politics and Property Rights: Links between Inequality and Growth," *Public Choice* 111: 127–54.

Kingston, Ch. and Caballero, G. (2009): "Comparing theories of institutional change," *Journal of Institutional Economics* 5, no. 2: 151–80.

Knight, J. (1992): *Institutions and Social Conflict*, Cambridge: Cambridge University Press.

La Porta, R., López de Silanes, F., Shleifer, A., and Vishny, R. W. (1999): "The Quality of Government," *Journal of Law, Economics and Organization* 15: 222–79.

Levi, M. (1988): *Of Rule and Revenue*, Berkeley, CA: University of California Press.

Levitsky, S. and Murillo, M. V. (2013): "Building institutions on weak foundations," *Journal of Democracy* 24, no. 2: 93–102.

Mahoney, J. and Thelen, K.(2009): "A theory of gradual institutional change," in J. Mahoney and K. Thelen (eds.), *Explaining Institutional Change*, Cambridge: Cambridge University Press.

Malito, D. V., Umbach, G., and Bhuta, N. (2018): *The Palgrave Handbook of Indicators in Global Governance*, London: Palgrave Macmillan.

Moore, M. (2004): "Revenues, State Formation and the Quality of Governance in Developing Countries," *International Political Science Review* 25: 297–319.

North, D. C. (1990): *Institutions, Institutional Change and Economic Performance*, Cambridge: Cambridge University Press.

North, D. C. (1991): "Institutions," *Journal of Economic Perspectives* 5, no. 1: 97–112.

North, D. C. (2005): *Understanding the Process of Economic Change*, Princeton, NJ: Princeton University Press.

North, D. C., Weingast, B., and Wallis, J. (2009): *Violence and Social Orders: A Conceptual Framework for Interpreting Recorded Human History*, Cambridge: Cambridge University Press.

Rigobon, R. and Rodrik, D. (2004): "Rule of Law, Democracy, Openness and Income: Estimating the Interrelationships," NBER Working Paper no. 10750.

Rodrik, D. (2007): *One Economics, Many Receipts. Globalization, Institutions, and Economic Growth*, Princeton, NJ: Princeton University Press.

Rodrik, D., Subramanian, A., and Trebbi, F. (2004): "Institutions Rule: The Primacy of Institutions over Geography and Integration in Economic Development," *Journal of Economic Growth* 9: 131–65.

Rolland, G. (2004): "Understanding institutional change: fast-moving and slow-moving institutions," *Studies in Comparative International Development* 38: 109–31.

Rotberg, R. I. (2014): "Good governance means performance and results," Governance, from http://onlinelibrary.wiley.com/doi/10.1111/gove.12084/full

Rothstein, B. (2011): *The Quality of Government: Corruption, Social Trust, and Inequality in International Perspective*, Chicago, Chicago University Press.

Solt, Frederick (2016): "The Standardized World Income Inequality Database," *Social Science Quarterly* 97, no. 5: 1267–81.

5

Centripetal Politics and Institution Building in Exiting the Middle-Income Trap

Richard Doner and Ben Ross Schneider

5.1 Introduction

Economists debate the nature and existence of a middle-income trap (MIT), but they generally agree on what to do to break out of it. First, unlike the factor and investment—driven shift from low-income (LI) to middle-income (MI), the move to sustained high-income (HI) requires skill and technology-driven productivity improvement and associated innovation often labeled as "upgrading."[1] Second, productivity improvement in turn requires policies that (1) raise the technical quality of the workforce through more and better education (especially higher and technical), (2) modernize infrastructure, and (3) deepen the stock of technical knowledge through R&D. Third, there is generally agreement on the importance of institutions appropriate for these new challenges. And lastly, most observers acknowledge political requisites—"political will"—for such institutional development, such as long-time horizons on the part of political leaders, broad societal consensus, business–government collaboration, and some degree of inclusive politics.[2]

The extensive writings on these issues leads to a question: Why—if experts and leaders are well aware of the weaknesses of their economies and the need for productivity improvement, if they are aware of the policies and related institutions required to raise productivity, and if they recognize the need for broad engagement and support—has it been so tough to make progress? Responding to this question requires a more systematic analysis of the political economy—the interests and institutions—common to middle-income countries (MICs).

[1] By upgrading, we refer to the production of goods and services with increasing value-added, with domestic linkages, and with levels of price, quality, and delivery required by global value chains (Doner 2009: 8–9).

[2] These issues are covered in greater depth in Doner and Schneider (2016) and Gill and Kharas (2015) and the introductory chapter to this volume.

Richard Doner and Ben Ross Schneider, *Centripetal Politics and Institution Building in Exiting the Middle-Income Trap* In: *Trapped in the Middle? Developmental Challenges for Middle-Income Countries.* Edited by: José Antonio Alonso and José Antonio Ocampo, Oxford University Press (2020). © OUP. DOI: 10.1093/oso/9780198852773.003.0005

We can illustrate the challenges facing MICs by comparing two sets of policies: macroeconomic policies (exchange rate, interest rate, and fiscal) required to provide assurance as to the stability of input costs and markets, and education reform required to improve productivity by raising the quality of the workforce. In the case of macroeconomic policies, information requirements are largely technical, with relatively clear templates. The number of participants is relatively narrow ("10 smart people"). Policy duration is relatively short as most measures can be carried out almost by fiat, with "the stroke of a pen." The most serious difficulties involve managing distributional consequences. By contrast, educational reforms:

> involve many more moving parts in terms of how they are planned and put into practice. They also require extensive consultation, negotiation and consensus building... decentralized forms of decision making and continual and time consuming monitoring and capacity building.... In contrast to... macroeconomic policy, many of the newer reforms do not have well recognized templates that explain the central problems and the appropriate solutions to it. Policymakers are thus... often walking blind as to what needs to be done... (Grindle, 2000: 371)

Specifying policy challenges allows us to go beyond the admonition that "institutions matter." As suggested by Grindle's description of education reforms, carrying out productivity-enhancing reforms requires institutions to monitor, coordinate, and reconcile the interests and information of many actors. Such institutions vary in design and by levels of operation, for example national ministries, peak and sectoral business federations, public–private consultative councils, investment coordinating boards, judicial agencies for effective contract enforcement, agencies specializing in testing and standards, and R&D promotion.

Two related factors make designing and establishing such institutions difficult. First, they require both (horizontal) coordination among state agencies, among firms, and between public and private actors (as in Peter Evans's (1995) concept of embedded autonomy), as well as (vertical) coordination of multiple providers, such as judges, teachers, researchers, curriculum developers, and test engineers, each of whom plays important roles in extended implementation chains. Second, although effective institutions may resolve market problems, they are typically created "not on the 'level playing field' of the market but rather within the political arena, in which some are endowed with greater power than others" (Bates, 1995: 42). This raises the political question of why self-interested economic and political elites would expend scarce resources to construct the complex institutions needed to formulate and implement initiatives in areas such as R&D and TVE (technical and vocational education). Our contention is that politics—defined here as the interests of, and relations among, key societal actors in MICs—inhibits such institution building.

Section 5.2 addresses the political factors accounting for the weakness of coalitions to support appropriate institutions. Unlike much of the existing literature that focuses on the supply of institutions, our emphasis is on *demand-side* weaknesses. MICs are often plagued by "disarticulation politics," in which growth trajectories on the way to MIC status fractured the groups—especially business and labor—that are the core potential constituencies for a big leap coalition. In Sections 5.3–5.6 we explore these dynamics in three constellations of institutions relevant for upgrading: taxation, quality infrastructure (testing and research centers, and sectoral institutes), and TVE.

5.2 Disarticulation Politics as Obstacles to Institution Building

Making enormous institutional investments requires extraordinary collective action and coalition building: "The most productive thing MICs can do to accelerate their transition to advanced economies is to establish a bipartisan political consensus" (Foxley and Sossdoff, 2011: 2).[3] Yet the evolving political economies of MICs have become especially inauspicious for such consensus and coalition building. More specifically, we believe that social cleavages—especially inequality, divisions between formal and informal workers, and divisions between foreign and domestic businesses—have weakened the potential for effective coalitions.

The justification for our focus on *coalitions of social groups* merits note at the outset. Historically, such coalitions were key for successful late industrialization and a move to high-income in the twentieth century.[4] These coalitions varied along several dimensions and ranged from "corporatism without labor" in post-war Japan, to "cohesive capitalist states" or "state corporatism" in the East Asian NICs, to the more horizontal, "societal" corporatist arrangements, typically involving labor as well as the state and business, as seen in small states of northern Europe and Ireland (Ornston 2012). Despite their variation, these arrangements all encouraged the inter-temporal bargains needed for investing in the upgrading-related investments that required extensive information, negotiation, monitoring, and short-term costs, but whose benefits would emerge only in the medium or long term. In the twenty-first century, such coalitions have become especially important in light of the short time horizons of politicians in both illiberal and more fully democratic regimes, including those increasingly prone to populist measures. If parties are weak and politicians short-sighted (as is common in MICs), then longer-term vision depends more on social coalitions that survive high turnover in politics. Yet three sets of socio-economic cleavages impede such coalitions.

[3] This section summarizes Doner and Schneider (2016).
[4] On the utility of a top-down, state-led approach to institution building see the Conclusion.

Inequality: Inequality has grown higher and endured longer in today's MICs than in earlier industrializers (van Zanden et al., 2014). For purposes of coalition building, this is problematic. Inequality weakens trust and makes politics more fractious and contentious (Gould and Hijzen, 2016). It also makes politics vulnerable to other kinds of political pathologies, such as elite capture, clientelism, economic entrenchment (as elites use resources to ensure privileges), and populism, all of which divert economic resources and political focus away from collective action in support of difficult-to-implement measures such as TVE, sophisticated investment promotion, and R&D. Further, the impact of overall social inequality may be intensified when it overlaps with other dimensions of social fragmentation, such as rural–urban or ethnic differences.

Labor and the Informality Problem: Earlier developers typically followed a "Lewis turning point" trajectory in which labor transited out of low-skill, rural informality into the formal, urban workforce (Ranis, 2004). The rising wages of these factory workers triggered investments in skills as the supply of surplus labor dried up. Many MICs are still waiting for the Lewis turning point as informality has persisted—a third to a half or more of workers in most MICs—and even grown despite overall economic growth and rising wages (Schneider, 2013). Various factors contribute to persistent informality, including inflows of migrant labor, the expansion of "contingent" labor through outsourcing and contract work, premature deindustrialization, low unionization levels, and weak enforcement capacity. Informality is thus often part of a broader pattern of labor market segmentation that involves migrants vs. indigenous citizens and temporary vs. permanent workers.

Regardless of the sources, the consequences of significant informality is a divergence of interests between informal and formal workers, corresponding to the well-known "insiders–outsider" split in Western Europe (Baker, 2019). Other things being equal, formal workers support subsidies for in-firm training owing to their longer job tenure and opportunities to benefit from on-the-job training. Informal workers, in contrast, would prefer active labor market policies such as public employment centers, investment in vocational schools offering general training, and subsidized employment (Wietzke, 2015). The upshot is a lack of labor cohesion on politics and institutions aimed at broad improvements in within-sector productivity (on exceptions in Latin America, see Garay, 2019).

Business Fragmentation: Given its structural power and stake in the supply of technical knowledge and qualified employees, it is safe to say that support from a broad segment of business, especially big business, is required for measures necessary to move into high income. Yet cleavages within business in most MICs weakens business' voice. A key cleavage—largely absent in most earlier industrializers—is between foreign and domestic firms. Although the stock of FDI in large MICs is not that high when compared to FDI in industrialized (OECD) countries today, it is much larger in today's MICs (34 percent of GDP in nine large MICs) than in high income countries in the twentieth century (4 percent of GDP for East Asia and 9 percent for OECD, Doner and Schneider, 2016). Foreign firms are not only numerically prominent (accounting for a third to a half of the largest firms in Latin America (Schneider, 2013)); they also dominate the manufacturing sectors of MICs.

In principle, market-seeking MNCs might be part of a coalition supporting policies such as technical-vocational training and technology promotion. But productive and technological heterogeneity in MICs, especially between foreign and indigenous firms, impedes the convergence of policy interests across the private sector. MNCs have their own, home market-based technology as well as options such as solving skill needs internally, depending on affiliated foreign suppliers, drawing on home-based R&D, or just shifting higher value-added production to other countries with the needed skills and infrastructure. When it comes to collective action and political engagement, the problem is less MNC dominance than disengagement from collective action with domestic firms (eg, by establishing separate associations).

The list of cleavages in MICs is longer and could include ethnic divisions, rural–urban splits, and other dimensions of firm heterogeneity. We highlight income inequality, formal versus informal labor markets, and domestic vs. foreign firm both because they seem more directly relevant for building consensus around upgrading institutions, and because these are new kinds of cleavages that earlier industrializers did not face, certainly not to the extent common in MICs in the twenty-first century (Doner and Schneider, 2016).

In the next sections we illustrate our preceding points by examining the nature and origins of three sets of institutions and related policy measures: taxation, quality infrastructure (especially in rubber and autos), and TVE. In previous work, we conducted similar analysis of R&D and education (Doner and Schneider, 2016). By selecting those policy areas and these here, we do not mean to argue that they should be higher priority or that they alone will resolve the MIC trap. Rather, these policy areas illustrate well our arguments on the challenges in institution building and politics.

5.3 Taxation: Truncated State Building

In the stylized history of earlier industrializers, states impose small taxes on many disbursed businesses and individuals (Tilly, 1992). Such a tax system depends on the creation of a large, effective, penetrating tax administration. Then, in the virtuous social contract, citizens (including the wealthy) are all taxed and in turn come to demand better, universal public services. In MICs, the stylized dynamic is quite different. States develop narrow tax bases, often primarily on commodity exports, and do not therefore build extensive tax administrations. Many individuals and firms are not taxed, especially in the informal sector, and the very rich,

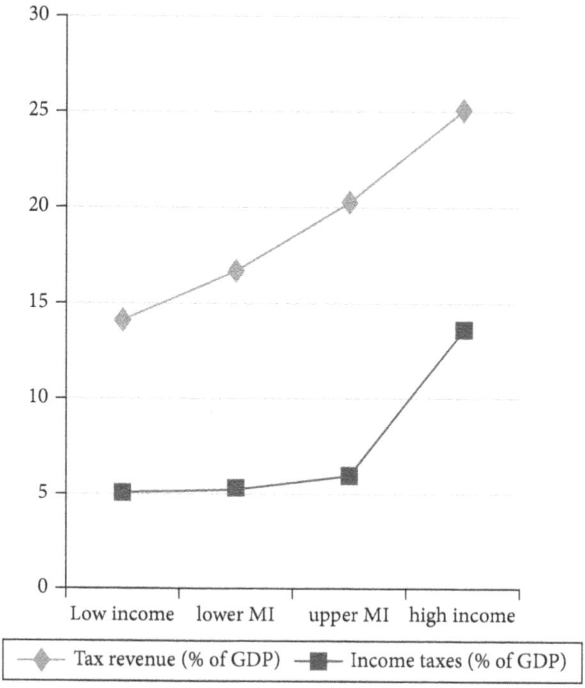

Figure 5.1 Total tax revenue and income taxes (as a percent of GDP)
Source: Calculated from Gordon and Li (2009: 856).

consequently, in a broken social contract, do not demand much in return from their states (Holland, 2017). MICs lag HICs in terms of total taxation; they lag even more in terms of income taxes as a share of GDP (Figure 5.1). Relatedly, the very wealthy pay little in taxes. The effective rate of taxation of the top 1 percent is only 7 percent in Colombia, 14 percent in Uruguay (one of the most redistributive governments in Latin America), and 15 percent in Chile compared with 21 percent in the United States and 31 percent in Germany (Fairfield 2019: 173).

The point is not just that states in MICs need more revenue, but also that their limited taxing capacity takes them out of the typical virtuous circle whereby states that penetrate fully their societies in order to tax everyone in turn develop more effective bureaucracies (that can also then be deployed for other policy goals) and create citizens with higher expectations (Persson and Rothstein, 2015). In MICs, the first link in the virtuous chain is broken by previous trajectory of growth based on various combinations of raw materials, informality, FDI, and inequality. For natural resource producers, weak fiscal capacity starts with the perverse petro-state dynamics, where the ease of taxing natural resources leads to relative underdevelopment of the capacity to tax society (as well as overall administrative weakness), as it is much simpler to skim the rents of natural resources as they pass through ports (Shafer, 1994). A large informal sector makes broad-based taxation of income next to impossible. In Thailand, for example, only two million of 36 million workers pay income taxes. Not surprisingly, higher levels of informality are correlated with lower levels of overall "tax morale" (disposition towards tax compliance) (Perry 2007: 13).

Inequality contributes to lower taxing capacity both because the poor have little to tax, but also because tiny wealthy elites have been effective in preventing states from taxing them though political opposition, evasion, or both (Fairfield, 2019). MICs often manage to increase total tax revenues, but they have a difficult time raising taxes on income (Figure 5.1). Raising income taxes requires power over wealthy elites and pro-tax coalitions to sustain that power, as well as building more sophisticated tax collection institutions.

Lastly, MNCs also escape taxation through several mechanisms including transfer pricing (which reduces declared income and profits in the host country) and race-to-the-bottom tax competition among MICs that offer potential MNC investors various tax exemptions (often institutionalized in export zones). Precise data do not exist, but estimates of tax revenues lost in developing countries due to transfer pricing range from $50 to $122 billion per year (Cooper et al., 2017: 10) to $160 billion (Murphy, 2012: 265). Given lower taxation in other realms (like income tax), corporate taxation accounts for a larger share of government revenue in MICs, and these losses thus hurt public accounts more.

Efforts to recoup these lost taxes face daunting administrative and political challenges. MNCs have many hard-to-detect-methods for transfer mispricing from the basics of under-pricing exports and over-pricing imports to excessive payments for intellectual property, consulting, or other miscellaneous services offered to MNC subsidiaries. Monitoring and regulating these flows require sophisticated state capacity, highly trained professional staff, and huge amounts of data.[5] In politics, problems of transfer pricing are technical and not electorally salient and so belong to the realm of 'quiet politics' where business usually prevails (Culpepper, 2010). Within the business community, domestic firms in principle should favor taxing MNCs at the same rates they pay, however collective action problems among domestic firms would be severe. Many business associations represent both domestic and foreign firms, making them unlikely to lead the charge. Moreover, individually, many domestic firms are deeply intertwined with MNCs as suppliers, partners, buyers, etc., and thus have no reason to antagonize MNCs.

5.4 Quality Infrastructure I: Cohesion and Fragmentation in Rubber

QI is a complex of institutions and policies designed to help firms meet global quality and standards levels. Here we explore two sets of QI institutions: public

[5] Cooper (2017) offers a book length manual on how to regulate transfer pricing.

Table 5.1 Core functions of public testing and research centers

Applied, contract research
Cooperative research
Information dissemination
Equipment loans
Training and use of laboratories
Technology transfer and diffusion
Diagnostic benchmarking
Instrument calibration (metrology, verification)
Testing and inspection (comparison measurements, proficiency tests)
Certification/accreditation (ISO, HACCP)

Source: Adapted from Shapira and Youtie (2013).

testing and research centers (PTRs) and sectoral institutes. By providing services such as testing, calibration, inspection, and certification, PTRs can help firms to upgrade their products and processes by absorbing technology "new" to them (Table 5.1). These institutions have been ubiquitous in earlier industrializers in Europe, North America, and especially Japan (Shapira and Youtie, 2013). They have also been central to the success of automotive industries in late developers Taiwan, the Republic of Korea, and China (as analyzed in Section 5.5).

Despite their benefits for upgrading, highlighted by a recent World Bank report (Kellermann, 2019), PTRs are far from ubiquitous. This gap can be explained in large part through the lens of the challenges identified earlier. Establishing QI institutions such as PTRs is information-intensive: they require not only an understanding of myriad product and process technologies but also site-specific information, that is, sensitivity to the specific quality and standard requirements of local firms and these firms' technological and managerial levels. Their effectiveness depends not only on officials and politicians allocating the necessary resources but also on cooperation among multiple agencies (eg, ministries of industry, standards agencies), and on engineers and technicians familiar with standards, certification, and testing equipment and capable of working with counterparts from myriad enterprises. In addition, the payoffs for such efforts are not very visible, especially in the short term. As the recent World Bank study notes, "QI can also be quite complex; thus, it is often sidelined from high-level political discussions or left out of a country's reform agenda" (Kellermann, 2019: ix).

In light of these challenges, it is useful to understand variation in effectiveness of PTRs. Here we briefly compare the experiences of the rubber value chains in two Southeast Asian countries.[6] Southeast Asia is the source of roughly 90 percent of the world's natural rubber as well as the largest source of rubber-based products such as gloves and condoms. Thailand and Malaysia have been regional

[6] Unless otherwise noted, this section is drawn from Doner (2016).

leaders in rubber, which is important to the economies of both. In Thailand, rubber employs some million families (six million people) in growing and processing and some 400,000 smallholding families (one million people) in Malaysia. Rubber is Thailand's single largest agricultural export and one of the country's top export earners, amounting to roughly 4 percent of total export earnings in 2013. Rubber has fallen in significance in Malaysia (from 25 percent of national exports in 1970, to 15 percent in 1980 to 5 percent in 2011), but it still accounts for a quarter of Malaysian commodity exports.

But the two industries differ in terms of performance in the key downstream segment of rubber-based products. Although both countries are major producers and exporters, Malaysia accounts for over 60 percent of global glove production and exports (vs. 18 percent for Thailand). Malaysia has been the leader in process and product innovation (eg, developing new processes to reduce the problem of latex allergies and pioneering the production of synthetic rubber gloves). Malaysia has also pioneered "engineering rubber products" such as seismic bearings. And while foreign firms have dominated the downstream sector in Thailand, large *domestic* producers have led the way in Malaysia (accounting for 80 percent of all rubber products and over 90 percent of gloves).

PTRs have been central to the successes of Malaysia's downstream producers. Domestic rubber product manufacturers have access to some fifteen testing facilities and labs that are part of a Rubber Technology Centre and a Global Testing and Consultancy for Rubber, all designed to promote value added in rubber. These public facilities operate in coordination with the private sector, including the use of firms' testing facilities (in some cases public and private labs benchmark off each other). Indeed, Malaysia's rubber testing facilities operate within a broad, relatively coherent institutional ecosystem involving a government coordinating body, the Malaysia Rubber Board, and powerful downstream business associations, especially the Malaysian Rubber Products Manufacturers Association and the Malaysian Rubber Glove Manufacturers' Association (MARGMA). It bears emphasis that this constellation of actors is devoted to *setting* as well as meeting global standards. As Malaysian producers move into more specialized products (eg, radiation protection gloves), the associations are striving to get member agreement on standards and the Malaysian Rubber Board now chairs the rubber panel of the International Standards Organization (ISO).[7]

For our purposes, the key point is that this "quality and standards ecosystem" is not only critical to the prominence of Malaysia's domestic rubber producers, it is also complex; it involves multiple actors, and it requires mastery of technical information about new and shifting product requirements, ranging from FDA phyto-sanitary rules for surgical gloves to seismic standards for "high damping

[7] Doner interview with of MARGMA official (Kuala Lumpur, November 27, 2017).

rubber isolators" for a 24km long bridge. Malaysia's success in addressing these challenges contrasts with the weak PTRs in the world's largest producer of natural rubber, Thailand. Until very recently, expansion of *upstream* production, especially through higher yields, has been the main area in which extension and research facilities have developed in the Thai rubber industry. Testing and research facilities devoted to downstream products have been largely limited to a modest Rubber Technology Research Center, especially its affiliated Research Development Center for Thai Rubber Industry (Somsak, 2009).

How then do we account for Malaysia's impressive quality infrastructure in rubber, especially in contrast with the Thai case, as well relative to other, weaker Malaysian sectors, such as autos (World Bank: 2010: 78)? The answer involves the relative degree of cohesion of business interests, as well as the institutional and political features associated with the structure of business. First, the Malaysian rubber products industry, with the exception of tires, is largely in domestic hands, ranging from giant glove and condom producers to smaller engineering product firms and a range of active supporting industries (eg, machine tools), all of whom are engaged in policy formulation and implementation. Thailand, on the other hand, exhibits the kind of disarticulation noted earlier: Foreign firms dominate downstream production and are minimally engaged with domestic producers in areas such as quality control and standards. Whereas the Malaysian industry is downstream-driven, the dominant domestic interests in Thailand are upstream farmers and exporters.

The contrasting degrees of cohesion are mirrored by relevant public and private sector governance institutions. In Malaysia, one ministry, the Ministry of Plantation Industries and Commodities, oversees the entire rubber value chain and views (semi-processed) natural rubber not as a source of export revenues but as feedstock for downstream, rubber-based products. In contrast, responsibility for the rubber value chain in Thailand is fragmented among the (often politicized) Ministry of Agriculture, Ministry of Commerce, and Ministry of Industry. The upstream Agriculture Ministry dominates while the Ministry of Industry has traditionally lacked interest or expertise in the development of rubber products, an area left largely to foreign producers. A sectoral governing body, the Rubber Authority of Thailand, established only in 2016, is dominated by upstream interests, and has focused more on helping farmers by propping up natural rubber prices than on supporting productivity improvement for downstream producers.[8] The two cases also differ with regard to politicization. Whereas the Malaysian Ministry of Plantation Industries and Commodities has been largely insulated from party politics, the Thai ministries have been the focus of inter-party maneuvering and rent-seeking.

[8] Doner interviews with officials of the Rubber Authority of Thailand, November 21, 2018 and members of Thai Polymer Association, November 12–13, 2018.

This variation in public sector governance arrangements is also seen in cross-national differences in relevant business associations. In Malaysia, MARGMA is dominated by large Malaysian glove producers, whereas domestic firms producing engineering products, such as auto parts and seismic equipment, dominate the Malaysian Rubber Products Manufacturers' Association (MRPMA). Both of these organizations are extensively involved in quality-related activities such as product validation, testing, and standards setting.[9] In Thailand, in contrast, domestic firms dominate only in upstream and midstream associations, whereas associations of downstream producers, such as the Thai Rubber Glove Manufacturers Association, are composed of smaller domestic producers with little focus on productivity issues. One of the most active groups of Thai-owned firms, the Rubber Products Industry Club, was weakened by the decision of foreign tire producers to split off and form a separate group.[10] In sum, the Malaysian associations and their members are central to a robust sectoral upgrading coalition, whereas fragmentation plagues rubber interests in Thailand.

5.5 Quality Infrastructure II: Continuing Fragmentation in Autos

Sectoral institutes are a second type of QI that involve public officials and producers in the same value chain with the goal of improving sectoral productivity.[11] They complement (and in some cases overlap with) PTRs by diffusing information and new technology to member firms, coordinating training in sector-required skills, testing and certifying vehicles, and undertaking research and development of technologies relevant to local markets. As with PTRs, successfully operating sectoral institutes is far from easy. They need to coordinate the activities of multiple firms, often smaller, local suppliers especially in need of technical support. And as with PTRs, some countries (and sectors) overcome these challenges more successfully than others.

To get a sense of this variation and its sources, we focus here on automotive institutes in several East Asian countries (Table 5.2). A first point to note is variation in the timing of establishment and abundance of resources, particularly personnel. These reveal a clear tripartite division, which corresponds to the strength of the national auto industries and domestic firms. Governments in the Republic ofKorea, China, and Taiwan—where significant technological development has occurred within domestic firms—established large and impressive automotive institutes relatively early. These Northeast Asian cases contrast with their Southeast Asian counterparts, where domestic producers are technologically

[9] Doner interview, MRPMA official and advisor to Kossan Industries, November 19, 2018.
[10] Doner interviews with founder of TRGMA and official of the RPIC, November 15, 16, 2017.
[11] Unless otherwise noted, this section draws on Doner, Noble, and Ravenhill (2021: ch 3).

Table 5.2 Automotive institutes in East Asia

	Institute	Year established	Staff	Functions
Republic of Korea	Korea Automotive Technology Institute (KATECH) Korea Automobile Testing and Research Institute (KATRI)	1990 1987	600 (300 each)	Testing/ assessment Research Forecast/ planning Training
China	China Automotive Technology and Research Center (CATARC)	1985	3,700	Testing/ assessment Research Forecast/ planning Training
Taiwan	Automotive Research & Testing Center (ARTC)	1990	300	Testing/ assessment Research Forecast/ Planning Training
Thailand	Thailand Automotive Institute (TAI)	1998	100	Forecast/ planning Training Testing (minimal)
Malaysia	Malaysia Automotive Institute (MAI)	2010	20	Forecast/ planning Training (?)
Indonesia	none	—	—	
Philippines	none	—	—	

weak and dwarfed by foreign assemblers and components producers. In Thailand and Malaysia, automotive institutes appeared later—well after the move toward trade policy liberalization—and remain far less developed. The Thai Automotive Institute has been principally concerned with financial survival owing to fragile support from the Ministry of Industry and private sector members (Patarapong 2018). Finally, institutions capable of filling even a small number of the functions noted above have yet to appear in Indonesia or the Philippines.

In contrast to their Northeast Asian neighbors, automotive institutes in Southeast Asia are closer to "too little, too late." Thailand established an automotive institute only in 1998, just as the Asian financial crisis pushed most Thai parts suppliers into bankruptcy or forced them to sell out to global parts giants. Until recently, the Institute lacked facilities, such as a dedicated building and test track. The staff of 100 has spent much of its time on industry planning, although more recently the Thai institute has focused on developing an industry training program. All these limitations are magnified in Malaysia, despite the country's aspirations to develop a "national car" beginning in the 1980s. Malaysia only established an automotive institute in 2010, staffed by only twenty personnel, most of whom specialize in industrial economics rather than auto technology.

As for rubber, cross-national variation in the strength of sectoral automotive institutes reflects contrasts in the position of foreign vs. domestic firms and, in turn, the cohesion of public and private sector governance arrangements. Here we focus on Thailand and Taiwan.[12] Despite Thailand's success in auto assembly and exports, reflected in its claim to be the "Detroit of Asia," public and private sector governance arrangements devoted to technological upgrading have been fragmented. There were several agencies devoted to improving technology competencies of local firms, but the impact of these institutions is limited, and there has been no agency designed to increase the value added and strengthen the backward linkages of Thai exports. Only after three decades of industry promotion, in May 2017, did the Thai Board of Investments (BOI) establish incentives to promote technological spillovers from foreign producers. Further, the BOI's principal ties are to foreign firms, whereas domestic producers typically operate under the purview of the more politicized Ministry of Industry.[13] Nor, until very recently, has there been much coordination between economic development agencies and the country's highly fractured education and training organizations. The most extensive study of the country's approach to innovation describes Thailand as "mismanaging innovation systems" (Patarapong 2018).

Weak public sector institutions are mirrored by fragmented private sector arrangements. Most critically, foreign auto parts producers have traditionally played a minimal role in the principal auto parts association, the Thai Auto Parts Manufacturers Association. TAPMA's major focus has traditionally been protecting market access for domestic firms. Technology transfer from foreign, especially Japanese, firms to local producers has emphasized goals such as quality control and cost reduction and has occurred through "cooperation clubs" operated by assemblers or large component producers. Only since around 2016 has TAPMA, working with a consortium of Japanese firms, begun to address issues of technological competence through a focus on "automotive human resource development."

Taiwan has largely forgone vehicle assembly and specialized in the production of automotive replacement parts by some 3,000 domestic producers. These are largely small and medium-sized firms for whom the key sectoral institution is the Automotive Testing and Research Institute (ATRI). The ATRI is supported both

[12] For analysis of the other Northeast and Southeast Asian cases, see Doner, Noble, and Ravenhill (2021).

[13] Doner interview, BOI official, May 23, 2018).

by a range of largely cohesive public sector agencies, beginning with the Ministry of Economic Affairs, as well as private associations, such as the Taiwan Auto Body Manufacturers Association. Two differences with the Thai system merit note: First, although foreign firms in Taiwan participate in these associations, the groups are clearly dominated by and devoted to domestic firms. Second, Taiwan's automotive associations work with associations and public–private institutions in other, related sectors, such as electronics, and in areas such as autonomous driving. In sum, Taiwan's status as the "Unsung Hero of Automotive Innovation" (GlobalFleet, 2018) stems from a cohesive set of interests and institutions that contrast sharply with Thailand's more fragmented automotive ecosystem.

5.6 Coalitions and Parties in Technical–Vocational Education

Developing a technically skilled workforce is not easy.[14] In addition to transaction and coordination, there are the intensive challenges of providing basic education (hundreds of thousands of teachers, curricula, text books, teacher training, etc.), technical–voactional education (TVE) involves additional challenges with regard to the need for more extensive training, for information on the needs of employers and future trends in employment, and for more complex and costly teaching materials and equipment.

In secondary enrollments, Europe is a global leader in technical education with, since the late twentieth century, around one-fourth of enrollments in TVE. Rates are lower in rich countries outside Europe like Japan (12 percent) and liberal Anglophone countries, and so too therefore is the average for the OECD overall (17 percent). For all MICs, the average enrollment has been low and flat at around 10 percent. Enrollment rates are higher and increasing among upper MICs (Table 5.3).

Weak coalitions for TVE helps to account for these low enrollments. Among firms, many of the largest producers of manufactured goods in the developing world are MNCs moving toward greater capital intensity (eg, increased reliance on robotics). Further, the need for flexibility in the face of shifting demand within global value chains has resulted in MNCs operating with a small percentage of permanent, relatively skilled workers backed up by a larger proportion of unskilled, contingent workers. And what demand for skills does exist can be satisfied by firm-specific programs. MNCs, then, are not likely to be active promoters of collective solutions for skill needs (Schneider 2013).

Nor is there reason to believe that large local firms in MIC countries will offset this flagging demand for TVE. In many MICs, the largest local enterprises are diversified business groups whose focus on natural resources, services, and

[14] This section draws on Doner and Schneider (2019).

Table 5.3 Percentage of secondary enrollment in vocational programs

	1990	2000	2013
European Union	27	24	27
OECD	18	16	17
United Kingdom	11	20	32
Japan	13	13	12
Republic of Korea			
Middle income	10	9	11
Upper middle-income	15	12	17
Lower middle-income	5	5	5
Latin America	16	9	10
Argentina		16	14
Brazil		2	4
Chile	23	27	21
Mexico	13	15	17
Turkey	23	20	22
Thailand	16	15	16
Malaysia	5	6	9

Source: Doner and Schneider (2019).

related non-tradeables may not stimulate demand for investments in skills. What training does occur is likely to be less sector-wide than highly specialized and in-house for a relatively small number of employees (Bassi et al., 2012). The overall result may be low effective demand for skill-formation programs and even, in some cases, as reportedly in Malaysia, an "increase in supply of skilled workers" but a "decline in the overall share of high-skill employment in the economy" and a rising share of low-skilled jobs (Jun 2016).

Further, small and medium-sized firms—those most in need of TVE programs—are unlikely to be effective advocates for skill formation measures. Preliminary analysis suggests that SME-targeted TVE programs are less present and effective in developing countries than in the industrialized world, with the revealing exception of Turkey (discussed later). SMEs suffer from the collective action challenges plaguing large numbers of smaller firms and economic and political dominance of MNCs and local business groups. Lastly, cleavages weaken labor's role in skills formation in MICs. The insider–outsider divisions noted in Europe (Rueda 2005) seem even more relevant for the MICs owing to de-industrialization and low levels of unionization, and the increasing role of contingent, informal sector workers (Schneider and Karcher, 2010). As noted in Section 5.2, formal sector workers tend to favor on-the-job training while workers in the informal sector prefer more vocational training and active labor market programs (Wietzke, 2015: 112).[15]

[15] However, the informal–formal distinction is blurred on other issues as workers often shift between formal and informal employment (Perry 2007; Baker 2019).

This social fragmentation is often mirrored in weak party systems. In most MICs, political parties—the institutions theoretically designed to "aggregate" interests—are weaker and less programmatic than the Social Democratic and Christian Democratic parties in Western Europe that provided lasting support for TVE (Busemeyer 2015; Bizzarro et al., 2018). In Thailand, for example, despite political conflict and massive demonstrations during the past decade and a half, civil society is disorganized and largely without ties to political parties (Unger and Mahakanjana 2016). Chile and Turkey are exceptions in part because their parties were stronger and more enduring than in other large MICs. Figure 5.2 shows a rough correlation overall between TVE enrollment and a composite measure of party institutionalization. Chile and Turkey are on the high end for party strength.

In Latin America, Chile has one of the largest and most developed systems of TVE in secondary education (Sevilla, 2017; Bogliaccini and Madariaga, 2020). Enrollments have expanded steadily from 27 percent of high school students in 1981 to 45 percent in 2007, almost doubling in absolute numbers from a little

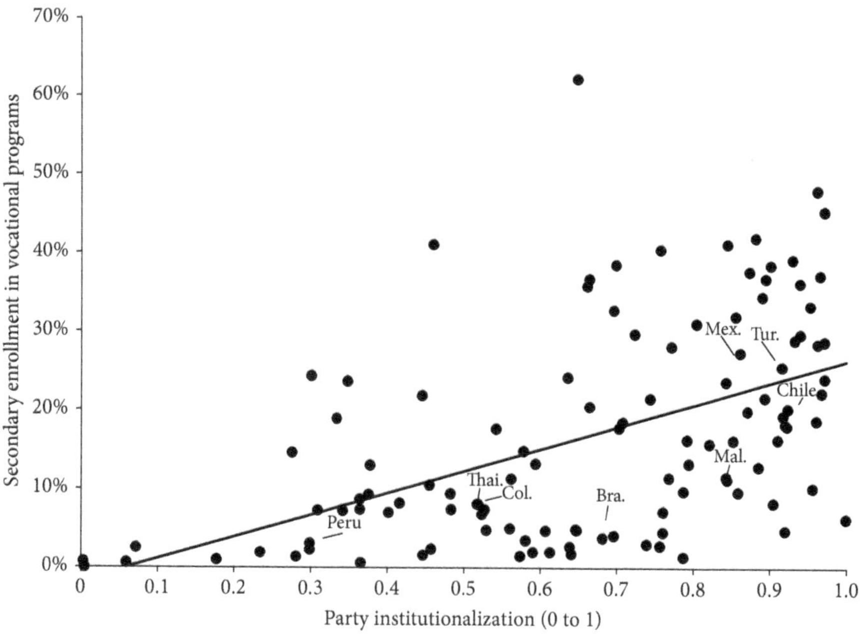

Figure 5.2 Secondary enrollment in vocational programs and party institutionalization (2015)

Notes: The index operationalizes institutionalization based on six indicators included in the Varieties of Democracy (VDEM) dataset, which aggregates expert responses to questions on the V-Dem survey. The indicators include the degree to which parties in a polity exhibit permanent national organizations, permanent local branches, centralized candidate selection, legislative cohesion, minimal party switching, and programmatic links to a social base (Bizzarro et al., 2018: 10).

Country n = 114.

Source: Doner and Schneider (2019).

over 200,000 students in 1990 to 400,000 in 2007. Families choose whether to send their children to academic or vocational secondary school, and over 90 percent of TVE students come from the poorest two quintiles in the income distribution (Iruarrizaga 2009: 7, 14). By 2010s, 55 percent of TVE secondary students were in private voucher schools, suggesting a strong market demand for technical education (CEPPE 2013: 3). Despite these achievements, Chile's heavy investment in secondary TVE is mostly school based with no close connections to business (as in European apprenticeship programs (Farías and Sevilla 2015)), and this investment in secondary TVE is not matched by the efforts to train adult or unemployed workers (Sehnbruch, 2006).

Chile's impressive but mixed record is mirrored by its political underpinnings. Through the late 2000s, the expansion of Chilean technical and general education was largely a story of top-down reform undertaken by a strong and lasting center-left coalition of parties called Concertación (Mizala and Schneider, 2014). For two decades from 1990 to 2010, voters consistently elected presidents from the Concertación coalition. As one of the few MICs with strong, programmatic parties, Chile's education trajectory is a good fit for Busemeyer's (2015) partisan and welfare state model of skill formation since the Concertación drew more support from poorer voters.

However, unlike social democrats in Europe, Concertación governments plowed resources into all levels of education, including higher education. Enrollments rose (especially in higher education), and Chile outscored the rest of Latin America in PISA league tables. Tellingly, business was on the sidelines (as was organized labor) through the three decades of the transformation of Chilean education. Throughout 2014–16, during the highly contentious and costly reforms to secondary education, business hardly appeared in the press (Mizala and Schneider, 2019). In sum, in Chile a more cohesive party system seems to have compensated for continuing disarticulation on the part of business and labor.

In Turkey, total enrollments in TVE nearly tripled from just over 1 million in 2000 to nearly 3 million in 2015 and total spending also nearly tripled but from 2011 to 2016 (Doner and Schneider, 2019). Turkey was one of the few MICs that maintained the proportion of TVE enrollments close to the European average of one-fourth and was also one of the few MICs that spent more per pupil on TVE students than on students in general education.

Over the course of the 2000s, prime minister Erdogan and the AKP (Justice and Development Party) increasingly alienated big business. As in other MICs, big business in Turkey was dominated by family owned, diversified business groups and MNCs (Colpan, 2010; Colpan, Hikino, and Lincoln 2010) that were well represented in an exclusive association for big business, TUSIAD. Big business was generally secular and internationalist and did not actively support Erdogan's nationalism, Islamism, or ultimately authoritarianism (Özel 2018).

As relations with big business soured, Erdogan courted associations of Muslim business (Musiad) and other associations with more SMEs (Sancak and Özel,

2018). As part of this courtship, the Erdogan government increased funding for technical education and vocational training and put representatives from business associations on boards to oversee TVE programs. Although large firms, represented by the association TUSIAD, did have a voice in workforce development efforts, the key private sector intermediary was the semi-public association, TOBB (Union of Chambers and Commodity Exchanges of Turkey, a federation of 365 local chambers). Given that most firms in Turkey are small, SMEs have a stronger voice in the compulsory TOBB than other voluntary associations (Sancak, 2017).

As discussed earlier, in most countries, the common trend is for big business to dominate relations with the government (and big business often solves its skills needs in-house) while at the same time SMEs (that have skill needs requiring public solutions) face barriers to collective action and access to political leaders. In Turkey, strained relations between big business and the AKP reduced the influence of big business and opened up opportunities for closer government collaboration with SMEs. However, these exceptional politics help to highlight how hard it is generally—in the absence of special organization and influence by small business, as well as a dominant party for whom small firms are a key constituency—to construct coalitions that are more attentive to the skill needs of SMEs.

5.7 Conclusions and Implications

We have sought to draw attention to the difficulties involved in developing institutions appropriate for the particular challenges of MICs. Our starting point is the need to distinguish among development policies and, more specifically, the challenges posed by within-sector productivity improvements faced by MICs. We have argued that such improvements involve policies, such as improved tax collection and quality infrastructure, whose implementation requires institutions capable of effective consultation, monitoring, and credible enforcement. Such institutions are difficult to construct not least because they require political support. Such support is in short supply owing to primary domestic cleavages among social groups that impede the coalitional support needed for institutional upgrading. Finally, we suggested that such (demand-side) disarticulation is often mirrored and intensified by more supply-side factors—namely weakly institutionalized party systems.

A fuller analysis of the MIC trap would need to incorporate further analysis of state capacity (and related pathologies of corruption and clientelism). As argued here, taxation is one core area of state capacity where MIC states lag in terms of their ability to collect revenue, overall and especially through income taxes, a weakness commonly associated with large informal sectors (Gordon and Li, 2009). Institution building of the sort analyzed here is costly and is likely to rely heavily on public sources, so tax capacity becomes a critical component.

While coalition building is decisive in our view, bureaucratic resistance and fragmentation of political institutions can pose additional obstacles to effective policy and institution building. In education, for example, it is important to understand why education bureaucracies are often large, politicized sources of rents at primary and secondary levels and fragmented at the tertiary level, while state-sponsored post-secondary vocational and technical education is fragmented and weakly related to business needs.

This concern with state capacity raises a further issue that merits examination: the potential for a more state-led, top-down development scenario. Our demand-side emphasis in this chapter has been more bottom-up, that is, focusing on the ways in which societal coalitions influence institutional strength. Yet the experiences of the Republic of Korea, Taiwan, and Singapore suggest that highly active, even decisive state roles influence societal demand by nurturing, discouraging, and channeling the interests and views of specific groups. Accounting for such a pattern requires a closer examination of the pressures on political elites, pressures that go beyond domestic coalitions to include external security challenges and ease of access to revenues, whether through natural resource rents or foreign funds (Doner et al., 2005).

5.8 Acknowledgments

We are grateful to José Antonio Alonso, Tom Remington, and participants at the June 2019 book workshop for comments on earlier versions. For fellowship support, Schneider thanks the Stellenbosch Institute of Advanced Study (Stias), Wallenberg Research Centre at Stellenbosch University, Stellenbosch 7600, South Africa.

References

Agénor, P.-R., Canuto, O., and Jelenic, M. (2012): "Avoiding Middle-Income Growth Traps," *World Bank Economic Premise* 98: 1–7.

Baker, Andy. (2019): "The Formal/Informal Labor Divide and Worker Attitudes toward Social Policy: Evidence from Mexico." APSA Annual Meeting. Washington DC.

Bassi, Marina, Busso, Matías, Urzúa, Sergio, and Vargas, Jaime (2012): *Disconnected: Skills, Education, and Employment in Latin America*, Washington, DC: Inter-American Development Bank.

Bates, Robert (1995): "Social Dilemmas and Rational Individuals: An Assessment of the New Institutionalism," in John Harris, Janet Hunter, and Colin Lewis (eds.), *The New Institutional Econonmics*, New York: Routledge, pp. 27–48.

Bhattacharya, Amar, Romani, Mattia, and Stern, Nicholas (2012): *Infrastructure for Development: Meeting the Challenge*, London: Center for Climate Change Economics and Policy.

Bizzarro, Fernando, Gerring, John, Knutsen, Carl Heinrik and Hicken, Allen (2018): "Party Strength and Economic Growth," *World Politics* 70, no. 2: 275–320.

Bogliaccini, Juan, and Madariaga, Aldo (2020): "Varieties of skills profiles in Latin America: a reassessment of the hierarchical model of capitalism," *Journal of Latin American Studies* 52: 1–31.

Busemeyer, Marius (2015): *Skills and Inequality: Partisan Politics and the Political Economy of Education Reforms in Western Welfare States*, New York: Cambridge University Press.

CEPPE (2013): *Formación de Técnicos Para Chile: Un Desafio Sin Políticas Públicas?* Santiago, Chile.

Colpan, Asli (2010): "Business Groups in Turkey," in Asli Colpan, Takashi Hikino, and James Lincoln(eds.), *The Oxford Handbook of Business Groups*, New York: Oxford University Press. doi:10.1093/oxfordhb/9780199552863.003.0017.

Colpan, Asli, Hikino, Takashi, and Lincoln, James (2010): *The Oxford Handbook of Business Groups*, New York: Oxford University Press.

Cooper, Joel, Fox, Randall, Loeprick, Jan, and Mohindra, Komal (2017): *Transfer Pricing and Developing Economies: A Handbook for Policy Makers and Practitioners.* Washington, DC: The World Bank. https://doi.org/10.1596/978-1-4648-0969-9.

Culpepper, Pepper (2010): *Quiet Politics and Business Power: Corporate Control in Europe and Japan*, New York: Cambridge University Press.

Doner, Richard F. (2009): *The Politics of Uneven Development: Thailand's Economic Growth in Comparative Perspective*, Cambridge: Cambridge University Press.

Doner, Richard F. (2016): "The Politics of Productivity Improvement: Quality Infrastructure and the Middle-Income Trap," *Thammasat Economic Journal* 34, no. 1: 1–56.

Doner, Richard F. and Schneider, Ben Ross (2016): "The Middle-Income Trap: More Politics than Economics," *World Politics* 68, no. 4: 608–44.

Doner, Richard F. and Schneider, Ben Ross (2019): "Technical Education in the Middle Income Trap: Missing Coalitions for Skill Formation," (with Richard Doner). *Journal of Development Studies* 56, no. 4: 680–97.

Doner, Richard F., Ritchie, Bryan, and Slater, Dan (2005): "Systemic Vulnerability and the Origins of Developmental States: Northeast and Southeast Asia in Comparative Perspective," *International Organization* 59, no. 2.

Doner, Richard F., Ravenhill, John, and Noble, Gregory W. Forthcoming (2021): *The Political Economy of East Asian Automotive Industrialization: Alternative Paths in East Asia*, New York: Oxford University Press.

Evans, Peter (1995): *Embedded Autonomy: States and Industrial Transformation*, Princeton, NJ: Princeton University Press.

Fairfield, Tasha (2019): "Taxing Latin American Economic Elites," in Gustavo Flores-Macías(ed.), *The Political Economy of Taxation in Latin America*, . New York: Cambridge University Press, pp. 172–93.

Farías, Mauricio and Sevilla, María Paola (2015): "Effectiveness of Vocational High Schools in Students' Access to and Persistence in Postsecondary Vocational Education," *Research in Higher Education* 56, no. 7: 693–718. doi:10.1007/s11162-015-9370-2.

Felipe, Jesus, Abdon, Arnelyn, and Kumar, Utsav (2012): "Tracking the Middle-Income Trap: What Is It, Who Is in It, and Why?" Working Paper. Annandaleon-Hudson, NY: Levy Economics Institute.

Foxley, Alejandro and Sossdorf, Fernando (2011): "Making the Transition: from Middle-Income to Advanced Economies," Washington, DC: The Carnegie Endowment. https://carnegieendowment.org/files/making_the_transition.pdf

Garay, Candelaria. (2019): "Labor Coalitions in Unequal Democracies," Book Prospectus.

Gill, Indermit, and Kharas, Homi (2015): *The Middle-income Trap Turns Ten*, Washington, DC: World Bank.

GlobalFleet (2018): "Taiwan—the Unsung Hero of Automotive Innovation," https://www.globalfleet.com/en/manufacturers/asia-pacific/features/taiwan-unsung-hero-automotive-innovation?a=FJA05&curl=1. Accessed October 28, 2019.

Gordon, Roger, and Li, Wei (2009): "Tax Structures in Developing Countries: Many Puzzles and a Possible Explanation," *Journal of Public Economics* 93, no. 7–8: 855–66.

Gould, Eric D. and Hijzen, Alexander (2016): "Growing Apart, Losing Trust? The Impact of Inequality on Social Capital," IMF Working Paper. WP/16/176 https://www.imf.org/external/pubs/ft/wp/2016/wp16176.pdf

Grindle, M. (2000): "In quest of the political: The political economy of development policymaking," in G. Meier, and J. Stiglitz, (eds.), *Frontiers of Development Economics: The Future In Perspective*, Washington, DC: The World Bank and Oxford University Press, pp. 345–81.

Hall, Peter and Soskice, David (2001): "An Introduction to Varieties of Capitalism," In Peter Hall and David Soskice(eds.), *Varieties of Capitalism*, . New York: Oxford University Press, pp. 1–68.

Holland, Alisha (2017): *Forbearance as Redistribution: The Politics of Informal Welfare in Latin America*, New York: Cambridge University Press.

Iruarrizaga, Francisca (2009): "Dos Miradas a La Educación Media En Chile," Chile: Universidad Católica.

Iversen, Torben, and Stephens, John (2008): "Partisan Politics, the Welfare State, and Three Worlds of Human Capital Formation," *Comparative Political Studies* 41, no. 4–5: 600–37. doi:10.1177/0010414007313117.

Jun, Lim Ping (2016): "Maylaysia's Labour Market and Job Creation under the Economic Transformation Program (ETP) 2011 to 2015." Penang (Malaysia): Penang Institute. https://penanginstitute.org/wp-content/uploads/jml/files/research_papers/Malaysia_s-labour-market-and-job-creation-under-the-ETP_5Apr2017_FINAL.pdf

Kellermann, Martin (2019): *Ensuring Quality to Gain Access to Global Markets: A Reform Toolkit. International Development in Practice*, Washington, DC: World Bank.

Kuruvilla, Sarosh, Gallagher, Mary, and Lee ,Ching-kwan (eds.) (2011): *From Iron Rice Bowl to Informalization: Markets, State and Workers in a Changing China*, Ithaca, NY: Cornell University Press.

Mizala, Alejandra and Schneider, Ben Ross (2014): "Negotiating Education Reform: Teacher Evaluations and Incentives in Chile (1990–2010)," *Governance* 27, no. 1: 87–109. doi:10.1111/gove.12020

Mizala, Alejandra and Schneider, Ben Ross. (2019): "Promoting Quality Education in Chile: The Politics of Reforming Teacher Careers," *Journal of Education Policy* 14: 1–27.

Moberg, Lotta (2015): "The political economy of special economic zones," *Journal of Institutional Economics* 11, no. 1: 167–90.

Murphy, Richard (2012): "Accounting for the Missing Billions," in Peter Reuter (ed.), *Draining Development. Controlling Flows of Illicit Funds from Developing Countries*,. Washington, DC: World Bank, pp. 265–307.

Naim, M. (1994): "Latin America: The second stage of reform," *Journal of Democracy* 5, no. 4: 32–48.

Nelson, J. M. (1999): *Reforming Health and Education: The World Bank, the IDB, and complex institutional change* (ODC Policy Essay No. 26). Washington, DC: Overseas Development Council.

Ornston, Darius (2012): *When Small States Make Big Leaps: Institutional Innovation and High-Tech Competition in Western Europe*. Ithaca, NY: Cornell University Press.

Özel, Işık. (2018): "Veiled Political Economy of an Apparent 'Culture War': Recent Education Policy Reforms in Turkey," In APSA Annual Meeting. Boston, MA.

Patarapong Intarakumnerd (2018): *Mismanaging Innovation Systems: Thailand and the Middle-Income Trap*, London: Routledge.

Paus, Eva (2014): "Latin America and the Middle Income Trap," ECLAC, Financing for Development Series, no. 250. Santiago, Chile: CEPAL.

Perry, Guillermo (2007): *Informality: Exit and Exclusion*, Washington, DC: World Bank Publications.

Persson, Anna, and Rothstein, Bo (2015): "It's My Money: Why Big Government May Be Good Government," *Comparative Politics* 47, no. 2: 231–49.

Pritchett, Lant and Woolcock, Michael (2004): "When the Solution is the Problem: Arraying the Disarray in Development," *World Development* 32, no. 2: 191–212.

Ranis, Gustav (2004): "Arthur Lewis' Contribution to Development Thinking and Policy," New Haven, CT: Economic Growth Center, Yale University. http://www.econ.yale.edu/growth_pdf/cdp891.pdf

Rueda, David (2005): "Insider–Outsider Politics in Industrialized Democracies: The Challenge to Social Democratic Parties," *American Political Science Review* 99, no. 01: 61–74. doi:10.1017/S000305540505149X.

Sancak, Merve (2017): *Vocational Training, Skills and Inequality: A Comparative Analysis of Mexican and Turkish Skill Systems*, Cambridge: Cambridge University Press.

Sancak, Merve and Özel, Işık (2018): "When politics gets in the way: Domestic coalitions and the making of skill systems," *Review of International Political Economy* 25, no. 3: 340–63.

Schneider, Ben Ross (2013): *Hierarchical Capitalism in Latin America: Business, Labor and the Challenges of Equitable Development*. New York: Cambridge University Press.

Schneider, Ben Ross and Karcher, Sebastian (2010): "Complementarities and Continuities in the Political Economy of Labour Markets in Latin America," *Socio-Economic Review* 8, no. 4: 623–51. doi:10.1093/ser/mwq022.

Sehnbruch, Kirsten (2006): *The Chilean Labor Market: A Key to Understanding Latin American Labor Markets*, New York: Palgrave Macmillan.

Sevilla, Maria Paola (2017): "Panorama de La Educación Técnica Profesional En América Latina y El Caribe," Santiago.

Shafer, Michael (1994): *Winners and Losers: How Sectors Shape the Developmental Prospects of States*, Ithaca, NY: Cornell University Press.

Shapira, Phillip and Youtie, Jan (2013): "Impact of Technology and Innovation Advisory Services," (December) Manchester, UK: Manchester Institute of Innovation Research, University of Manchester. http://research.mbs.ac.uk/innovation/

Somsak Tambunlertchai (2009): "Krongkhan Suksaa Sakayaphaap Phlit Phan Yang Nai Prataeth" ("Study Project on the Potential for Rubber Products in Thailand.") Report submitted to the Rubber Research Institute of Thailand, Dept. of Agriculture, MOAC.

Tilly, Charles (1992): *Coercion, Capital, and European States, AD 990–1992*, Cambridge: Blackwell.

Unger, Daniel H. and Chandra Mahakanjana (2016): *Thai Politics: Between Democracy and Its Discontents*, Boulder, CO: Lynne Rienner Publishers.

van Zanden, Luiten Jan, Baten, Joerg, d'Ercole, Marco Mira, Rijpma, Auke, Smith, Conal, and Timmer, Marcel (eds.) (2014): *How Was Life: Global Well-Being since 1820*, Paris, France: Organization of Economic Cooperation and Development.

Warr, Peter and Archanun Kohpaiboon (2017): "Thailand's Automotive Manufacturing Corridor," ADB Economics Working Paper Series #519 (September). Manila: Asian Development Bank.

Wietzke, Frank-Borge (2015): "Pathways from Jobs to Social Cohesion," *The World Bank Research Observer* 30, no. 1: 95–123. doi:10.1093/wbro/lku004.

World Bank (2010): *Malaysia Economic Monitor: Growth Through Innovation*, Washington, DC: World Bank.

Yusuf, S. and Nabeshima, K. (2009): *Tiger Economies under Threat: A Comparative Analysis of Malaysia's Industrial Prospects and Policy Options*, Washington, DC: World Bank.

6

Citizens' Rising Expectations

A Call to Rebuild the Social Contract?

Mario Pezzini

6.1 Introduction

Middle-income countries (MICs) are home to most of the world's population and are a growing economic force. A total of 106 countries are classified as middle-income: 56 upper middle-income and 50 lower middle-income. These countries have accounted for the majority of global poverty reduction over recent decades.

Yet as MICs move up the income ladder, they face increasingly complex international challenges, coupled with a growing demand from their new and still vulnerable middle-classes, for more and better public services. Discontent is increasing in many of these countries, going back to the Arab Spring, with Lebanon and Ecuador, and even high-income countries such as Chile, providing recent examples. Governments seem increasingly incapable of understanding people's perceptions of their quality of life, and of providing satisfactory responses. Domestically, development challenges that MICs face relate both to a lack of clear and shared development strategies and weak state capacities to mobilize resources and provide quality public goods. At a global level, MICs are highly exposed to the ease with which multinational enterprises (MNEs) are able to avoid and even evade tax, with less developed countries being most exposed to profit shifting. Moreover, MICs have to face illicit financial flows and deal with the consequences of digitalization on tax collection.

This chapter identifies two key priorities for MICs. First, countries should regenerate tailor-made national development strategies that take into account the voice of citizens, available resources, and possible fiscal reforms, and that mobilize national capabilities for designing and experimenting (democratically) with development options. Second, international cooperation should focus on improving government capacities in resource mobilization and strategy building.

The chapter starts by outlining the challenges faced by MICs in responding to increasing demand for public goods. These include the existence of an institutional development trap and the need to keep up with productive and digital transformation. In particular, it outlines mechanisms for increasing domestic

Mario Pezzini, *Citizens' Rising Expectations: A Call to Rebuild the Social Contract?* In: *Trapped in the Middle? Developmental Challenges for Middle-Income Countries*. Edited by: José Antonio Alonso and José Antonio Ocampo, Oxford University Press (2020). © OUP. DOI: 10.1093/oso/9780198852773.003.0006

revenues. These include reducing vulnerability to tax evasion and avoidance, enhancing tax structures and better addressing the political economy of fiscal reform. Finally, the chapter concludes with two overarching options for improving domestic resource mobilization nationally and internationally.

6.2 Middle-Income Countries: Challenges to Meeting Demand for Public Goods

In recent decades, national and local institutions in developing countries have often been unable to keep pace with their economies. Between 2000 and 2010, eighty-three developing economies grew at more than double the average GDP growth rate in the OECD over the same period. Many of these countries are or have become middle-income countries but their institutions have been struck by inertia. Moreover, their institutions confront phenomena that are new or rapidly growing in importance. These phenomena are often connected to globalization and technological innovation. In this chapter, we focus on three: increasing demand for public goods from the so-called new middle-classes; an increasing vulnerability to tax evasion and avoidance; and the impact of digital transformation on taxation and social protection systems.

6.2.1 Domestic Resource Mobilization and the Institutional Development Trap

Economic growth since the 1990s has resulted, among other things, in a reconfiguration of global economic geography and the emergence of a growing middle-class. Just over 50 percent of the world's population, or some 3.8 billion people, live in households with enough discretionary expenditure to be considered "middle-class" or "rich" (Kharas and Hamel, 2018). The expansion of the middle-class has come with growing aspirations and demands by citizens, among other things, for better quality public goods, better services and a more responsive and transparent state. More educated, better informed, and more connected than ever before, citizens of the growing middle-class are asking for more voice in public decisions (OECD, 2010).

The aspirations and demands of the newly formed middle-classes are often heightened by the fact that these classes remain highly vulnerable. A large number of citizens remain in vulnerable situations, for instance due to their informal status in the labor market or weak social protection systems. Two billion people (50 percent of the world's workforce) work informally today. Most of these workers are living in developing and emerging countries, have little or no formal education, unsophisticated skills, low access to social protection and little capacity to save (OECD/ILO, 2019). Aging, health problems, the death of a family member, or a divorce can cause a rapid descent into extreme poverty.

The growing aspirations and, in parallel, the chronic vulnerability of these "middle-classes" tend to generate frustration and, more and more frequently, social turbulence. MICs are under pressure to reform public programs and policies and, in turn, to mobilize additional resources to adequately respond to social demands. In other words, middle-income countries have to improve the functioning of the state, across levels of government, and with long overdue fiscal reforms.

Fiscal systems in MICs typically share five key features: (a) as a percentage of GDP, domestic fiscal revenues are usually far below those generated in high-income countries; (b) domestic fiscal revenues are the most important source of financing for national development; (c) flows of official development assistance (ODA, the technical term for aid) are declining both in absolute terms (by 2.7 percent between 2017 and 2018) and as a share of national income, at a faster rate than tax revenues are rising, resulting in an overall decline in public revenues; (d) private external sources such as remittances are a more important source of financing than ODA for many developing countries but are not sufficient to offset this decline, especially as the share of remittances to GDP peaks at around the low middle-income country threshold (Kharas et al., 2014), and (e) foreign direct investment to developing countries dropped by around a third over 2016–17, following a 12 percent drop in overall external finance from 2013 to 2016 (OECD, 2019).

This situation is exacerbated when countries are no longer eligible for ODA because their income per capita exceeds a certain threshold, without them necessarily having established an adequate level of institutional capacity. Between now and 2030, twenty-eight developing countries with a total population of 2 billion are projected to exceed the income threshold for ODA eligibility if current growth rates are maintained. All but fourteen of eighty-two countries currently eligible for concessional Multilateral Development Bank programs are projected to exceed their income criteria (OECD, 2014).

If fiscal reforms are needed and urgent, what obstacles constrain their scope and (even more so) their implementation? The combination of a growing demand for public goods and the lack of institutional capacity in MICs has often evolved into an "*institutional development trap*". Improvements in public services—such as education, health and social protection—do not keep pace with people's socio-economic conditions, creating high rates of dissatisfaction and a disconnect between citizens and institutions. In turn, citizens feel justified in avoiding their tax obligations, which results in lower resources to finance quality public services. This dynamic—essentially a self-reinforcing vicious circle—can keep countries trapped over time (OECD et al., 2019b). The institutional trap is both cause and consequence of countries finding themselves with insufficient resources, poor-quality public goods, and facing obstacles to development over and above fundamental challenges such as weak productivity and, increasingly, climate change. Tax evasion and avoidance by MNEs—analyzed in section 6.2.3—can further reduce citizens' willingness to pay taxes, as can the government's capacity to pursue certain fiscal reforms.

As a *lack of institutional capacity* makes it difficult to meet citizens' expectations, trust in institutions and satisfaction with public services have deteriorated in recent years. On average over the last decade, 62 percent of the Latin American population had little or no trust in their governments. In south-east Africa, up to 70 percent of the population feels there is corruption in their government (Gallup, 2018). Satisfaction with public services has also diminished in Latin America, with the share of people satisfied with the quality of healthcare falling from 57 percent to 41 percent between 2006 and 2016, and satisfaction with the education system falling from 63 percent to 56 percent over the same period (OECD/CAF/ECLAC, 2018). Effective government policies and performance are likely to have a significant impact on tax morale: higher tax morale is associated with individuals who trust their national government and consider fiscal redistribution to be essential (OECD, 2019g).

In short, MICs need to mobilize additional domestic resources to respond to new socio-economic challenges and increasing demand from their vulnerable "middle-classes." They must also show responsible use of these resources through good spending linked to sound national development strategies that are adapted to the complex environments they face. Building the right government capacities in this sense is essential.

6.2.2 What Are the Levels and What Are the Sources of Domestic Resources in MICs?

The road towards effective domestic resource mobilization (generation of government resources) is still long. As emphasized above, tax revenues in middle-income countries remain low. Tax revenues are far below the OECD average (34.2 percent of GDP in 2017) in Latin America and Africa. The tax-to-GDP ratio among the twenty-five countries in *Revenue Statistics in Latin America and the Caribbean* was 22.8 percent in 2017 and 17.2 percent in the twenty-six countries included in *Revenue Statistics in Africa*, just over half the OECD average (Figure 6.1). If only the eighteen middle-income countries in the African sample are considered, the average rises only slightly, to 18.3 percent of GDP. The largest economy in Africa, Nigeria, had a tax-to-GDP ratio of 5.7 percent in 2017, the lowest among the twenty-six. Meanwhile, the average tax-to-GDP ratio of the five Southeast Asian countries included in *Revenue Statistics in Asian and Pacific Economies*—Indonesia, Malaysia, Philippines, Singapore, and Thailand—was 14.9 percent (OECD, 2018c; OECD/ATAF/AUC, 2019; OECD et al., 2019c).

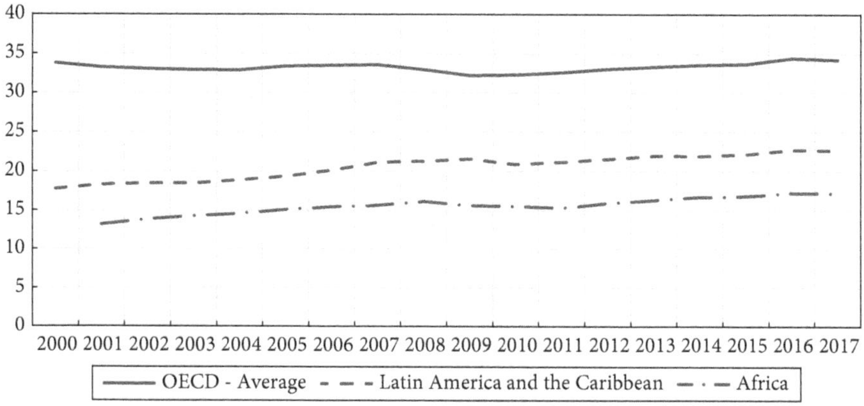

Figure 6.1 Tax-to-GDP ratios by region
Source: OECD (2019c).

The general picture is alarming not only because of the absolute level of fiscal revenues, but also because the tax mix in MICs is not conducive to redistribution: indirect taxes are far more prominent in the tax mix of developing countries than in the OECD. On average across OECD countries, taxes on goods and services accounted for 32.7 percent of tax revenues in 2017; they accounted for 49.8 percent of revenues in Latin America and the Caribbean (LAC), and 53.7 percent in Africa in the same year. On the other hand, social security contributions accounted for 26.2 percent of tax revenues in OECD countries but only 16.9 percent in LAC and 8.1 percent in Africa. Personal income tax generated a higher proportion of tax revenues in OECD countries (8.2 percent of GDP in 2017, versus 2.2 percent in LAC and 2.8 percent in Africa) than corporate income tax, while the opposite was true in LAC, and Africa (Figure 6.2).

The large differences in revenue generation through social security contributions and personal income tax account for most of the difference between the level of tax revenues as a percentage of GDP in OECD countries and developing regions respectively. This phenomenon also explains why fiscal systems in OECD countries tend to be far more redistributive than those in LAC or Africa. Overall, OECD countries are able to finance their welfare states (and other public programs) through taxes that themselves reinforce redistribution.[1]

[1] It should be noted that a number of developing countries have privatized (in part or in whole) their social security systems by introducing individual accounts, which are not redistributive, do not pool risks across the population or provide a state-guaranteed level of benefits. Contributions to these systems are not considered as taxes by the standard OECD methodology but, since they are mandatory, they add to the cost of labour. Measures of equivalent fiscal pressure, which include mandatory private social security contributions as well as resources from natural revenues, reduce the gap between OECD countries and those countries with private social security arrangements (Barreix et al., 2017).

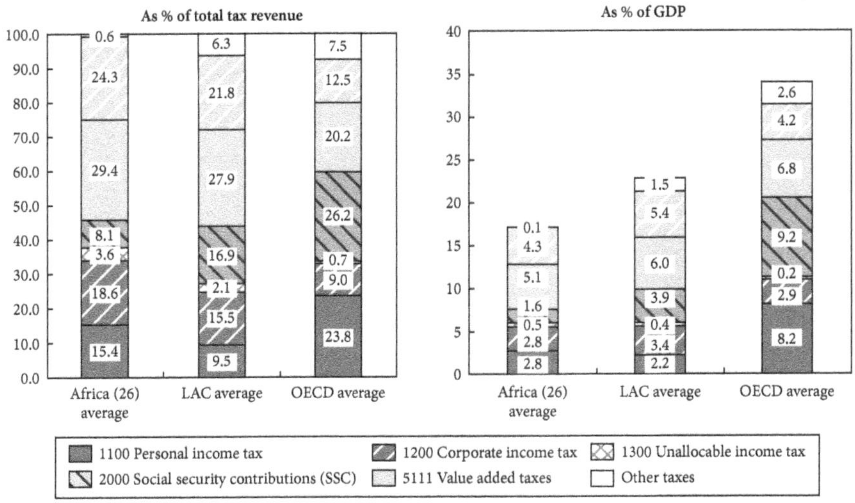

Figure 6.2 Tax structure for Africa (26), Latin America and the Caribbean (LAC), and OECD averages as a percentage of total tax revenues and as a percentage of GDP, 2017

Source: OECD/ATAF/AUC (2019).

So what is stopping developing countries from being more equitable and increasing personal income tax revenues and social security contributions? *Policymakers face at least two key dilemmas in developing countries.*

A first dilemma is how can governments generate higher revenues without pushing a higher proportion of the workforce into informal activities, precisely to avoid being taxed? The same challenge is echoed in social security coverage; in fact, it is even more pronounced because social security contributions tend to be payable at a lower income level. By examining the tax wedge at different income levels, the OECD (2016) was able to calculate the cost of formalizing across twenty LAC countries. In most cases, this cost exceeds 20 percent of workers' income on average and is higher for workers on the lowest incomes.

Labor market stratification is common in MICs and informality is often very high. Around two-thirds of Latin America's employed population were in wage employment in 2013. One in five of these individuals were employed informally, meaning they did not pay taxes or social security contributions. Informality levels were even higher when own-account, domestic, and unpaid family workers (who comprise the remaining third of the employed population) were taken into account. Across the LAC region, only 45.2 percent of the total employed population contributed to social security in 2013 and the magnitude of the coverage gap is likely to be in a similar range today.

A second related dilemma is how to reform tax systems in contexts of high income inequality. Across developing countries, poverty and vulnerability exert downwards pressure on tax rates or shrink tax bases—phenomena from which high-income earners frequently benefit. Where governments seek to stratify the tax system through simplified tax regimes for low-income enterprises, they run the risk of perverse incentives, distortions, fraud, and opacity.

What are the answers to these dilemmas?

Low revenues from personal income tax generated from a small tax base are a particular constraint in many MICs. High minimum thresholds for tax payments mean that only wage earners at the very top of the income distribution tend to pay. With the exception of Argentina and Uruguay, over 80 percent of personal income tax in LAC is paid by individuals in the top decile (BID, 2017). At the same time, large zero-rate bands mean that the average tax rates paid by high-income earners are far lower than the maximum statutory rates and that, in most countries, the "average worker" does not pay personal income tax. In addition, the benefits from certain tax exemptions on personal income taxes (e.g., interest rates on credit loans) mainly accrue to high paid workers.

A stronger reliance on indirect taxes has often been seen as a tactical way to introduce immediate reforms in tax systems. However, taxes on goods and services tend to be regressive. They impose a higher burden on low-income than on higher income groups, unlike personal income tax, which usually applies higher rates to higher earners. In practice, this *regressivity* is unlikely to be very pronounced, but in contexts of significant poverty and "middle-class" vulnerability, consumption taxes can nonetheless harm the living conditions of the lower segments of the population and further nourish social turbulence. As a result, it is common practice for governments to exclude certain goods (usually staple food and non-food items) from value-added tax. Yet these exemptions not only imply significant revenue losses but can also worsen distributional outcomes, since non-poor individuals consume the subsidized goods as well, often in greater volume. The fact that the population as a whole benefits from these subsidies makes them politically very difficult to eliminate.

A growing number of countries, particularly in Latin America, are implementing *Monotributos*, which combine simplified and lower-rate taxes for individuals in the informal sector with social security coverage (OECD, 2019h). Monotributos are gaining attention, particularly amongst the social protection community. The LAC region has also led innovation in matching social security contributions, whereby the government meets part of the cost of contributions. These innovations have not yet achieved dramatic success in terms of social security coverage or revenue generation. Yet, it is worth experimenting with them alongside initiatives targeting energy subsidies—with more or less success—as a source of fiscal space, and using social protection to mitigate political backlash. For example, successive administrations in Indonesia have increased cash transfers to poor individuals to compensate for reductions in fuel subsidies.

Achieving a step change in public revenues requires a new engaging and inclusive social contract, and self-reinforcing improvements in tax morale, public investments, and public services. We analyze some of these key issues further but first we must mention a series of additional obstacles preventing resource mobilization for development.

6.2.3 Middle-Income Countries are Vulnerable to Tax Evasion, Complexity and Avoidance

Developing countries are highly vulnerable to tax evasion, complexity, and avoidance. Such practices by MNEs and high-net-worth individuals can reduce the willingness to pay taxes among middle-class citizens. These issues require a broad and detailed analysis; for the sake of this chapter, we highlight three vulnerabilities that appear particularly relevant for our scope: fiscal behavior of MNEs, the complexity of taxing activities and profits of companies operating in the digital economy, and illicit financial flows.

First, MNEs' ability to avoid taxes in the countries where they make their profits is a practice that has spread across countries. Multinational companies make sizable tax savings by shifting profits from countries with high corporate taxes to countries with low corporate taxes. These practices are usually not illegal but have a significant impact on economies at all income levels. Some estimates show that close to 40 percent of multinational profits are declared offshore globally each year. As a result, governments the world over are found to be losing 10 percent of corporate tax revenues. The loss is estimated at 18 percent of corporate tax revenues in the European Union and roughly 14 percent of corporate revenues in the USA (Torslov et al., 2018).

Shifting profits to avoid taxes is likely to be more pervasive (and certainly more pernicious) in less developed countries. While the implied long-run revenue losses for OECD countries are in the order of 1 percent of GDP, revenue losses in developing countries have been calculated at around 1.3 percent of GDP (Crivelli et al., 2015; Johannesen et al., 2018). This is a significant amount, especially relative to their overall low tax-to-GDP ratios. Weaker institutional capacity leaves these countries more exposed to cross-border profit shifting and less prepared to adopt the best response to these increasingly common practices. This point is particularly relevant as developing countries—mostly low income and lower middle-income countries—tend to rely more on corporate income tax as a share of all tax revenue.

The inability to contain profit shifting pushes countries to lower their tax rates for the sake of competitive advantage in what has come to be termed a race to the bottom (Johannesen et al., 2018). Revenues lost to tax evasion in LAC have been calculated at USD 340 billion, or 6.7 percent of regional GDP: evasion of corporate income tax and personal income tax amounted to 4.3 percent of GDP and evasion of VAT amounted to 2.4 percent of GDP (ECLAC, 2016).

This is not the only challenge MICs face in trying to secure their tax base. Cross-border tax avoidance from high net worth individuals who hide their cash offshore is also a significant problem; developing countries are estimated to have some of the highest shares of financial wealth held offshore (22 percent in Latin America and 30 percent in Africa, compared with 10 percent in Europe) (Zucman, 2014). Allowing elites to hide their cash offshore makes it difficult for developing countries to encourage voluntary compliance from middle classes. Despite some recent successes, institutional capacities to confront these practices are still lacking in many developing countries.

Second, tax systems globally are finding it difficult to keep pace with the rapid growth of activity and profit of companies operating in the digital economy. A central challenge is how to tax the value generated by digital business models, where users, data, and intangible assets play a key role. A related challenge is more familiar to the above discussion: specifying the tax jurisdiction of digital companies in a context where they can provide services in many countries with minimal (or no) physical presence.

Just as these challenges affect every country's tax system, so the solution needs to be internationally binding to prevent digital companies from engaging in tax arbitrage (although this has not stopped a number of developed and developing economies from moving ahead unilaterally with digital tax policies while discussions at a global level continue). However, there will have to be compromise between developing and advanced economies, as to the rules of the game.

The institutions established to coordinate and regulate taxation of the digital economy are a topic of debate in themselves. Developing countries might be suspicious of arbitration processes that pit them against advanced economies. There are also fundamental capacity constraints in keeping up with a sector that is evolving so fast. Countries might not be fully aware of how their own economies are affected by the digital transformation; keeping pace with developments internationally and regularly contributing to global negotiations on the topic might be a challenge in itself. In this context, groups such as the African Tax Administration Forum are playing a crucial role in representing developing countries in ongoing negotiations related to the taxation of the digital economy.

Third, illicit financial flows (IFFs)—that include money-laundering, tax evasion, and bribery—tend to originate in developing countries, often in middle-income countries. While estimates may be and are greatly debated, it is widely thought that IFFs are likely to exceed aid flows and investment in volume (OECD, 2014a). An immediate impact of IFFs in developing countries is a decline in domestic spending and investment, both in the public and private sector; the social and economic impact in developing countries is more severe given their smaller resource base and markets.

IFFs from Africa (the majority from tax evasion) equaled USD 50 billion in 2015 (AU/ECA, 2015; OECD, 2019d). Global Financial Integrity (2015) found that IFFs from Asia between 2004 and 2013 were equivalent to 3.8 percent of GDP, that is, 38.3 percent of total losses incurred by developing countries over that period. Of the ten developing countries that experienced the highest volume of IFFs, five were in Asia, two in Africa, two in LAC, and one in Eastern Europe. Against this backdrop, the exchange of information across tax administrations, led by the Global Forum on Transparency and Exchange of Information for Tax Purposes, is crucial to support countries' domestic efforts in dealing with IFFs and contributing to international transparency on financial transactions.

In conclusion, the interconnected nature and impacts of taxation across countries requires an urgent, common, and global response. Increasing transparency and exchange of information would ensure that MNEs and high-net-worth individuals pay an appropriate amount of tax to the right jurisdiction. Renewed international cooperation involving information exchange among all actors—public and private and in all countries—would enable MICs to improve resource mobilization and respond to their citizens' needs. These countries need to strongly engage in such cooperation.

6.3 Not Just about Revenues: Navigating the Political Economy of Fiscal Reform and Good Spending

Changing the mind-set of citizens in MICs to increase tax paying and avoid the so-called "institutional trap" is only possible if taxation comes with effective expenditure. These expenditures must be visible in productive investments, an equitable system of transfers and quality public services, and they should be coherent with sound and agreed national development strategies. Effective and coherent expenditure is key for building trust between citizens and public institutions. Equally relevant is the ability of states to form and create capacity through fiscal reform by successfully navigating economic and political processes.

6.3.1 Navigating the Political Economy of Fiscal Reform

The political economy of fiscal reforms is particularly complex and requires sophisticated state capabilities. "State capability" is not simply an immutable inheritance or the immediate manifestation of certain principles, but rather the sedimentation of actions conducted by actors who are changing history all the time (Di John, 2006). Rights and institutions are formed as the by-products of bargains, or settlements of conflicts, in the course of cooperation or struggle between different stakeholders with different power and incentives. While this implies that action and reforms are possible, it also means that certain actors may have progressively captured more power than others. In middle-income countries, policymakers attempting tax reforms can be particularly influenced by different capture mechanisms, including financing campaigns, lobbying and "revolving doors" for high-level officials (Oxfam, 2018). Granting tax incentives to corporations, preferential rates on corporate income tax or personal income tax, as well as tax evasion and avoidance mechanisms to the private sector, often undermine the effectiveness of tax reforms and contributes to inequalities in Latin America (OECD et al., 2019b).

Given the need for fiscal reforms to enhance the quantity and quality of public goods, how should a country address these "capture mechanisms" that assign strong voices to rent seekers, limit tax revenue increases, or orient reforms in a partisan way? How can recent social discontent and lack of trust in institutions in middle-income countries and beyond be recognized, addressed, and translated into an intelligible voice? The answers are far from obvious; they require long-term analysis and "democratic experiments" (Dorf and Sabel, 2009) to extract some options. That being said, it seems likely that a new social contract in middle-income countries must include fiscal reforms and should address the following three key points (at least).

First, the policy making process for reform should include a participatory mechanism for consultation and dialog among stakeholders to co-design reforms. Governments should transparently "build" the components of proposed fiscal reforms with their citizens. Sometimes misunderstandings occur concerning the impact of reforms on citizens; it is essential to develop effective communications on the scope and segments of population affected by reforms. On other occasions, governments have asymmetric information, or suffer from capture, and the very design of the reform is biased; in this case, the design needs to be improved via feedback from the population. Equally important is the use of robust analytical tools and indicators, such as measures of well-being, when addressing the growing aspirations of middle classes and measuring the impact of policies.

Second, different reform components should be carefully sequenced. In recent decades, scholars have studied whether political leaders should push many reforms at once (a big bang approach) or introduce them one after the other (an unbundling strategy). There are strong arguments in favor of bundling reforms into a comprehensive package to build fiscal legitimacy (Dayton-Johnson et al., 2011), not least that bundling recognizes the multidimensional nature of development bottlenecks. The traditional sectoral approach of public administrations, however, sometimes faces difficulties in implementing pre-defined sectoral solutions. Bundling may require complex and long negotiations to reduce political constraints. However, it can help build wide programmatic and "constitutional" agreements that facilitate political support for fundamental reforms over different legislatures. This is because structural reforms to improve citizens' well-being that address distributional issues, may gain wider support and engagement from parliaments and from the population when they are explicitly weaved into a vision for the country and a renewed social contract. Finally, the scope for negotiation is wider and gains from one reform can compensate for losses associated with others.

Third, governments should complement reforms with more effective, efficient, and transparent public spending. How money is spent will significantly affect the overall developmental impact of fiscal policy. The quality and composition of spending and the alignment of fiscal policy to the business cycle and sound development strategies all affect the economy. Moreover, effective spending tends to be self-sustaining: it promotes economic growth and enhances tax morale, both of which should generate higher fiscal revenues. Stagnant tax-to-GDP ratios in many MICs suggest this virtuous circle is not taking hold. Public expenditure in LAC, for instance, has grown by 7 percent of GDP on average over the past 20 years but this increase was not reflected in a similar increase in quality physical and human capital or in lasting social outcomes (IDB, 2018).

If taken hand-in-hand, such actions can improve citizens' perceptions of comprehensive fiscal reforms and help build political support (OECD et al., 2019b). Let us now highlight some issues that could help to improve spending.

6.3.2 Good Spending

Quality spending requires allocations to be determined according to their impact on and alignment with agreed national priorities. Results-based budgeting is a critical means of incentivizing governments to align spending to national objectives, to improve implementation and to strengthen institutional cooperation. Results-based budgeting is demanding of governments' time, capacity, and resources. However, middle-income countries are not necessarily condemned to be second-comers in the use of results based budgeting. Uruguay made particularly rapid progress between 2007 and 2013 (IDB, 2018). Performance-based budgeting is also increasingly common in Africa, with over 80 percent of countries using it as a basis for allocations (CABRI, 2013). It has been a common feature of public-sector management reforms in Asia since 2000. However, progress in these areas has not been linear and the extent to which it has improved spending outcomes is often unclear. Amongst OECD countries, performance in this area has been highly variable in the 60 years since results-based budgeting first appeared (OECD, 2018b).

Focusing on the largest single component of public spending, the wage bill could also identify ways to improve the quality of spending. On average across LAC, the public sector wage bill accounts for 29.0 percent of spending, versus an average of 24.2 percent in the OECD. Public-sector employment in the region is nonetheless much lower as a proportion of total employment than in OECD countries (12.7 percent versus 17.4 percent respectively). This finding is echoed by the IMF (2016), which finds that the public sector wage bill averaged 27.2 percent of total spending in emerging economies globally, versus 24.5 percent in advanced economies. The IMF also confirms that public-sector employment, as a percentage of employment in emerging economies, is lower than in advanced economies. The reasons may include the effect of economies of scale in the public sector or a high wage premium, whereby workers with equivalent skills are paid much more in the public sector than in the private sector. The premium could be exacerbated by social security arrangements that in some cases provide more generous benefits than arrangements for the broader workforce. While in OECD countries there has been a tendency to merge arrangements for public and private sector workers, this has proved much rarer in developing countries (OECD, 2017, forthcoming). The matter deserves further exploration.

Finally, timing matters. Fiscal multipliers—the extent to which changes to taxes or spending impact the economy—vary according to the phase of the business cycle. An important objective of fiscal policy is to be counter-cyclical; meaning that it does not reinforce what is going on in the economy. A striking finding by (Vegh 2015) is that (with two exceptions) fiscal policy amongst advanced economies between 1960 and 2014 was counter-cyclical on average, while it was procyclical amongst the vast majority of emerging economies. If we look at spending over the long term, timing matters again. During the good times of the first decade of the 2000s, governments in LAC prioritized scaling-up transfer programs over capital investments, contributing to a significant fall in poverty and inequality over this period. Once fiscal consolidation was required, however, public investments were the first to suffer while transfers were protected even though reducing public investment has a much greater negative impact on the economy (Vegh et al., 2018).

As we have seen, spending and revenues need to be considered together. Only by looking at both together is it possible to understand: (a) the combined impact of fiscal and spending policies on inequality, poverty, and well-being; (b) the instruments that have the most impact on distributional outcomes; (c) the political economy of fiscal reforms. A well-known graph (Figure 6.3) helps to highlight this point. Through a combination of taxes and transfers, OECD countries reduce the Gini coefficient by approximately 16 percentage points; in LAC, the most unequal region on earth, the comparable reduction is only 2.2 percentage points on average (Lustig, 2017; OECD/CAF/ECLAC, 2018). Approximately two-thirds of the reduction in inequality in OECD countries is achieved by expenditure and a third by taxation.

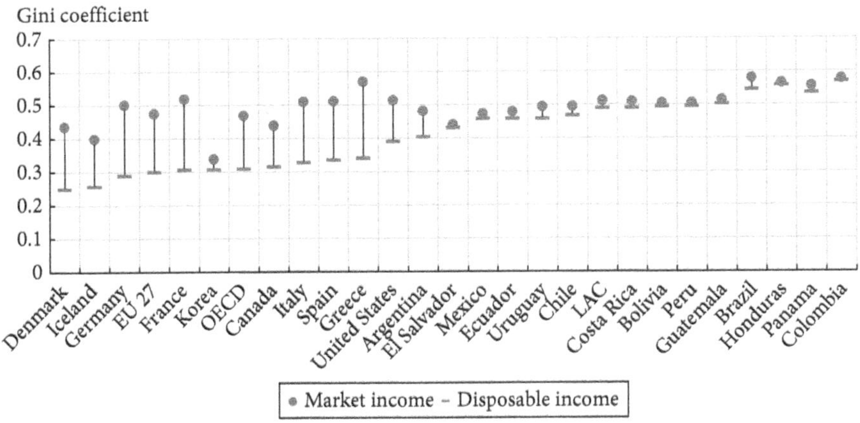

Figure 6.3 Impact of taxes and transfers on income distribution in Latin America, the European Union, and selected OECD economies
Source: Lustig (2017); OECD/CAF/ECLAC (2018).

6.4 There is No Magic Recipe: Two Proposals

Middle-income countries are at a turning point. How can their governments regain citizens' trust and respond to their demands and expectations? They need to upgrade their policies and capacities to adapt to a more complex national and international scenario. They need to build strong and shared narratives that address a broader and multidimensional vision of well-being and provide a strategic and encouraging vision toward progress. They need to renew the social contract.

The prospects for this upgrade are challenging, but there are some options to support middle-income countries taking on the task. We suggest improving and putting more emphasis on national development strategies. This would provide a platform for countries to re-discuss and agree on priorities. In turn, this would contribute to better navigating the political economy of reform and improve the quality of spending. Finally, it would provide more voice to citizens and allow the "negotiation" of a nationally agreed vision and plan for development. At the same time, we suggest increased coordination and cooperation at the international level to avoid tax evasion and avoidance, which is taking a heavy toll on middle-income countries. Cooperation would increase middle-income countries' institutional capacities by using existing global initiatives and efforts.

6.4.1 Rebuilding Citizens' Trust: A Focus on National Development Strategies

While middle-income countries may presently be experiencing common challenges in their development paths—persistent traps, rising inequality, increasing discontent—solutions remain framed by their cultural, geographical, and institutional specificities. A country must be able to analyze and reach consensus on the specific national bottlenecks to its development. It must put everything possible in place to anticipate future national trends beyond a single electoral cycle. A country has to design and implement commonly agreed national development strategies to help remove bottlenecks to development. Defining the right goals and priorities in a strategic, participatory and "negotiated" manner can be key for a country's long-term economic and social performance, as well as stability. This is relevant now more than ever, the situation appearing increasingly turbulent in many middle-income countries.

Not surprisingly, *national development plans* are re-emerging, following a weakening in the 1970s and 1980s and their near disappearance with the neoliberal approaches that prevailed thereafter. The number of countries with a national development plan has more than doubled in recent years, from about 62 in 2006 to 134 in 2018; more than 80 percent of the global population now lives in a country with a national development plan of one form or another. NDPs are increasingly recognized as tools that can help countries build shared development objectives with an agreed and long-term vision. This should not come as a surprise as the redefinition of the development models that have prevailed in recent decades, comes with the redefinition of social contracts and, in turn, of tax reform and quality-spending strategies. From this perspective, national development plans could help address development traps such as the institutional trap.

However, are the present planning experiences going in the right direction? Can plans provide, at least in part, alternatives to the weakened "intermediary bodies," that is, platforms such as traditional parties, strong unions, even religious institutions that in the past channeled citizens' voices towards the state, at both local and national levels? Studies have found a great variety of plans in terms of the evidence used, the degree of internal consistency between different parts of the same plan, the process of developing a plan (inclusive or elite-driven), and the extent to which they are clear on how they will be financed and turn aspirations into reality (Chimhowu, Hulme and Munro, 2019). In many cases, plans are not yet effective tools with which to build stronger links between governments and citizens. Nevertheless, efforts are multiplying to engage different actors and implement participatory processes ("Development à la base," shaped in Togo, is one example). These efforts should be better supported internationally, for example by pushing international cooperation to provide further multilateral knowledge-sharing for middle-income countries (see the more than fifteen Multidimensional Country Reviews carried out by countries with the OECD Development Centre).

More work needs to be done but some points can be drawn that would help tackle, at least in part, the consequences of decreased planning since the 1960s and 1970s. The redefinition of social contracts requires consensus-driven long-term visions and strategies. It should involve a broad range of actors, drawing on a variety of knowledge and viewpoints. These actors should identify and agree on unexploited development opportunities to be built or preserved. They should "negotiate" actions and identify their respective responsibilities. They should agree on transparent results frameworks. Plans should be place-based, reflecting differences in both rural and urban locations, as well as across a country's entire territory. Their unit of analysis and intervention should be not only national but also regional and local. Strategies should be multi-sectoral, with plans containing a clear and explicit policy mix and sequencing.

6.4.2 International Cooperation: A Tool to Fight Tax Avoidance and Evasion and to Build Countries' Institutional Capacities

Multilateral international cooperation can be crucial for knowledge-sharing in national planning processes; it is also fundamental in dealing with taxes, which are no longer just a domestic issue. International peer pressure on tax challenges can help to create the political space for action domestically including by increasing tax morale, plugging the leaks as well as showing that MNEs and elites are being taxed fairly. As we have seen for the middle-income countries, countries are highly vulnerable to tax evasion, complexity, and avoidance with the result that global responses are urgently needed. OECD calculations show that the erosion of the tax base and the transfer of benefits cost countries USD 100–240 billion in lost revenue annually, which is the equivalent to 4–10 percent of the global corporate income tax revenue (OECD, 2019e). Estimates by the IMF are even more pessimistic: losses go up to almost USD 200 billion, or 1.3 percent of GDP for developing countries, and between USD 400 and 500 billion, or 1 percent of GDP, for OECD countries (Crivelli et al., 2015).

Renewed international cooperation involving information exchange and reform of international standards on cross-border taxation would support MICs in improving resource mobilization and responding with upgraded policies to the increasing demand of their citizens and of their vulnerable middle classes. Fortunately, progress is being made. Information exchange has expanded dramatically since the global financial crisis, providing governments around the world with the policy space to put an end to bank secrecy and with a key tool to curtail Illicit Financial Flows. New tools and standards have also emerged to help address tax avoidance, complemented by increased capacity building for tax administrations. Finally, spaces have been created for inclusive and active discussion amongst countries at all income levels on tax matters. We emphasize three efforts that are particularly relevant.

First, bank secrecy has almost been eliminated globally, and through the Global Forum on Transparency and Exchange of Information for Tax Purposes, the 154 members hold each other mutually accountable for implementing and maintaining international standards on tax transparency. Joining the forum and becoming party to the multilateral instruments on exchange of information enables countries to access information on their taxpayers held in other signatory jurisdictions. The most recent advance provides for this information to be exchanged automatically. Over 100 billion euro of additional tax revenues have been identified through voluntary disclosure and tax investigations since the automatic exchange of information was agreed. In 2018, information on 47 million financial accounts with a total value of around 4.9 trillion euro was exchanged. However, a significant number of MICs are not part of these efforts. A new Toolkit for Becoming a Party to the Convention on Mutual Administrative Assistance in Tax Matters can help more of these countries fast track their participation to increase transparency and cooperation in tax matters (OECD, 2020). Increased political commitment is needed, alongside continued investment and support in technical capacities, for MICs to fully realize the potential of information exchange.

Second, the OECD and G20 initiated the Base Erosion and Profit Shifting (BEPS) initiative to address MNE tax avoidance strategies that exploit gaps and mismatches in tax rules. The Inclusive Framework on BEPS brings together over 130 countries to build common ground and implement legal instruments to fight tax avoidance. Moreover, tools and legal instruments are complemented by increased capacity building support. For example, Tax Inspectors Without Borders (TIWB), a joint OECD/UNDP initiative, facilitates the provision of experts to work with developing country tax administrations on real-time live audits. Around half a billion dollars in increased revenues have been raised as a result of TIWB programmes so far.

Third, there is a recognition that further reforms to the international tax system are needed. With the move to the digital age, for example, it has become clear that the existing approach to taxing multinationals requires updating. There has been a wide range of proposals made in response to this challenge, including from less traditional sources. One example is the proposal from the Independent Commission for the Reform of International Corporate Taxation (Ocampo, 2019), another one is the "Significant Economic Presence" or the "Marketing Intangibles and the "User Participation" proposals (OECD, 2019i).

MICs should use their existing seats at the table to make sure their needs are incorporated in upcoming reforms, with the focus on two main aspects. First, a focus on the allocation of taxing rights between jurisdictions should consider various proposals for new profit allocation and nexus rules that would enable multinationals' economic activity in a country to be taxed, even if there was no physical presence. Second, a focus on the establishment of an effective minimum corporate tax at the global level. This pillar should seek to develop rules that would provide jurisdictions with a right to "tax back" where other jurisdictions have not exercised their primary taxing rights or the payment is otherwise subject to low levels of effective taxation (OECD, 2019e).

The above initiatives show that international tax cooperation has already increased. However, there is still a long way to go. Looking ahead, international cooperation will continue to be essential for upgrading and creating instruments to face the challenges of an increased interconnected economy, including through the digital transformation. Middle-income countries have much to gain from this conversation if they take an active role in the debate and contribute to building an inclusive cooperation system. In other words, they not only need a seat at the table but they also need to make full and appropriate use of these spaces.

6.5 Conclusions

As a growing economic force, middle-income countries hold untapped potential, waiting to be unleashed. However, difficulties arise as these countries find themselves trapped between this potential and their remaining vulnerabilities. A general "geography of discontent" is taking shape as a response to the unmet demands of growing middle classes.

MICs should boost domestic resource mobilization and improve the quality of spending. However, given the complexity of the current context, these solutions can only be delivered by building on new national development strategies. Those strategies should be designed and implemented in ways that engage citizens in institutionalized democratic deliberation processes that provide spaces for local experimentation. In fact, achieving a step change in public revenues requires a new social contract that is engaging and inclusive. If achieved, such a contract could produce self-reinforcing improvements in tax morale, public investments, and public services.

For putting all these efforts in place, strengthening the capacities of MICs' governments is essential. To this end, MICs should make full use of the benefits of international cooperation, in particular on strategy building and on the mobilization of domestic resources.

6.6 Acknowledgments

The author wishes to thank several colleagues in particular who contributed greatly to the drafting of this chapter, including Adriana Caicedo, Rita Da Costa, Jason Gagnon, Sebastian Nieto-Parra, and Alexander Pick from the OECD Development Centre. Ben Dickinson and Joseph Stead from the Centre on Tax Policy and Administration provided constructive feedback and comments that enriched the document. The editing process by Elizabeth Holbourne from the OECD Development Centre was also fundamental for the final outcome.

References

AU/ECA (2015): Report of the High Level Panel on Illicit Financial Flows from Africa commissioned by the AU/ECA Conference of Ministers of Finance, Planning and Economic Development.

Barreix, A. et al. (2017): "Updating of equivalent fiscal pressure in Latin America and the Caribbean," Discussion Paper N° IDB-DP-548, https://publications.iadb.org/en/updating-equivalent-fiscal-pressure-latin-america-and-caribbean

BID (2017): "Revisando el impuesto a la renta personal en América Latina, Evolución e impacto, Banco Interamericano de Desarrollo," https://publications.iadb.org/publications/spanish/document/Revisando-el-impuesto-a-la-renta-personal-en-Am%C3%A9rica-Latina-Evoluci%C3%B3n-e-impacto.pdf

CABRI (2013): Performance and programme-based budgeting in Africa: A status report 2013, Collaborative African Budget Reform Initiative.

Chimhowu, A.O., Hulme, D., and Munro, L. T. (2019): "The 'New' national development planning and global development goals: Processes and partnerships," *World Development* 120: 76–89.

Crivelli, E., de Mooij, R., and Keen, M. (2015): "Base Erosion, Profit Shifting and Developing Countries," International Monetary Fund, Working Paper, WP/15/118.

Dayton-Johnson, J., Londoño, J., and Nieto Parra, S. (2011): "The process of reform in Latin America: A review essay," OECD Development Centre Working Paper, No. 304, Paris: OECD Publishing, https://doi.org/10.1787/5kg3mkvfcjxv-en

Di John, Jonathan (2006): *The Political Economy of Taxation and Tax Reform in Developing Countries*, United Nations University, UNU-WIDER World Institute for Development Economic Research, ISBN 92-9190-852-5

Dorf, M. and Sabel, C. (2009): "De la constitution de l'experimentalisme démocratique," *Cahiers Philosophiques*, n.119, October.

ECLAC (2016): "Tax Evasion in Latin America Totals $340 Billion Dollars and Represents 6.7% of Regional GDP," Article, https://www.cepal.org/en/news/tax-evasion-latin-america-totals-340-billion-dollars-and-represents-67-regional-gdp

ECLAC/OCDE (2018): *Emerging Challenges and Shifting Paradigms: New perspectives on international cooperation for development*, Santiago: ECLAC.

Gallup (2018): "World Gallup Poll, Gallup Analytics," https://ga.gallup.com/, accessed December 12, 2019.

Global Financial Integrity (2015): "Illicit Financial Flows from Developing Countries: 2004–2013," https://www.gfintegrity.org/wp-content/uploads/2015/12/IFF-Update_2015-Final-1.pdf

IDB (2018): *Better Spending for Better Lives, Development in the Americas*, Washington, DC: Inter-American Development Bank.

IMF (2016): *Managing Government Compensation and Employment—Institutions, Policies, and Reform Challenges*, Washington, DC: International Monetary Fund, http://www.imf.org/external/pp/ppindex.aspx

Johannesen, N., Torslov, T., and Wier, L. (2018): "Are less developed countries more exposed to multinational tax avoidance? Method and evidence from micro-data," University of Copenhagen.

Kharas, H. and Hamel, K. (2018): "A global tipping point: Half the world is now middle class or wealthier," Brookings Institute, https://www.brookings.edu/blog/future-development/2018/09/27/a-global-tipping-point-half-the-world-is-now-middle-class-or-wealthier/, accessed October 24, 2019.

Kharas, H., Prizzon, A., and Rogerson, A. (2014): *Financing the post-2015 Sustainable Development Goals, A rough roadmap*, London: Overseas Development Institute.

Lustig, N. (2017): "Commitment to Equity Handbook: A Guide to Estimating the Impact of Fiscal Policy on Inequality and Poverty," Department of Economics, Tulane University, New Orleans.

Ocampo, J. A. (2019): "International Tax emergency, A critical time for developing nations to speak up!," *Common Dreams*, https://www.commondreams.org/views/2019/10/21/international-tax-emergency-critical-time-developing-nations-speak, accessed October 28, 2019.

OECD (2010): *Latin American Economic Outlook 2011: How Middle-Class Is Latin America?* Paris: OECD Publishing. http://dx.doi.org/leo-2011-en

OECD (2014): "An outlook on ODA graduation in the post-2015 era," External financing for Development, https://www.oecd.org/dac/financing-sustainable-development/ODA-graduation.pdf

OECD (2014a): *Illicit Financial Flows from Developing Countries: Measuring OECD Responses*, Paris: OECD Publishing. https://www.oecd.org/corruption/Illicit_Financial_Flows_from_Developing_Countries.pdf

OECD (2015): "Recommendation of the Council on Budgetary Governance, Public governance and Territorial Development Directorate," https://www.oecd.org/gov/budgeting/Recommendation-of-the-Council-on-Budgetary-Governance.pdf

OECD (2016): *Government at a Glance: Latin America and the Caribbean 2017*, Paris: OECD Publishing, https://doi.org/10.1787/9789264265554-en.

OECD (2017): "Pensions at a Glance 2017: OECD and G20 Indicators," Paris: OECD Publishing. http://dx.doi.org/10.1787/pension_glance-2017-en

OECD (2018): "OECD Social Expenditure database (SOCX)," https://www.oecd.org/social/expenditure.htm

OECD (2018a): *Perspectives on Global Development 2019: Rethinking Development Strategies*, Perspectives on Global Development, Paris: OECD Publishing. https://doi.org/10.1787/persp_glob_dev-2019-en

OECD (2018b): "OECD Best Practices for Performance Budgeting," Public Governance Committee Working Party of Senior Budget Officials

OECD (2018c): *Revenue Statistics 2018*, Paris: OECD Publishing, https://doi.org/10.1787/rev_stats-2018-en

OECD (2019): "Development finance of countries beyond the DAC," accessed September 15, 2019, https://www.oecd.org/dac/stats/non-dac-reporting.htm

OECD (2019a): "Development aid drops in 2018, especially to neediest countries," http://www.oecd.org/development/development-aid-drops-in-2018-especially-to-neediest-countries.htm, accessed September 19, 2019.

OECD et al. (2019b): *Latin American Economic Outlook 2019: Development in Transition*, Paris: OECD Publishing, https://doi.org/10.1787/g2g9ff18-en

OECD, et al. (2019c): *Revenue Statistics in Latin America and the Caribbean 2019*, Paris: OECD Publishing. https://doi.org/10.1787/25666b8d-en-es

OECD (2019d): "Tax Transparency in Africa, Africa Initiative Progress Report 2018," https://www.oecd.org/tax/transparency/Tax-transparency-in-Africa-2018-progress-report.pdf

OECD (2019e): "OECD invites public input on the Secretariat Proposal for a 'Unified Approach'," under Pillar One, accessed 12 March, 2019.

OECD (2019g): *Tax Morale: What Drives People and Businesses to Pay Tax?*, Paris: OECD Publishing, https://doi.org/10.1787/f3d8ea10-en

OECD (2019h): *Multi-dimensional Review of Peru: Volume 3. From Analysis to Action*, OECD Development Pathways, Paris: OECD Publishing, https://doi.org/10.1787/c6c23d2c-en

OECD (2019i): "Addressing the Tax Challenges of the Digitalisation of the Economy," Public Consultation Document, Base Erosion and Profit Shifting Project, February 13–March 6, 2019, https://www.oecd.org/tax/beps/public-consultation-document-addressing-the-tax-challenges-of-the-digitalisation-of-the-economy.pdf

OECD (2020): *A Toolkit for Becoming a Party to the Convention on Mutual Administrative Assistance in Tax Matters*, Global Forum on Transparency and Exchange of Information for Tax Purposes http://www.oecd.org/tax/transparency/documents/MAAC-toolkit_en.pdf

OECD (forthcoming): "Civil service pension reform in developing countries: Experiences and lessons," OECD Development Centre.

OECD/ATAF/AUC (2019): Revenue Statistics in Africa 2019: 1990–2017, Paris: OECD Publishing, https://doi.org/10.1787/5daa24c1-en-fr

OECD/CAF/ECLAC (2018): *Latin American Economic Outlook 2018: Rethinking Institutions for Developm*ent, Paris: OECD Publishing. http://dx.doi.org/10.1787/leo-2018-en

OECD/ECLAC/CIAT/IDB (2018): "Revenue Statistics in Latin America and the Caribbean 2018," http://oe.cd/revenue-statistics-in-latin-america-and-the-caribbean

OECD/ILO (2019): "Tackling Vulnerability in the Informal Economy, Development Centre Studies," Paris: OECD Publishing, https://doi.org/10.1787/939b7bcd-en

Oxfam (2018): "Democracias capturadas: El gobierno de unos pocos. Mecanismos de captura de la política fiscal por parte de las élites y su impacto en la desigualdad en América Latina y el Caribe (1990–2017)", Oxford: Oxfam international, DOI 10.21201/2018.3521.

Torslov, T., Wier, L., and Zucman, G. (2018): "The missing profits of nations," NBER Working Paper No. 24701, June 2018.

Vegh, Carlos A. (2015): *Fiscal policy in emerging markets: Procyclicality and graduation*, NBER Reporter, Cambridge, MA: National Bureau of Economic Research (NBER), Iss. 4, pp. 8–12.

Vegh, Carlos A. et al. (2018): *Fiscal adjustment in Latin America and the Caribbean: short-run pain, long-run gain?* Semi-annual report (English). Washington, DC: World Bank Group, http://documents.worldbank.org/curated/en/458171524828617033/Fiscal-adjustment-in-Latin-America-and-the-Caribbean-short-run-pain-long-run-gain-semiannual-report

World Bank (2019): "World Bank County Lending Groups," https://datahelpdesk.worldbank.org/knowledgebase/articles/906519-world-bank%20country-and-lending-groups

Zucman, G. (2014): "Taxing across Borders: Tracking Personal Wealth and Corporate Profits," *Journal of Economic Perspectives* 28, no. 4: 121–48.

7

Is There New Capacity for Redistribution to End Poverty in MICs?

Christopher Hoy and Andy Sumner

7.1 Introduction

Amartya Sen's (1981) famous study of famines found that people died not because of a lack of food availability in a country but because some people lacked entitlements to that food. Is a similar situation now the case for global poverty, meaning that national resources are available but are not being used to end poverty? This chapter argues that up to three-fourths of global poverty, at least at the extreme poverty line of $1.90 a day and even at $5 a day, could now be eliminated—in principle—via the redistribution of nationally available resources.

To be clear at the outset: our purpose in this chapter is to demonstrate the *potential* fiscal space that many MICs have for tackling poverty even if that fiscal space is effectively "locked" by domestic political economy (eg, the highly regressive petrol subsidies that favor richer parts of society disproportionately and who will not willingly lose that cheap petrol). Furthermore, we are not proposing the reduction of development cooperation to MICs because of this potential fiscal space as the financing needs of MICs remain very substantial and way beyond the costs of ending absolute poverty even up to $5 per day. Our core argument is that if the resources exist in principle to end poverty then the causes of poverty, as per Sen's argument, are shifting towards questions of entitlement and political economy in MICs and the wider, possibly universal, funding of social policy measures is becoming increasingly plausible though dependent on domestic political economy and entitlements of poorer groups (see discussion of Martínez Franzoni and Sánchez-Ancochea, Chapter 8 in this collection).

The United Nations and member states have committed to ending poverty by 2030 in "all its forms" including monetary and other dimensions. This chapter makes conservative estimates of the capacity for national redistribution in the form of new taxes or the reallocation of public spending towards cash transfers to the poor. We focus on two global poverty lines to do this: at $1.90 (the World Bank's "extreme" global poverty line used in the Sustainable development Goals

Christopher Hoy and Andy Sumner, *Is There New Capacity for Redistribution to End Poverty in MICs?* In: *Trapped in the Middle? Developmental Challenges for Middle-Income Countries*. Edited by: José Antonio Alonso and José Antonio Ocampo, Oxford University Press (2020). © OUP. DOI: 10.1093/oso/9780198852773.003.0007

(SDGs)) and $5 (the median national poverty line of all countries) (see for discussion Hoy and Sumner, 2016).

Once the poverty line is set (with all the debates on the endeavor duly noted—see Jolliffe and Prydz, 2015, 2016; Lahoti and Reddy, 2015 as well as Ravallion, 2008; Reddy and Pogge, 2002, 2005), ending monetary poverty is a matter of either: a certain amount of economic growth—meaning output and consumption growth to achieve a household consumption per capita where no one is below the poverty line set OR a certain amount of redistribution from those above the chosen poverty line to those below it OR a mix of these (plus administrative costs of the transfers program, though most developing countries now have some kind of cash transfer program established). We focus in this chapter on the national capacity to redistribute.

We find that up to three-fourths of global poverty at the $1.90 per day poverty line and even three-fourths of global poverty at $5 per day could be eliminated with some form of nationally funded redistribution in the form of a reallocation of public finances and/or new taxes. We argue that our findings imply a rationale for a stronger consideration of some national redistribution for purely instrumental reasons: to end global poverty more quickly that waiting for growth.

The intended contribution of this chapter is as follows: First, we discuss some of the location of global poverty at the two poverty lines using (2011 purchasing power parity (PPP)) PovcalNet data.[1] It is often assumed that the severity of poverty is less acute in better-off developing countries, meaning MICs rather than in the world's poorest countries which may be labelled crudely as low-income countries (LICs) or least developed countries (LDCs). We find that the relationship between poverty severity and average consumption per capita is far from linear. Many countries that are unambiguously MICs and many upper middle-income countries (UMICs), have poverty severity, at various poverty lines, comparable to the very poorest countries, despite much higher gross national income (GNI) Atlas per capita (the basis of the World Bank country income classification) than the poorest countries. Conversely, poverty severity in some of the poorest countries is not uniformly high at any given poverty line.

Second, we consider the national capacity to end global poverty via redistribution in two forms. First, in terms of new taxation. We rerun with updated data the estimates of Ravallion's (2009) marginal tax rates (MTRs) to end poverty. Ravallion showed that only a small number of developing countries had the capacity for redistribution based on data from around the mid-2000s. We find that many more developing countries have emerging capacity. We also consider the reallocation of two illustrative public "bads." Specifically, regressive fossil-fuel subsidies (see discussion in Sumner, 2016a, 2016b and similar estimates at the

[1] This version of PovCal is October 2015.

$1.90 per day poverty line) which are an aspect of fiscal policy that is unequivocally pro-rich and something we have termed "surplus" military spending. We define "surplus" military spending relative to a country's neighbors. First, we identify the lowest military spending per capita of each region. Then we define "surplus" as that military spending a country makes above the lowest spend per capita of a country in the same region.

We appreciate that reducing military spending to this level may seem radical to some, as no doubt would the reallocation of fossil fuel subsidies away from cheap petrol. However, our estimates of the impact of such changes in fiscal policy show what is at stake—the end of three-fourths of global poverty—and our estimates are *deliberately* conservative for a number of reasons we outline. Our intention is not to annoy those who enjoy cheap petrol, for example, but to illustrate the resources now nationally available to governments and the implied *opportunity costs in terms of poverty*. We include a number of caveats on each of these estimates of reallocation of public finances. The reallocation of either spending would not be easily achieved, of course, given the political economy of fiscal policy. The argument we are seeking to sustain is that it is generally assumed that most or all developing countries have insufficient domestic capacity to raise taxes or reallocate public spending to address fully the aggregate poverty gap. We find that on average this is no longer the case: Much of the total poverty gap in MICs at the $1.90 poverty line, and potentially at $5 per day, could be addressed by national redistribution. However, above this level (which is required for a permanent escape from poverty), only a small share of the total poverty gap could be covered (see Hoy and Sumner, 2016). In short, most developing countries have the financial capacity to end poverty at the global poverty line of $1.90 and potentially $5 per day but not beyond this.

The chapter is structured as follows: Section 7.2 outlines the characteristics of global poverty. Section 7.3 makes new estimates of the national capacity to redistribute via new taxes and public finance reallocation. Section 7.4 concludes.

7.2 Global Poverty

7.2.1 The Location of Poverty

Approximately, 70 percent of global poverty is located in MICs—despite predictions of its evaporation over the last decade—and the majority of global poverty is likely to remain in MICs to 2030 and beyond. (See projections of Edward and Sumner, 2014; 2015 and for a range of discussions on poverty in MICs: Alkire et al., 2011, 2015a, 2015b; Alonso 2012; Alonso et al., 2014; Carbone, 2013; Clarke and Feeny, 2011; Edward and Sumner, 2014; Glennie, 2011; Haddad, 2012, 2014; Herbert, 2012; Kanbur and Sumner, 2012; Keeley, 2012; Koch, 2015;

Table 7.1 Global poverty and estimates of the mean consumption of the poor in countries which account for more than 1 percent of the global poverty headcount at $1.90, 2012

	$1.90 per day		$5 per day	
MICs with more than 1% of global poverty	% of total global poverty headcount	Mean consumption of poor	% of total global poverty headcount	Mean consumption of poor
Bangladesh	6.7	–	4.5	—
Brazil	1.1	$0.87	1.3	$3.00
China	10.2	$1.50	17.2	$3.13
India	26.9	$1.53	32.6	$2.72
Indonesia	3.4	$1.59	5.5	$2.90
Kenya	1.3	$1.27	1.0	$2.48
Nigeria	10.2	$1.14	4.9	$1.91
Pakistan	1.4	$1.63	4.5	$3.10
Philippines	1.5	$1.50	1.9	$2.86
South Africa	0.9	$1.34	0.9	$2.64
Zambia	1.0	$0.99	0.4	$1.59
Income groups				
LIC	26.8	$1.19	14.0	$1.98
LMIC	58.5	$1.34	62.4	$2.85
LMIC minus India	31.6	$1.33	29.7	$2.85
UMIC	14.6	$1.24	23.6	$3.36
UMIC minus China	4.4	$1.24	6.5	$3.37
All developing countries	100.0	$1.27	100.0	$2.91

Note: The full data are not available for Bangladesh in 2011 PPP but estimates are made in PovcalNet of headcounts at different poverty lines.

Source: Authors' estimates based on data from World Bank (2015).

Lundsgaarde, 2012; Madrueño-Aguilar, 2015; Ottersen et al. 2014; Poke and Whitman, 2011; Sumner, 2010, 2012; Sumner and Mallet, 2013; Tezanos and Sumner, 2013, 2016.)

Table 7.1 shows the MICs that each account for more than 1 percent of global poverty at the extreme poverty line ($1.90 per day). These countries (Bangladesh, Brazil, China, India, Indonesia, Kenya, Nigeria, Pakistan, the Philippines, South Africa, and Zambia) alone account for close to 60 percent of the world's poor at $1.90 and over 70 percent at the higher line of $5 per day.

This table also shows the mean consumption of those in poverty for each poverty line. A very clear pattern exists that there is only a relatively small difference between the average for LICs and MICs at the $1.90 per day lines. In contrast, there is quite a significant difference at the $5 line. We find that the average (mean) poor person living on under $1.90-per-day in Brazil is actually worse off than in the DRC. And the average poor person (under $1.90) in Ethiopia is only slightly worse off ($1.40) than the average poor person in China ($1.50) or India ($1.53), and the average poor person in Ethiopia is better off than the average poor person in South Africa ($1.34). On average the $1.90 poor in LICs consume almost the same as the poor in UMICs ($1.19 versus $1.24).

7.2.2 The Severity of Poverty

Discussion of the mean consumption of the poor raises the question of poverty severity (by which we mean how far the average person living in poverty is below the poverty line) and how this differs at different levels of average national income and consumption. It is often thought that poverty severity is far worse in poorer countries (taking national average income or consumption per capita). It is often also assumed that the severity of poverty is less acute in better off developing countries, which might be labeled crudely as MICs, than in the world's poorest countries, which may be labeled crudely as low-income or least developed countries. We find, however, that the relationship between poverty severity and income per capita is far from linear. Many MICs have poverty severity comparable to the poorest countries despite having much higher GNI per capita than the poorest countries. Conversely, poverty severity in some of the poorest countries is not uniformly high. Figures 7.1 and 7.2 show the average consumption of people living in poverty (y-axis) versus the average consumption for the whole population in a country (x-axis). Eight countries are labeled as they have at least 2 percent of

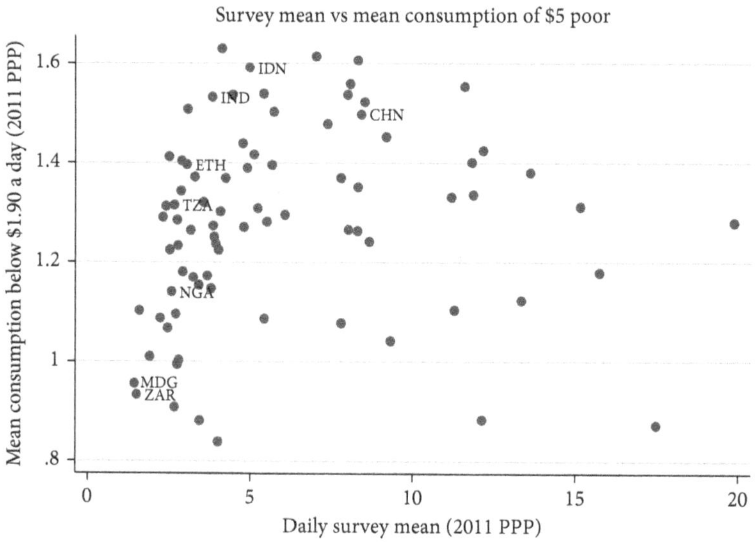

Figure 7.1 Poverty severity at $1.90-per-day compared to the mean survey consumption

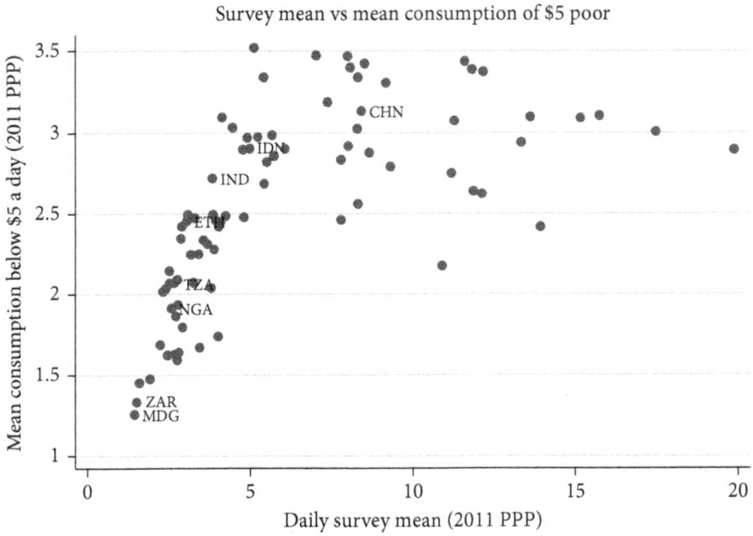

Figure 7.2 Poverty severity at $5-per-day compared to the mean survey consumption

Source: Authors' estimates processed from World Bank (2015, 2016).

the total share of world poverty (at $1.90). At the lower poverty line of $1.90 it is the case that poverty severity has little discernible relationship with average consumption. In contrast at $5 poverty severity has a clearer relationship with average consumption, whereby at higher average consumption levels poverty severity is lower. These are, of course, cross-sectional data but they have some important implications. On average, a person living in $1.90 poverty has a similar standard of deprivation in both low- and middle-income countries. In other words, people living in extreme poverty have similar levels of consumption regardless of the country they are in.[2] However, if a higher poverty line of say $5 is used, then one would find that a higher level of average poverty severity exists in poorer countries (see Figure 7.2). We next consider the end of poverty for both the $1.90 and $5 a day poverty line.

7.3 National Capacities for Redistribution to end poverty

7.3.1 Methodology

In this section we discuss the national capacity to redistribute via taxes and public finance reallocation towards cash transfers to the poor, to fill the total poverty gap in each country. As recently as the early to mid-2000s, estimates of redistributive

[2] This is the case even though LICs tend to have a much higher share of their population living in extreme poverty than MICs.

capacity suggested that the national capacity for redistribution was limited and would not cover the poverty gap unless the marginal tax rates (MTRs) on the "rich" were exorbitant for most developing countries. Ravallion (2009), taking survey data for the early to mid-2000s produced estimates for the $1.25 and $2 poverty gap (in 2005 PPP) and the taxation necessary to cover it. Ravallion estimated the MTRs for the "rich" (which he defined as those earning more than $13 per day in 2005 PPP which was based on an estimate of the US poverty line) that are required in order to end poverty in each country. He argued that MTRs over 60 percent would be prohibitive. While the MTRs needed to end poverty were less than 10 percent in many of the UMICs, in many LMICs they were much higher (see for estimates, Ravallion, 2009: 30–2).

We update these estimates using the latest data, which include almost another decade of growth in consumption, and thus a shrinking poverty gap and rising numbers in the "taxable" group. We replicate Ravallion's (2009) analysis estimating the US poverty line updated to $15 per day in 2011 PPP. Consistent with Ravallion (2009), we sourced the US Poverty line for a family of four from the US Department of Health and Human Services. This is the equivalent of $15.31 a day per person in 2011 dollars. We also use the $10-per-day "security-from-poverty" line (see López-Calva and Ortiz-Juarez, 2014). As above, we sourced data about poverty levels from PovcalNET (October 2015 Update).

An alternative to new taxes, given that new taxes tend to be unpopular, would be to reallocate public finances towards poverty transfers (eg, conditional or unconditional cash transfers). This raises the question of whether there are areas of public spending that might be reallocated from what might be labeled as a "public bad" (as opposed to a public good) to cash transfers to the poor. Here we take two areas purely for indicative assessments. The first is regressive fossil-fuel subsidies (see Sumner, 2016a; 2016b for further discussion). The second is what we have labeled "surplus" military spending (see Section 7.1). We use the following formulae to estimate the required marginal taxation on the "rich" and the reallocation of "surplus" military spending:

Marginal Tax Rate on the "Rich"

$$\text{Marginal Tax Rate} = \frac{PG_p PL_p}{SM - (1 - PG_R) PL_R}$$

Whereby:
PL_P = Poor Poverty Line
PL_R = 'Rich' Poverty Line
PG_P = Poor Poverty Gap
PG_R = 'Rich' Poverty Gap
SM = Survey Mean

"Surplus" Military Spending

$$\text{“Surplus” Military Spending (as a share of GDP)} = \frac{MS_{pc} - LMS_{pc}}{GDP_{pc}}$$

Whereby:
MSpc = Military Spending per capita (2011 PPP)
LMSpc = Lowest Military Spending per capita (2011 PPP)
GDPpc = GDP per capita (2011 PPP)
Note: Military Spending was converted from current $US to 2011 PPP using a price level ratio PPP conversion factor available in World Bank (2016).

Fossil Fuel Subsidies

Fossil fuel subsidies as a share of GDP were compared to the total poverty gap as a share of GDP in each country.

Clements et al. (2013) provide a data set on fossil-fuel subsidies by their components for each country.[3] Post-tax fossil-fuel subsidies in developing countries in 2011 amounted to $895 billion in current dollars (or almost two trillion in 2011 PPP dollars) (Clements et al., 2013). Such subsidies largely benefit the upper-middle classes and elite.[4] Some caveats are important to the estimates we make. First, that the calculations here are intended as indicative. Even though the cost of subsidies is conservatively estimated, oil prices fluctuate.[5] In years of higher energy prices relative to 2011 the estimates here will underestimate the poverty gap covered and vice versa. There are other methodological issues on the quantification of subsidies. Furthermore, the removal of the subsidies may raise transportation costs and thus prices of other goods such as food which may in turn impact on poverty. In short, the purpose of this exercise is solely to show that there are potentially sufficient public resources at *a national level*—in principle—to end much of global poverty. This is a relatively new phenomenon—that most countries may have the public resources to cover the poverty gap—even if their reallocation is not necessarily easy.

[3] Alternative estimates by Coady et al. (2015: 19) argue that the data in Clements et al. (2013) are too conservative and provide substantially higher estimates.

[4] Arze del Granado et al. (2012) in a sample of twenty developing countries during the 2005–09 period, including several of the LMICs such as Indonesia, Sri Lanka, India, and Ghana, find that, on average, the richest 20% of households gain six times more from such subsidies than the poorest 20% of households. The former capture, on average, 43% of the total subsidy value, the latter capture just 7%.

[5] Estimates of Clements et al. (2013: 42) take petroleum prices for 2000–11 and coal and natural gas prices for 2007–11. This would imply crude oil prices at an average of approximately $52/bbl; Coal at $92/mt, and natural gas at $6/mmbtu (bbl = barrel; mt = metric ton; mmbtu = one million British Thermal Units).

The second indicative estimate we make is with "surplus" military expenditure which as noted, we define as above the regional lowest per capita spend (see formulae). We recognize this will be contentious. There are of course other potential candidates (and thresholds). We take data from the Stockholm International Peace Research Institute (2016) which provides estimates for military spending. This includes all current and capital spending on: the armed forces, including peacekeeping forces; defence ministries and other government agencies engaged in defence projects; paramilitary forces, when judged to be trained and equipped for military operations; and military space activities. We estimate "surplus" military spending in developing countries in 2014 to be $792 billion in 2011 PPP. To reiterate, the estimates here are intended as indicative of resources now available.

The main limitation of our tax and reallocation estimates are that we assume no targeting and administrative costs (and of course there is the political economy of reallocating public spending noted). However, 57 developing countries already have conditional cash transfer programmes, and 114 developing countries had unconditional cash transfer schemes in 2014 (see data minus HICs in Honorati et al., 2015: 12). This would suggest that some of these issues are in hand. In addition, fuel subsidy programs of course come with substantial administrative costs that would be saved.

Furthermore, the estimates for reallocation of "surplus" military spending come with additional caveats which should not be forgotten. Unlike subsidies, military spending results in the actual production of goods and services, and is treated differently in national accounts for that reason. In other words, it is not a direct transfer though it is a form of public spending which could be spent differently on say cash transfers to the poor who would then most likely consume produced goods. Moreover, reducing military expenditure, like reducing fossil-fuel subsidies will have indirect impacts on the poor through, for example, reducing demand for small businesses, such as rural street food sellers, who sell food to soldiers.

We would argue though that our global estimates are conservative for several reasons (potentially with the exception of our definition of "surplus" military spending which of course can be contested as set too low). Our percentages only include in the numerator countries that can entirely eliminate the total poverty gap through redistribution. In other words, poverty reduction is only assumed to occur in countries where all poor people would be able to escape poverty through the redistribution. *As such, it is assumed that no reduction in poverty would occur in countries where redistribution would cover less than 100 percent of the total poverty gap. This dramatically underestimates the impact of redistribution on ending poverty.* However, we choose to present a conservative estimate that does not require assumptions to be made about which individuals living in poverty would receive the benefits from distribution and which would not. Finally, our combined estimates of taxation plus reallocation of fossil-fuel subsidies and "surplus" military spending only includes countries that can entirely eliminate the total poverty gap through a combination of the forms of redistribution. In other words, it includes countries whereby a combination of a tax on those living over the US poverty line (or over $10-per-day) and redistributing public spending on fossil-fuel subsidies and surplus military expenditure would cover the total poverty gap. For example, the additional tax could cover 40 percent of the total poverty gap and fossil-fuel subsidies plus surplus military spending could cover 60 percent, resulting in 100 percent of the total poverty gap covered.

7.3.2 The National Capacity for New Taxation

The findings are as follows. Figures 7.3 and 7.4 show the total poverty gap as a share of gross domestic product (GDP) using survey means in 2012. It is generally assumed that most or all developing countries have insufficient domestic capacity to raise taxes or reallocate public spending to fully address their aggregate poverty gap. We find that, in general, this is no longer the case at the $1.90 per day line as the total poverty gap represents less than 5 percent of GDP for all countries with mean per capita consumption above $3 a day. However, at the higher poverty line of $5, we find the average consumption per person is around twice as high before the aggregate poverty gap as a share of GDP falls below 5 percent. In short, most countries would need to find less than 5 percent of GDP

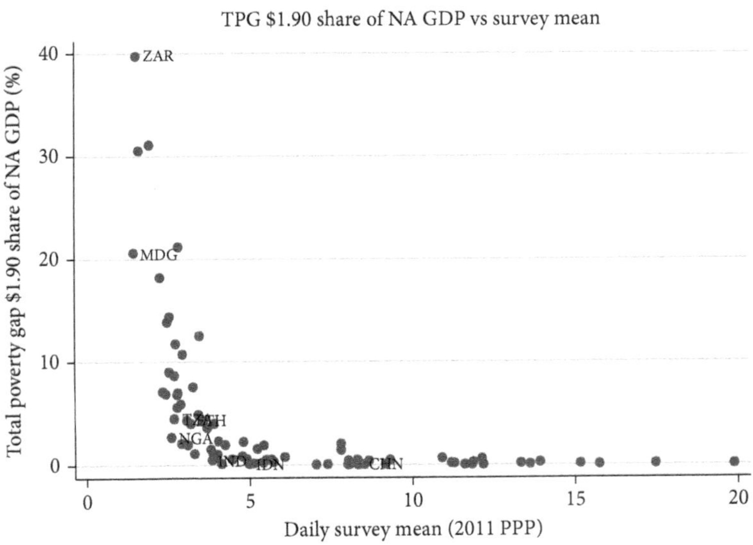

Figure 7.3 Total poverty gap at $1.90-per-day compared to the survey mean

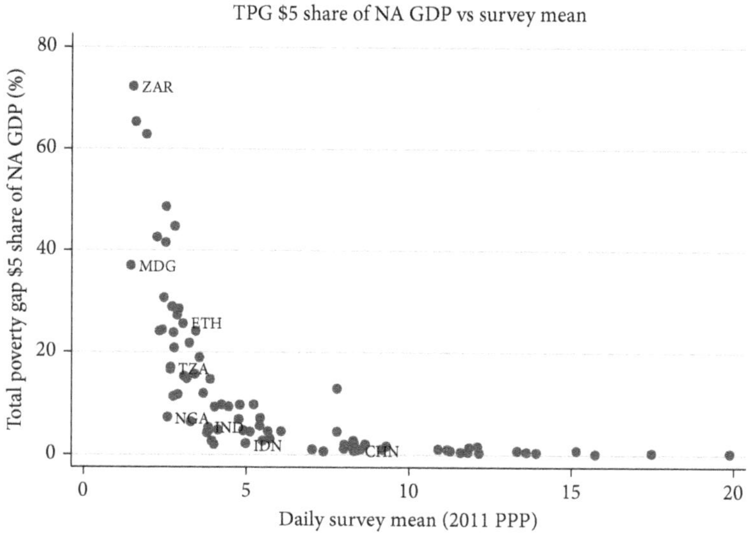

Figure 7.4 Total poverty gap at $5-per-day compared to the survey mean
Source: Authors' estimates based on data from World Bank (2015, 2016).

to dramatically speed up the end of poverty at the $1.90 line by closing the aggregate poverty gap through cash transfers; however, far fewer countries would be able to do so at a higher poverty line. The Section 7.3.3 discusses how these funds to close the aggregate poverty gap could be mobilized through new taxation and/or two examples of potential reallocation of public finances.[6]

If we take a closer look at the MTRs on those over the US poverty line and those over $10-per-day in the MICs where global poverty is focused (see Table 7.2), we find that the MTRs are far from prohibitive. For example, Brazil and China would only need at most an MTR on those groups above $10 or $15 per day of 1–2 percent to end $1.90 poverty, and Indonesia and the Philippines would need an MTR of about 6–10 percent to end $1.90 poverty. Pakistan and Kenya would need MTRs of 10–30 percent and India would need a 20–40 percent MTR. However, the remaining countries, Nigeria and Zambia, would need MTRs greater than 100 percent (ie, this is not possible without lowering people's income to below the threshold where the MTR starts to be implemented).

Could developing countries be classified by the capacity to end poverty rather than income or GDP per capita? Kanbur and Mukherjee (2007) outlined a means

[6] We find it tends to be the same countries that can afford redistribution using either new taxation or reallocation of fossil-fuel subsides or "surplus" military spending.

Table 7.2 Marginal tax rate (MTR) on those living above the US poverty line ($15/day) and over $10 per day to end poverty in countries which account for more than 1 percent of the global poverty headcount at $1.90, 2012

	MTR on people living above $15 a day		MTR on people living above $10 a day	
MICs	**$1.90 per day**	**$5 per day**	**$1.90 per day**	**$5 per day**
Brazil	0.64	5.58	0.49	4.26
China	2.30	65.19	1.25	35.45
India	38.95	>100	23.00	>100
Indonesia	10.61	>100	5.91	>100
Kenya	28.52	>100	18.64	>100
Nigeria	>100	>100	>100	>100
Pakistan	18.92	>100	8.84	>100
Philippines	10.66	>100	5.59	>100
South Africa	1.79	24.29	1.45	19.65
Zambia	>100	>100	>100	>100

Note: Data are not available for Bangladesh in 2011 PPP.

Source: Authors' estimates based on data from World Bank (2015, 2016).

of assessing the capacity to end poverty which we draw from.[7] We find in 2012 that countries cluster around four groups of ranges of MTRs to end poverty (based here on the $15 line of "taxable" population). There is one group of countries with MTRs of 200 percent or more to end poverty at $1.90 (see Table 7.3). Those groups correspond with an average survey consumption per capita in 2012 of approximately $1,000 per capita to end $1.90 poverty. Interestingly the corresponding GNI Atlas per capita lines (that are used in the World Bank's country income classification) for the upper limit of each MTR range are close to or not too far from the current low-income country upper threshold line ($1,045) at $965 (mean) and $675 (median) to end $1.90 poverty.

The average consumption per capita (survey mean) associated with the domestic capacity to end poverty, if that is defined as an MTR below 50 percent on those over $15 per day, are approximately $1,400 per capita to end $1.90 poverty. The corresponding GNI Atlas per capita upper limits on each MTR range are approximately $2,000 per capita to end $1.90 poverty. We do not classify countries based on the MTRs to end poverty at $5 a day. This is because most countries have MTRs well above 100 percent to end poverty at this line. For example, in Table 7.2 only three of the eleven MICs we examine have an MTR below 100 percent. All of the above would suggest that one could classify countries by their ability to end extreme poverty in terms of domestic taxation potential, though not the higher poverty line of $5-per-day.

[7] There is a wide ranging discussion on country classification (see Alonso, 2012; Fantom and Serajjudin, 2016; Kanbur and Sumner, 2012; Koch, 2015; Ottersen et al., 2014; Tezanos and Sumner, 2013, 2016).

Table 7.3 Country classifications based on capacity to end poverty by marginal tax rates on those above $15 (US poverty line) to end poverty at $1.90: Top of group threshold by survey means and GNI Atlas per capita, 2012

	$1.90 poverty			
	Survey Mean (2011 PPP)		GNI per capita (Atlas Method)	
MTRs	Mean	Median	Mean	Median
<5%	$5,147	$4,548	$8,069	$6,800
5–50%	$2,099	$1,974	$2,654	$1,813
50–200%	$1,371	$1,406	$2,281	$1,710
>200%	$936	$974	$965	$675

Note: Some countries do not have estimates because data were not available.
Source: Authors' estimates based on data from World Bank (2015, 2016).

7.3.3 The National Capacity to Reallocate Public Finances to Poverty

We focus once again on the countries that are home to much of global $1.90 poverty. Table 7.4 shows the estimates for the MICs with over 1 percent of global poverty of the reallocation of either the national fossil-fuel subsidy or "surplus" military spending. These estimates are without compensation for the poor for the loss of the subsidy, because earlier estimates for fossil-fuel coverage of the $1.90 poverty gaps at national level showed that this made little difference on national level estimates (see Sumner 2016a, 2016b).

Table 7.4 shows that the fossil-fuel subsidies alone would easily cover the $1.90 poverty gap in many of the MICs listed. Interestingly, in some of the large populous countries that dominate global poverty headcounts, such as India, China, Indonesia, and Pakistan, much or all of the $5 poverty gap might be covered by reallocation of the fossil-fuel subsidy. In a somewhat similar vein, the "surplus" military spending alone would cover all or most of the $1.90 poverty gap in China, India, Indonesia, Pakistan, and the Philippines. What is common, though, is that the reallocation of "surplus" military spending would not make much contribution to the $5 poverty gap.

Table 7.5 summarizes our estimates (and Table 7.6 shows the proportion of global poverty covered in the dataset). In terms of taxation we find that MTRs of 50 percent or less on those living above the US poverty line around the world or even those living on more than $10 per day would cover half of $1.90 poverty. However, if one were to reallocate fossil-fuel subsidies or "surplus" military spending (as we have defined), one might hope to fund cash transfers to cover 60–70 percent of global poverty at $1.90 or a third of global poverty at $5 poverty. If one adds together fossil-fuel subsidy reallocation and "surplus" military

Table 7.4 Fossil-fuel subsidy and "surplus" military spending coverage of total poverty gap (%), 2012

	Fossil-fuel subsidy coverage of total poverty gap		"Surplus" military spending coverage of total poverty gap		Total (fossil fuel subsidies plus "surplus" military spend) coverage of total poverty gap	
MICs	$1.90 per day	$5 per day	$1.90 per day	$5 per day	$1.90 per day	$5 per day
Brazil	177.01	53.67	1190.08	360.81	1367.09	414.48
China	4426.32	410.84	2473.61	229.60	6899.93	640.44
India	884.16	85.21	432.70	41.70	1316.86	126.91
Indonesia	3770.88	247.84	484.88	31.87	4255.76	279.71
Kenya	30.12	7.03	58.35	13.61	88.47	20.64
Nigeria	131.56	49.23	12.97	4.85	144.53	54.08
Pakistan	3936.46	127.02	1943.48	62.71	5879.94	189.73
Philippines	233.44	23.98	297.24	30.54	530.68	54.52
South Africa	1572.31	304.48	414.92	80.35	1987.23	384.83
Zambia	89.03	43.83	31.10	15.31	120.13	59.14
All developing countries	2411.64	186.76	826.31	89.52	3237.95	276.28

Note: Full data are not available for Bangladesh in 2011 PP.

Source: Authors' estimates based on data from World Bank (2015, 2016).

spending and tax on those over $10 or $15 per day, one could fund the end of much of poverty at not only $1.90- but potentially at $5-per-day too.

7.4 Conclusions

It is generally assumed that most or all developing countries have insufficient domestic capacity to raise taxes or reallocate public spending to address fully the aggregate poverty gap. The primary conclusion of this chapter is nuanced: much of global poverty at the poverty line of $1.90 per day (the World Bank extreme poverty line) and potentially higher poverty lines could now be ended via higher taxes on "richer" citizens and redistribution of national public expenditures currently allocated to regressive fossil-fuel subsidies and "surplus" military spending (defined as above the regional lowest per capita). In short, extreme poverty at least and potentially higher poverty lines are now much more of a matter of national inequality in MICs and thus domestic political economy as a national redistributive capacity to end poverty has emerged.

Table 7.5 Comparison of national capacity for redistribution to end global poverty at various poverty lines

Poverty Line	Percentage of global poverty eliminated by					
	Marginal tax rates of 50% or less on those living on $15/day or more	**Marginal tax rates of 50% or less on those living on $10/day or more**	**Reallocation of fossil-fuel subsidy to poverty transfers**	**Reallocation of surplus military spending to poverty transfers**	**Reallocation of fossil-fuel subsidies and surplus military plus new taxation on population living on over $15/day**	**Reallocation of fossil-fuel subsidies and surplus military plus new taxation on population living on over $10/day**
$1.90	50.47	52.39	69.08	59.38	74.98	76.95
$5	6.22	25.07	38.74	32.49	77.09	77.24

Notes: The total fraction of $5-per-day poverty that can be eliminated through a combination of the different types of redistributive policies (shown in columns 6 and 7) is far in excess of any of the policies individually (shown in columns 2 to 5). This is partly due to the fact we only count a country in the global total when poverty can be completely eliminated through redistribution. As such, in some countries any one of the redistributive policies eliminated most but not all $5-per-day poverty, whereas a combination of the policies completely eliminated poverty. In the case of the former they were not counted in the global poverty figures (shown in columns 2 to 5), but in the case of the latter they were (columns 6 and 7).

Source: Authors' estimates.

Table 7.6 Estimate of global poverty coverage in dataset used

Poverty line	$1.90	$5
Marginal tax rate on populations over $15/day and $10/day	92.92	94.91
Reallocation of fossil-fuel subsidies	89.35	92.17
Reallocation of "surplus" military spending	88.44	91.37

Notes: PovcalNet covers 92.4–95.5 percent of relevant population depending on poverty line; Ferreira et al. (2015) "fill" the remainder in global poverty estimates with regional averages (thus, for example, adding about 40m more $1.90 poor). Estimates in this table then take PovcalNet as 100 percent of global poverty on this basis and estimate additional gaps in our estimates.

Source: Authors' estimates.

7.5 Acknowledgment

Components of this chapter were published as C. Hoy and A. Sumner (2016): "Global Poverty and Inequality: Is There New Capacity for Redistribution in Developing Countries?" *Journal of Globalization and Development* 7 no. 1: 117–57. We would like to thank the editors, and the participants at the project workshop and two anonymous reviewers of an earlier version for their comments.

References

Aldenhoff, F. O. (2007): "Are economic forecasts of the International Monetary Fund politically biased? a public choice analysis," *Review of International Organization* 2, no. 3: 239–60.

Alkire, S., Roche, J., Santos, E., and Seth, S. (2011): *Multidimensional Poverty Index 2011*, Oxford: Oxford Poverty and Human Development Initiative (OPHI).

Alkire, S., Roche, J., Seth, S., and Sumner, A. (2015a): "Identifying the poorest people and groups: strategies using the Global Multidimensional Poverty Index," *Journal of International Development* 27, no. 3: 362–87.

Alkire, S., Roche, J., and Vas, A. (2015b): *Changes over Time in Multi-Dimensional Poverty: Methodology and Results for 34 Countries*, Oxford: Oxford Poverty and Human Development Initiative (OPHI).

Alonso, J. (2012): "From aid to global development policy," UNDESA Working Paper 121. New York: United Nations Department of Economic and Social Affairs (UNDESA).

Alonso, J., Cortez, A., and Klasen, S. (2014): "LDC and other country groupings: how useful are current approaches to classify countries in a more heterogeneous developing world?" UNDESA Working Paper. New York: United Nations Department of Economic and Social Affairs (UNDESA).

Arze del Granado, F. J., Coady, D., and Gillingham, R. (2012): "The unequal benefits of fuel subsidies: a review of evidence for developing countries," *World Development* 40, no. 11: 2234–48.

Carbone, M. (2013): "International development and the European Union's external policies: changing contexts, problematic nexuses, contested partnerships," *Cambridge Review of International Affairs* 26, no. 3: 483–96.

Clarke, M. and Feeny, S. (2011): "Old challenges and new opportunities for the MDGs: now and beyond 2015," *Journal of the Asia Pacific Economy* 16 (4): 509–19.

Clements, B., Coady, D., Fabrizio, S., Gupta, S., Alleyne, T., and Sdralevich, C. (2013): *Energy Subsidy Reform: Lessons and Implications*, Washington, DC: International Monetary Fund (IMF).

Coady, D., Parry, I., Sears, L., and Shang, B. (2015): "How Large Are Global Energy Subsidies?" IMF Working Paper. Washington DC: International Monetary Fund (IMF).

Edward, P. and Sumner, A. (2014): "Estimating the scale and geography of global poverty now and in the future: how much difference do method and assumptions make?" *World Development* 58: 67–82.

Edward, P. and Sumner, A. (2015): "New estimates of global poverty and inequality: how much difference do price data really make?" CGD Working Paper (and Data Set). Washington, DC: Centre for Global Development (CGD).

Fantom, N. and Serajjudin, U. (2016): "The World Bank's classification of countries by income," World Bank Policy Research Working Paper. Washington, DC: World Bank.

Ferreira, F. H. G., Chen, S., Dabalen, A., Dikhanov, Y., Hamadeh, N., Jolliffe, D. M., Narayan, A., Prydz, E. B., Revenga, A. L., Sangraula, P., Serajuddin, U., and Yoshida, N. (2015): "A global count of the extreme poor in 2012: data issues, methodology and initial results," World Bank Policy Research Working Paper. Washington, DC: World Bank.

Glennie, J. (2011): *The Role of Aid to Middle-Income Countries: A Contribution to Evolving EU Development Policy*. London: Overseas Development Institute.

Haddad, L. (2012): "Five assumptions of dominant thinking in international development," *Development* 55, no. 1: 34–44.

Haddad, L. (2014): "Equity: Not Only for Idealists," *Development Policy Review* 33, no. 1: 5–13.

Herbert, S. (2012): "Reassessing aid to middle-income countries: the implications of the European Commission's policy of differentiation for developing countries," ODI Working Paper. London: Overseas Development Institute (ODI).

Honorati, M., Gentilini, U., and Yemstov, R. (2015): *The State of Social Safety Nets 2015*. Washington, DC: World Bank.

Hoy, C. and Sumner, A. (2016): "Global poverty and inequality: is there new capacity for redistribution in developing countries?". *Journal of Globalization and Development* 7, no. 1: 117–57.

Jolliffe, D., and Prydz, E. (2015): "Global poverty goals and prices: how purchasing power parity matters," World Bank Policy Research Working Paper 7256. Washington, DC: World Bank.

Jolliffe, D., and Prydz, E. (2016): "Estimating international poverty lines from comparable national thresholds," World Bank Policy Research Working Paper 7606. Washington, DC: World Bank.

Kanbur, R. and Mukherjee, D. (2007): "Poverty, relative to the ability to eradicate: An index of poverty reduction failure,". *Economic Letters* 97, no. 1: 52–7.

Kanbur, R. and Sumner, A. (2012): "Poor countries or poor people? development assistance and the new geography of global poverty," *Journal of International Development* 24, no. 6: 686–95.

Keeley, B. (2012): *OECD Insights. From Aid to Development: The Global Fight Against Poverty*. Paris: Organisation for Economic Co-operation and Development (OECD).

Koch, S. (2015): "From poverty reduction to mutual interests? the debate on differentiation in EU development policy," *Development Policy Review* 33, no. 4: 479–502.

Lahoti, R. and Reddy, S. (2015): "$1.90: what does it say?" https://reddytoread.files.wordpress.com/2015/10/wbpovblogoct6final1.pdf.

López-Calva, Luis F. and Ortiz-Juarez, E. (2014): "A vulnerability approach to the definition of the middle class," *Journal of Economic Inequality* 12, no. 1: 23–47.

Lundsgaarde, E. (2012): *The Domestic Politics of Foreign Aid*, London: Routledge.

Madrueño-Aguilar, R. (2015): "Global income distribution and the middle-income strata: implications for the world development taxonomy debate." *European Journal of Development Research* doi:10.1057/ejdr.2015.61.

Ottersen, T., Kamath, A., Moon, S., andRøttingen, J. A. (2014): "Development Assistance for Health: Quantitative Allocation Criteria and Contribution Norms," Chatham House Working Paper. London: Chatham House.

Poke, N. and Whitman, J. (2011): "The Millennium Development Goals and development after 2015." *Third World Quarterly* 32, no. 1: 181–98.

Ravallion, M. (2008): "A Reply to Reddy and Pogge," In S. Anand, P. Segal, and J. Stiglitz (eds.), *Debates on the Measurement of Poverty*, Oxford: Oxford University Press, pp. 86–101.

Ravallion, M. (2009): "Do poorer countries have less capacity for redistribution?" PolicyResearch Working Paper 5046. Washington, DC: World Bank.

Reddy, S. and Pogge, T. (2002): "How not to count the poor (Version 3.0)." Mimeo. New York: Barnard College.

Reddy, S. and Pogge, T. (2005): "How not to count the poor (Version 6.2)." Mimeo. New York: Barnard College.

Sen, A. (1981): *Poverty and Famine: An Essay on Entitlement and Deprivation*. Oxford: Oxford University Press.

Sumner, A. (2010): "Global poverty and the new bottom billion: what if three-quarters of the world's poor live in middle-income countries?" Institute of Development Studies (IDS) Working Paper 349. Brighton: IDS.

Sumner, A. (2012): "Where do the Poor Live?" *World Development* 40, no. 5: 865–77.

Sumner, A. (2016a): *Global Poverty*. Oxford: Oxford University Press.

Sumner, A. (2016b): "Why are some people poor?" *European Journal of Development Research* 28: 130–42.

Sumner, A., and Mallet, R. (2013): *The Future of Foreign Aid*, Basingstoke: Palgrave Macmillan.

Tezanos, S. and Sumner, A. (2013): "Revisiting the meaning of development: a multidimensional taxonomy of developing countries," *Journal of Development Studies* 49, no. 12: 1728–45.

Tezanos, S. and Sumner, A. (2016): "Is the 'Developing World' Changing? A Dynamic and Multidimensional Taxonomy of Developing Countries," *European Journal of Development Research* 28, no. 5: 847–74.

World Bank. (2015): *PovcalNet (Oct 2015 update)*. Washington, DC: World BankFigure

World Bank. (2016): *World Development Indicators (Feb 2016 update)*. Washington, DC: World Bank.

8
Promoting Universal Social Policy in MICs

Juliana Martínez Franzoni and Diego Sánchez-Ancochea

8.1 Introduction

Reducing poverty levels, improving the distribution of income and improving people's capabilities are three key challenges of economic development. Many middle-income countries (MICs) have the state capacity and the resources needed to confront these challenges—as evident in Hoy and Sumner's discussion in chapter 7. Yet they have generally failed to meet these goals, failing to successfully provide healthcare, education, and income support to significant segments of the population. How can this problem be resolved? How should social benefits be provided in the MICs? Should services and transfers be for everyone or focus exclusively on the poor?

This chapter provides answers to these questions. Following our previous work and that of others, we argue that to be effective and successful, social policies should be universal, providing the whole population with similar, generous transfers and services (Martínez Franzoni and Sánchez-Ancochea, 2014a; Mkandawire, 2006a; Pribble, 2013). This will require active state intervention in funding, provision, and regulation. Universalism is likely to result in more resources spent on redistribution (Korpi and Palme, 1998), avoid the stigmatization of targeted approaches, increase the security of everyone in society, and—in many cases—contribute to more vibrant economies (Mkandawire, 2006b).

Yet delivering universal social policies in a development context is easier said than done. In the least developed countries, weak state capacity and insufficient revenues make it almost impossible. Universalism is more achievable in the MICs but, even there, informality, inequality, and power concentration have historically been insurmountable obstacles. How can we find credible paths to overcome these obstacles and move towards the goal of equitable social policies for all?

One recent popular response has been to propose a basic amount of benefits for all as a matter of rights, focusing initially on the poor. This approach was initially promoted by the International Labour Organization's Social Protection Floor, which aimed to provide a minimum level of healthcare, pensions, and other social rights to everyone. The accent here was on a *basic* guarantee, allowing public social security and markets to provide top-up services for those who can afford it.

Juliana Martínez Franzoni and Diego Sánchez-Ancochea, *Promoting Universal Social Policy in MICs* In: *Trapped in the Middle? Developmental Challenges for Middle-Income Countries.* Edited by: José Antonio Alonso and José Antonio Ocampo, Oxford University Press (2020). © OUP. DOI: 10.1093/oso/9780198852773.003.0008

This new approach has unquestionable strengths. By providing services as a matter of right, it can reduce stigma, encourage political engagement, and, under some circumstances, reduce social distance. By expanding the amount of resources available, it can highlight the importance of social policy. Yet their emphasis on *basic* benefits, the *de facto* role for markets concerning non-basic benefits and the lack of awareness of politics limits the positive impact of this policy approach. Vaccinating people but failing to treat them against cancer or providing a very low pension will not expand capabilities sufficiently. Providing unequal benefits for different citizens may not create much desired cross-class coalitions that support further expansions in the political process. At the end, there is a high risk that a large proportion of people in the MICs end up with inferior benefits.

We propose to take a step back and distinguish between what we want to achieve and how to achieve it. This requires separating the desired policy outputs (coverage, generosity, and equity of benefits) from the specific ways to secure them. To study the latter, we discuss the concept of the policy architecture: the combination of instruments that define what specific benefits are being offered, to whom, and how.

Choosing the desirable/feasible policy architecture—one that initially focuses on the poor or one that departs from other groups of the population as well—is both a technical and a political decision. When designing new architectures or reforming existing ones, policymakers must consider the incentives and constraints created in the long run. They should also be aware of the interactions between public and private arrangements and, more specifically, how the latter shapes the former.

The chapter does not offer a one-size-fits-all recipe, but a framework to think about universalism, particularly in the context of the MICs. Depending on pre-existing social programs, the quality of state institutions, the amount of resources available and the more or less unequal social structure, policymakers may opt for one policy architecture or another. In doing so, they should be aware that universal outputs can be secured through a combination of policy instruments; that creating opportunities for cross-class coalitions is important and, therefore, starting from the poor alone has significant risks and that thinking about long-term trajectories of change is essential.

We organize our argument in five sections. We start with a more detailed discussion of our framework, which separates between outputs and instruments. Section 8.3 further develops our definition of universalism, highlighting potential tradeoffs between the various dimensions it involves. Section 8.4 defines the concept of policy architecture and its influence in achieving pro-universal long-term trajectories. Recognizing that universal outputs will not be secured overnight, Section 8.5 explores trajectories that can contribute more or less towards positive results in the long run—whether a bottom-up strategy that starts from the poor or other alternatives that involve the non-poor from the onset. This chapter finishes with some analytical conclusions and policy recommendations, which further consider the role of politics and institutions.

8.2 Framework to Promote Universalism: Policy Outputs, Tools, and Trajectories

There is a growing consensus that universal policies can contribute to the expansion of people's capabilities both directly and indirectly. If people are to live the kind of lives they value, social rights must be guaranteed independently of people's resources and assets. Universal policies aim to secure these social rights for all regardless of income, occupational status, gendered relations, and the like. There is also growing evidence that many MICs have enough resources to implement these kinds of policies (see Hoy and Sumner, chapter 7, in this volume and also Ortíz et al., 2017).

But how can we promote universalism in social policy? This chapter offers a new framework to think about this challenge. Traditionally, the term universal has referred to a particular instrument to deliver social policies: programs that covered everyone as a matter of right with the same, generous benefits. For example, universal healthcare provides health services to all citizens in a society with general tax funding. Primary education is universal when it covers all children of a certain age free of charge.

Unfortunately, this definition conflates policy instruments and outputs—something that is particularly inappropriate in poor and unequal societies (Fischer, 2012). If the only road to offering a truly generous set of benefits for all is to rely on generous programs funded through general taxes, universalism becomes beyond reach for most MICs. As Jennifer Pribble argues for the Latin American case "the consolidation of such a welfare state is highly unlikely in the short-to-medium run" (Pribble, 2013: 8). There may simply be too many obstacles to secure tax-funded, citizenship-based, high quality programs in healthcare, pensions, or education in most developing countries. Yet it is pressing to look for ways to secure similar objectives through a diversity of instruments.

To do so, it is useful to separate the outputs that we want to achieve from the instruments to achieve them (see Figure 8.1). The main point is that there may be many different ways to provide benefits to the majority of the population using different policy instruments (social security, social assistance) and funding mechanisms (payroll taxes, general taxes, co-payments).

In clearly distinguishing between policy outputs and the specific ways in which those transfers and services are delivered, we join a previous body of knowledge. Our approach follows Jennifer Pribble's superb research on universal reforms in Chile and Uruguay—two of the most successful MICs in Latin America (Pribble,

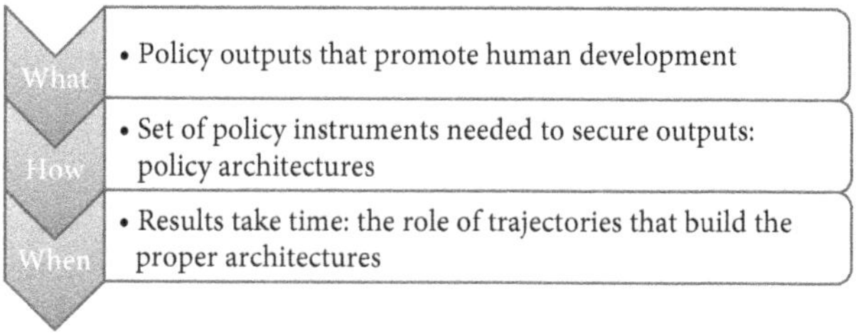

Figure 8.1 Distinguishing between outputs and instruments

2013). She avoids simplistic dichotomies (universalism vs. non-universalism) and focuses on the (gradual) process behind building expansionary welfare policies.

Andrew Fischer also moves away from oversimplifying dichotomies to distinguish degrees "towards stronger or weaker universalistic principles, along with their equalising or disequalising potentials, as well as the institutional obstacles potentially blocking such shifts" (Fischer, 2012: 12). His goals are similar to ours: to separate the definition of universalism from a specific historical experience, to establish the possibility of promoting universalism through different channels, and to consider different degrees.

Universal outputs do not automatically follow from explicit decisions to deliver them: even in developed countries, generous and equal benefits for all were neither created overnight nor can be easily assured today. Implementing new programs requires financial resources, new state capacities and coping with vetoes of different sorts. This is why the trajectories of change are important. As a recent research on universal healthcare explains, the road "often uses stepping stones. While some reforms create path dependence, others do not" (Cotlear et al., 2015: 6). Policymakers should make sure that the decisions they take today can create incentives (both financial and political) for further expansion in the future. Promoting universalism in the long run thus require thinking about trajectories of change as well and how they can overcome a diversity of obstacles.

8.3 Policy Outputs (the *What*): Trade-offs between Coverage, Generosity, and Equity

So what are universal policy outputs? In answering this question, it is useful to consider the objectives of the much-praised Scandinavian universal welfare regimes. They are characterized by a robust set of services available to everyone on the basis of citizenship principles and funded through general taxes. Rothstein (2008) contrasts this approach with liberal welfare regimes and with those where most benefits are concentrated in some privileged groups according to status. In doing so, he and other authors incorporate a strong normative thrust. Building on the Nordic experience, for example, Danson et al. are particularly clear that access to the same benefits in permanent—non-contingent—way is a social "right" (Danson et al. 2012: 3).

This approach to universalism in Scandinavian countries incorporates both specific instruments (citizenship-based services and transfers) and the set of outputs required to redistribute income and expand capabilities. These key outputs are full coverage of equal benefits for everyone. We are not the first to identify these features but we are probably the most emphatic on the need to distinguish outputs from instruments. Pribble (2013), for instance, focuses on coverage, quality of services, and the reduction of segmentation, but also includes transparency and financial sustainability—which we believe are more related to the instruments. Fischer (2012) includes three categories within universalism—access and coverage; costing and pricing; and financing—which also conflate policy outputs and policy instruments.

Social policies deliver universal outputs when they reach the entire population with similarly generous transfers and high-quality services. There are three dimensions involved: coverage, generosity (in level and quality), and equity. Few countries—at every stage of development—perform equally well on all three dimensions simultaneously. To illustrate this point, it is useful to compare the variety of non-contributory pensions across the world, considering both coverage and generosity. Although the analysis is incomplete—it does not evaluate equity for which we would need to include contributory pensions as well—it illustrates the way different countries deal with complex tradeoffs across dimensions of universalism.

Figure 8.2 presents data on coverage (measured by the percentage of the elderly population covered) and generosity (pension as a percentage of GDP per capita)

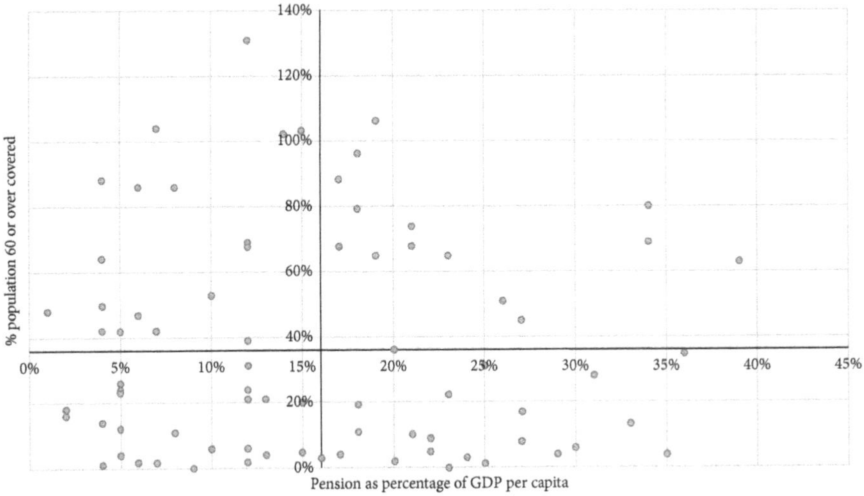

Figure 8.2 Non-contributory pensions across the world: Coverage vs. generosity
Source: Own elaboration with data from HelpAge (2015).

for non-contributory programs in eighty countries. The average for the sample is 36 percent and 16 percent, respectively, which we use to create four quadrants. There is no clear relationship between coverage and generosity, with countries located in all quadrants. Most of the best performing countries in both dimensions come from the OECD (eg, the Netherlands with 80 percent coverage and a pension that is a third of GDP per capita) but there are good performers among middle-income countries as well (eg, Lesotho and South Africa).

The weight that policymakers should place on coverage, equity, and generosity varies depending on policy realms and historical moments. For example, coverage in primary and secondary education has expanded rapidly across the world: the first has surpassed 80 percent of children in official school age in most of the world—with a large number of countries meeting the corresponding Millennium Development Goals (MDG). In recent decades, access to secondary education increased particularly fast in many MICs, which gradually converged towards the developed world.

Now dealing with quality concerns is much more urgent—and it is indispensable to improve equity as well. For example, almost half of Latin American students do not reach the minimum acceptable level of reading at age 15 compared to less than 20 percent in OECD countries. Regional disparities are also high: in Argentina, Mexico, and Panama, rural students lag more than one school year in terms of reading when compared to urban students (OECD, 2012). In Jordan and Tunisia, less than 35 percent of students at age 15 have basic competency in mathematics (Khrisnan et al., 2016). Lack of good teachers and poor infrastructure also contribute to high dropout rates (showing the connection between the dimensions of universalism): across the world 12 percent of children leave primary school and never complete (Murtin and Viarengo, 2013).

Much of the recent policy proposals revolve around coverage almost exclusively. For example, in referring to healthcare, Stuckler et al. argue that in developing countries universal healthcare is equivalent to universal healthcare *coverage* defined as "the existence of a legal mandate for universal access to health services and evidence that suggests the vast majority of the population has meaningful access to these services" (Stuckler et al., 2010: 2). A similar approach prevails in the post-MDGs agenda, which calls attention to a set of services the poor must receive as a matter of right. For example, the 2012 High Level Panel on Global Sustainability included "universal *access* to affordable sustainable energy" (Hoeven, 2012: 21, emphasis added).

Rights-based approaches to social policy share this accent on covering everyone with something, even if basic. For example, "basic universalism" is a notion put forward by Latin American scholars under the sponsorship of the Inter-American Development Bank in 2006. It refers to a set of essential benefits that governments should guarantee to everyone. The amount of benefits at a specific moment in time will depend on the state's fiscal capacity and the level of social and electoral support

(Molina, 2006). Essential transfers and services are those most capable of reducing inequality by redistributing present and future income: primary education, preventive medicine, and old-age monetary transfers. Targeting has a role to play in narrowing gaps and ensuring access and quality for all (Filgueira et al., 2006).

The basic social protection floor (SPF) shares a similar rationale of beginning by providing essential services and transfers for the poor. A commission led by Michelle Bachelet elaborated the proposal, defining SPF as "an integrated set of social policies designed to guarantee income security and access to essential social services for all, paying particular attention to vulnerable groups and protecting and empowering people across the life cycle" (Bachelet, 2011: 23). It initially included a range of social services such as healthcare, water and sanitation, education, food security, and housing, but its scope was narrowed to essential health and income security in the ILO Policy Recommendation 202. By 2012 it had gained the support of the United Nations, the World Bank, the G20, and many international non-governmental organizations (Deacon et al., 2013).

At some level, the SPF constitutes a significant departure from the previous minimalist approach based on compensatory measures in favor of the poor. The SPF sees social policy as a matter of right, calling for "the extension of social security that progressively ensures higher levels of social security to as many people as possible" (ILO, 2012: article 1b). Yet the approach is also rather contradictory. First, many of the interventions its proponents praise (like *Bolsa Familia* and other anti-poverty measures) are targeted at small segments of the population. Second, there is an accent on *basic* services and transfers, which may not expand capabilities sufficiently and be unattractive for the middle class. Third, while stressing the need for national adaptation, the SPF is generally unaware of political requirements.

Its accent on the "basic" and its limited attention to concrete political dynamics and path dependence—a problem basic universalism shares—is worrisome: it risks becoming a new way of targeting. Excessive accent on basic services for all can ultimately result in low quality services used only by those who cannot rely on private options. Moreover, if the SPF is not accompanied by strong regulation of private services, it could easily perpetuate fragmentation—a point to which we will return in Section 8.5.

8.4 Policy Architectures (the *How*): Constellation of Instruments that Deliver more or less Unification of Benefits

Delivering similar services for all may be desirable, but how likely is it in the MICs? The constraints are multiple and include weak taxing capacity and lack of political commitment. Of these, resources are first and foremost brought up in policy debates as the main bottleneck. These financial constraints are unquestionable, particularly in comparison with the many demands that countries face. Nevertheless, as we have already mentioned, a growing number of studies demonstrate that there is ample potential fiscal space in many middle-income countries.

What is also true is that achieving universalism in developing countries entails putting together different pieces. Policymakers should see this as puzzle, which is different depending on country context, political coalitions, and level of income—for example, lower middle-income and upper middle-income countries face distinct challenges. To help governments solve this puzzle, we introduce the notion of policy architectures. We define policy architectures as the combination of instruments addressing eligibility, funding, benefits, delivery, and outside market options for specific social policies. The architecture is the blueprint of a policy as defined not just by single components but by the interaction among them. Policy architectures can result from the explicit efforts of state building and/or from successive policy layers—that is, the incorporation of new elements to an existing arrangement (Thelen, 2004: 35).

Policy architectures involve five main components related to who access what, when and how (Figure 8.3):

a. *Eligibility* (*Under what criteria do people benefit?*): This dimension refers to who is entitled to receive benefits and under what criteria. The three eligibility criteria studied in the literature are citizenship, contributions, and

E + F + B + P + OO = Combined degree of unification/fragmentation

Figure 8.3 Dimensions of the policy architecture
Source: Martínez Franzoni and Sánchez-Ancochea (2016).

need (Esping-Andersen, 1990). Citizenship is associated with belonging to or residing in a given nation state. Contributions are related to the insurance of workers directly and of non-workers as economically dependent family members. Assistance responds to economic need. These three criteria can be displayed alone or in different combinations.

b. *Funding* (*Who pays and how?*): Financial resources may come from general revenues, earmarked taxes, and/or payroll contributions. The latter may involve different degrees of financial commitment by government, employers, and workers. Any of these funding sources may be complemented by co-payments.
c. *Benefits* (*Who defines them and how?*): States generally stipulate benefits in a statutory fashion. Public agencies can do this in a broad range of ways from assuming that all benefits are included by default to listing everything incorporated or listing only what is excluded. In some countries, businesses and/or workers also participate in the definition of benefits.
d. *Provision* (*Who does it?*): Delivery can be in the hands of public or private entities and, if private, for- and not-for-profit. Each of these arrangements is driven by particular goals that may favor or inhibit universal policy outputs. These outputs also depend on other factors such as efficiency, which we will briefly discuss in section 8.6.
e. *Outside option* (*How do governments manage market-based alternatives?*): This component refers to the existence of non-public options available to those who can afford them. The existence of market-based alternatives can trigger exit from state services and transfers (Korpi and Palme, 1998). Within the outside option, we do not only consider out-of-pocket funded private provision, but also the use of public resources for private gains (eg, doctors' conflicting dual practices).

Any policy architecture influences universalism in two ways. First, at any given point in time different combinations of policy instruments deliver different degrees of universalism (ie, the joint combination of coverage, generosity, and equity of benefits). Second, dynamically, different architectures create distinct opportunities and constraints for subsequent expansion—a point we discuss in the following section.

In the short run, building universalism in developing countries does not depend on a given funding mechanism or a single eligibility criterion. Instead, the likelihood of universal outputs depends on how effectively policy architectures cope with pressures towards fragmentation within and across policy components. In comparing different countries, we should thus not focus on individual programs (eg, public healthcare, social security, social assistance for the poor) but on how all of them interact. Ideally, this interaction would lead to unification: independently of funding sources, everyone would then get access to similar, generous services. In practice, there are several challenges to achieving this objective:

- Social insurance systems often provide different benefits to insured workers and to their family members. This can have negative implications for many women, who have access as a result of being economically dependent on the insured worker rather than for their contribution to unpaid work (or informal paid activities).
- In many countries, people accessing pensions or healthcare through non-contributory programs receive fewer benefits which can also be of poorer quality than those received by participants in social insurance. Since 2000 the expansion of these programs has had a significant impact on women's access to social protection, yet not necessarily on the generosity of the benefits they receive.
- A policy architecture that guarantees a small number of services or limited transfers, even if delivered as a matter of right by the public sector, may result in fragmentation in usage. Such fragmentation means that people strive to combine different public programs with non-public ones, each of them with different requirements and benefits.
- Some countries achieve unification in the first four components but fail to adequately regulate outside market options. As we will discuss later in the chapter, this can increase fragmentation by gradually weakening the commitment of the middle class to public services, eroding the quality of public benefits, and/or draining public resources.

The search for unification should be extended to the actual implementation of policies across regions and social groups. Most policy debates regarding the expansion of universalism has the nation states as the unit of deliberation and policy formation. Unfortunately, service delivery in healthcare, education, water, or housing varies significantly in sub-regions within each MIC. For example, in India, in the mid-2000s, 39 percent of children had full immunization coverage—theoretically a right provided by the public sector—compared to 59 percent in the urban population. Differences in service provision between states were significant: in Kerala, for example, there was one public hospital bed per 1,299 people compared to one per 20,041 people in Uttar Pradesh. Moreover, almost all deliveries in Kerala were attended by health personnel compared to just 27 percent in Uttar Pradesh (Baru et al., 2010). Meanwhile, according to World Bank statistics, in Tunisia 30 percent of the inequality in school attendance and almost half of the inequality in access to sanitation is explained by place of birth (rural vs. urban and region of the country). Geography counts much more than wealth, gender. and the level of education of the household head. Similar trends are observed in other Arab countries such as Egypt and Morocco (Krishnan et al., 2016: 63).

8.5 Trajectories (the *When*): The Order of Factors that Fuel or Deter Universalism over the Long Run

Coming up with fully unified policy architectures that deliver similar generous services and transfers for all and reduce spatial segmentation cannot be done from one day to another; it requires financial resources, personnel, bureaucratic support, and enhanced state capacity. One should only consider how long it took OECD countries to secure universalism: Austria and France required more than four decades to provide equal healthcare for all, something Germany did not achieve until 1992 (Bachelet, 2011).

The shape of the policy architecture at a given moment in time depends on the legacies created by previous architectures. There are three significant dynamic roles to consider:

- *Political incentives*. The initial policy architecture will shape "the distribution of power within the policy sector—in other words, emboldening some groups while weakening others" (Pribble, 2013: 27). In particular, some designs will be more successful in developing the type of cross-class coalitions required to support subsequent expansions.
- *Financial incentives*. Underfunded programs will become unpopular or will trigger demands for the expansion of revenues. These pressures will be different depending on the initial funding mechanisms (eg, payroll vs. income taxes) and the characteristics of the beneficiaries that are first incorporated.
- *Available reform alternatives*. The policy architectures also constrain the number of possible alternatives that social and state actors can pursue. For example, in countries with a large private sector, governments are unlikely to contemplate a full nationalization of healthcare or education.

Policymakers should be aware of the effects that their decisions will have in the long run. This requires attention to trajectories, that is, the way policy architectures change over time. Some trajectories are more likely to contribute to the eventual delivery of universal outcomes.

Below we go over three common trajectories many developed and middle-income countries have experienced and assess the positive and negative effects for universalism. Thinking about trajectories in this way is one of the main contributions of this chapter.

8.5.1 Top-down: The Legacy of Bisckmarkian Social Insurance

Historically, many MICs, particularly in Latin America, followed the European example of social insurance, adopting a so-called "top down" approach. Building

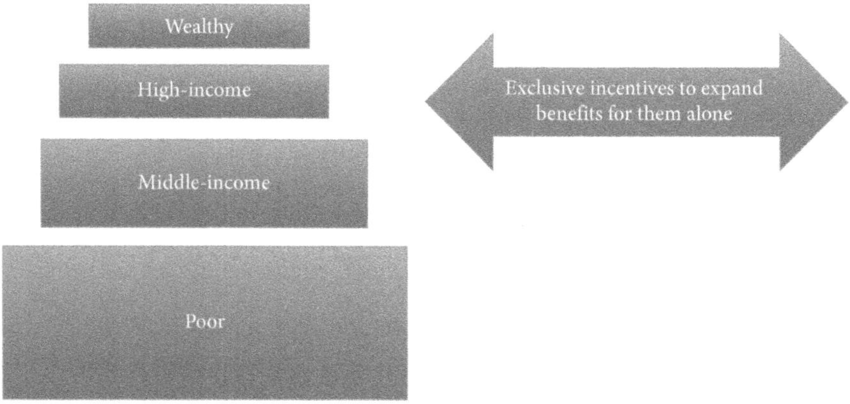

Figure 8.4 Corporatist, exclusionary model

on the principles of full employment and familiarism (Palier, 2010), these programs offered pension and healthcare rights to male workers in specific (formal) sectors. In countries with high levels of formality, the programs gradually expanded coverage to the whole population, even if problems of equity persisted. In countries with high informality—most of those in the South—universalism was almost impossible to reach.

A typical trajectory of these systems is summarized in Figure 8.4. There are at least two problems incorporating larger segments of the population in a similar way. On the one hand, different sub-groups within the middle class had access to different benefits. For example, Uruguay had nine pension funds in 1967, including those for civil servants, and nine autonomous health insurance funds for workers in different manufacturing activities. In exchange for a monthly premium, large parts of the middle class received services from mutual health associations, which spent 3.1 times more resources per person than the public system (Mesa-Lago, 1978). In Chile, social insurance involved more than ten different funds, with entitlements and obligations contained in more than 2,000 legal texts (Mesa-Lago, 1978; Segura-Ubiergo, 2007).

On the other hand, there was limited incentive to extend rights to other groups. Professionals such as teachers, doctors, army personnel, and other civil servants preferred not to incorporate lower-income groups into their programs. Instead, they applied pressure for the expansion of the number of benefits they had access to (by incorporating, for example, family allowances) even if this required higher payroll contributions (Mesa-Lago, 1978).

Most countries that followed this top-down trajectory incorporated low-income groups through non-contributory programs that were nominally for everyone in society. In general, these public services and transfers suffered from low generosity (both in quality and type) and underinvestment (Cotlear et al.,

2015). Politically, in most countries, "marginalized groups continue[d] to be excluded, not only because they lack[ed] class mobilization, but because the existing structure actively reinforce[d] their subordinate position" (Rudra, 2008: 220). Without the support of middle-income groups, the poor struggled to build the necessary political influence to change their situation.

8.5.2 Bottom-up: Creating Floors and Moving Up

The recent response to the problems of this kind of fragmented social architecture has been to promote "bottom-up" trajectories. In healthcare and pensions, this has involved creating new programs focused on the poor on top of the pre-existing ones. In new policy areas like childcare, policymakers have begun by incorporating the income poor first (Martínez Franzoni and Sánchez-Ancochea, 2019).

The belief in this case is that countries should focus initially on those groups in need, gradually expanding to other members of the population at a later stage. The SPF (and basic universalism) clearly has this kind of trajectory in mind: "The extension of social protection drawing on social floors is of course a progressive and gradual undertaking. Different contexts and conditions will determine how rapidly aspects of the floor can be implemented. However, it is important that there be a phased extension of coverage, with the eventual aim of full coverage" (Bachelet, 2011: 66).

This strategy of starting from the poor and then moving up the income ladder until the entire population is included has become popular across policy realms. In a recent World Bank study of universal health coverage, twenty-one of the twenty-four countries studied had implemented new programs for the poor that intended to reduce performance gaps with pre-existing interventions (Cotlear et al., 2015). In the case of pensions, non-contributory programs—most of which target low-income groups—have recently expanded in large number. More than 40 percent of the non-contributory pension programs collected in a recent database were introduced in the 2000s and an additional 18 percent in the 1990s (Figure 8.5).

This approach has also been adopted in the case of the new childcare programs, which have expanded rapidly in Latin America and other parts of the developing world. In countries like Brazil, Chile, and Ecuador, coverage for childcare services among children aged 0 to 3 years of age more than doubled over the course of a decade (see Figure 8.6).

Many of these initiatives aim to deliver universalism through a bottom-up strategy (Martínez Franzoni and Sánchez-Ancochea, 2019). In Costa Rica, for example, president Laura Chinchilla proclaimed in her 2011 state of the union address that "just as in the past we managed to universalize education and public health care, we will manage a universal integral attention to our young children" (Presidencia

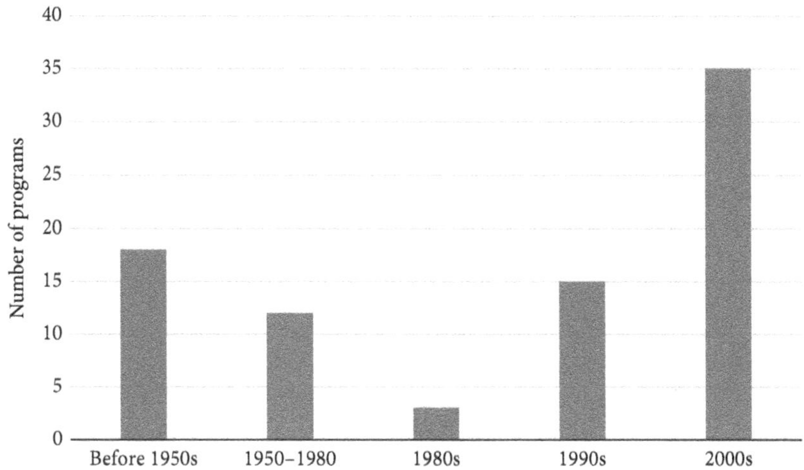

Figure 8.5 Number of non-contributory programs per decade of creation worldwide
Source: Own elaboration with data from Help Age (2015).

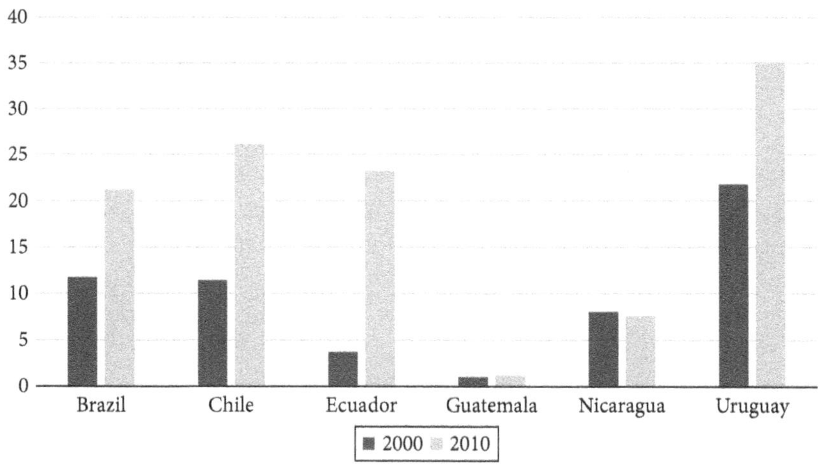

Figure 8.6 Enrollment in childcare services among children 0–3 years of age, 2000 and 2010
Source: Berlinski and Schady, 2015.

de la República, 2011: 9). This was to be done by starting from low-income groups and subsequently expanding to other groups in society. In Uruguay, the National Care Plan adopted the principle of "progressive universality": starting with poor children, it hoped to eventually incorporate all children above three years of age and a majority of younger children to the system by 2019 (SNC, 2015).

Proponents of this trajectory towards universalism highlight several strengths (Cotlear et al., 2015; Molina, 2006):

- Programs should start with those in most need, trying to reduce the benefit gaps between the poor and other social groups.
- It is easier to begin with a small number of benefits that can later be expanded than to promise everything from the beginning and make cuts later. In the case of healthcare, a recent study argues that "starting narrow and then broadening (from targeting the poor to broader population coverage) is relatively easy to do; starting broad and later narrowing (from having a wide benefit package and then curtailing items) is far harder" (Cotlear et al., 2015: 192). In the case of childcare, resources have initially been devoted to part-time services for the population unable to rely on market services.
- Funding constraints should be placed at the heart of any expansionary strategy. If benefits are nominally generous but funding is insufficient, countries will be forced to ration resources through waiting lists, geographical selection of schools, and other mechanisms that introduce *de facto* differentiation of benefits (eg, better performance among higher-income groups) and/or lack generosity across the board.
- Trying to fund programs with a combination of payroll and general taxes can create negative incentives in the labor market. Ideally, countries should start from the bottom through non-contributory mechanisms and gradually incorporate social insurance into this system (Levy, 2015).

Yet the bottom up strategy also has significant shortcomings, as reflected in Figure 8.7. Services for the poor tend to become poor services, and therefore insufficiently attractive for other social groups. Starting from the bottom of the income ladder is also unlikely to generate sufficient financial and political incentives to incorporate others. On the one hand, the middle class is likely to avoid services perceived as tailored for the poor, preferring to use market options

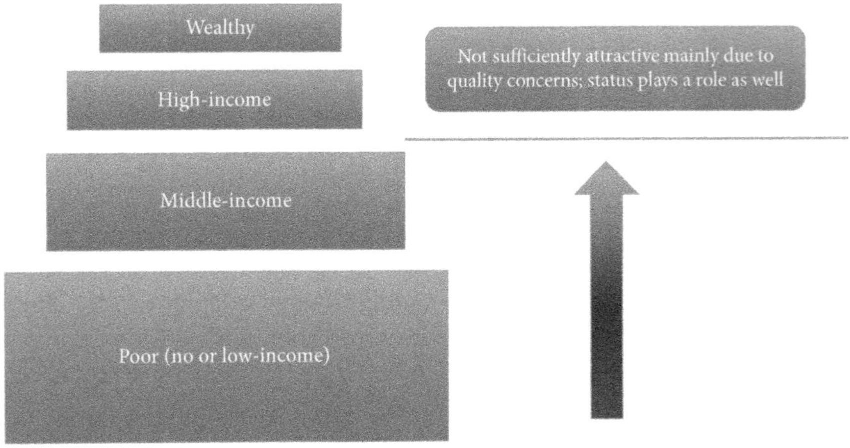

Figure 8.7 Bottom-up trajectories

instead. For example, in education, despite the clear expansion of social investment in public schools for all, between 2003 and 2011 private enrolment in Argentina went from 22 to 39 percent (Bayley, 2013 in Güemes and Paramio, 2014). On the other hand, sooner or later the upper middle class is likely to refuse to fund services that only benefit other groups. The greater the income inequality and the stratification of a country, the more likely it is that these problems will appear.

Focusing on the poor thus risks locking large segments of the population into the private sector—thus never creating sufficient social pressure toward the unification of services. In fact, even in OECD countries, a majority of the upper middle class relies on the market: in 2010 50 percent of children and the youth of families in the highest income quintiles went to private primary and secondary schools (against only 4–6 percent among the lowest income quintile) (Daude, 2012).

8.5.3 Lower-middle Up and Down: The Importance of Unification from the Start

There is a third trajectory that a few countries have adopted and that can theoretically deliver equitable advances in coverage and quality. As reflected in Figure 8.8, this is one that starts with a unified system (eg, social insurance with a single fund) that initially covers non-poor but vulnerable (eg, formal workers with low wages) and later expands upward and downward. In doing so, the risk of creating different programs for the poor and the non-poor is avoided.

Costa Rica's experience in building a policy architecture capable of promoting universalism probably constitutes the best illustration of this trajectory. During the second half of the twentieth century, Costa Rica became "the closest case of a

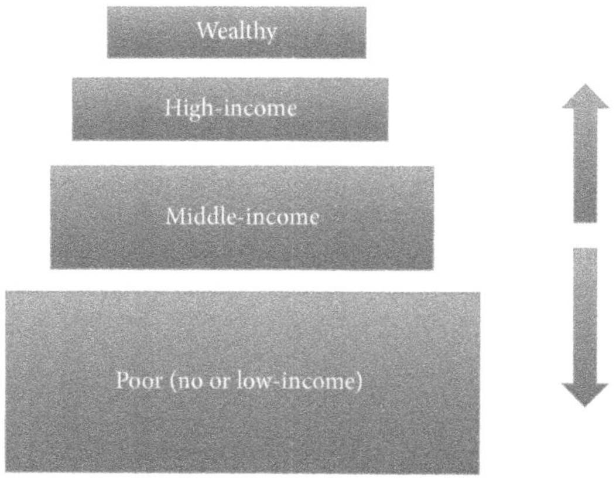

Figure 8.8 Lower-middle up and down trajectory

universalistic, egalitarian social state..." (Filgueira, 2007: 144) and the only one to "accomplish universalization of social-security coverage, integrating social assistance with social security" (Sandbrook et al., 2007: 40). This was rather unexpected since in the 1930s Costa Rican social policy was underdeveloped and its living conditions were not better than those found in neighboring countries. A majority of the population lacked running water, sanitation, and education (Rosero-Bixby, 1986) and at 159 per thousand, infant mortality was higher than that of Ecuador, El Salvador, or Mexico. By 1960, however, remarkable transformations had taken place in basic services, and Costa Rica outperformed Ecuador, El Salvador, and Mexico with an infant mortality rate of 87 per thousand (Hytrek, 1999).

In the 1940s, Costa Rica created a policy architecture for healthcare and pensions based on social insurance with three characteristics that facilitated a pro-universal expansion: (a) it first incorporated blue-collar urban workers who could exert voice but were not powerful enough to prevent the expansion to others; (b) it was a unified system with everyone incorporated to the same fund; and (c) it was funded through payroll taxes at a time when other resources were not available.

How did this foundational policy architecture shape incentive for subsequent expansion? Table 8.1 illustrates the main mechanisms through which this policy architecture led to a pro-universal expansion. Since the program started from lower middle-income groups, from the onset Costa Rican workers already insured had an incentive to support further expansion to higher-income groups who would bring larger tax contributions. This became evident in the 1970s when the government proposal to incorporate higher-income groups was supported by unions across the political spectrum.

Table 8.1 Trajectory of expansion in the Costa Rican case

Policy feature	Problem/opportunity	Consequence
Bottom-up expansion of mandatory social insurance for salaried workers	Financial constraints to meet the growing demand for services	Leads to lifting and eventually eliminating wage ceilings
	Most workers already insured would benefit from vertical expansion	Most workers and trade unions support the elimination of wage ceilings
Creation of a top-down unified system under a single agency	High investment in new medical facilities	In the absence of competing private services, the white collar workers and the better-off had incentives to join the system
Payroll taxes as primary funding source	Effective income-raising mechanism	Further expansion was managerially easy even to fund non-contributory access

Source: Martínez Franzoni and Sánchez-Ancochea (2014b).

The provision of the same high-quality healthcare benefits for everybody insured (whether workers or their dependent family members) created incentives for these high-income outsiders to join. As social security built new hospitals, its facilities became the newest and best funded and equipped. Coverage of the economically active population was 10 percent in 1944, 18 percent in 1945, 23 percent in 1950, 25 percent in 1960, 38 percent in 1970 and 54 percent in 1975. Coverage of the total population went from 12 percent in 1955 to 65 percent in 1975 (Rosenberg, 1979; own estimations). By 2000 coverage surpassed 90 percent and the 10 percent remaining outside the system were mostly the wealthy (Martínez Franzoni and Mesa-Lago, 2003).

The Costa Rican path towards universal pensions and healthcare was also politically easier than one based on general taxes because payroll taxes were relatively easy to collect and harder to oppose. This is an important point when considering the feasibility of different programs and ways to confront fiscal shortcomings. Payroll taxes expanded steadily to cover the insured but also funded other important components of the social policy regime (including professional training and non-contributory pensions). The total contribution to healthcare insurance alone started at 7 percent of the gross wage and was increased to 10.5 percent in 1965 and 16 percent in 1982. Meanwhile, expanding general taxation proved much harder—as in many other developing countries—due to strong opposition to direct income taxes; by 1970, its tax burden was just 12 percent of GDP compared to 15 percent in the poorer Dominican Republic.

The lessons we would like to draw from the Costa Rican case are not about a specific design but about a set of general guidelines. Probably the most important is the search for unification from the very beginning. Unification takes place when all beneficiaries receive the service or cash transfer in a similar fashion and the state plays a major role in defining benefits, acting as direct provider and effectively regulating the market. Creating public services that are not stigmatized can facilitate a subsequent expansion to all social groups.

Of course, as this chapter addressed earlier, the risk is that the poor remain excluded. This is why thinking hard about where to start is a second important guideline. In the Costa Rican case, incorporating the lower middle class first created incentives for subsequent expansion upward and enough resources to incorporate the poor as well. Other countries may try to search for ways to begin with specific groups of the poor and the middle class—trying to create as much mixing as possible. For example, in the case of childcare, this may require creating facilities in middle class neighborhoods but creating incentives for low-income groups to attend as well.

The last, yet not least, important guideline refers to the convenience of linking services to funding sources. This way, a growing demand for services will come together with more income. Otherwise, countries run the risk of developing underfunded programs that cannot be effectively expanded over time.

8.5.4 Are There some Ideal Policy Architectures for Universalism?

So what should be the characteristics of the initial policy architecture in new policy realms? In the case of policies already in place, how should policymakers reform pre-existing architectures? In this section, we identify two potential trajectories: one that focuses on the poor exclusively and another that tries to incorporate segments of the middle class from the very beginning. This distinction is also at the heart of recommendations by the Lancet Commission on Global Health 2035, which sees two main paths towards universalism in healthcare (Jamison et al., 2013):

- A tax-funded, defined benefit package, which targets health interventions that disproportionally affect the poor. This kind of program—which may exist in parallel to social insurance or to an expanding private sector—will focus on expanding coverage of basic benefits. Cotlear et al. (2015: 26) proposes a sub-type of this modality, calling for "bottom-up" approaches that are fiscally sensible, moderate in terms of benefits and "give preferential treatment to segments that had traditionally been left behind in the expansion of health coverage."
- A more generous package of interventions aimed at the entire population that includes some patient co-payment, which the poor will not have to pay. In this case, there will be a diversity of financing mechanisms, including general taxes, payroll taxes, mandatory insurance premiums, and co-payments, all as part of a single set of benefits.

In education, programs focusing exclusively on the poor have often relied on private providers. They include lost-cost primary and secondary schools as well as subsidies to attend private universities—usually with lower quality than private ones—in countries like Brazil.

For economists like Santiago Levy, the tax-funded programs targeted at the poor are preferable and should gradually replace social insurance. By eliminating the distinction between programs for formal and informal workers, this approach could avoid the negative incentives against formal employment that social security programs often create. In the case of pensions, countries will try to guarantee a minimum pension to as many people as possible, leaving the rest to private funds.

Is this trajectory actually feasible? Given the low-tax capacity in developing countries, this kind of strategy risks insufficient investment, low-quality services and low transfers. In light of these shortcomings, the middle class and the wealthy would likely "exit" the public sector and resort to the market—consolidating fragmentation and thus failing to improve equity.

Maybe a better strategy of unification of the policy architecture is one that tackles benefits and suppliers but maintains different funding mechanisms. Both in healthcare and pensions, this would imply the maintenance of social security and social assistance programs but with convergent benefits. For example, this has been the experience with pensions in Brazil, where the maximum non-contributory pension is equal to the minimum contributory one, but the two separate programs persist.

At the end, there cannot be one size-fits all but context-specific decisions that pursue the maximum degree of unification of the policy architecture attainable at each moment in time. Countries where social insurance reaches less than 20 percent of the population make for a very different scenario than one where social insurance reaches more than 60 percent. In the first case, the best strategy may be an aggressive expansion of social assistance but with generous benefits and trying to attract as many members of the middle class as possible. Revenues would ideally come from a diversity of sources, including co-payments for those who can afford them, payroll contributions, and general taxes. Where successful social insurance programs (or high-quality education in parts of the country) are already present, the challenge will be to unify the benefits different groups receive—something a few countries, like Uruguay, have done particularly well (Martínez Franzoni and Sánchez-Ancochea, 2016).

8.6 Conclusions

Universal social policies should be at the heart of any strategy to promote human development. In contrast with segmented policies—including those based on targeting—universal social policies are likely to guarantee better health, education, and insurance against risks. By giving these benefits to everyone, they will also avoid stigma and uncertainty. Additionally, this policy approach will have social advantages, promoting cohesion and often creating more dynamic economies. In this way, universal social interventions can be a key instrument to resolve the middle-income trap discussed in other parts of this book.

Yet what exactly do we mean by universalism? Much of the social science literature defines it as a set of tax-funded programs that provide everyone with an equal amount of generous services and transfers. Benefit allocation is based on a single rule of access based on the principle of citizenship. Using this standard, few MICs will create universal social policies any time soon. They face too many obstacles, including lack of tax capacity, weak bureaucracies, and powerful (conservative) elites. We thus need to develop an analytical and policy approach that delivers the results we want, but through an array of means.

Building on our previous work (particularly Martínez Franzoni and Sánchez-Ancochea, 2016), this chapter has proposed such an approach. We separated the universal outputs from the strategies to achieve them both in the short and long term. To do so, we introduced the concepts of policy architectures and trajectories.

A second contribution of the chapter was to link the discussion of instruments and politics. Research on social (and economic) policy in MICs takes place in silos. Political scientists focused on the conditions needed to develop universal social policies. Their recent work has emphasized the role of democracy (Filgueira, 2007; Lehouqc, 2012; McGuire, 2010; Rudra and Haggard, 2005; Segura-Ubiergo, 2007), progressive political parties (Huber and Stephens 2012; Pribble, 2013), adequate economic models (Haggard and Kauffman, 2008), and international policy diffusion (Deacon, 2005). These authors generally downplay the role of policy instruments and their interactions with political variables. In contrast, the abundant expert literature on healthcare, education, and pensions deals with technical issues such as funding mechanisms, rules of allocation and principal–agent problems without considering the political implications of decisions about them. Understanding the process of development and how to overcome social challenges and the middle-income trap will demand more active conversations from economists and political scientists as well as policy recommendations that creatively link technical and political dimensions.

8.7 Acknowledgment

This chapter draws on the following working paper "Achieving Universalism in Developing Countries," *Background paper for the UNDP Human Development Report 2016.*

References

Bachelet, Michele (2011): *Social Protection for a Fair and Inclusive Globalization. Report of the Social Protection Floor Advisory Group*, Geneva: International Labor Organization.

Baru, Rama, Acharya, Arnab, Acharya, Sanghimitra, ShivaKumar, A. K. and Nagaraj, K. (2010): "Inequities in access to health services in India: Caste, class and region," *Economic and Political Weekly* 45, no. 38: 49–58.

Berlinski, Samuel and Schady, Norbert (2015): *Los primeros años: el bienestar infantil y el papel de las políticas públicas.* Washington, DC: BID.

Cotlear, Daniel, Nagpal, Somil, Smith, Owen, Tandon, Ajay, and Cortez, Rafael (2015): *Going Universal: How 24 Developing Countries Are Implementing Universal Health Coverage Reforms from the Bottom Up.* Washington, DC: World Bank Group.

Danson, Mike; McAlpine, Robin, Spicker, Paul, and Sullivan, Willie (2012): "The case for universalism: An assessment of the evidence on the effectiveness and efficiency of the universal welfarestate," *The Jimmy Reid Foundation.*

Daude, Christian (2012): "Educación, clases medias y movilidad social en América Latina," in Ludolfo Paramio and Rebeca Grynspan (eds.), *Clases medias en sociedades emergentes*, Madrid, España: Fundación Carolina.

Deacon, Bob (2005): "Social policy in the context of new global actors: How far is China's developmental model in Africa impacting traditional donors?" *Global Social Policy* 13: 261–79.

Deacon, Bob, Cimadamore, Alberto, Grønmo, Sigmund, Koehler, Gabriele, Lie, Gro Therese, O'Brien, Karen, Ortiz, Isabel, Pogge, Thomas, St. Clair, Asuncion (2013): "Mobilizing critical research for preventing and eradicating poverty," Crop Poverty Brief, *January.*

Esping-Andersen, Gosta (1990): *The Three Worlds of Welfare Capitalism*. Princeton. NJ: Princeton University Press.

Filgueira, Fernando (2007): "The Latin American social states: Critical juncture and critical choices," in Yusuf Bangura (ed.), *Democracy and Social Policy*, New York: Palgrave/UNRISD, pp. 136–63.

Filgueira, Fernando, Molina, Carlos Gerardo, Papadópulos, Jorge, and Tobar, Federico (2006): "Universalismo básico: una alternativa posible y necesaria para mejorar las condiciones de vida," in Carlos Gerardo Molina (ed.), *Universalismo básico. Una nueva política social para América Latina*,. Washington, DC: Inter-American Development Bank, pp. 19–58.

Fischer, Andrew (2012): *Inequality and the Universalistic Principle in the Post-2015 Development Agenda*. Institute of Social Studies (The Hague), Erasmus University Rotterdam, November.

Güemes, Cecilia and Paramio, Ludolfo (2014): "Las nuevas clases medias y el legado social y urbano del neoliberalismo," in Juan José Michelini (ed.), *Desafíos metropolitanos*, Madrid: Libros de La Catarata, pp. 212–30.

Haggard, Stephan and Kaufman, Robert (2008): *Development, Democracy, and Welfare States: Latin America, East Asia, and Eastern Europe*. Princeton, NJ: Princeton University Press.

HelpAge (2015): *HelpAge International Pension Watch Database*. http://www.pensionwatch.net/social-pensions-database/social-pensions-database--/

Hoeven, Rolph van der (2012): "MDGs Post-2015: beacons in turbulent times or false lights?" Paper prepared for the UN System Task Team on the Post-2015 UN Development.

Huber, Evelyne and Stephens, John D. (2012): *Democracy and the Left: Social Policy and Inequality in Latin America*. Chicago: Chicago University Press.

Hytrek, Gary (1999): "Insurgent labour, economic change and social development: Costa Rica 1900–1948", *Journal of Historical Sociology* 12, no. 1.

ILO (2012): *The strategy of the International Labour Organization. Social Security for All. Building Social Protection Floors and ′*. Geneva: International Labour Organization.

Jamison, Dean, Summers, Lawrence, Alleyne, George, et al. (2013): "Global health 2035: a world converging within a generation," *Lancet* 382: 1898–955.

Korpi, Walter and Palme, Joakim (1998): "The paradox of redistribution and strategies of equality: welfare state institutions, inequality, and poverty in the Western Countries," *American Sociological Review* 63, no. 5: 661–87.

Krishnan, Nandini, Ibarra, Gabriel Lara, Narayan, Ambar, Tiwari, Sailesh, and Vishwanath, Tara (2016): *Uneven Odds, Unequal Outcomes: Inequality of Opportunity in the Middle East and North Africa*, Washington, DC: World Bank (Directions in Development).

Lehoucq, Fabrice (2012): *The Politics of Modern Central America: Civil War, Democratization and Underdevelopment.* Cambridge: Cambridge University Press.

Levy, Santiago (2015): "Is social policy in Latin America heading in the right direction? Beyond conditional cash transfer programs," Brookings Opinion at http://www.brookings.edu/research/opinions/2015/05/21-social-policy-latin-america-levy (last accessed 9 July 2016).

Martínez Franzoni, Juliana and Mesa-Lago, Carmelo (2003): *Las reformas inconclusas: pensiones y salud en Costa Rica: avances, problemas y recomendaciones.* San José: Fundación Ebert.

Martínez Franzoni, Juliana and Sánchez-Ancochea, Diego (2014a): "Should policy aim at having all people on the same boat? the definition, relevance and challenges of universalism in Latin America" Desigualdades.net Working Paper No 70.

Martínez Franzoni, Juliana and Sánchez-Ancochea, Diego (2014b): "Filling in the missing link between universalism and democracy: The case of Costa Rica," Latin American Politics and Society 56, no. 4: 98–118.

Martínez Franzoni, Juliana and Sánchez-Ancochea, Diego (2016): *The Quest for Universal Social Policy in the South: Actors, Ideas and Architectures*, Cambridge: Cambridge University Press.

Martínez Franzoni, Juliana and Sánchez-Ancochea, Diego (2019): "Overcoming segmentation in social policy? comparing new early education and child care efforts in Costa Rica and Uruguay", *Bulletin of Latin American Research*, 38(4): 423–37.

McGuire, James (2010): *Wealth, Health and Democracy in East Asia and Latin America.* Cambridge: Cambridge University Press.

Mesa-Lago, Carmelo (1978): *Social Security in Latin America: Pressure Groups, Stratification and Inequality.* Pittsburgh: University of Pittsburgh Press.

Mkandawire, Thandika (2006a): "Targeting and universalism in poverty reduction," *Social Policy and Development Programme Paper 23*, Geneva, UNRISD.

Mkandawire, Thandika (2006b): *Social Policy in a Development Context.* Geneva: UNRISD.

Molina, Carlos Gerardo (2006): *Universalismo básico.* México, DC: Editorial Planeta Mexicana.

Murtin, Fabrice and Martina Viarengo (2013): "The expansion and convergence of compulsory schooling: Lessons for developing countries," Vox at http://voxeu.org/article/expansion-and-convergence-compulsory-schooling-lessons-developing-countries

OECD (Organisation for Economic Co-operation and Development). (2012): *Latin American Economic Outlook 2012: Transforming the State for Development.* Paris: OECD and the UN Economic Commission for Latin America and the Caribbean.

OECD (2016): "OECD Reviews of Health Care Systems: Mexico 2016," http://dx.doi.org/10.1787/9789264230491-en. OECD.

Ortiz, Isabel, Cummins, Mathew, and Karunanethy, Kalaivani (2017): "Fiscal space for social protection and the SDGs: Options to expand social investments in 187 countries", ESS Working Paper No. 48, ILO, UNICEF, and UN-Women.

Palier, Bruno (2010): *A Long Goodbye to Bismarck? The Politics of Welfare Reforms in Continental Europe*, Amsterdam: Amsterdam University Press.

Presidencia de la República. (2011): "Mensaje de la Señora Presidenta de la República Laura Chinchilla", Asamblea Legislativa, May 1, 9.

Pribble, Jennifer (2013): *Welfare and Party Politics in Latin America.* Cambridge: Cambridge University Press.

Rothstein, Bo. (2008): "Is the universal welfare state a cause or an effect of social capital?" QoG Working Paper Series 16.

Rosenberg, Mark (1979): "Social security policy making in Costa Rica," *Latin American Research Review* 14, no. 1: 116–33.

Rosero-Bixby, Luis (1986): "Infant mortality in Costa Rica: explaining the recent decline," *Studies in Family Planning* 17, no. 2: 57–65.

Rudra, Nita (2008): *Globalization and the Rate to the Bottom in Developing Countries: Who Really Gets Hurt?* New York: Cambridge University Press.

Rudra, Nita and Haggard, Stephan (2005): "Globalization, democracy, and effective welfare spending in the Developing World," *Comparative Political Studies* 38, no. 9: 1015–49.

Sandbrook Richard, Edelman, Marc, Heller, Patrick, and Teichman, Judith (2007): *Social Democracy in the Global Periphery: Origins and Prospects*, Cambridge: Cambridge University Press.

Segura-Ubiergo, Alex (2007): *The Political Economy of the Welfare State in Latin America*, Cambridge: Cambridge University Press.

SNC. (2015): *Plan Nacional de Cuidados: 2016–2020.* Montevideo: Junta Nacional de Cuidados.

Stuckler, David, Feigl, Andrea B., Basu, Sanjay, and McKee, Martin (2010): "The political economy of universal health coverage," Background paper for the global symposium on health systems research. Switzerland.

Thelen, Kathleen (2004): *How Institutions Evolve: The Political Economy of Skills in Germany, Britain, the United States, and Japan*, Cambridge: Cambridge University Press.

9

Employment and Labor Markets in MICs

How to Cope with Technological Change and Global Challenges

Rolph van der Hoeven

9.1 Introduction and Overview

Fostering (formal) employment has been one of the most effective ways to reduce poverty and (until recently) inequality in high-income countries. One would expect middle-income countries (MICs) to follow this trend. However, it is questionable whether such a trend in MICs will be similar to that in high-income counties (HICs), because HICs themselves are undergoing a process of de-formalization as a consequence of the liberalization of labor and other markets (partly policy-induced and partly driven by technological change). Also, international competition has increased, and various MICs are undergoing, for internal and external reasons, a process of premature de-industrialization. This chapter briefly discusses in section 9.2 various interpretations of the informal sector and the informal economy followed by section 9.3 on how economic growth and labor markets in MICs have been evolving and how, over time, this has affected their classification as lower- and upper middle- and high-income countries in the global South. Section 9.4 gives an overview of economic and labor market developments in MICs for three geographical regions and it singles out which MICs managed to have a virtuous growth path, combining fast economic growth with better labor market performance coupled with a faster decline in informality. Section 9.5 discusses how institutions in and the policies of these MICs led to such a virtuous growth path. Section 9.6 discusses whether conclusions from past experiences of these successful MICs are still relevant in the light of current and future challenges to the world of work. Section 9.7 concludes.

9.2 The Informal Sector, Informal Employment, and Informal Economy

The notion of the informal sector is not uncontested. For some scholars the informal sector is a temporary phenomenon that would disappear with the transition

Rolph van der Hoeven, *Employment and Labor Markets in MICs: How to Cope with Technological Change and Global Challenges* In: *Trapped in the Middle? Developmental Challenges for Middle-Income Countries.* Edited by: José Antonio Alonso and José Antonio Ocampo, Oxford University Press (2020). © OUP. DOI: 10.1093/oso/9780198852773.003.0009

from agriculture to industrialization. Giving this sector too much attention would only cause a country's development path to deviate. Yet the reality is different. Neglecting the informal sector, and those working in the informal sector, would bypass a large, and often the poorest, part of the population. But for others, the informal sector is seen not as a problem but as a solution (de Soto, 1989; Maloney, 2004). These authors lament the overbearing role of the central state and local authorities in halting any private sector initiative. Supporting and stimulating the informal sector is thus not seen as a way of helping workers in a transition process, but rather as an important way of liberalizing the economy and so, in the view of these proponents, of fostering growth through liberalization. Under pressure from developing countries and scholars, in 2003 the statistical bureau of the International Labour Organization (ILO) developed a comprehensive classification of informal sector activities and employment patterns. One consequence of that classification is that it *rejects the existence of an informal sector* per se, but rather acknowledges the existence *of informal activities and an informal economy* that are sometimes closely intertwined with the formal economy. There can be informal employment in the formal sector (Breman, 2013). Often, households cannot be exclusively classified as belonging to the informal or formal sector, and economic activities can be a blend of informal and formal activities. A remaining problem is that informal employment is difficult to measure. In developing countries, the unemployment rate is not an appropriate measure for distinguishing whether a country belongs to a good or weak labor market regime: in countries with no decent form of unemployment benefits, poor and middle-income workers cannot afford to be unemployed, whereas richer and educated jobseekers are listed as unemployed waiting for more highly paid jobs (Ghose et al., 2008; 79). For example, China, with a rapidly expanding labor market, has consistently higher unemployment figures than India. Thus the unemployment rate is not a very accurate measure *for comparing* the functioning of labor markets in MICs.[1] We therefore use the better statistically documented category of wage and salaried workers.

9.3 Labor Market Characteristics of Middle-Income Countries

Various indicators for labor market characteristics and income levels and how these relate to economic growth are used in this chapter: Economic status and growth is measured by level and growth in gross domestic product (GDP) per

[1] *This is not to say that unemployment figures are without use.* For example, increases in unemployment figures do signal cyclical or structural slack in activities in the modern sector that need to be acted upon. Also breaking unemployment figures down into figures for males and females can give an indication of the involvement of males and females in the labor market in a particular country.

capita, and economic structure by the percentage of workers in agriculture and industry. Poverty rates and the percentage of working poor are indications of socio-economic progress. Indicators of labor market performance are employment to population rate, labor force participation rate, unemployment rates, and the percentage of wage and salaried workers. Literacy rates and secondary school participation rates are not only indicators of the quality of the labor force, contributing to higher productivity, but are also worthwhile goals in themselves. *Using such an elaborate set of labor market indicators to get a picture of the employment problem in MICs recognizes that in the relationship between labor markets, employment, and development, causation can run in both directions, thus considering development, good labor markets, and employment both as a means and an end.*

International organizations make a distinction between low-, middle-, and high-income countries. But as the group of middle-income countries nowadays comprises the majority of the countries in the world, a further distinction is made between lower and upper middle-income countries. A number of low-income countries, mainly in Asia and some in sub-Saharan Africa have moved from the low-income category to the lower middle-income or even to the upper middle-income category, while also (mainly in Latin America) a number of countries moved up from the lower middle-income category to the upper middle-income category. However, outside eastern and western Europe *only five countries moved fully out of the middle-income category*: The Republic of Korea, Chile, Uruguay, and Panama, while Argentina because of its volatile development path moved in and out the category of high-income countries. Thus, it is instructive not only to investigate how labor markets have performed in MICs but also to investigate whether some common economic and labor market factors made these countries graduate, or whether it was just a lucky streak.[2]

Considerable differences exist in labor market and growth performances between lower middle-income, upper middle-income, and graduated countries, illustrated in Table 9.1. The four graduated MICs started in 1992 with higher than average per capita incomes and also much higher per capita incomes in 2017, but showed different per capita growth rates. Korea and Chile grew much faster than in Argentina and Uruguay.

Lower middle-income countries are still characterized by having the largest share of employment working in agriculture and less working in industry and services. Upper middle-income countries are characterized by a greater decline in the share of employment in agriculture, but only a slight increase in the share in industry. The quantum increase was in employment in services. These last shifting patterns in sectoral employment are even stronger in the set of graduated countries: much lower and declining shares of employment in agriculture and, for

[2] Panama, because of its small size and geopolitical situation has not been retained in this investigation.

all four countries, not an increasing but a decreasing share of industrial employment and a strong increase in service employment, with levels being much higher than in upper middle-income countries. *In this respect labor market composition in these graduated countries shows similar patterns as those in high-income countries, to which group they now belong.*

Labor market characteristics in lower and upper middle-income countries and graduated countries show different patterns. The labor force participation rate is low and even decreasing in lower middle-income countries and it is much higher, though also decreasing, in upper middle-income countries. The graduated countries show a different trend in that labor force participation, although somewhat lower than in the upper middle-income countries, increased in all four countries. A similar trend for the employment to population rate can be seen. Except for Uruguay, unemployment rates in lower and upper middle-income countries and

Table 9.1 Economic and labor market characteristics of lower and upper middle-income countries and of four graduated countries (Argentina, Chile, Republic of Korea, and Uruguay)

		LMIC	UMIC	ARG	CHI	KOR	URU
GDP percentage const. 2010$	2017	2199	8228	10397	15060	26152	14363
	1992	979	3097	7261	6904	9719	7576
%GDP percentage growth		3.6	4.4	1.6	3.2	3.9	2.6
%Poverty HC at $3.20 day	2017	*50.6*	*15.0*	2.0	1.8	*0.5*	0.4
	1992	*78.6*	*60.7*	4.9	16.7	n.a.	n.a
%Employed agriculture	2017	40.0	22.1	0.1	9.3	4.8	8.7
	1992	57.2	47.6	0.4	16.1	14.0	12.3
%Employed industry	2017	22.0	27.0	22.4	22.7	25.1	19.7
	1992	15.6	23.6	32.4	27.1	35.8	21.5
%Employed, services	2017	38.0	50.9	77.5	68.0	70.1	71.5
	1992	27.3	28.9	67.2	56.8	50.2	66.1
Labor force PR	2017	59.9	71.5	68.5	68.5	68.9	75.5
	1992	62.2	76.3	67.3	59.7	63.1	70.9
Employment to population rate	2017	55.3	61.2	55.6	58.0	60.6	59.1
	1992	58.1	68.5	56.6	59.7	50.2	53.3
Unemployment rate	2017	4.0	6.0	8.3	7.0	3.7	7.9
	1992	3.4	4.1	6.4	4.3	2.5	12.9
%Wage & salaried workers	2017	34.1	58.9	74.7	71.3	74.6	72.0
	1992	25.6	43.6	70.2	69.4	62.7	72.7
Secondary school enrollment (gross)	2017	69.6	92.7	*105.2*	99.7	98.1	n.a.
	1992	42.4	57.9	*70.0*	94.3	91.8	82.5
Literacy rate	2017	*74.2*	*94.3*	*99.1*	n.a	n.a	98.6
	1992	59.2	83.1	n.a.	94.3	n.a	n.a.

Source: World Bank: World Development Indicators (WDI) and ILO: World Employment and Social Survey WESO), accessed 7 May 2019.

in three out of four graduated countries are all higher for 2017 than for 1992.[3] Education and literacy levels, an indication of the quality of the labor force, also differ considerably between the various income groupings. In the lower middle-income countries less than three-fourths of the population in 2017 is literate while the literacy rate in upper middle-income countries is almost 95 percent. For the four graduated countries literacy rates are not fully available in the database used, however using other sources shows that literacy rates in these countries were already very high in 1992 and have attained their maximum in 2012.

9.4 The Improvement of Labor Markets and Economic Progress in MICs and Graduating Countries

The discussion on the characteristics of labor markets in middle-income countries and graduate countries gives several pointers for further analysis. First, there is a definite improvement in labor market indicators when countries reach a higher stage of per capita income, *but one can not determine from a first look whether growth propelled the improvement in labor market indicators or whether the opposite is the case: improvements in labor market indicators propelled growth.* There is, furthermore, a wide variation in labor market indicators at a similar level of income.

The World Bank's classification of MICs in 1991 and 2017 and the changes in classification between these years, point to strongly different (sub) regional patterns.

- First, countries in Asia, many of which belonged to low-income or lower middle-income countries in 1991 have moved upwards. *There are, with rare exceptions of war torn countries, no low-income countries left in Asia.*
- Second, in 1991 many countries in sub-Saharan Africa belonged to the group of low-income countries and several have graduated to the middle-income country category. However, this not true of them all: *sub-Saharan Africa is the only region where low-income countries (with a few exceptions) are still situated.*
- Third, *Latin American countries (save a few) belong to the group of middle-income countries*, often shifting upwards to upper middle-income countries.

Since these continental regions are quite distinct, we analyze the economic and labor market developments in these three regions separately.[4] In order to establish whether a country belongs to a good or weak labor market regime, we use a

[3] As discussed in section 9.2, the unemployment rate is not always a good inter country comparison indicator.

[4] The group of MICs comprises countries in the Middle East and North Africa (MENA) region and in Europe and West Asia (mainly countries of the former USSR). Because of very distinct geo-political specificities in the latter two regions, we exclude these two regions from the detailed analysis on developing and emerging countries that follows.

Table 9.2 Annual percentage GDP growth in constant $1986–2015 to define regional growth criteria

	High growth	Intermediate growth	Slow growth
Asia	> 4.5%	< 4.5% and > 3.0%	< 3.0%
Latin America	> 2.0%	< 2.0% and > 1.5%	< 1.5%
Sub-Saharan Africa	> 2.0%	< 2.0% and > 0.0%	< 0.0%

mixed set of labor market indicators such as working poor, employment in agriculture, employment to population ratio, labor force participation rates, percentage wage, and salaried workers, literacy rate, and secondary school completion as indicators of the quality of the labor force itself (see the Appendix). Also because of the great diversity in growth performance in the MICs, it is more appropriate, for analytical purposes, to distinguish not between two, but between three middle-income country groupings differentiated by their growth performance and also to use different criteria to define good economic performance for each region, as summarized in Table 9.2. *Had we used the same criteria for economic performance we applied in Asia in Latin America and in sub-Saharan Africa, no single country in Latin America or in sub-Saharan Africa would have belonged to the group of fast growers as defined for Asia.*

9.4.1 Diverse Developing Experience in Asian Countries

In the Asian group, Cambodia, Bhutan, and Myanmar were not retained due to a lack of consistent time series, while Taiwan could not be retained, as it is not included in comparative international databases. Furthermore, for reasons explained in Nayyar (2013), the city economies of Singapore and Hong Kong were not retained either. This leaves a group of thirteen East, South, and Southeast Asian middle-income countries (see also Appendix Table 9.A1).

9.4.1.1 The Growth Regimes in Asia

The first group of fast growers, in descending order of per capita growth, comprises of China, Republic of Korea, Vietnam, and India; however with considerable variation in growth performance over the 1986–2015 period. China shows a fairly consistent trend over the 30 years under consideration with per capita growth rates nearing 9 percent. Vietnam's growth rate was steady at around 5 percent throughout the period. The Republic of Korea still had high growth rates in 1986–95, following earlier decades of fast growth, but suffered from the East Asian crisis in the 1990s and has since had a slower growth rate, more that of a high-income country, to which category it belongs. India stepped up its annual per capita growth rates over the three 10-year periods from 3.2 to 5.8 percent.

The second group, that of steady growers, contains Laos, Sri Lanka, Thailand, Malaysia, Bangladesh, and Indonesia. Laos, though starting at a low annual growth level of 2.9 percent in the period from 1986 to 1995, gradually increased annual growth to 6.4 percent in the period from 2006 to 2015. Sri Lanka's growth rate increased gradually over the three 10-year periods. Thailand had growth that peaked in the decade from 1986 to 1995 and then fell back, partly as a consequence of the Asian crisis in 1998, to more modest growth rates of 2.5 percent and 2.75 percent in the 1996–2005 and the 2006–15 periods. Malaysia also had strong annual growth during the 1986–95 period (and before), but then tapered off over the last two 10-year periods, dropping to below 4 percent. Indonesia grew annually by more than 4 percent for the first three 10-year periods, but had an exceptionally weak performance of only 0.85 percent annual growth during the period from 1996 to 2005. Bangladesh displays the opposite pattern, starting from low growth in the 1986–95 period and then moving to much higher growth over 2006 to 2015. Indonesia's growth pattern was erratic, high in 1986–95 and in 2006–15 period, but very low in the 1996–2005 period, caused—likeas in Thailand—by the Asian crisis.

The group of slow growers consists of Nepal, the Philippines, and Pakistan. Nepal's growth is fairly stable and slightly increased in the last period. The Philippines show improving growth rates over the three 10-year periods under consideration. However, Pakistan's growth rate has been continuously decreasing from 2.1 percent in the 1986–95 period to 1 percent in 2005–15.

9.4.1.2 Labor Market Regimes in Asia

The group of fast growers shows a mixed pattern in terms of labor market regimes: in Korea, China, and Vietnam fast declining poverty rates and a declining percentage of working poor, as well as a rapid or steady decline of the percentage of workers in agriculture, combined with high and increasing literacy rates and a high employment to population rate of over or near 70 percent.[5] Furthermore, China and Korea have a high percentage of wage and salaried workers. Yet, the share of wage and salaried workers in Vietnam falls into the same range as that of countries in the group of steady growers and slow growers. In contrast, India's structural and labor market profile is more like that of countries with a lower growth rate: high levels of poverty, a high percentage of workers working in agriculture, lower levels of labor force participation rate, low levels and only gradually increasing levels of wage and salary workers, and low and only slowly increasing literacy rates. The only indicator where India levels with the other countries in the group of high-growth countries is that of secondary school completion rates.

[5] Because of its developed country status in later periods, the employment-to-population rate in Korea is now lower than that for the developing or emerging countries in the Asian region.

Table 9.3 Country classifications by growth and labor market regime in Asia, 1986–2015

	High growth	Medium growth	Low growth
Good labor market regime	China, Republic of Korea, Vietnam,	Malaysia, Indonesia, Thailand	
Weak labor market regime	India	Laos, Sri Lanka, Bangladesh,	Pakistan, Nepal, Philippines

Source: See Appendix.

The labor market outcomes of the group of steady growers are rather diverse. In Laos and Bangladesh, the poverty rate has declined by less than in other countries, resulting in a still substantial level of working poor. Sri Lanka, Malaysia, Thailand, and Indonesia have had much faster poverty reduction than Laos and Bangladesh. Literacy rates have declined in Laos and, though growing, remain low in Bangladesh. Only in Malaysia is the share of wage and salaried workers high. The number of individuals who have completed secondary school education varies substantially in this group of steady growers, with the lowest in Bangladesh and the highest in Malaysia (56 percent).

The group of slow growers all still have high poverty rates. Pakistan and the Philippines also have low employment to population rates. The rate in Nepal, in contrast, is the highest in the region. The percentage of persons employed in agriculture varies considerably in this group, with relatively lower rates in Pakistan and the Philippines and a rather higher rate in Nepal. Literacy rates and secondary school completion rates are also very low in this group, except for the Philippines, which has high literacy and secondary school completion rates.

The considerations discussed in this sub-section lead to the country groupings for the various growth and labor market regimes shown in Table 9.3.

9.4.2 Diverse Developing Experience in Latin American Countries

As indicated, most Latin American countries belong to the upper middle-income group of countries. They also show variation in their growth performance, although at a much lower level than in Asia. Caribbean countries and Central American countries, with the exception of Mexico, are, because of their small size and atypical economic structures, excluded from this analysis.

The Latin American countries that do not belong to the group of upper middle-income countries are Bolivia (a lower middle-income country) and Argentina, Chile, and Uruguay, which all graduated to the status of high-income country (although Argentina moves in and out of MIC status).

9.4.2.1 The Growth Regimes in Latin America

The group of fast growers comprises two countries with the highest and the third highest per capita incomes in the region (Chile and Uruguay) and one country belonging to a middle GDP level group. Chile is the only country that had an annual per capita growth rate of over 2.5 percent over all three 10-year periods under study. The growth patterns of Uruguay and Peru were much more erratic, with both countries each having a 10-year period with negative per capita growth. Peru, however, shows increasing annual growth rates over the three 10-year periods under consideration.

The group of steady growers—Colombia, Bolivia, and Argentina—had a dip in the their growth performance during the 1996–2005 period but recovered from that in the last 10-year period. Argentina is, however, rapidly deindustrializing. The experience of the slow growers is mixed: Brazil and Ecuador demonstrated increasing levels of annual per capita growth over the three 10-year periods, Paraguay and Venezuela show dips in annual growth rates for the 1996–2005 period, while Mexico has an inverse pattern as its annual per capita growth rate peaked, albeit at a low-level, during 1996–2005.

9.4.2.2 The Labor Market Regime in Latin America

The group of fast growers in Latin America show, over the 1986–2015, period a mixed pattern in terms of labor market regimes. There were rapidly declining poverty rates and abolition of the working poor in Chile and Uruguay, while Peru showed a three-fourths decline in the percentage of the working poor. All three countries had high and increasing literacy rates. Notable also is a decline of the percentage of workers in agriculture (however, similar magnitudes of decline were also seen in slower growing countries). The share of employment in industry declined slightly in Chile, remained constant in Uruguay, and increased somewhat in Peru. Furthermore, Chile and Uruguay have the highest (save for Argentina) percentage of wage and salaried workers of all Latin American countries, while Peru, on the contrary, has the one but lowest percentage.

The labor market outcomes of the group of steady growers are rather diverse. In Argentina and Bolivia the poverty rate remained stable or even increased, but it fell in Colombia. In all three countries the percentage of working poor decreased substantially. Although the share of workers in agriculture in Bolivia did decline by a quarter, the share of employment in manufacturing barely increases. A similar pattern can be observed in Colombia. Many workers ended up in the service sector. The labor force participation rate is lower in these three countries, and so is the literacy rate except for that of Argentina.

Two countries in the group of slow growers manifested sizable declines in their poverty rate (Brazil and Ecuador). The poverty rate in Venezuela went up. Except for Venezuela, the percentage of working poor went down substantially. Ecuador and Paraguay still have a quarter of employment in agriculture. The share of

Table 9.4 Country classifications by growth and labor market regime in selected Latin American countries, 1986–2015

	High growth	Medium growth	Low growth
Good labor market regime	Chile, Uruguay	Colombia	Brazil, Ecuador
Weak labor market regime	Peru	Bolivia, Argentina	Paraguay, Mexico, Venezuela

Source: See Appendix.

employment in industry remained more or less stable in Brazil and Mexico, but went down in Ecuador (one of the countries with the lowest per capita income in the region) and in Venezuela, and increased in Paraguay. Literacy rates are more or less the same for the group of fast and steady growers, but secondary school enrollment rates are generally lower (though having increased considerably in all countries in this group).

The considerations discussed in this sub-section lead to country groupings depicting various growth and labor market regimes as shown in Table 9.4.

9.4.3 Diverse Developing Experience in Sub-Saharan African Countries

Almost all the low-income countries (LICs) in the world are located in sub-Saharan Africa, which also contains a group of middle-income countries, of which Botswana, Gabon, Namibia, Mauritius, and South Africa sit in the group of upper middle-income countries, while Angola, Cameroon, Republic of Congo, Côte d'Ivoire, Ghana, Kenya, Nigeria, and Zambia belong to the group of lower middle-income countries. These MICs in sub-Saharan Africa show great variations in their growth performances amongst themselves and over time.

The group of fast growers (with a percentage GDP growth rate of over 2 percent) contains Mauritius, growing annually at 4 percent (higher that any Latin American middle-income country) but sub-Saharan Africa also has a group of MICs that had negative growth from 1986 to 2015 (Congo Republic, Cameroon, Côte d'Ivoire, and Gabon).

9.4.3.1 The Growth Regime in Sub-Saharan Africa

The group of fast growers comprises two of the four upper middle-income countries in sub-Saharan Africa: Mauritius and Botswana, which both grew much faster in the 1986–95 decade than in later decades. Ghana and Nigeria, lower middle-income countries in this group, grew faster in the last 10-year period under consideration. In the group of countries with a per capita growth rate between 0 and 2 percent, Namibia, Zambia, and Kenya grew faster over the last 10-year period than over other periods, while the growth rates in Angola and South Africa varied considerably over the three 10-year periods. The countries with an average negative growth rate over the three 10-year growth periods (Congo Republic, Cameroon, Côte d'Ivoire, and Gabon) all showed a positive growth rate over the last 10-year period (2006–15).

9.4.3.2 The Labor Market Regime in Sub Saharan Africa

The group of fast growers among the sub-Saharan countries (Mauritius, Ghana, Botswana, and Nigeria) show, over the 1986–2015, period a rather mixed pattern in terms of labor market regimes (see Appendix Table 9.A3). Poverty declined the fastest in Ghana, more modestly in Botswana, and not at all in Nigeria. While Mauritius has hardly any working poor, and rates dropped considerably in Botswana and Ghana, the poverty rate in Nigeria remained rather high. There is a mixed picture concerning the percentage of workers in agriculture (slightly down in Nigeria and Ghana but also in Mauritius where it was already low in earlier periods, but up in Botswana). A worrying sign is that the share of employment in industry declined in three out of the four countries (Ghana being the exception). The employment to population rate declined in three of the four countries. The percentage of waged and salaried workers increased only slightly. Literacy rates generally went up, but declined however in Nigeria.

The labor market outcomes of the group of countries with a growth rate below 2 percent per annum are also rather mixed. The share of working poor went down in Namibia and South Africa but increased in Angola, Zambia, and Kenya. There was also little structural transformation. The share of employment in agriculture rose in Angola and Kenya and remained high in Zambia. The share of employment in industry declined in Namibia, Angola, South Africa, and Kenya. The employment to population rate remained extremely low in Namibia and South Africa, and dropped in Kenya. The share of waged and salaried workers showed hardly any change between the 1986–95 and 2006–15 periods. Literacy rates increased but still remained—except for South Africa—at modest levels. Secondary school enrollment increased, but still remained very low in Kenya (54 percent) and in Angola (24 percent).

A lack of data prevents a proper analysis of poverty in the group of countries with negative growth. The rate of working poor increased in Côte d'Ivoire, and remained high in Congo republic and Cameroon. This group is also characterized by a lack of structural transformation in that the share of employment in agriculture remained high and that in industry shows little change. With the exception of Cameroon, employment to population rates are low and not showing much upward movement. The share of waged and salaried workers increased somewhat in Cameroon and Gabon. A lack of data also prevents any assessment of whether high literacy rates developed. The secondary school enrollment rate declined in Congo republic and increased in Cameroon and Côte d'Ivoire.

Table 9.5 Country classifications by growth and labor market regime in African countries, 1986–2015

	High growth	Medium growth	No or declining growth
Good labor market regime	Mauritius, Ghana		
Weak labor market regime	Botswana, Nigeria	Namibia, Angola, Zambia, South Africa, Kenya	Congo rep. Cameroon, Côte d'Ivoire, Gabon

Source: See Appendix.

The considerations discussed in this sub-section lead to country groupings which depict various growth and labor market regimes and are summarized in Table 9.5.

9.5 Policies and Institutions in Middle-Income Countries for Virtuous Growth and Employment Creation

The challenge is to distinguish specific policies and institutions for the group of countries with high or medium growth and good labor market outcomes. Kahn (2012) explains the superior performance of the Asian sub-regions, especially that of East Asia, by continued intensive growth in employment, stimulated initially by a transformation in agriculture, caused by more egalitarian landholdings, and by a consequent increase in industrial activities, with initial high output employment elasticities, stimulated by a strong final demand regime, either through exports or through internal consumption. Jessen and Kluve (2019), analyzing more than 150 case studies on reducing the size of the informal sector conclude "interventions appear to be more effective under favourable economic conditions (lower unemployment and poverty and higher growth)" (Jessen and Kluve 2019: 24).

There are a number of common characteristics of the fast-growing countries with good labor market outcomes in Asia (Korea, China, Vietnam). These countries did not rely exclusively on the market for the allocation of resources and their macroeconomic policies did not correspond to neoclassical macroeconomic prescriptions, in contrast to policies in the fast growers with good labor market outcomes in Latin America (Chile and Uruguay). Another important characteristic for most fast growers in Asia was their initially low household income inequality. In Asia the low household income inequality was itself the result of more equal factor distribution of income, labeled by Adelman (1979) as redistribution before growth. The most salient examples of equal factor distribution were programs of land redistribution and early investment in education. This distribution in land and human capital assets resulted in higher factor rewards for workers and peasants when the economic process started to take off, and left fewer factor rewards for capital owners, thus creating spells of virtuous growth. Amsden (2011), in her assessment of early developments in East Asia, argues that the institutions in these countries constrained, in the development process, the influence of capital ("taming capital"), not through social contracts or labor market agreements—as happened in the equitable high-growth episode in Europe in the aftermath of the Second World War—but through state interventions by an enlightened bureaucracy, which either directly (China) or indirectly forced firms to invest, to expand, and to create employment. However, the effect was the same: productivity gains were used to invest, to expand employment, and to increase wages. Taylor (2010) labels such a virtuous growth regime as mildly profit-led, where there is room for wage growth and where profits were reinvested in the economy. On the one hand, this created additional demand but, on the other hand, it also led, through productivity gains, to an expansion of supply (the so-called Kaldor–Verdoorn mechanism). This virtuous growth pattern of fast-growing Asian countries was the result of what Khan (2007) calls growth-enhancing governance. Kahn contrasts growth-enhancing governance with market-enhanced governance, a set of policies advocated by the Bretton Woods institutions in the 1980s and 1990s as part of the Washington Consensus. Two important observations are in order. First, although the fast-growing countries with good labor market regimes in Asia started their development process with low inequality regimes, in some of these countries household inequality has since risen substantially (for example, in China where income inequality is reaching a Gini ratio of 0.5 or more (UNU-WIDER, n.d.—see Appendix data sources)). This begs the question of the sustainability of current growth regimes, an issue that we will take up in more detail in section 9.6 on future prospects. A second observation is that several countries that did not manifest a high-growth regime also have, or at least had in the past, a low inequality regime. Hence, a low inequality regime is a necessary but certainly not a sufficient condition for embarking on a virtuous growth and employment pattern.

Therefore, other drivers of growth must be sought for the three fast-growing and the three not so fast-growing countries with good labor market outcomes in Asia. All the countries in this group made use of external markets to sustain a demand-led growth regime. However, as in the case of their investment regime, external demand was not left to an invisible hand. On the contrary, firms were encouraged to export, with clear export targets. South Korean firms were not allocated foreign exchange or further export licenses if they had not met previously agreed export targets and levels of investment (Amsden, 2007). In the African region, Mauritius applied the same strategy. All the virtuous growing countries defied the lessons from the "Washington Consensus," which came to dominate policy advice from Bretton Woods institutions in the 1980s (van der Hoeven and Taylor, 2000).

The countries with fast and median growth with a good labor market regime in Asia, despite different political constellations, manifested a Lewisian development process where labor could move to industry. Countries in Asia with an explicit growth regime based on strong demand and managing a fair income distribution regime, showed better performances in the labor market as employment generation and increasing rewards on the labor factor made a virtuous growth path possible. Comparing the trajectories of India and China shows how important a well-coordinated industrialization policy is for good labor market outcomes. The success of China's industrialization compared to India's is well demonstrated by Felipe (2012: 101): whereas the actual share of manufacturing to total output in China is *higher* than its predicted share based on its GDP per capita level (34.5 percent vs. 27.3 percent), the actual share in India is *lower* than the predicted share (15.85 percent vs. 19.55 percent, figures for 2000). Female labor force participation, the percentage of waged and salaried workers, the employment to population rate, and the literacy rate are all higher in China than in India. While India has made efforts to boost industrialization since 2000, its share of manufacturing remains far below its potential. Various policy deficiencies have contributed to this. Nayyar (2018) points to the low level of loans from development banks in India, where the percentage of outstanding loans from development banks to GDP dropped over the period from 2000 to 2010 from 7.4 percent to 0.8 percent, while the percentage in China rose from 6.2 percent to 11.2 percent. The amalgam of economic and labor market policies in China led to a process of "cumulative causation" that fostered an effective transformation and good labor market outcomes, in contrast to those in India.

As in India, vibrant industrial development was also lacking in Latin America, resulting in slower per capita growth than in other emerging countries. This lack of dynamism in Latin America can be explained by two missing "middles" (McKinsey 2019). The first missing middle is demonstrated by the extreme polarization of large and small firms, resulting in a continual large proportion of informal sector workers. The second missing middle is the virtual absence of a cohort of upwardly mobile consumers whose rising incomes from productive jobs drive economic demand and investment. (Latin America's bottom 90 percent of earners—of whom many work in the informal economy—accounts for less than two-thirds of domestic consumption, the lowest of all regions). Paus (2019), comparing three different approaches to development in Latin America (state led, fully market led, and moderately market led), concludes that under all three strategies private sector demand tended to be weak throughout (Paus 2019: 17). The surge in the price of primary resources on the international market at the beginning of the twenty-first century compensated for the lack of internal demand, and various countries (notably Brazil) used these increases in final demand to contain, and even reduce, high income inequality and to introduce improved social and labor market policies that could potentially stimulate internal demand. Ocampo (2019) argues that Latin America has faced a strong "middle-income trap," the conditions for which were sown in the last stages of state-led industrialization, when the region failed to transition to the development of strong innovation systems and higher levels of research and development. The challenges that the region faces have mounted with the recent collapse of the super-cycle of commodity prices, which had delivered the only period since market reforms began when performance approached the records achieved during the period of state-led industrialization.

In Africa, Mauritius combined fast growth with good labor market performance. Growth in Mauritius was driven by three subsequent industrialization strategies: inward-looking import-substituting industrialization (ISI) that can be dated to between 1968 and 1972; a heterodox mix of ISI and export-oriented industrialization (EOI) between 1972 and 2006; and a globally competitive paradigm from 2006 onward (Narrainen, 2013). Mauritius' industrialization drive was part of a developmental state concept that Mauritius applied through a mix of state participation in industries, regulation, support for private initiatives, the maintenance of social expenditure and harmonious labor relations, and flexible structural policies.

Countries with fast growth and a good labor market regime also showed the fastest increase in formal wage employment as measured by the percentage of waged and salaried workers[6] which, over the period 1995–2015, more than doubled in Vietnam from 15.5 to 35.7 percent, in China rose from 40.4 to 62.9 percent, in Ghana from 16.6 to 24.4 percent, while these percentages remained high in Mauritius, Chile, and Uruguay (around 79 percent, 72 percent, and 73 percent respectively). The virtuous path of fast growth and good labor market development is the best recipe foe reduced informality.

9.6 Future challenges

What are the future challenges[7] for MICs with a virtuous growth path (combining steady growth with improved labor market characteristics and a decline in informal employment) as well as for MICs that did not manage to develop a virtuous growth path, and are therefore perhaps even more vulnerable? Various important, though not entirely independent, factors strongly influence the future development of these economies and their labor markets.

[6] As indicated earlier we have chosen this metric rather than the percentage of informal sector workers, as no long time series and comparable figures for this share of informal sector workers is available.

[7] Challenges stemming from measures to combat climate change are discussed in chapter 10.

Just before the great recession, the IMF (2007) as well as several academic studies, brought forward the notion of "decoupling," arguing that development paths in Southern MICs were becoming increasingly decoupled from those of Northern countries. However, the great recession of 2007–08, that had its roots in the collapse of American and European banking systems, resulted in severe recessions in the MICs, and demonstrated that the economies of Southern countries were not isolated from development in the North. Yet, through pragmatic crisis resolution, especially through appropriate monetary and fiscal policies in some important MICs, the consequences for Southern countries were less severe (although they nevertheless affected a large number of poor in these countries, Ghosh, 2011). The current efforts to create Southern-based financial institutions to face a future crisis and to bolster development in Southern countries could result in more decoupling in the future, but it would be illusory to envisage a full decoupling over the coming 25 years. Economic and social developments in MICs therefore remain influenced to a certain extent by economic development in Northern countries and by how the international economic and financial system is able to cope with these (Lin, 2017). Ocampo (2019) argues, that given the sluggish growth of international trade—which has become an essential feature of the world economy since the North Atlantic financial crisis—it is essential that Latin American MICs not only boost competitiveness and improve the quality of their export basket, but also strike a balance between the domestic and external markets.

Technological development and industrialization have played a major role in the fast-growing MICs with a virtuous growth path and superior labor market outcomes (Lin, 2012). For the fast-growing countries that have a reached a certain level of industrialization and have good labor market performances (such as China), the question is whether further industrialization should be pursued or whether more attention should be given to developing various activities in the high-end service sector, as manufacturing costs are rapidly rising (McKinsey 2017a). Ocampo (2019) argues, especially with respect to Latin American countries, that renewing economic growth will require a return to active production sector strategies, breaking those policy patterns that became entrenched during the period of market reform. The essential focus of the new strategies must be the increased knowledge content of the new economic activities. This should include re-industrialization but also modern services and the opportunities provided by exploiting technological upgrades of natural resources.

In the transition to more service-oriented activities, artificial technologies can dramatically boost productivity. McKinsey (2017b) argues that this increased productivity could be a crucial way for China to sustain its future economic growth as the country's working-age population declines. It estimates that automating workplaces with artificial intelligence could add 0.8 to 1.4 percentage points to GDP growth annually, depending on the speed of adoption. However, realizing this potential in China also depends on automating workplaces across

China's traditional industries and not just among the technology giants. UNCTAD (2017) observes that robotization has been primarily employed in the automotive, electrical, and electronics industries, but that in many labor-intensive industries, such as garment making, widespread automatization is not yet suitable and that in countries with large numbers of low-skilled workers entering the labor force automatization may still drive up production costs. Governments in these countries therefore need to apply judicious policies for encouraging new technologies but not rely on the effects of these solely, or massively subsidize such technologies. The experience of China of "walking on two legs" when it developed its industrial base while maintaining agricultural output and employment, could also be applied by combining more traditional labor-intensive manufacturing and high technological activities.

Lower middle-income countries in sub-Saharan Africa would still gain from industrialization. Hallward-Driemeier and Nayyar (2017) conclude that:

> With reform priorities becoming more urgent, one key lesson is that new technologies and changing globalization patterns increase the complementarities between economy wide and targeted approaches. Yet it may be more feasible, at least in the immediate future, to meet the requirements to be competitive by targeting locations and sectors rather than attempting to reform and provide public investments throughout the whole economy and that given the growing uncertainty about the pace of technological change, horizontal policies that develop transferable skills would reduce risks in the future. (Hallward-Driemeier and Nayyar, 2017: 6)

High literacy and secondary education completion rates, or a strong improvement of these levels, are a common characteristic of MICs that had high or medium growth rates and had good labor market outcomes. This conclusion has at least two important pointers for the future development of MICs and their labor markets. First, in countries that lag behind in achieving full literacy and secondary education, growth and productive employment will remain constrained. Attaining full literacy and investing in education as part of an overall growth strategy is warranted in these countries. Second, countries that have progressed well in these areas need to be cognizant of the fast changes in the labor market caused by the technological development discussed above. This requires changes in school curricula and in developing systems for continuous learning and the upgrading of skills. Failing in this will lead to a slowdown in growth, deteriorating labor market conditions, and increasing wage and income inequality (Stiglitz and Greenwald, 2014).

Income inequality shows a varied pattern in MICs. Most notable is the increase in income inequality in India and China (both countries with initially low inequality) where the Gini ratio increased from the 0.26–0.35 range in the 1966–70 period to the 0.45–0.55 range in the 2011–15 period (UNU-WIDER, n.d.).

Some Latin American countries showed modest declines in their high levels of initial income inequality, during the commodity price boom of the early twenty-first century, but the tendency for most other MICs has been for stable or increasing income inequality. Income inequality has widened for various reasons, but a strong overall contributing factor is the declining wage share, indicating that capital owners capture productivity gains to a larger degree than workers. This, combined with increases in wealth inequality, is leading to an increased share of the top 1 percent of the population. McKinsey (2017b) argues that the rapidly increasing use of artificial intelligence in China and in other fast-growing Asian countries will raise the premium placed on digital skills, while reducing the demand for medium- and low-skilled workers, potentially exacerbating income inequality. It is difficult to predict whether this trend of rising inequality will continue, but there are clear signs that a continuing rise in inequality is socially and economically untenable. Few countries in the region have explicit policies for reducing income and wealth inequality. With rising inequality, the economic growth of the past is not sustainable (van der Hoeven, 2011; Nayyar, 2013), and high inequality and faltering growth will lead to social unrest and to deteriorating labor market outcomes, undoing, for some countries, the gains achieved in this area (Nayyar, 2017). Domestic policies to face these challenges can be reinforced or compromised by international developments. If, as the Trade and Development Report of UNCTAD (2017) strongly advocates, a global social contract on global growth and employment creation could be achieved (van der Hoeven, 2012), then economic and social developments in MICs would certainly progress faster than they would without such a global social contract. But whether such a global social contract will emerge is not at all a given in the current international political constellation.

9.7 Conclusions

This chapter has juxtaposed a discussion of challenges for the MICs and analysis of those MICs that have fared better in terms of virtuous growth (solid GDP growth, better labor market performance, a rapid decline of poverty, and a reduction in the share of informal workers). The discussion highlights the need for a continuation, or stronger adoption, of managed demand-led growth with good labor market outcomes which has been so successful in several of the fast growing MICs, and those that have graduated. Productive transformation from commodity production to higher value-added activities is also at the heart of the transition from a middle-income to a high-income economy. What is key is the development of domestic innovation capabilities to move up the value chain on a broad enough basis to generate sustained productivity growth. Since World War II few countries have achieved this transition. Under the market-led strategies of the past 30–40 years, Latin American countries and sub-Saharan countries have become trapped at the middle-income level. Current globalization processes, particularly the rise of China, have shifted the goal posts for middle-income countries and increased the urgency for domestic innovation capabilities (Paus, 2019). Diao, McMillan, and Rodrik (2019) have shown that (re-)industrialization in Latin American and sub Saharan countries might well be a determining factor in achieving a virtuous growth path. Given current geo-political changes, this challenge becomes more difficult but it must certainly be pursued.

In order to face current challenges, however, the emphasis can no longer be put on industrialization per se. The general principles of successful industrial policies apply in any successful multi-faceted strategy, not just to manufacturing, but also to agriculture, services, and natural resources (Stiglitz, 2018: 27). In facing technological challenges policymakers in MICs should be aware that excessive optimism as well as excessive pessimism both lead to a passive policy stance (UNDESA, 2017) and to undermining adequate responses to technological change. A comprehensive development strategy is called for with a balance between markets, government, and society, based on a new understanding of what leads to successful economic and societal transformation (Stiglitz, 2018: 31).

To restore balance in society, development policies need to be strengthened by good labor market policies. These should not only reduce income inequalities in general but also reverse the declining share of labor income in national income and protects workers against the inevitable economic transformation by introducing or strengthening unemployment insurance and basic social protection independent of job status (van der Hoeven, 2019). Given the challenges of technological change and the increasing flexibility in the economy, a rethink of the traditional social protection based on employment in large conglomerates is needed in the form of citizen's dividends or basic income (Basu, 2019). Labor market performance also improves when the education system better prepares workers for coping with and mastering new technologies, leading to a "learning society" (Stiglitz and Greenwald, 2014).

9.8 Acknowledgment

Passages discussing Asian performances draw partly on van der Hoeven (2019).

References

Adelman, I. (1979): "Redistribution before Growth," in Institute of Social Studies, *Development of Societies, the Next Twenty-five Years*. The Hague: Martinus Nijhoff.

Amsden, A. H. (2007): *Escape from Empire, the Developing World's Journey through Heaven and Hell*. Boston, MA: MIT Press.

Amsden, A. H. (2011): "Say's Law, Poverty Persistence, and Employment Neglect," in R. van der Hoeven (ed.), *Employment, Inequality and Globalization: A Continuous Concern*. London: Routledge.

Basu, K. (2019): "Technology, Labor and Globalization: Contemporary Challenges," *The Indian Journal of Labour Economics*, Published online April 24, 2019.

Breman, J. (2013): *At Work in the Informal Economy of India: A Perspective from the Bottom up*, Delhi: Oxford University Press.

de Soto, H. (1989): *The Other Path: The Invisible Revolution in the Third World*, New York, NY: Harper and Row.

Diao, X., McMillan, M.,and Rodrik, D. (2019): "The recent growth boom in developing economies: a structural change perspective," in M. Nissanke and J. A. Ocampo (eds.), *The Palgrave Handbook of Development Economics, Critical Reflections on Globalisation and Development*, https//doi.org/10.1007/978-3-030-1400-7.

The Economist (2017): "Asia's looming Labour Shortage," February 11.

Felipe, J. (2012): *Inclusive Growth, Full Employment, and Structural Change: Implications and Policies for Developing Asia*. London and Manila: Anthem Press and Asian Development Bank.

Ghose, A. K., Majid, N.,and Ernst, C. (2008): *The Global Employment Challenge*, Geneva: ILO.

Ghosh, J. (2011): "*Reorienting Development in uncertain Times*," in P. A. G. Bergeijk, A. de Haan, and R. van der Hoeven (eds.), *The Financial Crisis and Developing Countries*, Cheltenham: Edward Elgar.

Hallward-Driemeier, M. and Nayyar, G. (2017): *Trouble in the Making? The Future of Manufacturing-Led Development*. Washington, DC: World Bank.

IMF (2007): *World Economic Outlook*, Washington, DC: IMF.

Jessen, J. and Kluve, Jochen(2019): "The effectiveness of interventions to reduce informality in low- and middle income countries," IZA DP No. 12487, IZA— Bonn: Institute of Labor Economics.

Khan, M. H. (2007): "Governance, economic growth and development since the 1960s," UNDESA Working Paper 54, New York: United Nations.

Khan, A. R. (2012): "Employment in Sub Saharan Africa: Lessons to Be Learnt from the East Asian Experience," In A. Noman, K. Botchwey, H. Stein, and J. E. Stiglitz (eds.), *Good Growth and Governance in Africa, Rethinking Development Strategies*, New York: Oxford University Press.

Lin, J. (2012): *The Quest for Prosperity: How Developing Economies Can Take Off*, Princeton, NJ: Princeton University Press.

Lin, J. (2017): "Development beyond Aid," May 8, 2017, Project Syndicate https://www.project-syndicate.org/commentary/china-development-patient-capital-by-justin-yifu-lin-and-yan-wang-2-2017-05?barrier=accesspaylog

Maloney, W. S. (2004): "Informality Revisited," *World Development* 32, no. 7: 1159–78.

McKinsey Global Institute. (2017a): *Artificial Intelligence: Implications for China*, London and Shanghai: McKinsey.

McKinsey Global Institute. (2017b): *Jobs Lost, Jobs Gained: Workforce Transitions in a Time of Automation* San Francisco, CA, London and Shanghai: McKinsey.

McKinsey Global Institute. (2019): *Latin America's Missing Middle, Rebooting Inclusive Growth*, Brussels, San Francisco, Shanghai: McKinsey.

Narrainen, S. P. (2013): "Industrialization: The Mauritian Model," in J. E. Stiglitz et al. (eds.), *The Industrial Policy Revolution II*, © International Economic Association 2013.

Nayyar, D. (2013): *Catch Up, Developing Countries in the World Economy*, Oxford: Oxford iversity Press.

Nayyar, D. (2017): "Can Catch up Reduce Inequality?" in P. A. G. Bergeijk and R. van der Hoeven (eds.), *Sustainable Development Goals and Income Inequality*, Cheltenham: Edward Elgar.

Nayyar, D. (2018): "Financing Reindustrialization: Bring Back Development Banks?" New Delhi: MINT, May, 11.

Ocampo, J. A. (2019): "Latin America's Structural Transformation patterns," in J. Lin and C. Monga (eds.), *Oxford Handbook of Structural Transformation*, Oxford: Oxford University Press, pp. 439–64.

Paus, E. (2019): "Innovation Strategies Matter: Latin America's Middle-Income Trap Meets China and Globalisation," *The Journal of Development Studies*, 36, no. 4: 657–79.

Stiglitz, J. (2018): "From Manufacturing Led Export Growth to a 21th Century Incluisve Growth Strategy: Explaining the Demise of a successful growth Model and what to Do About it," Paper presented at UNU-WIDER Conference, Helsinki, Finland, September 15, 2018.

Stiglitz, J. E. and Greenwald, B. C. (2014): *Creating a Learning Society.* New York: Columbia University Press.

Taylor, L. (2010): *Maynard's Revenge: The Collapse of Free Market Macroeconomics*, Cambridge, MA: Harvard University Press.

UNDESA. (2017): "Frontier Issues: The impact of the technological revolution on labour market and income distribution," Working Paper July 31, 2017, New York: United Nations.

UNCTAD. (2017): *Trade and Development Report. Beyond austerity: Towards a global new deal*, Geneva: UNCTAD.

van der Hoeven, R. (ed.) (2011): *Employment, Inequality and Globalization: A Continuous Concern*. London: Routledge.

van der Hoeven, R. (2012): *Emerging Voices: A Global Social Contract to Follow the Millennium Development Goals*. Washington, DC: Council on Foreign Relations.

van der Hoeven, R. (2019): "Unemployment, Employment and Development," in D. Nayyar (ed.), *Asian Transformations, An Inquiry into the Development of Nations*. Oxford: Oxford University Press.

van der Hoeven, R. and Taylor, L. (2000): "Introduction: Structural Adjustment, Labour Markets and Employment: Some Considerations for Sensible People", Special Section on Structural Adjustment and the Labour Markets, *Journal of Development Studies*, 36, no. 4: 20–32.

Appendix

Data sources for Tables 9A1–9A3
Data used to assess country economic and labor market performances have been drawn from November 2018 till June 2019 from the following data sets:
ILO: online Data Bank
UNU-WIDER: "WIID—World Income Inequality Database"
World Bank: World Development Indicators

Table 9A1 Growth and labor market characteristics, selected Asian countries, 1986–2015, ten-year averages (unless otherwise indicated)

Variables	Chi	Vie	Kor	Indi	Lao	Sri	Tha	Mal	Bdh	Indo	Nep	Phi	Pak
Average % per capita GDP growth													
86–15	9.0	5.4	5.0	4.7	4.5	4.3	3.8	3.5	3.2	3.1	2.5	2,0	1.8
86–95	8.38	4.85	7.81	3.18	2.93	3.24	8.34	6.22	1.74	4.99	2.47	0.47	2.18
96–05	8.13	5.09	4.58	4.22	4.32	3.44	2.45	1.92	2.95	0.85	2.10	1.60	1.61
Av. 06–15	8.56	4.78	2.73	5.84	6.37	5.49	2.72	2.66	4.85	4.33	3.37	3.64	1.08
PC GDP 2010 US$													
06–15	4,770	1,373	22,227	1,376	1,199	2,958	5,130	9,409	789	3,209	599	2,198	1,062
% Poverty ($3.20 per day)													
86–95	86.8	78.3		80.8	69.3	42.3	14.7	11.9	80.6	88.2	86.6	53.6	87.3
06–15	23.7	28.1	0.7	65.2	62.2	19.3	2.9	3.3	59.2	48.8	50.9	37.9	47.3
% Working Poor													
2000	34.4	36.4	0.0	41.0	75.8	6.0	1.1	4.1	80.7	47.6	46.2	15.2	16.7
2015	4.7	4.0	0.0	13.2	49.3	4.1	0.1	3.0	66.2	10.4	8.2	8.0	7.8
% Employed, Agriculture													
86–95	58.2	63.8	17.7	55.8		41.9	61.4	26.1	62.8	52.8	70.9	45.9	49.7
06–15	35.5	46.5	6.6	51.1		31.2	39.6	13.3	47.5	37.9	73.9	33.0	43.9
% Employed, Industry													
86–95	22.1	13.5	34.2	19.0		21.4		27.0	13.6	13.3	11.6	15.3	19.4
06–15	28.5	21.6	25.0	22.4		25.8		28.2	17.7	19.7	10.8	15.4	20.6

Continued

Table 9A1 *Continued*

	Chin	Kor	Vie	Indi	Lao	Sri	Tha	Mal	Bdh	Indo	Nep	Phil	Pak
Employment to Population ratio													
86–95	75.6	59.4	76.5	58.3	79.3	49.8	75.0	59.7	71.7	63.1	83.3	60.0	47.6
06–15	68.3	58.6	75.6	53.6	76.5	51.5	72.0	59.3	60.4	62.7	81.1	59.9	50.7
Total LFPR													
86–95	79.2	60.8	78.5	60.7	81.3	58.5	77.1	61.9	74.2	65.8	85.8	65.6	50.2
06–15	71.4	60.7	77.3	55.7	77.6	54.2	72.7	61.3	63.0	67.7	83.4	64.5	53.8
Unemployment Rate													
96–05	4.5	4.1	2.3	4.2	1.8	8.9	2.0	3.2	3.4	5.9	2.3	3.7	6.9
06–15	4.3	3.4	2.2	3.7	0.8	5.0	0.9	3.2	4.1	5.7	2.3	3.6	3.3
% Wage & Salaried Workers													
96–05	46.2	61.5	21.2	13.6	11.1	58.6	39.8	74.7	34.5	36.2	20.5	50.0	36.8
06–15	59.7	67.6	33.5	17.6	14.7	56.2	43.9	74.7	37.6	42.4	18.4	55.0	38.1
Literacy Rate													
96–05	90.9		90.2	61.0	70.3	90.7	93.1	88.7	47.5	90.4	48.6	92.6	49.9
06–15	95.1		93.5	66.0	58.3	90.8	94.3	93.1	46.9	93.3	59.6	95.9	55.5
%Sec. School Completion Rate													
06–15	22.3	69.4	25.7	26.9		56.1	26.4	50.2	17.1	28.4	35.2	57.2	24.6

Table 9A2 Growth and labor market characteristics, selected Latin American countries, 1986–2015, ten-year averages (unless otherwise indicated)

	Chili	Urug	Peru	Col	Bol	Arg	Brazil	Ecuad	Para	Mex	Ven
Average % per capita GDP growth											
86–15	3.9	2.5	2.3	2.0	1.9	1.6	1.4	1.3	1.1	0.9	0.5
86–95	5.6	3.0	−2.3	2.3	1.5	1.0	0.1	0.5	2.2	0.7	0.6
96–05	2.9	−0.2	1.7	0.4	1.0	−0.4	0.9	0.7	−1.3	1.5	−1.4
06–15	2.9	4.7	4.6	3.4	3.3	1.8	2.2	2.6	3.3	0.5	1.0
Per capita GDP 2010$											
Average 06–15	13167	11715	5000	6398	2022	10014	10935	4831	4288	9283	13831
% Poverty ($3.20 per day)											
86–95	7.2	0.7	na	9.0	6.7	1.7	14.8	14.9	5.9	6.8	6.9
06–15	1.8	0.3	5.8	6.3	8.1	1.7	4.3	5.0	4.2	3.9	9.8
% Working Poor											
2000	2.0	0.1	16.2	11.7	26.3	3.1	8.3	25.3	5.2	6.8	8.6
2015	0.3	0.0	4.2	2.2	6.2	0.2	0.8	3.7	0.5	1.9	6.3
% Employed, Agriculture											
86–95	16.4	12.2	36.5	23.7	40.9	0.4	22.0	31.3	35.5	25.2	12.0
06–15	10.7	10.0	28.7	17.7	30.8	0.9	14.6	27.6	25.4	13.8	8.3
% Employed, Industry											
86–95	26.7	21.5	14.7	18.9	18.9	30.1	22.4	20.4	15.8	22.6	25.2
06–15	23.4	21.2	16.4	20.1	20.4	23.7	22.3	18.7	18.2	24.9	21.0

Continued

Table 9A2 *Continued*

	Chili	Urug	Peru	Col	Bol	Arg	Brazil	Ecuad	Para	Mex	Ven
Employment to Population ratio											
86–95	74.0	68.2	72.3	77.9	79.8	68.5	77.7	78.7	79.1	81.3	74.6
06–15	69.8	71.9	82.7	75.7	79.8	68.3	72.0	78.9	80.7	76.7	73.6
Total LFPR											
86–95	59.8	70.7	62.7	70.2	70.6	67.3	66.4	66.4	72.4	61.5	66.3
06–15	66.4	76.0	80.4	72.4	72.8	68.4	69.8	68.8	73.0	64.7	68.0
Unemployment Rate											
86–95	4.9	13.1	5.4	8.9	3.1	10.5	6.2	4.7	8.9	4.1	8.5
06–15	8.0	7.6	3.6	10.3	2.5	7.9	7.7	3.6	4.7	4.6	7.3
% Wage & Salaried Workers											
86–95	69.6	72.7	37.9	48.0	29.8	70.0	62.5	53.0	41.5	56.3	61.9
06–15	72.7	71.6	43.9	47.9	39.2	76.3	67.8	54.8	52.4	66.6	64.6
Literacy Rate											
86–95	94.3	98.2	87.2	91.1	80.0	96.1	90.8	88.3	90.3	87.6	89.8
06–15	97.4	98.5	92.0	93.4	92.0	99.0	92.0	92.7	94.4	93.5	96.5
% Sec. School Enrollment (gross)											
86–95	82.0	79.3	66.2	54.9	n.a.	70.4	n.a.	57.9	33.4	53.8	55.8
06–15	95.3	100.3	93.6	97.6	84.7	101.2	97.5	92.2	68.9	86.3	83.4

Table 9A3 Growth and labor market characteristics, selected African countries, 1986–2015, ten-year averages (unless otherwise indicated)

	Maur	Bots	Ghana	Nig'a	Namb	Angol	Zamb	S. Afr	Kenya	Cong rp	Cam	C d'Iv	Gabon
Av percentage GDP growth													
86–15	4.0	3.2	2.6	2.3	1.7	1.7	1.5	1.0	0.5	−0.1	−0.3	−0.7	−0.9
86–95	5.0	5.2	1.7	0.5	−0.5	−5.1	−2.1	−1.2	−0.2	−2.1	−6.1	−2.7	0.1
96–05	3.5	2.5	2.0	3.4	2.0	3.2	1.8	1.6	−0.2	0.2	1.8	−1.4	−2.3
06–15	3.7	2.7	5.0	3.4	2.7	1.8	4.0	0.9	2.4	2.0	1.4	1.9	0.8
Percentage GDP 2010$													
Av.06–15	9477	7309	1640	2563	6112	3752	1619	7576	1108	2926	1467	1470	9598
% Poverty $3.20													
86–95	n.a	59.9	76.3	77.8	n.a	n.a	71.6	50.1	57.4	n.a	n.a	33.0	n.a
06–15	3.4	37.8	32.5	77.5	38.5	55.7	77.2	36.8	66.2	61.3	50.2	57.3	n.a
% Working poor													
2000	0.2	26.2	28.2	54.2	30.0	27.9	43.1	11.6	30.4	50.2	26.0	24.4	6.0
2015	0.1	11.7	5.4	44.9	7.7	30.3	53.8	6.1	32.9	35.1	20.1	27.2	2.1
% Employed, Agriculture													
86–95	14.3	16.2	56.7	49.7	45.0	40.2	72.1	10.8	46.9	39.6	67.3	49.1	43.8
06–15	8.4	24.3	47.9	40.3	29.8	47.3	63.0	5.4	59.5	38.5	53.9	46.6	36.9
% Employed, Industry													
86–95	39.8	25.8	13.9	12.0	14.8	9.1	7.1	28.3	13.2	22.2	9.8	11.8	9.6
06–15	29.6	18.8	14.7	11.7	14.1	8.4	8.8	25.4	7.0	23.3	12.4	11.1	10.0

Continued

Table 9A3 *Continued*

	Maur	Bots	Ghana	Nig'a	Namb	Angol	Zamb	S.Afr.	Kenya	CongRp	Cam	C d'Iv	Gabon
Employment to population rate													
86–95	54.2	49.8	70.9	53.6	45.2	61.2	64.9	39.1	65.5	54.0	76.4	63.1	37.5
06–15	53.8	54.5	65.4	52.8	46.9	70.0	69.3	40.4	59.7	60.3	75.0	56.9	39.8
Total LFPR													
98–95	63.4	62.3	75.8	56.6	58.0	78.5	79.8	57.8	73.3	68.7	83.6	67.4	48.0
06–15	63.9	67.9	70.6	55.0	60.0	78.3	77.2	57.3	66.4	70.6	78.7	61.0	51.6
Unemployment Rate													
86–15	9.3	18.2	5.4	3.8	19.6	21.4	18.5	29.1	9.4	20.0	7.7	5.7	17.4
06–15	7.7	17.5	5.6	3.9	20.0	10.1	9.5	25.0	9.5	13.2	3.6	5.6	19.2
% Wage & Salaried Workers													
86–95	79.8	66.1	16.2	15.0	64.4	33.8	19.0	82.8	33.6	20.3	14.8	21.0	50.5
06–15	79.1	71.3	21.1	18.3	64.7	30.2	19.5	84.1	36.1	22.3	20.4	22.4	65.7
Literacy Rate													
86–95	79.9	68.6	n.a.	55.4	75.8	n.a	65.0	n.a.	n.a.	n.a.	n.a.	34.1	72.2
06–15	91.5	87.7	71.5	51.1	82.4	66.0	72.5	92.8	75.4	79.3	71.0	42.4	82.3
% Sec. School Enrollment (gross)													
86–95	50.0	41.9	36.9	25.8	43.8	8.9	19.9	68.1	40.2	55.2	26.1	18.5	38.7
06–15	91.1	81.5	55.8	42.6	64.1	24.4	n.a.	94.9	54.1	52.1	46.0	41.5	n.a.

10

Should Middle-Income Countries Implement Environmental Policies?

Emilio Padilla Rosa

10.1 Introduction

The 1992 United Nations Conference on Environment and Development (UNCED) recognized the principle of common but differentiated responsibilities. That is, all countries contribute to environmental problems, but there is a clear difference in their degree of responsibility on present environmental problems. High-income countries have obtained their material prosperity through the overuse of natural resources, contributing disproportionally to environmental problems such as deforestation, exhaustion of resources, climate change, and biodiversity loss. Besides these great differences in historical liability for environmental problems, low- and middle-income countries have more pressing social and economic needs than high-income countries. In short, middle-income countries concentrate more than two-thirds of the total poor population (Alonso, 2014). It may seem unfair to ask them to make strong sacrifices for the common good. From an extreme interpretation of the "common but differentiated responsibilities" principle some may argue that these differentiated responsibilities provide a good reason for inaction on environmental issues, and that all the efforts on environmental pressures mitigation should be made by countries with greater responsibility and more available financial resources. However, this might not be a smart strategy as we will discuss in this chapter.

As regards global environmental problems, according to most projections and research, the poor populations of low- and middle-income countries are those that will have to face the worst consequences of them, which is clearly the case of climate change (IPCC, 2014). Therefore, these countries are greatly interested in the enforcement and success of global environmental agreements, which requires the active participation of middle-income countries. In the case of global warming, a great share of the growth in greenhouse emissions in recent decades occurred in middle-income countries, which were not affected by the emissions control agreed in the Kyoto Protocol. They are also the countries that are projected to grow more in the coming years. No agreement will have any significant impact on global

Emilio Padilla Rosa, *Should Middle-Income Countries Implement Environmental Policies?* In: *Trapped in the Middle? Developmental Challenges for Middle-Income Countries.* Edited by: José Antonio Alonso and José Antonio Ocampo, Oxford University Press (2020). © OUP. DOI: 10.1093/oso/9780198852773.003.0010

emissions without the participation of these countries. This was made clear in the Paris Agreement, to which they all committed. This is also the case for other global environmental problems, such as biodiversity loss or ozone depletion. The Montreal protocol on substances that deplete the ozone layer, signed in 1987, included a special treatment for low- and middle-income countries, which facilitated its success. We will see in this chapter how participation in these agreements may be convenient and provide potential co-benefits for middle-income countries.

As to local environmental pressures, they strongly impact on the welfare of poorer populations in low- and middle-income countries, due to their strong dependence on natural resources for the direct satisfaction of their needs and as a source of income generation. In addition, this group of people are more vulnerable to environmental risks due to their lower resources and capacity to adapt to environmental degradation. This is the case for water and air pollution, soil erosion, natural resources depletion, among other environmental problems that cause direct damage on poorer populations, who are concentrated to a great extent in middle-income countries. Therefore, inaction on these environmental issues do not seem to favor their interests.

10.2 Should Middle-Income Countries Grow First and Clean up Later?

An argument that is often made to support deferring the application of stringent environmental policies is that economic growth will facilitate the solution to environmental problems, so that it would be preferable to just promote economic growth. Actually, the debate on the relationship between economic growth and environmental pressures has been dominated in recent decades by the environmental Kuznets curve hypothesis (Figure 10.1).[1] This optimistic hypothesis

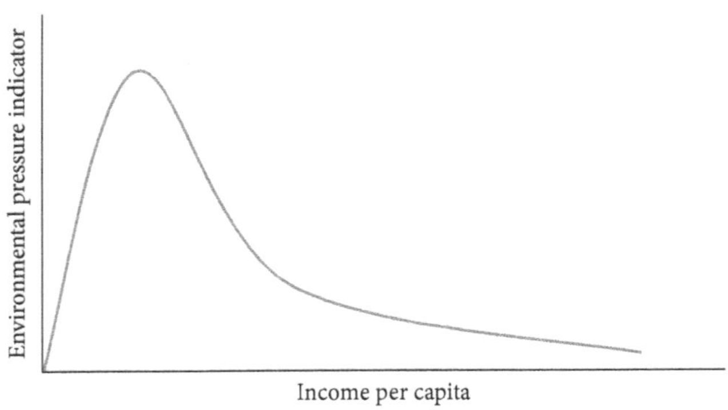

Figure 10.1 The environmental Kuznets curve

[1] The hypothesis owes its name to its analogy with the relationship between income per capita and inequality found by Kuznets (1955) in his empirical analysis.

assumes that, while at the initial stages of development economic growth involves greater environmental pressures, there will be a turning point from which the relationship changes and more economic growth will lead to a reduction in environmental pressures. In the case of middle-income countries, these would still typically be in the phase when the relationship shows a positive slope, though the transition to become a high-income country would eventually lead to a change in this relationship. Grossman and Krueger (1991) found in their seminal paper that for some pollutants there was an inverted-U relationship with income. Several papers have tested the hypothesis for different sets of countries and environmental pressures (see a review in Sarkodie and Strezov, 2019). A number of authors even used some partial evidence in favor of the hypothesis to suggest that the best environmental policy is just to pursue economic growth (Beckerman, 1992).

Grossman and Krueger (1991) identified three effects that would explain the relationship: scale, composition, and technology effects. The growth of the economy, the scale effect, would lead to a proportional increase in environmental pressure. The change in the composition of production resulting from structural changes to the economy, the composition effect, would first lead to an increase in environmental pressures during the process of industrialization, and later to a reduction of these pressures during the tertiarization of the economy. The technology effect refers to the improvement in the techniques of production that would come with economic development and that would allegedly lead to reduced environmental pressures. At a certain level of income per capita, the composition and technology effects would overcome the scale effect and lead to a change in the relationship between income per capita and environmental pressures; so that, after this point, economic affluence would facilitate the improvement in environmental quality.

However, the explanation of the hypothesis based on these effects has several drawbacks. As regards the composition effect, it is not certain that an increasing proportion of services necessarily involves less environmental pressure. Some services, such as transport, or some types of tourism, involve high direct environmental pressures, while other service activities consume many inputs from polluting sectors, so that their demand causes a greater environmental impact than the one initially assumed (Alcántara and Padilla, 2009; Piaggio et al., 2015). Even if we assumed that services are, on average, less polluting than other sectors, an increase in the share of services would not mean lower total environmental pressure, but lower pressure per unit of production (Roca et al., 2001).

As regards the technology effect, we cannot just assume that any new technology that comes with economic development is going to be better for the environment. Many new technologies that have appeared in high-income countries have just served to deplete natural resources at a quicker pace, for example, consider the cases of fracking or new fish techniques. Moreover, new production processes entail new environmental pressures that are not always better for the environment.

Even when the technological improvement consists of an efficiency improvement (less use of the resource per unit of the same product or service in a given production process) the final outcome on the environment is not clear as this increase in efficiency uses to lead to a rebound effect (an increase in the use of the resource as demand for the product or service increases due to its lower price) (Khazzoom, 1980; Greening et al., 2000). Energy policies generally ignore the rebound effects, while pricing policies seem to be the best option for limiting their impact (Baranzini et al., 2017). The rebound effects may be particularly significant in middle-income countries: they experience important improvements in energy efficiency, their demand for energy services is far from satiation level (Sorrell, 2007), and there is a rapid accumulation of technologies using energy (van den Bergh, 2011). Therefore, technological change needs to be directed with appropriate policies in order to achieve the desired impact on the environment.

An alternative explanation of the environmental Kuznets curve hypothesis considers environmental quality as a luxury good (Selden and Song, 1995; McConnell, 1997). The demand for environmental quality would increase as income increases in such a way that, above a certain income level, there would be a change in the relationship between economic growth and environmental pressure. However, this hypothesis ignores the fact that the welfare of poor populations depends critically on the quality of environmental services and resources. In addition, these models do not consider income inequality across individuals, so that different distributions lead to different environmental outcomes (Roca, 2003), and income distributions are quite varied across middle-income countries. Furthermore, the models explaining the hypothesis assume that environmental quality is like a good tradable in a market, while it is actually a public good that depends to a great extent on measures decided politically (Roca et al., 2001). People act against pollution and put pressure on political institutions when they are affected by it, not just when they become richer. Environmental quality will thus depend on the quality of the institutions and democratic systems, as well as on income distributions, so that we may find strong differences across middle-income countries with similar income per capita.

Besides the problems in the justifications of the environmental Kuznets curve hypothesis, the empirical evidence has also put it into question. There is no unambiguous evidence for any environmental pressure indicator. There seems to be more evidence in favor of the hypothesis for the case of local environmental pressures, while in the case of global problems (where the benefits of changing behaviors or policies are less clear for those taking pro-environmental actions) the hypothesis is rejected more often. Therefore, the hypothesis could not be generalized to explain the global relationship between the economy and the environment. There is also the problem that in some cases some environmental pressure indicators improve at the cost of the deterioration of others. Some analyses suggest that improvements for some countries have been achieved through the offshoring of extractive and polluting activities to other countries (Ekins, 1997; Stern et al., 1996; Suri and Chapman, 1998), without the consumption composition varying substantially. This process of specialization would make it more difficult for several middle-income countries that have specialized in resource- or pollution-intensive industries to show the same "greening path" as high-income countries in the future. In addition, the environmental Kuznets curve hypothesis is generally weakened when additional variables are introduced, so that in some cases it may arise due to the omission of relevant variables in econometric estimations. In many studies finding evidence supporting the hypothesis, the turning point is far above the income per capita of most middle-income countries so that arriving at this point would involve huge levels of pollution and environmental degradation if resolute environmental policies were not applied (Selden and Song, 1995; Stern et al., 1996). This is particularly relevant when some environmental damage is irrreversible, so that, even when there is evidence in favor of the hypothesis for some environmental pressure, it is not possible to return to the previous situation of environmental quality (Arrow et al., 1995), and so the recipe "growing first and cleaning later" would not make much sense for low- and middle-income countries. Most studies apply cross-section or panel data analysis in which they assume the same functional form and turning point in the relationship between environmental pressure and income per capita for all countries. However, the empirical evidence rejecting this homogeneity is clear (Dijkgraaf and Vollebergh, 2005; Piaggio and Padilla, 2012), so that what is found for the set of countries cannot be extrapolated as the individual behavior of each country, as they may be following different paths. It is more appropriate in the analysis of the relationship for individual countries, taking into account their economic structure and institutional context (Stern et al., 1996; de Bruyn et al., 1998).

The literature on the environmental Kuznets curve hypothesis makes clear that we cannot expect growth alone to solve the environmental problems of middle-income countries. Quite the opposite, it has served to highlight that resolute environmental policies are necessary. In the cases in which there seems to be a "delinking" between economic growth and environmental pressure, this has usually been achieved through determined environmental policies (Ekins, 1997). Moreover, policies can allow less damaging paths in the process of industrialization of middle-income countries (Dasgupta et al., 2002). Middle-income countries can avoid the worse environmental degradation phases by adopting and adapting efficient processes already proven in high-income countries, which may also be facilitated by the falling costs of clean technologies, without repeating the polluting path followed by them and avoiding the high costs of a late transition.

10.3 Potential Gains of the Enforcement of Environmental Policies in Middle-Income Countries

There is one argument that says that environmental policies may be prohibitively expensive for middle-income countries with other urgent needs. Nevertheless, many environmental policies are affordable and can even be accompanied by economic and social gains (Padilla, 2017), which may be particularly the case for climate action (NCE, 2018) and adaptation (GCA, 2019). When these potential gains are realized the greening of the economy is not just compatible but may facilitate the achievement of economic and social goals. There are important market failures (such as environmental and knowledge externalities) and government failures, and correcting them could pay from an economic point of view and would facilitate the achievement of a more sustainable development trajectory in middle-income countries.

10.3.1 Welfare and Health Improvement

The welfare of poor populations of low- and middle-income countries is closely related to access to (and the quality of) environmental goods and services. These are clearly the populations suffering the worst consequences of environmental degradation (Jehan and Umana, 2003; Bowen and Fankhauser, 2011; World Bank, 2012; Uitto, 2016). In addition, the lack of financial resources and proper institutions in these countries limits their capacity to react and makes them more vulnerable to environmental problems (IPCC, 2014). Measures to increase the availability of freshwater and reduce air pollution could have a significant impact on the welfare of poor populations, improving health and even labor force productivity (OECD, 2001). Outdoors pollution was estimated to cause 4.2 million premature deaths in the world in 2016, 91 percent of which were in low- and middle-income countries, the greatest number in the South-East Asia and Western Pacific regions (WHO, 2018a). As regards indoor pollution, around three billion people in low- and middle-income countries cook with and heat their homes using coal, kerosene, and biomass, with the consequence of 3.8 million people a year dying prematurely (WHO, 2018b). Substituting these inefficient devices with clean alternatives could significantly reduce these figures at a modest cost. Small solar power generators can provide energy at lower cost and pollution (IFC, 2007; Bowen and Fankhauser, 2011; REN21, 2016). With respect to water accessibility, according to the WHO (2019) in 2017 more than 2 billion people used a drinking water source contaminated with feces and 785 million people lacked a basic drinking-water service, including 144 million people who were dependent on surface water, most of them in low- and middle-income countries. Contaminated water can transmit several diseases, such as diarrhea caused by contaminated drinking water, which is estimated to cause 485,000 deaths each year. These deaths and morbidity could be significantly reduced with a moderate investment and proper regulation and management of water resources in order to secure clean water for all.

10.3.2 Increase in Efficiency, Productivity and the Potential for Future Growth

Economic growth requires sufficient availability of natural resources and services for production. It is not a sound policy to cause irreversible damage to the capacity of the environment to provide resources just in order to obtain greater economic growth which will only last for few years. Poor populations of low- and middle-income countries depend highly on natural resources for consumption and income generation. Moreover, their economies are already suffering high costs due to environmental degradation. A World Bank (2012) study estimated that this degradation averaged a cost of 8 percent of GDP per year across a sample of low- and middle-income countries. This figure is subject to some uncertainties and measurement difficulties, but it makes clear that environmental degradation is already imposing difficulties for the development of some low- and middle-income countries, which will worsen without proper adaptation measures. According to GCA (2019) more efficient water management and investment to adapt to climate risks are vital to economic growth; without them GCA estimate that the GDPs of India, China, and Central Asia could be about 6 percent lower by 2050.

The overuse of common-pool natural resources reduces their productivity. These shared natural resources are characterized by rivalry in their consumption and the difficulty of excluding users. They often suffer the problem of "open access" where there is no management restricting their use (Ostrom, 1990; Aguilera, 1994); that is, the resources are overexploited by users that obtain the immediate benefits of their use but share the costs with the rest of users. Many populations in low- and middle-income countries depend on these resources (such as fisheries, forests, or pastureland). Proper management of them would avoid their overexploitation and lead to increases in their productivity. Moreover, stable and sustainable harvests make the development of resource processing industries more feasible. Therefore, better management of common-pool resources clearly pays in environmental and economic terms. Depending on the specific resource and context, different measures may be appropriate. In some cases economic incentives can play a decisive role, though they should be carefully adapted to each context in order to avoid crowding out other motivations for conservation. One example is payment for environmental services, which could help to reduce the degradation of environmental services and poverty (Pagiola et al., 2005), though it has limitations and its appropriateness may depend on the context and design (Martínez-Tuna, 2008; Wunder, 2013). In the case of fisheries, limiting total captures through the distribution of tradable quotas may be an efficient way to reduce overexploitation in some cases (Costello et al., 2008; Heal and Schlenker, 2008). However, a FAO (2005) study suggests that in the context of small fisheries in low- and middle-income countries community rights-based management could be more appropriate as a contribution to poverty alleviation.

An improvement in the management of natural resources and services can certainly increase their productivity and their contribution to welfare. Some measures to reduce resource overexploitation may temporarily lead to lower production, as renewable natural resources are replenished, but will result in faster growth in the long-run (Ocampo, 2012), while contributing to the reduction of environmental risks and poverty alleviation through their greater productivity.

Climate change is expected to seriously affect agriculture productivity. More resilient food availability relies on increases in agricultural R&D to adapt to climate change, which, according to GCA (2019), has a high benefit–cost ratio. One example is drip irrigation technologies, which, besides facing water scarcity leads to higher crop productivity. Mangrove forest protection is also an area were actions provide a strong benefit–cost ratio due to avoiding losses from coastal flooding in addition to their contribution to fisheries, forestry, and recreation (GCA, 2019).

Many measures to increase environmental efficiency—lower resource use or pollution per unit of production—can translate into economic gains. Resources are often wasted due to inefficient processes, market distortions, inertia, lack of information, or bad management. The solution for many of these market failures and problems would pay in environmental and economic terms in a short period of time. In the case of energy efficiency improvements, they can provide a triple dividend: energy savings, fewer emissions, and more jobs (World Bank, 2010). According to McKingsey & Company (2009) energy efficiency regulation can overcome market imperfections and result in a net economic benefit, so that the costs savings of reducing energy consumption are greater than the investment in energy efficiency. Many of these measures are concentrated in technical standards for transport and particularly for building (such as standards for insulation, lighting systems, water heating, or air conditioning). In the case of many middle-income countries, they are quickly building infrastructure for coming decades and building standards are still to be imposed, so that the potential savings for energy efficiency in buildings are particularly significant (World Bank, 2010). There may also be possibilities in the power sector in low- and middle-income countries such as the use of off-grid solar power electricity systems in rural areas, which are cheaper than diesel generators. As regards manufacturing, there is also the potential to significantly improve efficiency with the application of best practices and existing technologies, without compromising growth (IEA, 2008). The potential gains are also particularly high in low- and middle-income countries due to their lower efficiency levels and the fact that they are still in the process of industrializing.

Better urban planning may help to improve environmental and economic efficiency. Avoiding city sprawl models and favoring more compact and dense city layouts enable cheaper service delivery and involve lower energy consumption and pollution, particularly in transport (Rickwood et al., 2008; OECD; 2012a). Commuting hours and exposure to polluted air would be reduced. In addition, livable compact, connected, and coordinated cities facilitate movement, may spur economic dynamism and provide better access to jobs, while higher densities may enable affordable housing (NCE, 2018). Middle-income countries are still urbanizing at a rapid pace and building their infrastructure, so that they can gain much from proper planning. The economic costs of greening at a later stage of development might be too high due to the increasing costs of high-carbon development and the high costs to reverse inefficient urbanization and infrastructure. In addition, climate adaptation efforts in urban areas could generate high economic returns, providing more resilient urban services and avoiding several risks of climate change associated with a business as usual situation. For instance, the cost of action in coastal cities is estimated as one-tenth the cost of no action (GCA, 2019).

Making infrastructures more sustainable and climate-resilient would slightly increase their upfront costs but have a very high benefit–cost ratio, making sound economic sense (GCA, 2019). The falling cost of clean alternatives is making sustainable investments even more attractive (NCE, 2018). Strategic infrastructure investment, such as the public clean transport networks can help to reduce congestion and pollution for more livable cities. There are also clear co-benefits of investing in resilient power and water systems and housing that resist increasingly frequent extreme climate events. Global projected infrastructure investments between 2020 and 2030 are $60 trillion according to GCA (2019) or $90 trillion according to NCE (2018); in any case more than the current stock. Ensuring that this infrastructure is sustainable will critically determine future economic prosperity. Investing it properly will help to drive innovation, improve health, facilitate new jobs, and tackle the risks of climate change (NCE, 2018). The challenge is particularly relevant for middle-income countries, which are in the phase of building much of their infrastructure for the next decade.

10.3.3 Avoiding Government Failures Produces Environmental and Economic Benefits

There are many policy measures that still encourage pollution and the overexploitation of natural resources. One obvious way to improve the environment and economic efficiency is to eliminate such measures. These inefficient incentives, that usually take the form of subsidies, move market prices away from the value of resources and the cost of pollution, leading to the overuse of natural resources and the assimilative capacity of nature.

The most important subsidies are the ones for fossil fuels, but there are also subsidies for the consumption of electricity, fisheries capture, mineral extraction, water irrigation, and intensive agriculture. Dobbs et al. (2011) and the World Bank (2012) estimated the total annual support to natural resource overexploitation to be around US$1–1.2 trillion annually. Coady et al. (2017) estimates that eliminating fossil-fuel subsidies in 2013 would have reduced air pollution deaths by 55 percent, cut emissions by 21 percent, at the same time having a positive impact on revenues and social welfare. According to Coady et al. (2017), three-fourths of total energy subsidies in the world are provided by the governments of low- and middle-income countries. Energy subsidies lock economies into inefficient technologies that will be more difficult and costly to replace in the future, which is especially counterproductive for low- and middle-income countries that are still industrializing and also have to build much of their infrastructure and buildings. Actually, energy efficiency across non-OECD countries tends to be the lowest in those countries where subsidies are the highest (Ellis, 2010).

Despite their negative environmental and economic impacts, subsidies are maintained due to the pressure of interest groups and the fear of social conflict if they are suppressed. However, the beneficiaries of these subsidies are often the people with higher incomes in low- and middle-income countries (Clements et al. 2014). Arze del Granado et al. (2012) analyzed twenty low- and middle-income countries between 2005 and 2009 and found that the richest 20 percent captured six times more in fossil-fuel subsidies than the poorest 20 percent. The evidence of their negative environmental, economic, and distributive effects is clear; however, fiscal reforms oriented to suppress them still find strong social contestation, as the recent example of protests in Ecuador shows (Guardian, 2019). Several countries have taken measures to phase out energy subsidies, including Indonesia, Colombia, Ghana, Malaysia, Turkey, Zimbabwe, and Iran (OECD, 2012b), and more recently Ecuador. However, even those that were initially successful tend to unravel at election time or when energy prices increase (OECD, 2012b), and some even stopped the reforms to appease the social unrest motivated by them.

There are clear benefits in cutting these subsidies. However, any change has its winners and losers and will surely find some opposition. Part of this resistance may be based on false information or a false perception of who benefits by these subsidies, which may be used by different interest and political groups. Therefore, any reform should be accompanied by better information presenting the damage caused by these distorting incentives, including their negative redistribution impacts. Such campaigns, however, need to be credible, something that depends on the perceived quality of institutions and public information, which is an important challenge in many middle-income countries. Only then will this information be able to prevail to misinformation campaigns, which nowadays can be rapidly promoted and spread through social networks. Reforms should also be accompanied by measures targeting the low- and middle-income populations affected. The new available public resources provided by this cut in expenditure could provide the necessary resources for programs that can increase the acceptance of the reform (information campaigns, social cushioning, and measures for a green transition). These reforms may be especially challenging in those middle-income countries with poor institutions and where interest and pressure groups are often able to guide the use of public revenues toward their own interest.

Finally, the elimination of fossil-fuel subsidies, together with other measures to promote the production of clean energy, can contribute to reducing oil dependence, with positive economic impacts. This would increase energy security, as it would reduce the dependence of middle-income economies on fuel imports, and it would also reduce their vulnerability to oil price shocks. In addition, those middle-income countries without fossil-fuel endowments would improve their balance of payments.

10.4 Development through Green Industrial Policies

Various middle-income countries have successfully developed new sectors on green goods oriented to export. Some middle-income countries, such as China, hold a growing proportion of patents in various renewable technologies, such as solar photovoltaic and wind power (Ocampo, 2012). China is the top exporter of solar panels and cells, and both China and India are among the top global suppliers of wind turbines. These countries have increasingly big domestic markets and the associated scale economies have helped the development of their export sectors (Cosbey, 2012). While these countries can compete in green innovation areas in the development of top technologies, other middle-income countries may find it more difficult. The production of green products often requires advanced technical training, supporting technological industries, access to finance, government support, and a certain size of domestic demand, which seem to favor large emerging economies, such as China and India (Cosbey, 2012). For many low- and middle-income countries there is a lack of financial resources and human capital. These countries can, anyway, focus on facilitating diffusion and adaptation of existing green technologies that are new to their firms, which can reduce the environmental impact and improve the competitiveness of their industries.

The process of adoption, adaptation, and deployment of green technologies can be facilitated by international openness (World Bank, 2012). Policies should facilitate foreign direct investment and the import and deployment of greener and more efficient technologies. In addition, capacity development is necessary to facilitate the adoption of green technologies, customizing them to local needs to maximize the benefits obtained (World Bank, 2012). Moreover, to maximize improvements for poorer populations, there should be an important focus on innovations that can be adapted to meet the needs of poor consumers at a low cost (Prahalad and Mashelkar, 2010; World Bank, 2012).

However, green products are heterogeneous, and biofuels, solar thermal, and geothermal are lower-tech technologies in which less developed countries have either expertise or potential for developing competitive export sectors (Steenblik, 2006; Cosbey, 2012). Besides China and India, Brazil, Pakistan, Thailand, and Malaysia, among others, have also developed biofuel industries, which would indicate that this sector has low barriers to entry (Ocampo, 2012). Moreover, some middle-income countries have a rich natural environment that may facilitate the development of a number of green industries with the appropriate support policies, such as, eg, solar energy in North Africa (World Bank, 2012; Vidican Auktor, 2017), where Morocco is investing public resources in wind energy and in large scale electricity production with solar power to sell it to Europe. Morocco is taking advantage of its favorable conditions for solar and wind generation to reduce fossil-fuel import dependence and to trigger its industrial development (Vidican Auktor, 2017). These new green sectors have, in most cases, appeared and been consolidated with the active support of governments through industrial policies, such as subsidizing research and development and industrial production (World Bank, 2012).

Environmental awareness and increasingly demanding environmental standards is leading the global market of green products and services to grow year after year. The growth of middle-income countries in coming decades may depend on being able to seize these opportunities and green their economies. Middle-income countries have to exploit their latent comparative advantages (such as their abundance of natural resources and services), to benefit from this growing market. In addition, efforts to reduce energy and resource inputs in production and reducing and reusing wastes, make products more competitive and reduce their environmental impact, but can also facilitate the development of exportable services and technologies (Cosbey, 2012). These opportunities may also be encouraged by the WTO mandate to reduce or eliminate barriers and liberalize trade in so-called environmental goods and services, though there is controversy on which goods should be included in this category (Cosbey, 2012; Khor, 2012). According to Dutz and Sharma (2012), in 2010 the shares for green and "close-to-green" product exports (13 vs. 15 percent) were closer between developing and high-income countries that the shares for green products (3.4 vs. 6 percent). This would indicate that the production structure of low- and middle-income countries could allow them to catch up gradually, increasing their share of green exports and taking advantage of these development opportunities. Some sectors will suffer with the changes in international preferences for greener productions. The situation might be particularly challenging for middle-income countries relying on commodity exports (energy and resource intensive sectors), as they will require a structural shift to a more diversified economy (Cosbey, 2012).

Present decisions affecting sectoral and technological specializations may lock countries into a high-carbon economy that will involve much greater costs in a future decarbonization, such as the costs of replacing long-lived carbon-intensive equipment and infrastructure. Focusing on long-term development, it would be better to avoid carbon intensive development using current knowledge to minimize economic and environmental costs of the development path chosen. Moreover, if middle-income countries make an early start in transforming their economies, they may gain early mover advantages on low-carbon industries and the production of green goods, besides avoiding the costs of a later transition.

Green sectors and technologies are more labor-intensive and so may provide more jobs in the medium to long term. Moreover, in situations of high unemployment, public investment to develop green production and technologies can contribute to generating jobs. There is also the possibility to generate a double dividend, when changing from taxing labor to taxing environmental damage, which results from penalizing environmental harm at the same time that the penalization of economic goods or labor is reduced (Pearce, 1991). There may, however, be transition costs when polluting industries are phased out and new green alternatives emerge slowly (World Bank 2012; UNIDO and GGGI, 2015), and there is also the risk of losing a part of domestic demand if the transformation involves changes in cost and prices.

10.5 Consequences for Middle-Income Countries of International Environmental Policies and Agreements

Countries adopting more stringent policies on environmental issues are often worried about the consequences of these measures. The main concern is the potential consequences over the competitiveness of the industries that see their costs and prices affected by these measures and face the competition from imported products that do not have to bear similar measures. Several proposals to tackle the problem involve imposing sanctions on countries not participating in the agreements. One option is the imposition of a "border tax adjustment." The idea is to "level the playing field" between the industries of the countries subject to stringent policies and those that are not subject to similar policies. In the case of climate change, there is a growing debate on the possibility to establish a "climate club" (Nordhaus, 2015), where those participating impose trade sanctions on those outside the agreement to avoid any incentive to free ride. It is also the case of the proposals on "carbon border tax adjustments," that would charge imports from "free riding" countries proportionally to their carbon content as if they were subject to the policy (Lockwood and Whalley, 2010), or the alternative of making them buy emission allowances (from emission trading systems) with the same purpose (Houser et al., 2008). There is debate on how these measures should be designed to be consistent with WTO rules (Cottier et al., 2009; Mattoo et al., 2009; Jakob et al., 2015). However, many developing countries may oppose these policies, as they might consider them to be protectionist measures penalizing countries that do not have the relevant resources or access to low-emission technologies. Some could even see border tax adjustments as measures against the principle of "common but differentiated responsibilities" (Khor, 2012). Therefore, if these types of measures are applied, they should be combined with appropriate finance and technological help to developing countries, so that they do not impose an additional impediment to their development. The measures to support developing countries will logically depend on their will to green their economies and participate in the agreements. Increasing environmental awareness, a greater stringency of environmental policies, and possible measures against "free riding" countries mean that not participating in international environmental agreements and continuing with a high-polluting development path would undermine the long-term potential for exports and industrial development of middle-income countries.

International agreements on environmental issues actually involve economic opportunities and transfers of technology for low- and middle-income countries. These countries have many possibilities for reducing emissions at a low cost—such is the case of land use change (eg, reducing deforestation and changing agricultural practices) (Bowen and Fankauser, 2011). Flexible mechanisms, such as the clean development mechanism, allow funds to be obtained for reducing emissions, especially in the manufacturing and energy sectors. They also involve financial and technological transfers, and support the capacity development of developing countries, which may facilitate the transformation of their manufacturing and energy sectors. These mechanisms provide incentives to low- and middle-income countries to participate and to transform their economies. The payment for reduced emission from deforestation, or international carbon trading may also provide gains for those countries performing well and following a low-carbon development path. All these flexible mechanisms allow a given global mitigation to be obtained at a lower cost, so that, from a global perspective, they are efficient tools for reducing emissions.

However, in order to be successful, any international agreement has to take fairly into account the potential of the different countries. The principle of "common but differentiated responsibilities" has to guide its design in such a way that low- and middle-income countries can make environmental goals compatible with their economic development. Global agreements must include additional finance transfers to help developing countries' mitigation and adaptation. Furthermore, it is argued that flows obtained from flexibility mechanisms should not be considered as contributions from high-income countries to the financing of the mitigation and adaptation needs of low- and middle-income countries, as they actually substitute for the commitments that these countries have to meet (Ocampo, 2012). The priority of these funds is poorer countries, though this finance should not just substitute current aid to development but be additional to it. There are arguments, however, for also implementing these transfers for middle-income countries to help their contribution to global public environmental goods, such as protection of the biodiversity, forests, and climate stability, as payment for the environmental services provided (Dervis, 2008; Ocampo, 2012).

Finance transfers must encourage developing countries to participate in environmental agreements and take adequate measures. In this respect, however, it seems that the Paris Agreement plan to provide US$100 billion per year for 2020–25 to developing countries to help their adaptation and mitigation efforts seems fairly insufficient (GCF, 2016). The agreement stated that this amount, provided through the Green Climate Fund, would be progressively increased after this period. In order to benefit from these funds, developing countries must participate in global climate agreements. A previous agreement on another global environmental problem that succeeded in obtaining universal ratification was the Montreal Protocol on substances that deplete the ozone layer (UNEP, 2015). Its success was to a great extent based on special treatment to developing countries, including longer periods and financial assistance for meeting the stated targets. Finally, we can mention the Global Environment Facility (a partnership of 183 countries), which provides funds for the development of projects with environmental benefits. This fund has facilitated the participation of low- and middle-income countries in various international agreements.

10.6 Conclusions

Despite there being a wide agreement on the principle of "differentiated responsibilities," it does not seem that its acceptance must lead to the conclusion that implementing environmental policies in low- and middle-income countries is not a good idea. Moreover, we have seen that waiting until economic growth provides the solution to environmental problems may be counterproductive in environmental and economic terms.

Several environmental policies are affordable and may even provide welfare enhancement and economic and social gains for middle-income countries. However, if some green policies could be implemented at a negative cost, one may question why they are not being enforced. The answer is that the government and market failures whose solution may involve these gains require appropriate policy measures that are not always easy to implement. Moreover, this implementation is even more challenging in many low- and middle-income countries suffering from economic and institutional limitations that hamper the application of appropriate measures. Environmental and green industrial policies require the good governance and high quality of institutions in order to avoid rent-seeking and political capture. Governments and institutions should be able to control pressure groups and manage public resources wisely. Some middle-income countries suffer from poor quality institutions. Institutional quality tends to be particularly low in middle-income countries with lower taxes, income, and education levels, and more unequal income distribution (Alonso, 2013). In addition, the lack of proper financial institutions in these countries also hampers the implementation of policies providing benefits in the long term.

There are no unique measures that should be applied in the same way to all countries. Each middle-income country should assess the potential risks and benefits of the different feasible green policies, balancing the costs of early action against the costs of lock in. Therefore, policy measures may be combined in a different way depending on each specific situation. Some middle-income countries, such as China, have been able to develop top new technologies and become leaders in a range of green industries. However, for most middle-income countries there is less risk when they adapt already tested technologies to their local context. Middle-income countries can also use some competitive advantages, such as those provided by rich natural environments, and develop new green industries in sectors with lower entry barriers if they have the appropriate policy support.

The international context, such as environmental awareness, the stringency of policies in rich nations, and international agreements, play an important role in the potential gains of implementing environmental policies and promoting a green transformation in middle-income countries. Keeping with a brown specialization may make the future development of these countries difficult. Furthermore, high-income countries should provide support to developing countries in the form of adequate finance transfers and financial mechanisms, but also by facilitating technology transmission and capacity development, and providing institutional support. In this way, it will also be feasible for middle-income countries to take advantage of the potential co-benefits that environmental policies can provide them.

10.7 Acknowledgments

This chapter is based on a presentation in the "Workshop on trapped in the middle? developmental challenges for middle-income countries", sponsored by the

Fundación Ramón Areces and the Spanish Ministry of Foreign Affairs, European Union and Cooperation, in Madrid on June 10 and 11, 2019. It extends some of the arguments presented in Padilla (2017) for the case of developing countries. I acknowledge support from project RTI2018-095484-B-I00 (Spanish Ministry of Economics and Competitiveness and ERDF).

References

Aguilera, F. (1994): "Some notes on the misuse of classic writings in economics on the subject of common property," *Ecological Economics* 9: 221–8.

Alcántara, V. and Padilla, E. (2009): "Input–output subsystems and pollution: An application to the service sector and CO_2 emissions in Spain," *Ecological Economics* 68: 905–14.

Alonso, J. A. (2013): "The determinants of institutional quality. More on the debate," *Journal of International Development*, 25, no. 2: 206–26.

Alonso, J. A. (2014): "Cooperation with middle-income countries: an incentive based approach," Spanish Cooperation Working Papers 2014, AECID.

Arrow, K., Boling, B., Costanza, R., Dasgupta, P., Folke, C., Holling, S., Jansson, B.-O, Levin, S., Mäler, K.-G., Perrings, C., and Pimentel, D. (1995): "Economic growth, carrying capacity and the environment," *Science* 268: 520–1.

Arze del Granado, F. J. A., Coady, D., and Gillingham, R. (2012): "The unequal benefits of fuel subsidies: A review of evidence for developing countries," *World Development*, 40, no. 11: 2234–48.

Baranzini, A., van den Bergh, J., Carattini, S., Howarth, R., Padilla, E., and Roca, J. (2017): "Carbon pricing in climate policy: Seven reasons, complementary instruments, and political-economy considerations," *WIREs Climate Change*, 8, no. 4: 1–17.

Beckerman, W. (1992): "Economic growth and the environment: whose growth? Whose environment?" *World Development* 20: 481–96.

Bowen, A. and Fankhauser, S. (2011): "Low-carbon development for the least developed countries", *World Economics* 2: 145–62.

Clements, B., Coady, D., Fabrizio, S., Gupta, S., and Shang, B. (2014): "Energy subsidies: How large are they and how can they be reformed?" *Economics of Energy & Environmental Policy* 3, no. 1: 1–18.

Coady, D., Parry, I., Sears, L., and Shang, B. (2017): "How large are global fossil fuel subsidies?" *World Development* 91: 11–27.

Cosbey, A. (2012): "Trade, sustainable development and a green economy: Benefits, challenges and risks," in J. A. Ocampo, A. Cosbey, and M. Khor (eds.), "The Transition to a Green Economy: Benefits, challenges and risks from a sustainable development perspective", Report to Second Preparatory Committee Meeting for UN Conference on Sustainable Development, under the direction of UNDESA, UNCTAD, UN Environment.

Costello, C., Gaines, S. D., and Lynham, J. (2008): "Can Catch Shares Prevent Fisheries Collapse?", Science 321: 1678–81.

Cottier, T., Nartova, O., and Bigdeli, S. Z. (eds.) (2009): *International Trade Regulation and the Mitigation of Climate Change: World Trade Forum*, Cambridge, New York: Cambridge University Press.

Dasgupta, S., Laplante, B., Wang, H., and Wheeler, D. (2002): "Confronting the environmental Kuznets curve," *Journal of Economic Perspectives* 16: 147–68.

de Bruyn, S.M., van den Bergh, J. C. and Opschoor, J. B. (1998): "Economic growth and emissions: reconsidering the empirical basis of environmental Kuznets curves," *Ecological Economics* 25: 161–75.

Dervis, K. (2008): "The Climate Change Challenge: WIDER Annual Lecture 11," Helsinki: UNU-WIDER,.

Dijkgraaf, E. and Vollebergh, H. (2005): "A Test on parameter heterogeneity in CO_2 panel EKC estimations," *Environmental and Resource Economics* 32, no. 2: 229–39.

Dobbs, R., Oppenheim, J., Thompson, F., Brinkman, M., and Zornes, M. (2011): *Resource Revolution: Meeting the World's Energy, Materials, Food, and Water Needs*, London: McKinsey & Company.

Dutz, M. A. and Sharma, S. (2012): "Green growth, technology, and innovation", Policy Research Working Paper 5932, Washington, DC: World Bank.

Ekins, P. (1997): "The Kuznets curve for the environment and economic growth: examining the evidence", *Environment and Planning A*, 29, 805–30.

Ellis, J. (2010): "The effects of fossil-fuel subsidy reform: A review of modelling and empirical studies", Winnipeg: Global Subsidies Initiative, International Institute for Sustainable Development.

FAO. (2005): *Increasing the Contribution of Small-Scale Fisheries to Poverty Alleviation and Food Security*, FAO Technical Guidelines for Responsible Fisheries, No. 10. Rome: FAO.

Global Commission on Adaptation (GCA) (2019): *Adapt Now. A Global Call For Leadership on Climate Resilience*, Rotterdam and Washington: Global Center on Adaptation and World Resources Institute.

Green Climate Fund (GCF) (2016): "Green Climate Fund. Global context," https://www.greenclimate.fund/about-gcf/global-context, accessed December 10, 2016.

Greening, L. A., Greene, D. L., and Difiglio, C. (2000): "Energy efficiency and consumption—the rebound effect—a survey," *Energy Policy* 28, no. 6–7: 389–401.

Grossman, G. and Krueger, A. (1991): "Environmental impacts of a North American free trade agreement," NBER working paper, on. 3914.

The Guardian (2019): "Ecuador declares state of emergency as protesters decry end to fuel subsidies," 3 October 2019, https://www.theguardian.com/world/2019/oct/03/ecuador-state-of-emergency-fuel-subsidies-protest (accessed on October 7, 2019).

Heal, G. and Schlenker, W. (2008): "Economics: sustainable fisheries," *Nature* 455, no. 7216: 1044–5.

Houser, T., Bradley, R., Childs, B., Werksman, J., and Heilmayr, R. (2008): "Leveling the Carbon Playing Field: International Competition and US Climate Policy Design," Washington: Peterson Institute for International Economics and World Resources Institute.

International Energy Agency (IEA). (2008): *Energy Technology Perspective 2008: Scenarios and Strategies to 2050*, Paris: IEA.

IFC. (2007): *Selling Solar. Lessons from More than a Decade of IFC's Experience.* Washington, DC: International Finance Corporation.

Intergovernmental Panel on Climate Change (IPCC). (2014): *Climate Change 2014: Impacts, Adaptation, and Vulnerability.* Working Group II Contribution to the Fifth Assessment Report of the Intergovernmental Panel on Climate Change. Cambridge: Cambridge University Press.

Jakob, M., Chen, C., Fuss, S., Marxen, A., and Edenhofer, O. (2015): "Development incentives for fossil fuel subsidy reform," *Nature Climate Change* 5, no. 8: 709–12.

Jehan, S. and Umana, A. (2003): "The environment–poverty nexus," *Development Policy Journal* 3: 53–70.

Khazzoom, J. D. (1980): "Economic implications of mandated efficiency in standards for household appliances," *The Energy Journal* 1, no. 4: 21–40.

Khor, M. (2012): "Challenges of the green economy concept and policies in the context of sustainable development, poverty and equity," in J. A. Ocampo, A. Cosbey, and M. Khor (eds.), "The Transition to a Green Economy: Benefits, challenges and risks from a sustainable development perspective", Report to Second Preparatory Committee Meeting for UN Conference on Sustainable Development, under the direction of UNDESA, UNCTAD, UN Environment.

Kuznets, S. (1955): "Economic growth and income inequality," *American Economic Review* 45: 1–28.

Lockwood, B. and Whalley, J. (2010): "Carbon-motivated border tax adjustments: old wine in green bottles?", *The World Economy* 33, no. 6: 810–19.

Martínez-Tuna, M. (2008): "¿Mercados de servicios ambientales? Análisis de tres experiencias Centroamericanas de pago por servicios ambientales," PhD thesis, ICTA, Universidad Autónoma de Barcelona.

Mattoo, A., Subramanian, A., van der Mensbrugghe, D., and He, J. (2009): "Reconciling climate change and trade policy," Policy Research Working Papers. The World Bank.

McConnell, K. (1997): "Income and demand for environmental quality," *Environment and Development Economics* 2: 383–99.

McKinsey & Company. (2009): *Pathways to a Low-Carbon Economy. Version 2 of the Global Greenhouse Gas Abatement Cost Curve.* McKinsey & Company.

New Climate Economy (NCE) (2018): *Unlocking the Inclusive Growth Story of the 21st Century*, Washington, DC: New Climate Economy.

Nordhaus, W. (2015): "Climate clubs: overcoming free-riding in international climate policy," American Economic Review 105, no.4: 1339–70.

Ocampo, J. A. (2012): "The macroeconomics of the green economy," in J. A. Ocampo, A. Cosbey, and M. Khor (eds.), "The Transition to a Green Economy: Benefits, challenges and risks from a sustainable development perspective", Report to Second Preparatory Committee Meeting for UN Conference on Sustainable Development, under the direction of UNDESA, UNCTAD, UN Environment.

OECD. (2001): "Human health and the environment," In OECD, *OECD Environmental Outlook*, Paris: OECD.

OECD. (2012a): *Compact City Policies. A Comparative Assessment*, OECD Green Growth Studies, Paris: OECD Publishing,.

OECD. (2012b): *Green Growth and Developing Countries—Consultation Draft*, Paris: OECD.

Ostrom, E. (1990): *Governing the Commons. The Evolution of Institutions for Collective Action*, Cambridge: Cambridge University Press.

Padilla, E. (2017): "What can developing countries gain from a green transformation?"

Pagiola, S., Arcenas, A., and Platais, G. (2005): "Can payments for environmental services help reduce poverty? An exploration of the issues and evidence to date from Latin America," *World Development* 33, no. 2: 237–53.

Pearce, D. (1991): "The role of carbon taxes in adjusting global warming," *The Economic Journal* 101: 938–48.

Piaggio, M. and Padilla, E. (2012): "CO_2 emissions and economic activity: heterogeneity across countries and non stationary series," *Energy Policy* 46: 370–81.

Piaggio, M., Alcántara, V., and Padilla, E. (2015): "The materiality of the immaterial. Services sectors and CO_2 emissions in Uruguay," *Ecological Economics* 110: 1–10.

Prahalad, C. K. and Mashelkar, R. A. (2010): "Innovation's Holy Grail," *Harvard Business Review* (July–August): 132–41.

REN21. (2016): "Renewables 2016 Global Status Report," REN21 Secretariat, Paris. http://www.ren21.net/GSR-2016-Report-Full-report-EN

Rickwood, P., Glazebrook, G., and Searle, G. (2008): "Urban structure and energy—a review," *Urban Policy and Research* 26, no. 1: 57–81

Roca, J. (2003): "Do individual preferences explain the Environmental Kuznets curve?", *Ecological Economics* 45: 3–10.

Roca, J., Padilla, E., Farré, M., and Galletto, V. (2001): "Economic Growth and Atmospheric Pollution in Spain: Discussing the Environmental Kuznets Curve Hypothesis," *Ecological Economics* 39, no. 1: 85–99.

Sarkodie, S. A. and Strezov, V. (2019): "A review on environmental Kuznets curve hypothesis using bibliometric and meta-analysis," *Science of the Total Environment* 649, no. 1: 128–45.

Selden, T. M. and Song, D. (1995): "Neoclassical growth, the J curve for abatement and the inverted U curve for pollution," *Journal of Environmental Economics and Management* 29: 162–8.

Sorrell, S. (2007): *The Rebound Effect: An Assessment of the Evidence for Economy-Wide Energy Savings from Improved Energy Efficiency*, London: UK Energy Research Centre.

Steenblik, R. (2006): "Liberalisation of trade in renewable energy and associated technologies: biodiesel, solar thermal and geothermal energy," OECD Trade and Environment Working Paper 2006–01. Paris: OECD.

Stern, D. I., Common, M. S. and Barbier, E. B. (1996): "Economic growth, trade and the environment: implications for the environmental Kuznets curve," *World Development* 24: 1151–60.

Suri, V. and Chapman, D. (1998): "Economic growth, trade and energy: implications for the environmental Kuznets curve," *Ecological Economics* 25: 195–208.

Uitto, J. I. (2016): "The environment–poverty nexus in evaluation: implications for the Sustainable Development Goals," *Global Policy* 7, no. 3: 441–7.

UNEP. (2015): "The Montreal Protocol on Substances that Deplete the Ozone Layer", UNEP, Ozone Secretariat; http://ozone.unep.org/en/treaties-and-decisions/montreal-protocol-substances-deplete-ozone-layer; (accessed on May 5, 2016).

UNIDO and GGGI. (2015): *Global Green Growth: Clean Energy Industry Investments and Expanding Job Opportunities. Volume I: Overall Findings*, Vienna and Seoul: UNIDO and GGGI.

van den Bergh, J. C. (2011): "Energy conservation more effective with rebound policy," *Environmental and Resource Economics* 48, no. 1: 43–58.

Vidican Auktor, G. (2017): "Renewable energy as a trigger for industrial development in Morocco", in T. Altenburg, C. Assmann (eds.), *Green Industrial Policy: Concept, Policies Country Experiences*, Geneva, Bonn: UN Environment and German Development Institute (DIE).

World Bank. (2010): *World Development Report 10. Development and Climate Change*, Washington, DC: The World Bank.

World Bank. (2012): *Inclusive Green Growth. The Pathway to Sustainable Development*, Washington, DC: The World Bank.

World Health Organization (WHO). (2018a): "Ambient (outdoor) air quality and health," Fact sheet, Updated May 2, 2018; https://www.who.int/news-room/fact-sheets/detail/ambient-(outdoor)-air-quality-and-health, accessed October 7, 2019.

World Health Organization (WHO). (2018b): "Household air pollution and health," Fact sheet, Updated May 8, 2018; https://www.who.int/news-room/fact-sheets/detail/household-air-pollution-and-health, accessed October 7, 2019.

World Health Organization (WHO). (2019): "Drinking-water," Fact sheet, Updated June 14, 2019; https://www.who.int/news-room/fact-sheets/detail/drinking-water, accessed October 7, 2019.

Wunder, S. (2013): "When payments for environmental services will work for conservation," *Conservation Letters* 6, no. 4: 230–7.

11

National Development Finance in Middle-Income Countries

The Role of National Development Banks

Stephany Griffith-Jones

11.1 Introduction

National development finance is crucial for funding sufficient investment, a pre-condition to allow middle-income countries to grow in a macroeconomically and environmentally sustainable way, and thus help them escape the middle-income trap (MIT). Therefore, this chapter looks at the role of domestic financial intermediation and its potential contributions to dynamic, sustainable, and inclusive development, and specifically to structural change, necessary to achieve such development.

There are several main reasons why domestic finance is essential and, in several aspects, preferable to external finance. One is that it tends to be a more stable source of funding, and can be more easily regulated than external capital flows. A second reason is that it does not generate payments in foreign currency abroad, which become especially onerous if there is a balance of payment crisis linked to a constraint of foreign exchange. Associated with this is a third reason, which is that domestic finance does not generate currency mismatches, as foreign flows often do. Currency mismatches are particularly problematic if the foreign lending or investment in foreign currency is to borrowers, whose sales only or mainly generate domestic currency, or to banks, which either have currency mismatches themselves or pass them on to their borrowers (see chapter 15 by Ocampo in this volume, Ocampo, 2017, and Ffrench Davis and Griffith-Jones, 2019). Though having these important advantages over international capital flows, domestic finance needs to be complemented by such external capital flows, for example to finance trade and to attract foreign direct investment, that contributes new technologies, access to markets, and other benefits. Very short-term private external flows, not linked to funding trade, can be highly problematic, if they are excessive and come in waves.

Stephany Griffith-Jones, *National Development Finance in Middle-Income Countries: The Role of National Development Banks* In: *Trapped in the Middle? Developmental Challenges for Middle-Income Countries.* Edited by: José Antonio Alonso and José Antonio Ocampo, Oxford University Press (2020). © OUP. DOI: 10.1093/oso/9780198852773.003.0011

As regards domestic finance, the role of National Development Banks (NDBs) will be emphasized, as in many emerging, and in some developing, economies, they play a major role in financing sectors key for dynamic and sustainable growth and are a valuable instrument for supporting investment in sectors prioritized in countries' national development policies. They do this both through their own lending, but also in some cases, by catalyzing private finance.

It is important to stress the need to avoid domestic financial instability. This might lead to developmentally costly debt or banking crises, which in many cases relate to boom–bust cycles in external financing (as emphasized in chapter 15 by Ocampo in this volume), but may also have domestic dimensions that generate new shocks or amplify external ones. Actually, there is a link between these two issues, as some of the market failures that may be the source of domestic financial instability also justify the need for development banks. An important point here is that by diversifying the financial system to include development banks, systemic risk may be reduced, especially if the risks taken by development banks are not correlated to those taken by private banks.

After this Introduction, section 11.2, looks at the limitations of private finance, section 11.3 examines the roles and main features of NDBs. Then in section 11.4, the chapter looks at the counter-cyclical, innovation, and inclusion roles of NDBs, and section 11.5 at NDBs' role in infrastructure, including green infrastructure. Section 11.6 examines the desirable scale of NDBs, while section 11.7 considers new issues on financial instruments, illustrated by the recent European experience, and its lessons. Section 11.8 concludes.

11.2 Limitations of Private Finance

A key problem for many emerging countries is that their domestic financial markets are thin. They have a high prevalence of short-term financial assets and liabilities. This means that their capacity to finance investment that requires patient or long-term finance is limited. This obliges firms to rely on short-term loans, or limit their investment to what they can finance with their own resources, such as retained profits. However, the latter route is limited to existing firms, and thus financial constraints particularly limit new activities associated with structural change. Consequently there are problems of fair access to finance, as only the largest established firms can tap international financial markets. Furthermore, firms in relatively poorer and less dynamic regions will also face greater difficulty accessing finance than those in more prosperous areas, leading to a vicious circle of increased regional inequality. In sectors like investment in infrastructure, private finance for long-term investment is very limited.

More generally, the insufficiency of long-term domestic funding contributes to insufficient levels of investment, which then becomes a barrier for emerging countries trying to escape the middle-income trap. In fact, many of the countries that seem most likely to escape the middle-income trap are those, as in Asia, that have had systematically high levels of investment. Furthermore, those high levels of investment are to an important extent funded in such countries by high levels of domestic savings; NDBs play a key role in many of these economies.

In addition, emerging and developing economies face a variable mix of maturity and currency mismatches in portfolios. This poses the risk that during crises, creditors may not roll over short-term loans, or may force borrowers to pay higher interest rates when their revenues could be falling. Domestic bond markets—if sufficiently developed—will also face a reduction in the financing available, plus shorter maturities and/or higher interest rates, for those firms still able to borrow. This can pose risks to financial stability.

Maturity and currency mismatches are especially problematic in countries, including many middle-income ones, that lack adequate development of futures markets where firms could hedge their risks. Such markets, if available, tend to be relatively short-term and become even shorter-term or stop operating during crises. In turn, the increasing use of derivative products, when they exist, may become an additional source of volatility. Therefore, although the growth of derivative markets helps reduce "micro-instability," by creating new hedging techniques that allow individual companies to cover their risks, it may become an additional source of "macro-instability" (see, for example, Dodd and Griffith-Jones, 2006, for the cases of Chile and Brazil).

The broad conclusion is that in emerging and even more so in developing countries, private finance on its own cannot fund many key investments, especially those that require long-term finance—"patient capital"—and more generally are seen by private lenders and investors to be too risky.

11.3 The Roles and Main Features of National Development Banks

Given the limitations (both in terms of market gaps and market failures) and stability issues that private financial sectors have, development banks play an essential role from the perspective of both growth and stability. As extensively argued in the conclusions of a recent research project and book, led by José Antonio Ocampo and the author of this chapter (Griffith-Jones and Ocampo, 2018), on which important parts of this chapter draw, NDBs' main functions are: (i) providing counter-cyclical financing; (ii) promoting innovation and structural transformation; (iii) supporting infrastructure investment; (iv) enhancing financial inclusion; and (v) supporting the provision of public goods, particularly combating climate change.

Function (ii) seems particularly worth emphasizing in the context of trying to overcome the MIT, but other dimensions also are significant. Function (i) makes development banks an additional and valuable instrument of counter-cyclical macroeconomic policy and function (iii)—financial support for infrastructure—is also essential for dynamic growth in both the domestic and international markets. Promoting small start-ups or SMEs linked to more dynamic growth, as part of the broader objective of financial inclusion (iv), is also crucial for structural change. And many of the activities associated with mitigating and adapting to climate change, included under (v) are innovative activities, linked to the development of new technologies.

The failure of private financial and banking markets, on their own, to deliver adequate funding in a stable manner, at sufficient maturities, and at reasonable cost in local currencies has led many governments to rely more on NDBs. The importance of these banks is a crucial feature of financial sectors in successful emerging economies such as China, India, and the Republic of Korea, but also of successful developed countries, notably Germany. The scale of several existing NDBs is very large, and therefore they have a large impact in several countries: the level of total assets reached approximately $5 trillion in 2015, about five times the level of loans of all Multilateral Development Banks (MDBs) in the same year. Several African and Asian countries recently created NDBs, and a number of European countries (eg Portugal and Ireland) also did so, while others expanded existing ones (BPI France, as one example of several).

For a long time, the topic of NDBs was largely neglected in the academic and policy literature. Since the 2007–09 North Atlantic financial crisis, support for these institutions increased, alongside that for MDBs. This has led to a need to understand key issues in relation to NDBs: how they operate; which instruments, incentives, and governance work better; how they link to broader government policies; and, very importantly, how they link with private financial agents and the private sector in general, as their major objective should be to promote private investment.

Griffith-Jones and Ocampo (2018) analyzed NDBs in seven countries (Germany, China, Brazil, Chile, Colombia, Mexico, and Peru). The authors conclude that overall these banks tend to be successful at what they do—albeit with varying levels of success, associated with their relative size. They have been broadly efficient development policy instruments, helping to overcome major market failures, and doing so in a flexible and dynamic way over time. Furthermore, they have played an important role in funding structural adjustment as part of national development strategies.

There is diversity in the modalities of national development banks. There are countries with individual banks (Germany, Brazil, and Chile), others in which they are part of a system of NDBs with sectorial functions (Colombia and Peru), and a final group in which there is a system, but it is dominated by an individual bank (China and Mexico). Some are second-tier institutions, which lend via financial intermediaries that are usually private, but others are first-tier and lend directly themselves. In addition there are several that combine both functions.

NDB funding strategies vary: as well as having paid-in capital provided by governments, they also raise funds on national and international private capital markets, mixing—in a variety of ways—special fiscal resources channeled through them, bond issues, deposits (generally long-term), and external credit, for example that provided by multilateral banks.

In the case of first-tier lending, typically NDB loans are co-financed by private agents, and of course in second-tier lending by private financial agents—as well as state-owned commercial banks—directly provide the loans that are rediscounted by the development banks.

Leveraging public resources with private funds is especially valuable in contexts of limited fiscal space, usually during and after crises, particularly the 2007–09 North Atlantic crisis. Aside from lending and equity investment in new firms, there are novel instruments that are increasingly used by these institutions, both to achieve new aims, such increasing equity stakes in diversified portfolios, and to increase greater leverage. These new instruments include guarantees, as well as venture capital and debt funds (see section 11.8).

The size of the NDB institutions varies significantly among the countries studied (see Figure 11.1). China, Germany, and Brazil have very large NDBs, with assets in the range of 15–19 percent of GDP. In contrast, the size of NDBs is only about 2–3 percent of GDP in Chile, Colombia, and Mexico. Peru is an intermediate case, but if we exclude the largest institution (Banco de la Nación), which has only some limited development functions, it belongs to the second category.

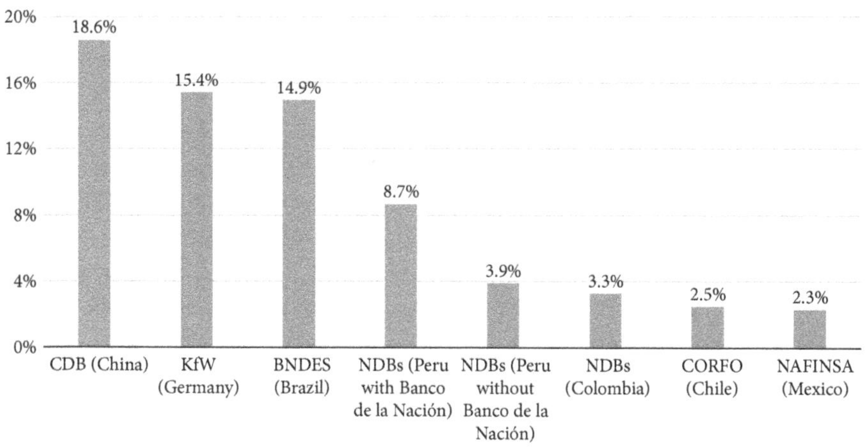

Figure 11.1 Assets of NDBs as a proportion of GDP, 2015

Source: Banscope and NDBs.

11.4 The Counter-Cyclical Role of NDBs

Among the functions mentioned in section 11.3, it is important to stress that NDBs were clearly counter-cyclical after the North Atlantic financial crisis. According to World Bank data (Luna-Martinez and Vicente, 2012), NDBs increased their lending from \$1.16 trillion to \$1.58 trillion between 2007 and 2009, that is by 36 percent; this increase in lending in hard times was far higher than the mere 10 percent increase in private bank credit in the same countries. For Latin America, the research in the Griffith-Jones and Ocampo research project and book shows that NDBs increased lending by 3.4 percent annually in normal times and by over 10 percent in crisis periods; on the other hand, private banks behaved pro-cyclically and reduced the growth of lending in crisis periods (Brei and Schlarek, 2018).

The counter-cyclical role of NDBs should be seen as a complement to counter-cyclical fiscal, monetary, and foreign exchange policies. Just as central banks provide key liquidity in bad times, NDBs provide crucial finance in those periods, particularly of a long-term character, to support economic recovery and help finance and maintain investment levels, as well as specific projects or programs. This is especially important in sectors essential for the process of structural transformation, such as new companies and new technologies, as well as for the funding of infrastructure. One example, amongst many, of such a specific and significant program that was supported by an NDB, was that by NAFINSA, to continue the introduction of wind energy in Mexico. The companies attempting to invest in the sector found that they were unable to raise finance through private bank loans and on the private capital markets, during and after the 2007–09 financial crisis (see Griffith-Jones and Attridge, forthcoming).

The scale of NDB institutions is also very important from the perspective of properly fulfilling their counter-cyclical role in the economy; this is the case for all categories of countries, developing, emerging, and even developed ones. If NDBs are large, and represent a high proportion of the financial sector of the particular economy, they can have a bigger impact in helping to maintain key investment during and after financial crises. On the other hand, if NDBs are relatively small, as proportion of the financial system of a country, their counter-cyclical impact will be limited, even if they significantly increase their lending. The counter-cyclical role that NDBs play implies, of course that they should not only expand financing during crises, but also moderate it during booms.

11.5 The Innovation and Inclusion Roles of NDBs

NDBs have played a key role in fostering innovation and entrepreneurship in national economies, essential to achieve the structural transformation needed to overcome the MIT. As Mazzucato and Penna (2018) argue, there is mounting evidence that NDBs have fostered patient, long-term committed finance for mission-oriented investment in innovative activities. For example, they are increasingly providing long-term venture capital for innovation projects. Because these projects are risky and uncertain, private finance is reluctant to support them, thus also making the role of NDBs crucial as catalysts of private finance. If successful, these projects generate positive externalities, inducing further innovations. Often, private investors join NDBs in providing venture capital funds, thus helping to channel private investment into sectors of high priority for dynamic growth.

KfW, the German development bank, for example, invests in the modernization of industries and has encouraged the development of new sectors, notably renewable energy, over the past decade. CDB, the Chinese development bank, the largest NDB in the world, has supported and nurtured new ventures and innovations since the 2000s, some of which have been behind the continued success of the Chinese economy. It also played a key role in financing renewable energy, and making, for example, solar panels cheaper in China and also in the rest of the world. BNDES, the Brazilian development bank, began to experiment with financing programs targeted at high-tech firms and innovation development in the 1990s; it has a venture capital fund, CRIATEC, whose results are striking: in its first four years of existence, the value of the CRIATEC portfolio grew at a rate of 50 percent per annum.

CORFO, the Chilean development agency, has provided long-term resources to expand the role of risk capital funds. Moreover, it created a start-up program, which has received international recognition. This program has encouraged the improvement and broadening of the policy mix to support these companies in Chile. Relevant regulations have been simplified and financing has also been expanded to support different phases of the projects. Finally, CORFO has helped the government design a more detailed industrial strategy. However, the institution lacks sufficient scale to deliver significant impact.

BANCOLDEX, as a bank for trade and industrial growth in Colombia, manages a specific innovation program, iNNpulsa Colombia. The program supports innovation for business growth for firms of all sizes and ages, and in all sectors and regions of the country. Among its specific instruments is the national network of "angel investors," which it co-finances, and different regional initiatives to promote the incubation and growth of firms, training in technology transfer and commercialization, and support strategies to encourage rapid business growth. As in the case of CORFO, the major problem of these programs is their small scale.

The activities of NDBs supporting key new sectors serve as an important leverage to attract private investors. A remarkable case is renewable energy and energy efficiency. For example, KfW was initially the sole lender to private companies investing in solar energy in Germany, but later private banks followed. In China, CDB helped to design broad policy to encourage investment in renewables, especially solar energy, as well as playing a major role in initial funding. Germany and especially China have been major actors in promoting the spread of solar energy worldwide, at an increasingly competitive cost with fossil fuels. Their NDBs played a key role in catalyzing this, thus contributing in a significant way to international climate change mitigation, as their financing contributed to a dramatic reduction in the cost of solar panels, and that has made solar energy competitive with fossil-fuel generated energy.

NDBs have developed new instruments, such as guarantees and equity—including venture capital and debt funds. Loan instruments continue to be important, though a greater emphasis than in the past is placed on second-tier loans, which may make it more difficult to use NDBs as a direct instrument for industrial policy This factor may be particularly important for escaping from the middle-income trap. We return to this discussion in more detail in Section 11.8.2.

In the area of financial inclusion, correspondent stores have been an important new instrument, which has been widely used in Colombia. Mexican NAFINSA also operates an online reverse factoring system called Productive Chains. It allows SMEs to sell their accounts receivables from large companies to private banks and get their money immediately; this program, which provides working capital to SMEs, is considered to have been very successful, and is now being implemented in other Latin American countries.

NDBs do and should play an important role in providing access to financing for microenterprises and SMEs (MSMEs). A common rationale for development banks to provide financing for MSMEs is that these tend to be too small, implying high transactions costs, and too risky to be of interest to most commercial lenders. Development banks like NAFINSA, CORFO, KfW, BANCOLDEX, and FINAGRO, among others, have provided financing to reach different segments of MSMEs and meet their distinct needs through a series of instruments, mainly second-tier credits, first-tier lending to associations of producers, and guarantees. These products are essentially channeled through different types of financial intermediaries: commercial banks, specialized financial institutions, and micro-financing institutions.

In NAFINSA, 71 percent of its second-tier credit has gone to their innovative program, Productive Chains, which helps potential borrowers rediscount their bill, through an electronic platform, as already mentioned in this section. NAFINSA also provides guarantees to improve the conditions under which loans are granted and to increase the overall supply of credit. These guarantees are first-loss, and participant firms do not directly apply for the guarantee, which is given against a portfolio of loans. In the case of Colombian BANCOLDEX, close to half of its rediscounts are destined to MSMEs, which are complemented by the guarantees externally provided by the national or regional guarantee funds.

BANCOLDEX also manages a major Colombian government program to support financial inclusion, Banca de las Oportunidades. The achievements of this program include the promotion of a program of bank correspondents in municipalities or poor urban neighborhoods where formal financial institutions are absent. By 2016, all Colombian municipalities had at least one correspondent.

11.6 NDBs' Role in Infrastructure Finance

NDBs, because they can provide the long-term financing needed for infrastructure investment, are especially well suited in this sector. This is the case given the large scale of the initial investment and the long period for amortizations. Development banks can finance at relatively low cost, as they often have very high credit ratings and can, therefore, borrow relatively cheaply at long maturities on capital markets and pass on that cost and maturity advantage to their borrowers. This role is particularly crucial as the deficit in infrastructure investments has created enduring challenges for many countries, which may contribute to them suffering from the middle-income trap. NDBs also can provide valuable expertise in helping to design projects, as well as making them replicable, so the investments can be scaled up, something which has for example been done by KfW in energy efficiency projects. This is an approach that can help attract institutional investors, who tend to require large-scale packages to invest in.

Banks like CDB, FDN, FINDETER, and BNDES are very active in long-term infrastructure financing. Additionally, these development banks have been also important players in the financing of sustainable infrastructure projects.

CDB has been a key player in the development of the Chinese financial market and credit system by reshaping the local government credit system, including through a local government financial vehicle (LGFV) model. As local governments had restricted capacity to invest in infrastructure, in 1998 CDB created a model in which the local government creates an LGFV, a legal company registered as a local state-owned enterprise. The local government promises to inject its quality assets to the LGFV, and if these assets—eg highways—are profitable, the LGFV can take the future profits as collateral and borrow from CDB. Under this model, loans can be bundled and local government revenues—including those associated with profits from managing land owned by local governments—can also be transferred to the LGFV. Despite its benefits, it seems that the LGFV model had opened a Pandora's box because, with the explosion of local government debt burden, this model has made financial supervision less effective.

BNDES, as part of the government's initiative to build the market for infrastructure bonds, expanded guarantee-sharing clauses in its financing contracts, equalizing the level of seniority of bondholder to loans it co-financed. Through its subsidiary BNDESPAR, it has also bought stakes in companies that could prospect for new business in the sector.

In Colombia, FDN has developed a myriad of products—senior and subordinated credits and credit enhancements—to catalyze resources into infrastructure projects, mainly highways, using project finance arrangements. FINDETER has continued providing rediscount facilities for urban and local projects and has implemented key programs of the national government with a regional content.

In terms of green growth, development banks bring the advantages of accumulated expertise, administrative efficiencies, and convening power. They can help mobilize additional funding, contribute to designing the necessary policy frameworks, and implementing effective projects that can showcase the viability of certain green investments, as in renewable energy. KfW, BNDES, CDB, and CORFO, to name a few examples, have played important roles in supporting the development and use of green technology, including green infrastructure. This has become increasingly important, as climate mitigation investment acquires much higher priority in governments' development plans, and as Climate Finance Funds may increase the amounts they are channeling via NDBs, as is for example the case in DBSA in South Africa.

This has been particularly important in the case of KfW. One prominent aspect ofKfW's mandate is the support of the structural change towards a low-carbon economy. This is particularly evident in two areas: energy-efficient housing for consumers, and energy saving and renewable energy promotion for businesses. In energy-efficient housing, KfW contributed to the design of the strategy put forward by the Ministry for the Economy, defined the standards for an energy-efficient house, engaged in monitoring and evaluation, and provided loans at slightly below-market rates. In improving energy savings and the use of renewables by businesses, KfW was involved in all stages of the policy cycle of a program targeting SMEs using clean energy.

Chilean CORFO helped design a National Strategic Solar Industry program and, as part of it, designed specific credit lines to provide stable funding to producers capable of adapting to local conditions and fostering local value added. BNDES has a technology fund FUNTEC, which targeted resources to very specific technologies, such as alternative energy, specifically bioenergy, solar energy, and thermal energy; nanotech and biotech solutions to address issues of waste disposal, land, and water pollution; and electric-drive vehicles.

As already indicated, CDB invests significantly in renewable energy projects as well, particularly solar panels. The CDB has a track record of funding alternative energy firms to develop their technologies, such as, for example, the solar company *Yingli Green Energy*, which has a US$5.3 billion line of credit opened for it at CDB.

11.7 Pre-conditions for Successful NDBs

11.7.1 Scale of NDBs

A key question is whether, given major current development challenges, NDBs do enough, especially in Latin American and African countries, but also more broadly. In particular, is their current scale large enough for the structural transformation and development needs of their countries?

The case studies in Griffith-Jones and Ocampo (2018) and other research show that there is a greater need for larger scale NDB activity in most Latin American countries—the major exception being, of course, Brazil, which already has a large NDB, though its scale is being decreased by the current and previous administrations. Preliminary evidence from Africa leads to similar conclusions. This is due to the low levels of both private and public investment. In the case of private investment, this is linked in part to the limitations of private finance, in particular its capacity to fund long-term investment, particularly that associated with innovative activities. Furthermore, Latin American countries have limited fiscal space, which bounds public sector investment. The leverage of public resources provided by NDBs therefore becomes particularly attractive as a way to boost investment.

There is, at the same time, a greater need for higher investment in Latin America and Africa as the challenges of structural transformation become more urgent, and are linked to the need for a radically different economic model. This model should be more dynamic and smarter, with better innovation and improved ability to adapt to increase productivity more rapidly; it should be more inclusive, to reduce the large income inequalities; and it needs to be greener, to make it consistent with the needs of the environment. In all these cases, reversing premature de-industrialization must be a key element of this strategy, which would help emerging countries avoid falling into the middle-income trap.

In the case of Africa, there are major unmet needs, for example in infrastructure investment, as well as for poverty reduction. The needs of infrastructure investment are difficult to meet with purely private investment, either national or foreign. Private investment provides less than 7 percent of total infrastructure investment, is heavily concentrated in more profitable sectors, like energy, as well as in larger and relatively richer countries, and is pro-cyclical (Griffith-Jones and Flament, forthcoming). Government investment is an important source of funding infrastructure, but is constrained in many countries by limited public resources. Therefore, there seems to be an important role for NDBs, especially if they can leverage private finance, particularly in countries with deep capital markets. One example is DBSA in South Africa, which mainly funds infrastructure and is able to raise money on domestic capital markets. Furthermore, in smaller African economies, NDBs are effective instruments for channeling international public funds, such as from the World Bank, the African Development Bank, bilateral donors, and international climate finance.

An additional challenge is that the new development model may become less reliant on international trade, which has grown more slowly since the North Atlantic financial crisis, thus turning into a less dynamic engine for growth. It is now also threatened by protectionist tendencies in some major developed economies, especially the USA. In both Latin America and Africa, regional integration can help counteract this trend, and is particularly important for encouraging innovation in broader regional markets, and creating dynamic regional value chains. Perhaps most importantly, the end of the super-cycle of commodity prices is creating an urgent need for investment in new sources of exports and growth. NDBs need to play a significant role in supporting such investment in new areas, which would help overcome the middle-income trap.

Investment in new sectors and technologies is dominated by uncertainty, and is unlikely in most cases to be funded purely by private financial institutions, which are unwilling to take large risks, especially for long maturities. Therefore, NDB finance, which has the virtue of being long term (as over 50 percent of NDB lending is for over 10 years' maturity) and includes innovative activities, is needed on a significant scale. It may also facilitate the use of subsidies to provide for cheaper loans to SMEs, for example SMEs that are more innovative or are based in poorer regions; such subsidies are usually funded by government grants, or can be based on cross-subsidization from other more profitable activities of the NDB.

The need for larger scale has been understood in the highly successful economies of Germany and China, where the scale of NDB assets, in proportion to the country's GDP is fairly large. Within the Latin American region, we see different scales and trends (see Figure 6.1). Brazil's BNDES has continued to be an important and large institution in recent decades, though its scale has been shrinking recently. On the other hand, countries like Chile, Colombia, and Mexico have seen the scale of their NDBs fall, though in the case of Colombia the scale has seen some resurgence in recent years. Peru also lacks a sizable NDB system, if we exclude the major state-owned commercial bank.

It therefore seems a key conclusion that, in countries such as Chile, Colombia, Mexico, and Peru, the scale of operations of NDBs should be significantly increased, so they can have a more meaningful impact on increasing investment for structural transformation and development, and help these countries avoid falling into the middle-income trap. This does not necessarily imply large government resources, as the only public contributions would be an increase in their paid-in capital and special programs that governments want to promote; these NDBs could then fund their operations on the private domestic market—fairly developed in some of the Latin American countries, notably Chile, as well as international capital markets. Furthermore, more international resources, for example climate finance, should be channeled through NDBs (Attridge and Griffith-Jones, forthcoming).

Although the conclusion that NDBs need to be larger and more active focuses on Latin America, it can certainly be extended to other regions of the developing world—notably, as already pointed out, to Africa (see for example, Griffith-Jones and Flament, forthcoming, for the infrastructure sector in Africa and the potential role of NDBs). It can even be applied to developed countries, where NDBs can play an important role, as the very successful experience of KfW indicates.

Increasing the role of NDBs in countries that have them, or creating them in those that do not, would help to create, therefore, a financial system that better serves the needs of the real economy and society in general, and of structural transformation in particular. Indeed, the existence of a more mixed financial sector, that combines both public and private institutions in a creative and efficient way, may be a new paradigm for funding structural transformation, and thus avoiding the middle-income trap, as well as helping to green the economy, transforming it to a low carbon economy.

11.7.2 Other Key Pre-conditions for Successful NDBs

The broader context in which development banks operate is key for their success. Thus, good macroeconomic policies—in particular, active counter-cyclical policies, relatively low inflation, moderate real interest rates, and competitive and stable real exchange rates—are essential for successful NDBs. A well-functioning financial sector is another important pre-condition for the smooth running of an effective NDB, and for helping NDBs fund themselves on local capital markets, as they do in most developed economies. NDBs can help develop a deeper and better capital market. CDB, for example, played a key role in the development of the Chinese bond market. More generally, a number of NDBs have helped the introduction of local currency and green bonds in their own local capital market.

Furthermore, and perhaps most importantly, an NDB can operate far more effectively if the country has a clear national development strategy, ideally linked to a modern industrial policy, which should focus on promoting innovative sectors and guaranteeing competitiveness in different sectors, building on the comparative advantages, existing and potential, and accumulated capacities of different economies. Development banks like KfW, CDB, and CORFO operate broadly in the context of a clear strategic direction. Policy mandates are particularly valuable if they do not change too much with different governments, but adapt to changing national and international circumstances, allowing continuity and long-term planning for the NDBs and their support for development. As discussed below, the greater emphasis on maximizing leverage by development banks, and the greater use of increasingly indirect instruments (like guarantees) may reduce the ability of development banks to help implement a modern industrial policy, by reducing their ability to give policy steer.

In recent years, and especially since the Paris Climate Summit, a priority area for development plans is the aim of making an urgent transition to a low carbon economy, given the climate emergency. It is vital that NDBs play a central role in implementing that aim, as well as contributing to the sustainable development strategy at a national level.

It is important to underscore, finally, that what should be promoted are "good" development banks. This implies having institutions with clear mandates, a good governance structure, and that are well managed, transparent, and accountable, so they fulfill their functions well. The main objective of NDBs is to maximize their development impact rather than profits, though assuring at least minimal returns. NDBs should be profit making, but not profit maximizing.

11.8 New Issues on Financial Instruments: Lessons from the European Experience

There have been important recent debates on the type of instruments that NDBs should use. This is part of the broader conversation of how to maximize the impact of development banks in general (including multilateral and regional development banks, as well as NDBs), mainly by maximizing their leverage via private resources. As discussed below, this has potentially great advantages, in terms of mobilizing far larger resources, particularly for essential investment in more innovative and high productivity activities that could help countries escape from the middle-income trap. However, this approach also has some problems, which we discuss in this section. We will illustrate this issue with the role of the European Investment Bank (EIB) and European NDBs, but it is also relevant for NDBs in other regions, and is very relevant for emerging economies, as they are encouraged to follow such a path, for example by the World Bank.

We start by briefly outlining the expanded role of the European Investment Bank Group (EIBG), and then evaluate different instruments. In the wake of the financial crisis of 2007–09, and the Eurozone debt crisis of 2009–10, there has been renewed support in Europe for public regional and national development banks, as the limitations and problems of a purely private financial sector became more evident.

In this context, the EIBG, the largest multilateral development bank in the world, with a long track record of successfully playing a key and large role in funding intra-European infrastructure, including renewable energy, as well as SMEs and innovation, took on renewed importance, as have European NDBs. In 2012 the EIB's paid-in capital was doubled with contributions from all member states, leading to significant increases in its operations (Griffith-Jones and Kollatz, 2012). In 2014 the EIBG began to implement the European Fund for Strategic Investment (EFSI), which aimed to provide much needed investment for Europe, in the wake of austerity, as well as facilitate much needed structural change to a greener, more dynamic, and equal economy.

EFSI is a EUR 26 billion guarantee from the European Union budget, complemented by a EUR 7.5 billion allocation of the EIB's own capital. The total amount of EUR 33.5 billion aims to leverage additional investment of at least EUR 500bn between 2015 and 2020. It seems that EFSI will meet this target. Essentially, a small fraction of the EU budget is used as a guarantee for EIB projects that have a higher risk profile than more usual projects. The aim is to push the EIBG to finance valuable but risky projects that could not secure funding on their own, to reduce risks taken by private investors, to increase the chances of attracting their investment.

EFSI has two components: the innovation and infrastructure window managed by the EIB, and the SME window implemented by the EIF (European Investment Fund). The EIF, part of the EIBG, is focused mainly on providing guarantees, to increase private lending to SMEs. About a fourth of the transactions of EFSI are estimated to have been channeled through NDBs, increasing their role. For the next EU budget (2021–27), the European Commission is developing the continuation of EFSI, with some modifications, as InvestEU Fund. InvestEU will follow the Juncker Plan in mobilizing additional private funds for additional investment.

11.8.1 A Framework for Evaluating EFSI, as well as Other Similar Initiatives

In evaluating these instruments, two related issues emerge. The first concerns the types of risks various instruments entail for the public sector. The second concerns the trade-off between increasing loan volume through leverage and policy steer, to achieve specific policy objectives, such as structural transformation that could help countries overcome the middle-income trap.

There is a key distinction on the nature of risk that it is essential to clarify, both from an analytical point of view and a policy perspective. This should be important when evaluating initiatives like EFSI and InvestEU, but also initiatives by institutions such as the World Bank, and their application to NDBs, in the aim to convert "billions to trillions," that is, catalyze large amounts of private funding via limited public resources.

There are first the "economic" risks; these are basically associated with the natural uncertainty related to projects or sectors. They are typically of the following kinds:

(1) Occurring in infrastructure projects (risks of construction difficulties and delays, especially in engineering ambitious projects, like the Channel Tunnel), as well as in the financing of new green energy technologies, or their improvement.
(2) Such risks are also very prevalent in the funding of innovative companies, such as start-ups, often based on potentially excellent ideas, but lacking assets for guarantees, and/or a proven track record.
(3) Financing SMEs is generally considered more risky in most countries, except in countries such as Germany, with very decentralized banking systems, which allow for greater knowledge of companies, thus reducing asymmetries of information (Stiglitz and Weiss, 1981), and a long tradition

of successful lending to SMEs. SME financing becomes riskier if financial crises happen, when the benefits of diversification are reduced.

(4) Very importantly, economic risks can also relate to sectorial or cross-sectorial innovation, that may lead to major increases in productivity and/or significant structural transformation, for example to a greener economy (see Mazzucato, 2013).

These economic risks contrast sharply with "financial engineering" risks, created by financial actors, often partly hidden by opaque and complex structures, and whose impact often only emerges ex-post in crisis situations. The alleged, and sometimes legitimate, aim may be to increase the leverage of public resources, and for this reason may be backed by policymakers who aim to do "more with less." However, the main general aim of creating instruments with "financial engineering" risk is to increase profitability for private financial actors, at the same time as minimizing their risk of losses. While the mobilization of private capital brings potential benefits in terms of leveraging scarce budgetary resources, it also generates potential fiscal risks, via contingent liabilities, that need to be properly accounted and provisioned for.

While the distinction between "economic" and "financial" risk was less important in the aftermath of the Eurozone debt crisis (and in general after any financial crisis), as there was a great need to increase counter-cyclically lending volumes to maintain investment, as the private financial sector became risk averse. However, as the private financial sector became more willing to lend, there is not much benefit in most countries and sectors to further de-risking.

However, there remains a need to take economic risks, especially for sectors important for industrial policy/structural transformation, or sustainable developmental objectives. Financial risk needs to be limited in total scale, very carefully evaluated ex-ante, to avoid large contingent liabilities, and thus possible significant losses. It has been argued, therefore, that EFSI and InvestEU must have a greater focus on the final beneficiaries of projects rather than on the private financial intermediaries, in order to avoid the moral hazard of transferring public resources or guarantees to private financial institutions (Griffith-Jones and Naqvi, forthcoming). This seems even more relevant for NDBs in emerging economies, where public resources need to be channeled carefully to encourage investment in structural transformation, something that is essential to avoid the middle-income trap.

Thus, the concept of the "de-risking" of private banks and investor's transactions by public development banks, currently fashionable in some circles, is imprecise. The issue is really centered on how public and private institutions share risks, how these risks are priced, and provisioned for. Furthermore, if risks are shared, it is also important that mechanisms are created to share profits. One such mechanism is equity investment by NDBs; the other is to have loans, with equity kickers. This implies that, if a company which has been given a loan by the development bank has been very profitable, the development bank can transform its loan into equity, and thus benefit from the upside of the project. It is interesting, that in the context of EFSI, the EIB created such a mechanism, called venture debt, which seems to be rather successful. NDBs in emerging economies could explore the feasibility of using such instruments.

11.8.2 EFSI and Industrial Policy: Leverage vs. Policy Steer

Industrial policy can be defined as "any policy that attempts to affect the evolution of specific industries through state intervention in order to effect national efficiency and growth" (Chang, 1994). It includes the allocation of subsidies or guarantees against risks, by, for example, NDBs to private actors, in exchange for these actors performing economically valuable functions, such as helping finance certain sectors or activities that they otherwise would not. For this to work, it is vital the public sector can strictly monitor and enforce performance related conditionality on the recipients of subsidies, and withdraw support if the conditions are not being met (Amsden, 1992).

There is some trade-off between the European Commission's objectives of achieving policy steer, for example as part of an industrial policy, and achieving the highest possible loan volume through leverage, because the instruments that provide leverage also make the activity much more indirect. This is also very relevant for NDBs in emerging economies (see Griffith-Jones and Ocampo, 2018).

On the one hand, increasing the loan volume through leverage is positive, as it should facilitate higher levels of investment in the context of budget constraints by "doing more with less fiscal resources." (There is, of course, the option of increasing taxation to finance more public investment.) However, there is a risk that the greater the loan volume achieved through involving private intermediaries, the more indirect the instruments and operations become, and the less strategic direction public institutions are able to exert over the choice of sectors and projects. Involving intermediaries makes monitoring and enforcing conditionalities more difficult. While high leverage at the expense of policy steer may have been more appropriate for EFSI as it focused on counter-cyclical provision of finance in the wake of the Eurozone crisis, in InvestEU there is more focus on industrial policy, and therefore the balance between leverage and policy steer needs rethinking. In emerging economies, a greater emphasis on helping kick start private lending via NDB lending is more important during times of economic slowdown (counter-cyclical role), but less important for funding long-term industrial policy, essential for avoiding a middle-income trap.

11.9 Conclusions

For NDBs to contribute significantly to helping to avoid a middle-income trap, several conditions need to be fulfilled: (1) they must be "good" development banks, with good governance, including efficient management, clear accountability and transparency, as well as independence from narrow public or private interests, while working closely to implement public policies and aims, as well as interacting with the private sector; (2) their scale must be sufficiently large to help meet investment needs on a significant scale, as well as to perform NDB roles at a sufficiently significant level; (3) there must be a clear national development strategy, and the NDBs must be active in implementing it, so as to support structural transformation.

This chapter has stressed NDBs' contribution to supporting innovative sectors, as well as sectors such as infrastructure, with long-term funding. The support of innovation with long-term financing is complementary to other functions of these institutions, including supporting the provision of public goods, particularly through financing investments that help combat climate change, and financial inclusion, particularly by supporting small start-up firms and SMEs linked to innovative sectors, as well as in poorer regions. In all cases, NDBs should not supplant private financing but should complement it and leverage additional private funds for innovative activities. However, as discussed in the last section, indirect instruments such as guarantees should be used with care, and be carefully evaluated, both to avoid excessive contingent liabilities, and to ensure the NDBs are able to give sufficient policy steer, to facilitate the allocation of resources for the structural transformations needed to achieve national development aims, and help avoid the middle-income trap.

NDBs should be active in the provision of counter-cyclical financing at the national level, both during busts, when privately-financed investment tends to decline or grow less and NDB lending should be increased to help maintain crucial investment, and during booms, when lending by NDBs should slow down, or even decrease.

References

Amsden, A. H. (1992): *Asia's Next Giant: South Korea and Late Industrialization*, Oxford: Oxford University Press on Demand.

Brei, M. and Schlarek, A. (2018): "The Counter-Cyclical Behaviour of National Development Bank in Latin America and the Caribbean," in S. Griffith-Jones and J. A. Ocampo (eds.), *The Future of National Development Banks*, Oxford and New York: Oxford University Press.

Chang, H.-J. (1994): *The Political Economy of Industrial Policy*, New York: St. Martin's Press.

Dodd, R. and Griffith-Jones, S. (2006): "Report on derivatives markets: stabilizing or speculative impact on Chile and a comparison with Brazil". ECLAC. https://pdfs.semanticscholar.org/e76b/b025b070f177965a6b29fee70c26f8b176de.pdf?_ga=2.256214795.18047313.1573046395-341071677.1569748714

Ffrench-Davis, R. and Griffith-Jones, S. (2019): "*Financial Globalization and Its Implications for Development*," in M. Nissanke and J. A. Ocampo (eds.), *Handbook of Development: Critical Reflections on Globalisation and Development*, Berlin: Springer.

Griffith-Jones, S. and Flament,V. (forthcoming): " The role of development banks in innovative long-term financing of the private Sector," UN Economic Commission for Africa. Addis Ababa.

Griffith-Jones, S. and Kollatz Ahnen, M. (2012): *Financial Times*, http://www.stephanygj.net/press/sgj-e-forum.pdf

Griffith-Jones, S. and Naqvi, N. (forthcoming): "EFSI (Junker Plan), InvestEU and the EIB: Increased leverage, but could risk distribution and policy steer be improved?" FEPS Working Paper.

Griffith-Jones, S. and Ocampo, J. A. (eds.) (2018): *The Future of National Development Banks*, Oxford and New York: Oxford University Press.

Griffith-Jones, S. and Attridge, S. (2020): "The role of NDBs in supporting the transition to a low carbon economy," ODI and AfD. https://www.odi.org/publications/16552-securing-climate-finance-through-national-development-banks

Luna-Martinez, J. de and Vicente, C. L. (2012): "Global survey of development banks,. World Bank Policy Research Working Paper No. 5969.

Mazzucato, Mariana (2013): *The Entrepreneurial State—Debunking Public vs. Private Sector Myths*, New York: Anthem Press.

Mazzucato, M. and Penna, C. C. R. (2018): "National development banks and mission-oriented finance for innovation," in S. Griffith-Jones and J. A. Ocampo (eds.), *The Future of National Development Banks*, Oxford and New York: Oxford University Press.

Ocampo, J. A. (2017): *Resetting the International Monetary (Non) System*, Oxford and Helsinki: Oxford University Press and UNU-WIDER.

Stiglitz, J. E. and Weiss, A. (1981): "Credit rationing in markets with imperfect information," *The American Economic Review* 71, no. 3: 393–410.

12
Middle-Income Countries and Multilateral Development Banks
Traps on the Way to Graduation

Otaviano Canuto, Matheus Cavallari, and Tiago Ribeiro dos Santos

12.1 Introduction

Multilateral Development Banks (MDBs) have two financing windows, with different terms, dedicated to low- and middle-income countries. Countries are presumed to cross those windows as their income per capita rises, with middle-income countries (MICs) eventually "graduating" to non-client status once they reach certain criteria. However, due to what may be called "middle-income traps," such progression toward graduation has been limited to a small number of countries.

In this chapter, we suggest areas where support by MDBs would yield the highest results toward the "graduation" of MICs. Item 1 reviews the criteria that have been used to justify graduation, whereas item 2 approaches middle-income levels as a stage of growth and development. Finally, item 3 proposes an interface between MDBs' support to MICs and the policy agenda to overcome middle-income traps.

12.2 Graduation Redux

MDBs have different financing windows for low-income countries (LICs) and MICs, for which different country eligibility criteria are applied. Besides levels of income per capita, both the availability and terms of country access to international financial markets are also considered in the definition of which window a country is to be situated in as a potential financial resource taker.

Those financing windows differ in terms of implicit subsidies. While financing to LICs carry high degrees of concessionality—corresponding to grants or finance with very low interest rates and long maturities—the cost differential embedded in financing MICs corresponds to the difference between interest rates charged by

Otaviano Canuto, Matheus Cavallari, and Tiago Ribeiro dos Santos, *Middle-Income Countries and Multilateral Development Banks: Traps on the Way to Graduation* In: *Trapped in the Middle? Developmental Challenges for Middle-Income Countries.* Edited by: José Antonio Alonso and José Antonio Ocampo, Oxford University Press (2020). © OUP.
DOI: 10.1093/oso/9780198852773.003.0012

MDBs and financial markets. MDBs are capable of typically offering finance at lower prices than—or close to—markets because of their ability to raise funds at very low costs, as a reflection of the "preferred creditor status" enjoyed by their operations, the "callable capital" pledged by shareholders,[1] and the high levels of capitalization.

Thresholds of income per capita and country-specific classifications per window are periodically reviewed. For instance, in the case of the World Bank Group, which we use here as a reference for MDBs, the soft-loan window for LICs—International Development Agency (IDA)—implemented a graduation policy review in 2016 to be followed in the IDA18 3-year round of pledges by donors (World Bank, 2016).

In the case of the World Bank's lending for MICs—the International Bank for Reconstruction and Development (IBRD)—the Articles of Agreement contain broad references to country eligibility and to graduation criteria, referring to capital availability at reasonable or suitable conditions—articles I (Purpose) and III (Conditions on which the Bank may Guarantee or Make Loans) (World Bank, 1944). Over the years, the interpretation of those references has served as a basis for IBRD graduation policy.

For example, according to a 1982 President's Memorandum on the subject, two conditions would justify an IBRD member's graduation: the level of development and overall economic situation, and the capacity to sustain long-term development process without relying on financial support from the Bank. This memorandum was followed by a statement by the Board of Executive Directors in 1984 to further clarify the discussions about eligibility. The substantive factors underlying such process would be reached by assessing three factors:

(1) the country's ability to access external capital markets on reasonable terms;
(2) the progress in the establishment of key institutions for economic and social development;
(3) the achievement of a minimum level of GNI per capita (currently close to US$7,000).

The 1984 Board statement clarified that member countries would not automatically lose access to IBRD lending by reaching such a GNI per capita level, and only by reaching all substantive factors. After those understandings, repetitive

[1] The relative weight of the preferred creditor status and the significant amount of callable capital in explaining the low-cost funding of most MDBs is an unsettled issue. If the "preferred creditor status" matters most, MDBs' operations benefit from a partial transfer of risks to other foreign liabilities of the country, whereas the role played by callable capital corresponds to implicit guarantees also provided by non-client shareholders, especially those with high credit ratings. There is a long discussion with respect to how much—and if—such loans are "subsidized," or if they are merely solving market failures in capital markets. See Clemens and Kremer (2016).

interactions among Bank Management and Executive Directors have broadly agreed that the graduation policy has been sufficiently flexible to underlie appropriate graduation decisions.

Since 1973, seventeen countries went through the IBRD graduation process.[2] Five of those later reversed their graduation (Iraq, Gabon, Trinidad and Tobago, Republic of Korea, and Venezuela), and only one re-graduated in 2016 (Republic of Korea). Currently, seventy-four countries have financial obligations with the IBRD.

Figure 12.1 depicts levels and composition of outstanding lending commitments of some MDBs to different country income groups. Different shares by income groups in each MDB's balance sheet reflect differences in "missions" and in regional exposure of each institution.

Knack et al. (2012) used different econometric specifications and found empirical evidence that both income and non-income factors have been significant determinants of IBRD graduation. On the upgrade side, the determinants are: income relative to graduation threshold, length of time above this threshold, institutional quality, and creditworthiness. On the downgrade, the occurrence of crises and being a small country have also mattered. These findings suggest that the graduation policy has been applied in a consistent manner.

Another way to look at the historical evolution of the graduation process is by assessing each of the graduation criteria. The GNI-per-capita threshold was first adopted at US$1,000 in 1973, as a proxy for structural development. This level was later updated in 1980 to US$2,650, being annually updated for price changes and exchange rates, without additional discussion about its meaning in terms of structural development. While in 1982 this threshold represented 110 percent of world average income and 29 percent of the average GNI per capita of high-income countries, in 2015 it had dropped to only 67 percent and 17 percent, respectively. Additionally, the median GNI per capita income of graduated countries, excluding the cases of reversion, is above US$16,000 at 2010 prices (Figure 12.2).[3]

The next criterion, access to external capital markets on "reasonable terms" can be approached with a comparison of the level of sovereign bond spreads vs. the IBRD spreads for those countries with GNI per capita above the income threshold. As one would suspect, sovereign spreads have a closer link to creditworthiness than to GNI per capita, especially for upper middle-income countries. In other words, sovereign spreads vary considerably for similar levels of GNI per

[2] Graduated countries: Iraq, Venezuela, Gabon, Trinidad and Tobago, Oman, Portugal, The Bahamas, Cyprus, Barbados, Republic of Korea, Slovenia, Czech Republic, Estonia, Lithuania, Hungary, Latvia, and Slovak Republic.

[3] Interestingly, it is worth noting that countries considered to be still fighting "middle-income traps"—as approached below—have remained well below that median income.

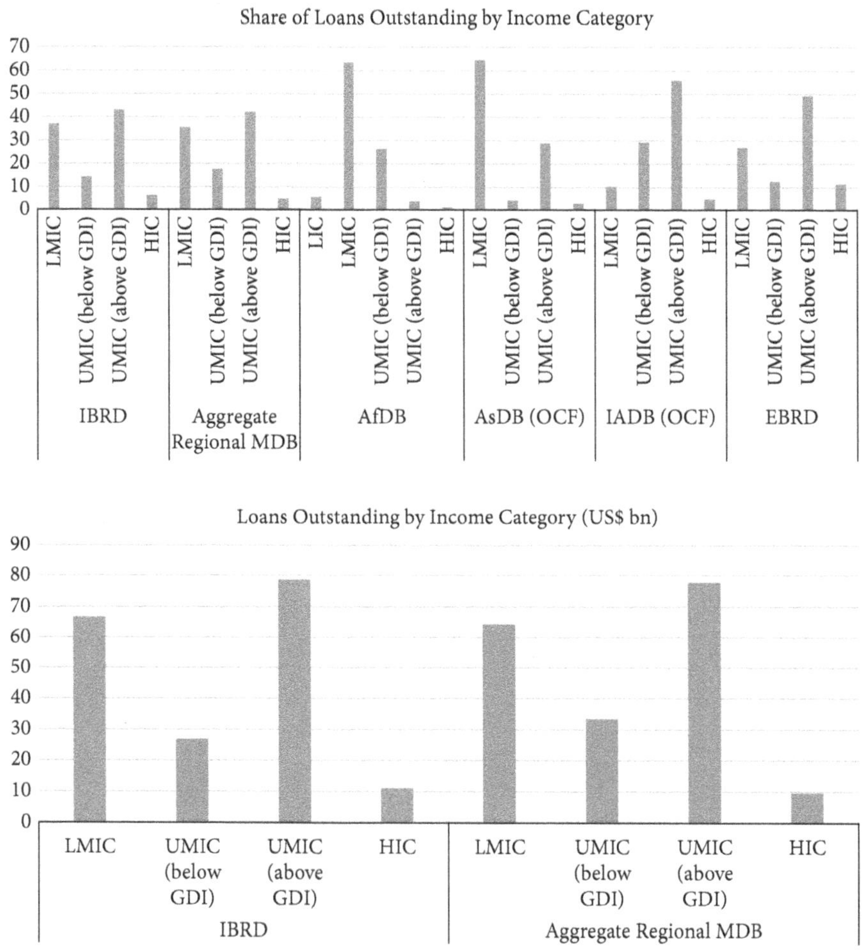

Figure 12.1 Loans outstanding by income category (share and volume)
Source: WBG Finances, IBRD Statement of Loans by Country as at September 30, 2017. Annual reports for AfDB, AsDB, IADB, and EBRD for year ending December 31, 2016. Analysis by World Bank using World Bank FY2018 income classifications.

capita (Figure 12.3). Furthermore, access to capital markets shifts often and abruptly during crises, which would make the assessment of "reasonable terms" a complex task, even for high-income countries—for example during the global financial crisis in 2007–09 or the European debt crisis in 2010.

As for the third criterion, the comparison of GNI per capita and institutional strength shows that similar levels of per capita income may be associated with substantially different levels in the quality of institutions (Figure 12.4).

One may therefore notice how flexible and inevitably discretionary tends to be any country-specific use of the set of criteria for IBRD graduation.

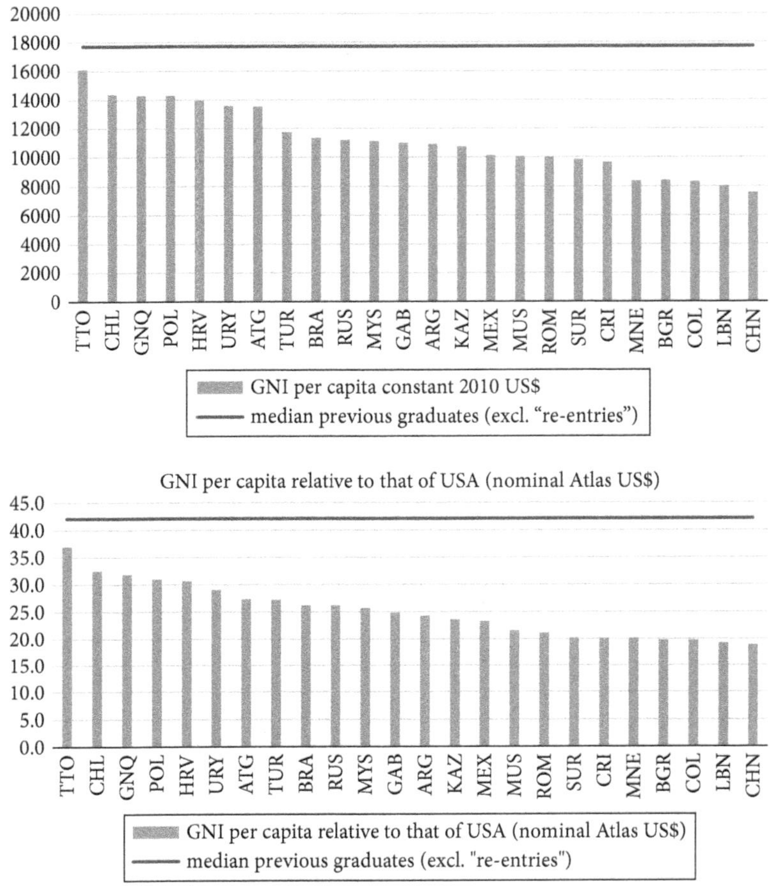

Figure 12.2 GNI per capita constant and relative to that of the USA, US$2010
Source: World Bank Indicators.

A new round of intensive discussion around the graduation of MICs is poised to take place in the near future. In 2018, when World Bank governors agreed on a capital increase package for IBRD, it was announced that the institution "commits to a more systematic application of its graduation policy" (Development Committee, 2018). Interactions shall occur in the periodic strategic discussion between IBRD and every client member country, once the country achieved the above-mentioned income threshold. Such strategic engagement shall focus on strengthening policies and institutions to sustain development, aiming ultimately at its graduation.

A diverse range of views is at stake (Canuto, 2019a). At one extreme, one may point out the view in favor of MDBs narrowing lending windows and moving toward providing grants wherever applicable (eg, Meltzer 2000). More moderate views on focusing access to IBRD finance go from a strict enforcement of

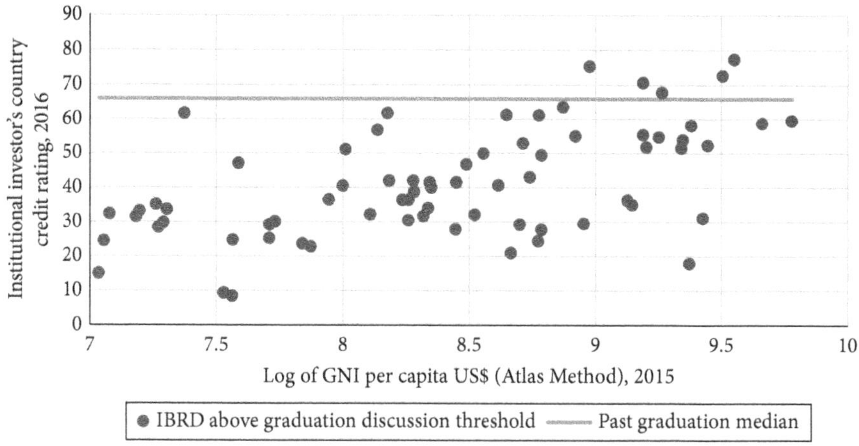

Figure 12.3 Country creditworthiness against GNI per capita for IBRD countries
Source: World Bank Indicators and Institutional Investor, Inc.

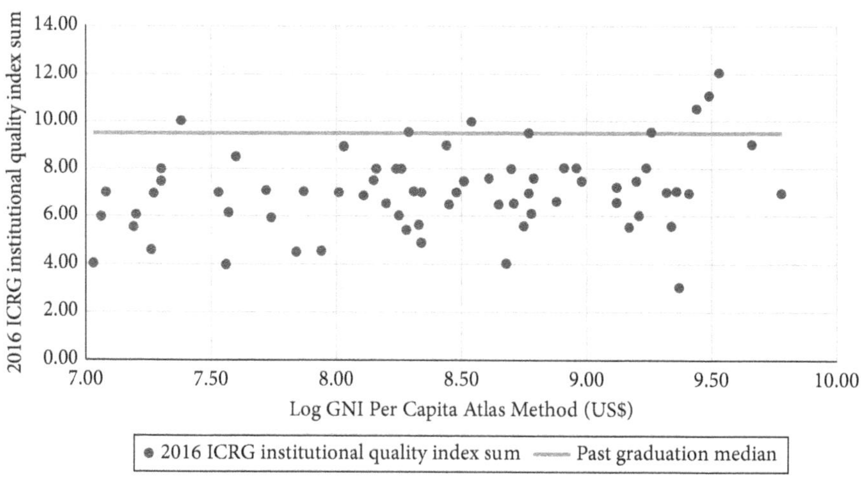

Figure 12.4 Institutional quality index against GNI per capita for IBRD countries
Source: ICRG for institutional quality and WDI for 2015 GNI per capita data.

income-based graduation to charging higher interest rates and capping the lending space to those MICs with income above graduation levels—without taking into account other criteria. The latter two features were ultimately included in the terms agreed in the 2018 IBRD capital increase agreement.

On the other hand, several arguments in favor of a cautionary approach to the graduation of MICs can also be pointed out: while lending to MICs with above-graduation levels of GNI per capita may dispute the use of scarce lending space with below-graduation MICs, the favorable composition of risk-adjusted returns obtained with the former may also crowd in lending space and minimize capital replenishments.

Second, a differential factor of MDB lending vis-à-vis market finance is the knowledge content embedded. In some cases, even MICs with cheaper access to foreign credit opt for using it. While those who lean in favor of graduation refer to the possibility of MICs purchasing technical assistance from MDBs, instead of borrowing, there is also a feedback loop for MDBs in terms of "learning by operating" with these countries. The "hummingbird" role played by MDBs, pollenizing knowledge throughout the whole range of non-advanced economies, might lose one of its major learning sources (Canuto, 2019b).

Third, the role played by MDBs in the provision of global public goods benefits from having a set of tools to interact with all MICs, which includes financial operations. As of 2015, member countries of IBRD with GNI per capita above the graduation level hosted 30 percent of the world population and 33 percent of the world GDP in PPP terms. Their carbon emissions increased from 31 percent as a share of the world's during 2002–04 to 41 percent during 2011–13, while hosting 9.9 percent of the global poor in 2013, considering US$3.1 a day (PPP) as a poverty line. Narrowing the set of options to support the provision of global public goods by those countries, including its spillovers, as an outcome of a premature graduation must also be considered.

Regardless of where decision lines with respect to MIC effective graduation are to be drawn, one may presume that a country's attainment of graduation conditions is a common desire for both client and non-client MDB shareholders. In the following items, we approach how the three-pronged set of graduation criteria—GNI per capita, access to external capital markets on reasonable terms, and domestic institutions key for economic and social development—are intertwined in the process of successfully overcoming "middle-income traps." Supporting MICs through such processes is an obvious agenda for MDBs.

12.3 Middle-Income as a Stage of Growth and Development

The "middle-income trap" has become a broad designation trying to capture the many cases of developing countries that have succeeded in evolving from low- to middle-levels of per capita income, but then appeared to stall, losing momentum along the route toward the higher-income levels of advanced economies. Such a trap may well characterize the experience of most of Latin America since the 1980s, and in recent years middle-income countries elsewhere have expressed fears of following a similar path. Underlying these views is a more general feeling that moving up the income ladder gets harder the higher one climbs.

There are two different ways in which the concept has been approached since its first use 12 years ago by Gill and Kharas (2007).[4] One has been empirical,

[4] On those two approaches, see Canuto (2019c).

whereby a search is made to identify—or deny—breaks or turning points in time-series data exhibiting "growth traps" for middle-income economies. The other approach, closer to the way it was originally suggested, refers to the need for policy and institutional change for a country to keep climbing the income ladder after a transition from low levels. Traps are seen as shortcomings resulting from the absence of any of those policy and institutional changes considered key to gearing up the transition from middle- to upper-income levels. In most cases of successful evolution from low- to middle-income per capita in recent history, the underlying development process has been broadly similar. Typically, there is a large pool of unskilled labor that is transferred from subsistence-level occupations to more modern manufacturing or service activities that do not require a great deal of skill upgrade for those workers, but nonetheless employ higher levels of capital and embedded technology. The associated technology is available from richer countries and easy to adapt to local circumstances. The gross effect of such a transfer—usually happening in tandem with urbanization—is a substantial increase in "total factor productivity", that is, an expansion of the value of GDP that goes beyond what can be explained by the expansion of labor, capital, and other physical factors of production in the economy.

Reaping the gains from such "low-hanging fruits" in terms of growth opportunities sooner or later faces limits, after which growth may slow down, and the economy may get trapped at middle-income levels. The turning point in this transition occurs either when the pool of transferrable unskilled labor is exhausted, or in some cases, when the expansion of labor-absorbing modern activities peaks before that exhaustion happens.

Beyond this point, raising total factor productivity and maintaining the pace of fast growth becomes dependent on the economy's domestic ability to move upward in manufacturing, service, or agricultural value chains, *toward* activities characterized by technological sophistication. It also requires high levels of human capital and intangible assets such as design and organizational capabilities. The path from low- to middle- and then to high-income per capita corresponds to increasing the shares of the population moved from subsistence activities to simple modern tasks and then to sophisticated ones. Within-sector productivity gains and "moving up value chains" increase in weight relative to productivity-lifting cross-sector structural change (Gill and Kharas, 2015).

An institutional setting supportive of innovation and complex chains of market transactions is of the essence. Instead of mastering existing standardized technologies, the challenge becomes the local creation of domestic capabilities and institutions, which cannot be simply brought in or copied from abroad. The provision of education to labor and of appropriate infrastructure becomes a minimum condition.

Current middle-income countries in Latin America decelerated their labor-transfer process from subsistence before exhausting labor surpluses, as macroeconomic mismanagement and inward orientation until the 1990s established early limits to that process. Nevertheless, some enclaves up on the ladder of value chains have been established (for instance, technology-intensive agriculture and sophisticated capabilities of deep-sea oil drilling and aircraft design in Brazil).

By contrast, Asian fast-growth economies have relied extensively on international trade to scale-up their labor transfer through insertion into the unskilled labor-intensive segments of global value chains. This has been facilitated by advances in information and communication technologies, combined with decreasing transport costs and lower international trade barriers. Taken together, these factors made possible the unbundling of production lines in chains of tasks with different degrees of sophistication requirements that can be geographically dispersed (Canuto, 2017, 2018a).

Figure 12.5 shows the structure of wealth for economies by income group and they illustrate the path of evolution that a country is expected to cross on the way up the ladder. It displays averages and individual countries will differ, for example because of different levels of natural wealth (Canuto and Cavallari, 2012). However, three broad features may be highlighted: the high and increasing weight of human capital (World Bank, 2018a); the weight of produced capital—physical capital—stabilizes in relative terms after the ascent from low-income levels; and, regardless of country-specific natural resource richness, its weight decreases relatively along the ascent.

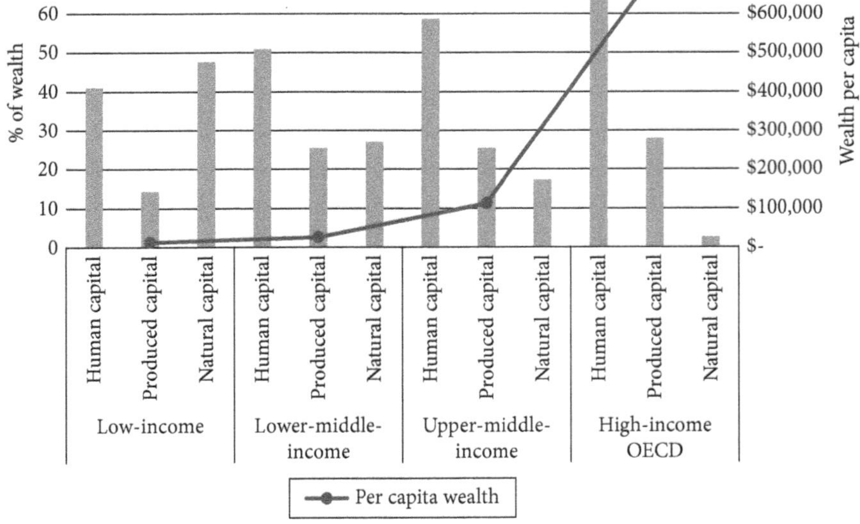

Figure 12.5 Composition of wealth by country income levels, 2014

Source: World Bank (2018b).

Natural resource-rich middle-income countries face a road of their own. Unlike manufacturing, natural resource use is to a large extent idiosyncratic, in the sense that each concrete experience is unique. That creates privileged scope for the local creation of capabilities in sophisticated upstream and downstream activities, with the corresponding challenge to do so in a sustainable fashion. Nevertheless, an institutional setting supportive of innovations and complex chains of market transactions, high-level education, and local building of intangible assets are also preconditions.

Although not included in the data displayed, one may expect a strong correlation between the human capital accumulation and the local development of intangible assets (capabilities to adapt technologies and innovate; managerial and organizational capabilities; rules and institutions that do not impose costs and waste on chains of transactions which tend to become dense and complex as the economy climbs the ladder). One may expect the return from these assets to underlie what Moses Abramovitz called our "measured ignorance"—namely, total factor productivity increases not explained by the accumulation of production factors in exercises of production function-based GDP and productivity decomposition.

Local development of capabilities of imitation and creative adaptation of existing technologies, followed by or in tandem with capabilities to innovate, is a requisite to raising productivity, upgrading, occupation and moving up the income ladder. Any application of technology needs locally specific content that cannot be acquired or transferred by means of textbooks or other codifiable forms of knowledge transmission. This knowledge cannot be made explicit, simply transmissible in blueprints, and thus cannot be perfectly diffused as either public information or private property. It must be developed locally. Production, technology adoption, and invention requires a relatively high level of such idiosyncratic knowledge and local capabilities (Canuto, 1995).

While technology originators tend to follow a reversed sequence to that off latecomers, it is typical for the latter to start from production and technological adoption and only then move on to invention. That has been the case in the Republic of Korea and China (Canuto, 2018b). These countries have developed innovation capabilities after intense learning through using and adapting existing technologies.

Simple interconnectedness does not automatically spark productivity increases and local innovation. Success depends on the presence of a broad set of complementary factors: access to finance, infrastructure, skilled labor, and good managerial and organizational practices. In the absence of these factors, returns from investing in the development of capabilities are likely to be low (Canuto et al., 2010; Cirera and Maloney, 2017).

Solutions must be found to market failures that generate disincentives to the accumulation of knowledge, but the private and public sector interaction cannot be unfriendly to the rising density and complexity of chains of transactions accompanying progression. Transaction costs associated with "doing business"—such as trading across borders, hiring and enforcing contracts—cannot be too high, whereas other dimensions of the "investment climate"—policy uncertainty, macroeconomic instability, corruption, losses due to crime, infrastructure and others (Canuto, 2007)—must be favorable so as to not disincentivize investment in the acquisition of capabilities. In a broad sense, the structure of incentives for economic agents must be such as to favor the search for efficiency rather than seeking "rents" (Canuto and Ribeiro dos Santos, 2018).

International trade and technology transfer have proven to be important boosts on such a journey, but institutional change, high-level education, and local building of intangible assets are also essential for sustaining this over the long run. The Republic of Korea is a prime example of a country that exploited these opportunities to move all the way up the ladder.

It is worth remarking that, particularly in the case of large economies, heterogeneity and diversity of states is to be expected. Brazil's per-capita income, classified as upper-middle by the World Bank, is associated with an economic structure where one locates both high- and low-income types of activities and jobs. Overcoming middle-income traps in such a case means upgrading a substantial share of overall employment, including by rescuing low-income agents left behind as such by the previous transition (Canuto, 2011).

Traps may take place in situations when upgrading faces high obstacles to gaining competitiveness because of incumbents in global markets. Gill and Kharas (2007) used the phrase "middle-income trap" to designate economies that were being "squeezed between the low-wage poor country competitors that dominate in mature industries and the rich-country innovators that dominate in industries undergoing rapid technological change." To a large extent, manufacturing in Latin America was relatively squeezed by the large addition of cheaper labor to the global economy resulting from the downfall of the Soviet Union and China's economic integration.

Ultimately, however, one may point to local insufficiency or appropriateness of some of the policies and institutions necessary to underpin the transition upward as potential causes of middle-income traps. Agenor and Canuto (2015, 2017) developed analytical models of multiple equilibria in which distorted incentives and the misallocation of talent, weak contract enforcement and protection of intellectual property rights, a lack of access to advanced infrastructure, and a lack of access to finance create the possibility of a middle-income economy settling on a "bad" low-growth path. In turn, Aiyar et al. (2013) and Han and Wei (2017) approach the negative implications for growth of a high frequency of macroeconomic booms-and-busts.

12.4 Policies and Institutions Needed to Climb up the Income Ladder and Graduate

We have analyzed the challenges of middle-income traps and the prima facie case for the engagement of MDBs with middle-income countries. What are the actions that these countries can take which would benefit from engagement with MDBs? They are very different from the original actions that MDBs first took upon themselves, which were basically addressed at solving capital market failures. Indeed, they involve a wide array of topics and the greatest challenges for these countries. We present below a non-exhaustive list of what are some of the most promising areas and corresponding actions that MDBs could take to help countries overcome the trap: (a) accumulate human capital and develop high cognitive skills; (b) foster entrepreneurship; (c) increase complexity; (d) provide access to advanced infrastructure; (e) pursue macroeconomic stability; (f) climate change mitigation.

12.4.1 Accumulate Human Capital and Develop High Cognitive Skills

As economies evolve from low- to middle-income status, so do their growth drivers. While accumulating physical capital remains important for growth in middle-income economies, *human capital accumulation* and total factor productivity improvement—or growth in production not derived from higher use of inputs—acquire larger weights in growth determination. Productivity-centered growth is needed to reach high income.

Human capital accumulation supports both growth and equity and the emphasis must be on ramping up the quality of education. Economies with relatively *high cognitive skills* benefit from having a critical mass of students likely to become innovators. As economies move closer to the technological frontier, the returns on research-oriented innovation pick up tangibly.

World Bank (2017a) recognizes the difficult pass from the recognition of the importance of education for development to the establishment of effective policies which increase human capital in the population. But it also provides directions for successful policies, and we underscore two of the most promising areas.

Teaching to the level of the student is a crucial recommendation. If a student is not following lessons, they may become completely demotivated and give up on schooling altogether. Effective policies need not involve the personalization of teaching for every student, which would imply daunting costs. They can be as simple as reassigning students to classes based on their current level of understanding of the material, instead of the blunt age criteria currently implemented in most countries. According to the Chief Economist for the United Kingdom's foreign aid agency, Rachel Glennerster,[5] such policies could deliver the equivalent of 460 learning-adjusted school years (LAYs) for as little as US$130. Other promising areas for teaching to the level of the student include remedial support and computer-assisted learning. The latter, however, needs to be implemented as an auxiliary tool for teachers, instead of replacing them.

Investing in early years education is another policy identified by the World Development Report 2018 which has a large body of evidence to support it. The economist James Heckman and others have produced several studies documenting how crucial it is to properly stimulate children from an early age so that they can develop not only cognitive but also non-cognitive skills. While many countries only offer public schooling from age six until high school (and many of them spend vast resources in university education), the greatest returns for human capital formation are, by far, concentrated in early childhood.

A role for MDBs may lie in helping countries adopt those policies themselves. Education is one of the highest government expenditures, and they are increasing. The World Bank estimates that governments spent on average 4.8 percent of GDP on education in 2015, which amounts to around US$3.5 trillion, which is orders of magnitude higher than MDBs financial capacities. Their greatest impact, therefore, will be related to properly informing the debates around the world, providing evidence which will not be directly linked to any of the main groups of interest, and designing programs, such as Development Policy Loans (DPLs), which may provide the incentives for the transition towards more effective policies. This is not a vain hope. There is now good evidence[6] that governments in developing countries do pay attention to the results of studies when formulating their policies.

Even though governments have been involved in education for a long time, and devote so many resources to it, there is still so much we do not know. What is the ideal class size? What is the most important material that should be taught? What sequence should be adopted?

MDBs are uniquely placed in conducting studies to better understand what are the most effective and efficient education policies. They have the necessary expertise to study in the most rigorous way possible the consequences of different approaches to education, in different settings. They have the scale to conduct these studies which are often linked to investments in the millions of dollars. Lastly, they have the standing. Given that learning what works in building human capital is in many ways a global public good,[7] it only makes sense that collective

[5] https://80000hours.org/podcast/episodes/rachel-glennerster-best-buys-in-international-development/?utm_campaign=podcast_rachel-glennerster&utm_source=80000+Hours+Podcast&utm_medium=podcast

[6] https://www.povertyactionlab.org/evaluation/informing-policy-research-brazil

[7] Although there will be regional differences, which should also be studied.

entities such as MDBs should be at the forefront of financing them. The recent award of the Nobel prize to the so-called *randomistas*, Banerjee, Duflo, and Kremer, highlights the importance of using these studies to fight poverty. The success of their approach should inspire MDBs to scale up the conduction of RCTs, including by incorporating the component of randomization to future projects. This way, learning and doing go hand-in-hand, much like what happens with current tech companies, obsessed with A/B testing.

12.4.2 Foster Entrepreneurship

Innovation matters more as economies approach the technological frontier and entrepreneurship turns new ideas or technology into innovation-based growth. Opportunity-driven *entrepreneurship*, which is often built on new ideas or technology, increasingly outweighs necessity-driven entrepreneurship, which responds to existing market needs.

Risk-taking entrepreneurs take the lead in fostering innovation, and these individuals respond to incentives that are either strengthened or weakened by economic policies and institutions. Governments can promote innovative entrepreneurship through stronger intellectual property protection and the rule of law, better access to finance, and effective competition policies.

The main takeaway for fostering entrepreneurship is that countries should strive to create the conditions by which private actors are able to implement their visions, instead of trying to evaluate ex-ante which proposals have a greater chance of success. In that vein, improving the business environment is an essential task. World Bank (2017b) provides some of the most important measures that can be taken: business entry reforms, making it easier for people to start their own businesses; business licensing and inspections reform, making sure that licensing is not used as a source of revenue which increases the cost of business; construction-permitting reform, which can both decrease the costs for formal businesses to be physically established or to expand, but also avoid unsafe construction in the informal sector; and quality infrastructure and standards reforms. The general theme above is one of decreasing rent-seeking on the part of governments. This means that the particular aspects of governance reforms should also be addressed, especially in order to raise rewards of efficiency-seeking behavior relative to rent-seeking—Canuto and Ribeiro dos Santos (2018).

A crucial role for MDBs is one they already fulfill but could expand on: documenting in the most objective way possible the current state of the business environment across the world. This not only helps empower administrations which pursue improving business environments for their own sake, but also creates incentives for politicians, whoh are merely expecting to remain on the job, to take measures which may improve the situation of their country.

The World Bank's Doing Business Report, for example, provides information on the ease of doing business in the different countries of the world. This information, in turn, is actively used by governments to pursue improvements in their business environments, and it also helps investors' assessment of opportunities. In many ways, however, it is still a rough measure. Usually the World Bank assesses the environment of only the largest commercial city. The assessment of the different policy stances must rely on a just a few indicators. This limitation of scope creates two problems: one, it is not as representative as it should be of the real business environment of countries as a whole. The changes in scores due to changes in methodologies reflect that. Second, because of the low number of indicators, this might create a race between some country leaders too aware of the reputational risks of a low score, which will concentrate all their efforts in improving only those few indicators instead of the whole business environment. Given the importance of the project, much greater investment for a more complete picture of the business environment is called for.

12.4.3 Increase Complexity

Graduation to high-income status requires a diverse and sophisticated product mix. In addition to producing a wider range of goods, middle-income economies must aim to produce more *complex* goods and services, which support higher productivity and better wages.

Rising total factor productivity (TFP) levels reflect the accumulation and development of domestic capabilities of production, organization, and management. These capabilities, in turn, keep a feedback loop of learning relationships with the complexity of production processes. This is illustrated in the correlation depicted in Figure 12.6 between GDP per capita and the Economic Complexity Index—see the MIT's Observatory of Economic Complexity and Harvard's Atlas of Economic Complexity.[8]

While this diagnosis is well-established, there is much less agreement over what governments should do to increase complexity in such a way that reliably advances along a sustained growth and development path. The most obvious remedy would be direct industrial policies to stimulate sectors which embed that complexity, such as high-technology industries and services. But properly conducting industrial policies is a very hard task which is often subject to capture by beneficiaries, leading over time to rent appropriation outweighing gains in complexity and the development of capabilities—an issue that even proponents of these measures recognize (Warwick, 2013). On the other hand, one may be sure

[8] http://globe.cid.harvard.edu/

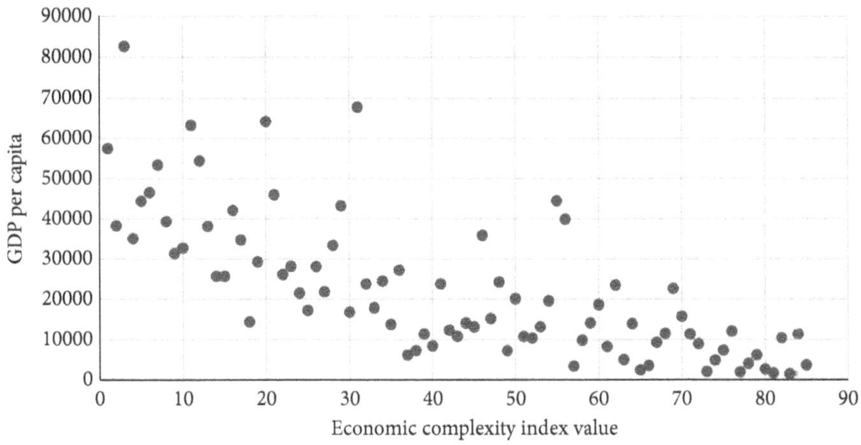

Figure 12.6 Economic complexity
Source: Our World in Data, https://ourworldindata.org/how-and-why-econ-complexity.

that the accumulation of human capital and cognitive skills, as well as microeconomic incentives rewarding learning efforts are requisites for any deepening of complexity and local development of capabilities.

12.4.4 Provide Access to Advanced Infrastructure

Investments in infrastructure are a component of the produced capital accumulated as a country climbs up the income ladder, as depicted in Figure 12.5. However, infrastructure needs shift as an economy becomes more complex and sophisticated at upper income levels. There is a nexus of *advanced infrastructure*, highly developed skills, and innovation. Fine-tuning infrastructure regulation and the labor division between public and private sectors in the provision of services and investment finance must be made in order to lift investment in corresponding sectors.

It should be noted that the world economy—and emerging market and developing economies in particular—have displayed a gap between infrastructure needs and its finance during recent decades. On the one hand, infrastructure investment has fallen far short of what would be necessary to support potential growth. On the other, abundant financial resources in world markets have been facing very low and decreasing interest rates, whereas opportunities for a higher return from potential infrastructure assets are missed.

A better match between private sector finance and infrastructure can be obtained if properly structured projects are developed, with risks and returns distributed in accordance with different incentives for stakeholders (Canuto and

Liaplina, 2017). Investments may also be maximized if financial operations by public-sector entities—and MDBs—are designed so as to crowd-in—rather than crowd-out—private participation, as in the World Bank's approach of "maximizing finance for development" (Development Committee, 2017).

12.4.5 Pursue Macroeconomic Stability

An environment conducive to growth needs *macroeconomic stability*. When a country attains middle-income status, its growth rate tends to become more vulnerable to indicators affecting macroeconomic stability—such as whether the country faces a banking or a currency crisis, the extent of capital inflows other than foreign investment, and government debt as a share of GDP. Climbing up the income ladder becomes harder to obtain with a high frequency of booms and busts, as it runs against higher-risk, long-term investment decisions.

Even though the major responsibility for pursuing macroeconomic stability lies inevitably with country policymakers, the Bretton Woods model established in the 1940s assigned a responsibility of supporting it to the IMF (Canuto, 2019a). There are still some products by MDBs and other multilateral financial institutions that can help achieve that objective—such as Public Expenditure Reviews (PERs), Financial Sector Assessment Programs (FSAP), etc.—by shedding light on the challenges to be faced by authorities themselves. Development Policy Lending (DPL) operations may also be used to support these changes.

In short, the role of the government necessarily evolves as an economy progresses, becoming more of a supportive type as the private sector fully fledges. The government must shape an environment conducive to innovative entrepreneurship by promoting investment in education and infrastructure, as well as macroeconomic stability.

12.4.6 Climate Change Mitigation

It is a truism to point out that climate change is a truly global problem. One non-obvious consequence of this truism is that climate change can be fought anywhere, but the costs should be borne by all, according to their contribution, which is enshrined in the principle of "common but differentiated responsibilities." In practice, this means that there are many opportunities for MDBs to invest in climate change mitigation efforts in middle-income countries, because if countries are to pay collectively for a global public good, MDBs are the best tool, and because some of the very low-hanging fruits for climate change mitigation are in middle-income countries.

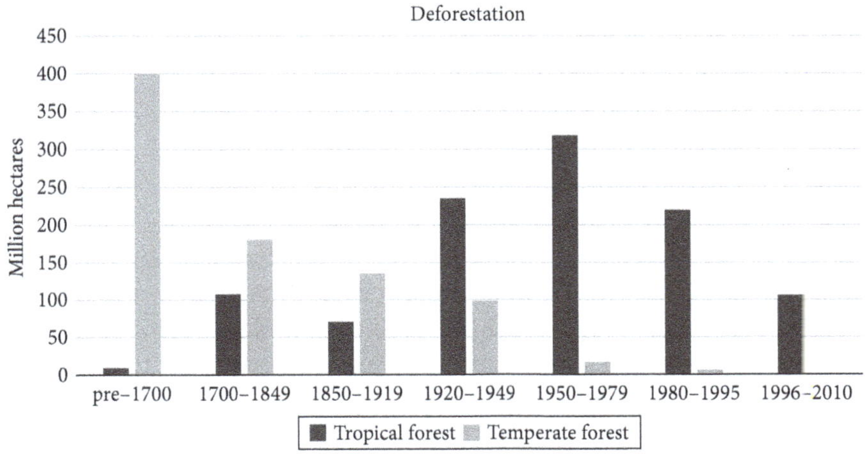

Figure 12.7 Deforestation
Source: Our World in Data—forests, https://ourworldindata.org/forests.

MICs are "just right" for climate change mitigation because they have much higher emissions than LICs, so there is a lot to cut, but a large share of these emissions can be avoided with relatively cheap changes (which is not the case in the high emission HICs).

Initiatives such as the Climate Investment Fund should have even greater priority, then. The opportunities for higher engagement with MICs abound. For example, reforestation in tropical climates (typical for MICs) is one of the most promising forms of carbon sequestration. Likewise, preventing further deforestation is one of the best ways of reducing emissions.

As it turns out, not only are tropical climates better at carbon sequestration, most of the opportunities for reforestation and deforestation prevention are also in tropical countries. The graph in Figure 12.7 shows that there is no more deforestation in temperate climates (typically developed). Deforestation in tropical forests, while decreasing, is still going on.

The comparative advantage of fighting climate change in MICs is not limited to forests, however. The environmental Kuznets curve shows that MICs have the highest CO_2 content of consumption, which implies great opportunities for improvement (Caron and Fally 2018).

12.5 Concluding Remarks

The qualitatively distinctive nature of the middle-income stage of development differentiates it from both high- and low-income phases, demanding an effort to go beyond generalizations about growth and productivity. In our view, the relevance of the concept of middle-income traps stems not from being a hypothesis about deterministic trends in growth, but rather as a warning shot about "complacency" risks of casting forward past transition successes. Instead, updating and prioritizing policies and strengthening institutions to new requirements are paramount. Individual middle-income country experiences of falling into a "trap" could also be approached as cases of a lack of—or failing performance in—footing the bill in terms of appropriate foundations for development.

Human capital accumulation, development of high cognitive skills, fostering entrepreneurship, advanced infrastructure availability, macroeconomic stability, and deepening of complexity in production all relate to "domestic institutions key for economic and social development." Macro-financial stability is, in turn, a precondition to "access to external capital markets on reasonable terms." As they are all policy priorities for an economy to move beyond the track from low- to middle-income stages and reach high-income levels, one may notice a convergence between overcoming growth traps and crossing the way to MIC graduation in MDBs.

References

Agenor, P.-R. and Canuto, O. (2015): "Middle-income growth traps," *Research in Economics* 69, (no.) 4: 641–60.

Agenor, P.-R. and Canuto, O. (2017): "Access to finance, product innovation and middle-income traps," *Research in Economics* 71 (no.) 2: 337–55.

Aiyar, S., Duval, R., Puy, D., Wu, Y., and Zhang, L. (2013): "Growth Slowdowns and the Middle-Income Trap," IMF Working Paper. No. 13/71. Washington, DC.

Canuto, O. (1995): "Competition and endogenous technological change: an evolutionary model," *Revista Brasileira de Economia* 49 no. I: 21–33.

Canuto, O. (2007): "Investment climate and microeconomic reforms," *Roubini's EconoMonitor*.

Canuto, O. (2011): "Navigating the road to riches," Project Syndicate, July 12.

Canuto, O. (2017): "Overlapping globalizations," Policy Center for the New South, November, PB 17–42.

Canuto, O. (2018a): "Can services replace manufacturing as an engine for development?" *Capital Finance International*, summer issue.

Canuto, O. (2018b): "Making Returns on Knowledge—How Innovation Can Flow from Globalisation," *Capital Finance International*, autumn issue.

Canuto, O. (2019a): *New Challenges Faced by the Bretton Woods Institutions*, Center for Macroeconomics and Development, April.

Canuto, O. (2019b): "World Bank: A Hummingbird on the Firing Line," Policy Center for the New South, January.

Canuto, O. (2019c): "Traps on the road to high income," Policy Center for the New South, Policy Brief PB-19/14, April.

Canuto, O. and Cavallari, M. (2012): *Natural Wealth: Is It a Blessing or a Curse?*, Economic Premise n.83, Washington, DC: World Bank.

Canuto, O. and Liaplina, A. (2017): "Matchmaking Finance and Infrastructure," *Capital Finance International*, summer.

Canuto, O. and Ribeiro dos Santos, T. (2018): "It's evolution, baby—how institutions can improve without critical junctures," Policy Center for the New South, November, PB 18–39.

Canuto, O., Dutz, M., and Reis, J.G. (2010): "Technological Learning and Innovation: Climbing a Tall Ladder," in O. Canuto and M. Giugale (eds.), *The Day after Tomorrow: A Handbook on the Future of Economic Policy in the Developing World*, Washington, DC: World Bank.

Caron, J. and Fally, T. (2018): "Per capita income, consumption patterns, and carbon dioxide emissions," VoxEU, December 1st.

Cirera, X. and Maloney, W. F. (2017): *The Innovation Paradox: Developing-country Capabilities and the Unrealized Promise of Technological Catch-up*, Washington, DC: World Bank

Clemens, M. A. and Kremer, M. (2016): "The new role for the World Bank," *Journal of Economic Perspectives* 30, no. 1: 53–76.

Development Committee (2017): *Maximizing Finance for Development: Leveraging the Private Sector for Growth and Sustainable Development*, September 19.

Development Committee (2018): *Sustainable Financing for Sustainable Development: World Bank Group Capital Package Proposal*, April 21.

Gill, I. and Kharas, H. (2007): *An East Asian Renaissance: Ideas for Economic Growth*, Washington, DC: World Bank

Gill, I. S. and Kharas, H. (2015): "The Middle-Income Trap Turns Ten," Policy Research Working Paper 7403. Washington, DC: World Bank.

Han, X. and Wei, S.-J. (2017): "Re-examining the middle-income trap hypothesis (MITH): What to reject and what to revive?" *Journal of International Money and Finance* 73: 41–61.

Knack, S., Rogers, F., and Heckelman, J. (2012): "Crossing the threshold: A positive analysis of IBRD graduation policy", *The Review of International Organizations* 7, no. 2: 145–76.

Meltzer, A. (2000): *The report of the International Financial Institution Advisory Commission: comments on the critics; reform of the international architecture*, Washington, DC.

Warwick, K. (2013): "Beyond Industrial Policy: Emerging Issues and New Trends," OECD Science, Technology and Industry Policy Papers, No. 2, Paris: OECD Publishing.

World Bank (1944): *International Bank for Reconstruction and Development—articles of agreement.* Washington, DC: World Bank.

World Bank (2011): *Latin American and the Caribbean's long-term growth: made in China?*, Washington, DC: World Bank.

World Bank. (2016): *Review of IDA's graduation policy. IDA18*, Washington, DC: World Bank.

World Bank (2017a): *World Development Report 2018—LEARNING to Realize Education's Promise*, Washington, DC: World Bank.

World Bank (2017b): *Business environment*, Washington, DC: World Bank

World Bank (2018a): *World Development Report 2019—The changing nature of work*, Washington, DC: World Bank.

World Bank (2018b): *The Changing Wealth of Nations 2018: Building a Sustainable Future*, Washington, DC: World Bank.

13

The Disruptive Role of MICs in the Development Cooperation System

Providers and Recipients

José Antonio Alonso and Jonathan Glennie

13.1 Introduction

Because of its ambition and comprehensiveness, the 2030 Agenda for Sustainable Development obliges the international community to move towards a radically new development cooperation framework. The realm of "donors and recipients" and unilateral transfers of official concessional funds via vertical decision-making structures is under stress. The (re)emergence of official providers from the South, the more active involvement of private actors, the advent of new instruments and modalities of cooperation, and the shrinking relative weight of official funds in development financing are all factors in the tectonic mutation that the development cooperation system is currently undergoing (Alonso, 2018).

This context of change offers a valuable opportunity for building a more inclusive and transformative system of development cooperation that: (i) embraces all providers across more horizontal and cooperative relations; and (ii) uses a wider spectrum of instruments in order to mobilize resources beyond the concessional ones coming from official sources. Thus, the first step in driving international support to serve the 2030 Agenda should be to *upsize and democratize* the development cooperation system, moving from an exclusive domain of a few countries towards a system that belongs to all countries and that brings diverse players and resources together to contribute and cooperate. That is what the 2030 Agenda proclaims when it seeks to "revitalize the global partnership for sustainable development."

The emergence of MICs in the international scenario has become an important driver for pushing these changes in the development cooperation system. On the one hand, the progress of some MICs has increased the heterogeneity and complexity of the international system, promoted new voices and actors in the international arena and opened the space to a more comprehensive and universal development agenda. On the other hand, through their role as providers of South–South cooperation (SSC), MICs have broken the strict donor/recipient

José Antonio Alonso and Jonathan Glennie, *The Disruptive Role of MICs in the Development Cooperation System: Providers and Recipients* In: *Trapped in the Middle? Developmental Challenges for Middle-Income Countries*. Edited by: José Antonio Alonso and José Antonio Ocampo, Oxford University Press (2020). © OUP. DOI: 10.1093/oso/9780198852773.003.0013

duality and have widened the options for poor countries to receive international support. Additionally, through their rivalry with traditional donors, the new providers have obliged OECD countries to review their priorities and procedures.

This chapter first discusses the foundations on which a revamped development cooperation system should be based, taking into account current tendencies in both the global context and the development agenda. Additionally, it sheds some light on the role that MICs can play in the new development cooperation system, considering their dual role, as recipients and providers, as well as the implications that this engagement has for the rules, standards, and governance of the system.

13.2 Foundations of a New Development Cooperation Policy

Conceived as a policy primarily by rich countries, "international aid" was born, in the 1950s, as a response to the North–South divide. At that time, national poverty was mainly considered a self-perpetuating phenomenon, with low-income countries (LICs) caught in a vicious cycle ("poverty trap") of paralyzing factors that mutually reinforced each other. It required a massive investment effort (a *big push*) for developing countries to break out of the "low-level equilibrium trap" and achieve self-sustained growth. In this context, external official concessional funds were considered an important ingredient for enabling the world's poorer countries to escape poverty. This international support was considered as only a temporary requirement: once a country overcame the poverty trap, aid would become unnecessary. Being unilateral in nature, international aid was left to discretionary decisions by donors, conditioned only by voluntary standards and rules agreed within an exclusive committee of the OECD donors (the Development Assistance Committee, DAC). Thus, the development cooperation system was built on mostly vertical and hierarchical relationships.

Most of these foundational principles of international aid are either outdated or, at least, under severe stress, as a consequence of important changes in both the international system and in the theory and experience of development. As a consequence, a reassessment of development cooperation policy is needed. The developing world is now more heterogeneous and the development agenda more comprehensive than in the past, and the development cooperation system should be prepared to deal with such diversity. Many of these changes can be presented as a tension between alternative options. We consider four sources of tension in sub-sections 13.2.1–13.2.4.

13.2.1 Focused Policy vs. Wide-scope policy

The North–South dichotomy was an imperfect description of the world in the 1950s and 1960s, but it is an even more obviously inappropriate image for capturing the complexity of the international realm nowadays. In the last three decades, developing economies have followed very disparate trajectories: a handful of countries (mainly in Asia) have shown intense rates of growth, allowing them a process of sustained economic convergence; an ample group of economies (in Latin America and North Africa, for example) have followed rather unstable trends, but with average rates of growth higher than those of the developed world and, finally, a group of countries have achieved very poor results in terms of growth, and some of them (mainly in Sub Saharan Africa) have shown a rather stagnant trajectory.

As a consequence of these processes, inequalities at the international level remain significant, but with countries distributed along a more graduated spectrum of development levels. This process has led to an enlargement of the MIC group that embraced 107 countries in 2018 and three-quarters of the world population, while the LIC group comprises just 31 countries and 9 percent of the world population. This situation is very different from 1990 when only 20 percent of the world population was located in MICs and 57 percent in LICs (see Chapter 1). As a consequence, levels of heterogeneity among developing countries have significantly increased.

The need to respond to this growing heterogeneity constitutes a challenge for the development cooperation system, presented with two extreme options: either to focus it, aiming to specialize in fighting extreme poverty, mainly in the poorest countries (a dwindling group) through highly concessional funds, or else to maintain an integral perspective, working through differentiated agendas and different mixes of instruments and type of funds in accordance with the heterogeneous conditions of developing countries.

It is understandable that many analysts and donors think that the first option is the most suitable. Since aid resources are scarce, they argue, they should be focused on the poorer countries (the *bottom billion* in terms of Collier, 2007). Implicitly, and often explicitly, it is assumed that MICs have sufficient resources to deal with their own development problems by themselves, including the eradication of poverty. However, it is equally reasonable to consider that the current world requires an international development policy with a wider scope, able to calibrate policy measures and support in accordance with countries' capacities and needs.

This approach is based on the idea that, although MICs have fewer shortages than LICs, they tend to suffer diverse gaps and vulnerabilities that could be more easily relieved with international support. Often, their deficiencies are not caused by absolute deprivations, but from specific bottlenecks faced by the processes of productive change, institutional improvement, social gap reduction, or international markets integration. These problems lead countries to fall into repeated slowdowns, hindering their convergence process towards higher-income levels (Fallon et al., 2001; Alonso, 2007; Agenor and Canuto, 2012; Aiyar et al., 2013). Development cooperation can make a difference in helping countries to overcome these structural blockages and supporting their involvement in the international development agenda through selective measures of support, sometimes funded with non-concessional funds.

This wide-scope approach seems to be in accordance with the spirit of the 2030 Agenda. While the Millennium Agenda still responded to a dual world of "donors and recipients" and adopted a narrow approach focused on combating extreme poverty, mainly in the poorest countries, the 2030 Agenda has assumed a more comprehensive, ambitious, and universal approach. On this occasion, all countries (not only the poorest) are called to push transformative measures for sustainable and inclusive development strategies. Certainly, the SDGs will not become a reality without the full engagement of MICs, both national and internationally.

In sum, making the SDGs a reality will require countries to adopt vigorous transformative measures at both domestic and international levels, and the development cooperation policy should support these efforts. For doing that, it should go beyond fighting extreme poverty—important as it is—and operate in three broad domains (Alonso, 2018). First, *guaranteeing minimum social standards* for all people, wherever they live: this would be a way to reduce poverty and vulnerability, promote social justice, and realize human rights; second, *reducing international inequality*, encouraging the process of convergence in terms of living conditions across countries, which not only implies transfers of income between countries, but also the promotion of an international framework (rules and incentives) that contributes to better distribution of development opportunities among countries; finally, *providing international public goods*, particularly those related to development achievements.

This approach seems more feasible at a time when the development cooperation policy has widened the range of its instruments beyond those strictly computable as Official Development Assistance (ODA). Besides grants and concessional funds, the perimeter of development cooperation embraces other official non-concessional funds channeled by an ample rage of institutions (such as multilateral and bilateral development finance institutions, environment facilities, or sovereign funds), as well as those private resources mobilized with official support. This broader perimeter is to be captured by the new concept of Total Official Support for Sustainable Development (TOSSD) that the OECD is promoting: tentative estimates suggest that TOSSD is double or triple the figures of ODA.

13.2.2 Transfers of Income vs. Incentive for Change

ODA was created to support developing countries to escape from "poverty traps," when physical capital was seen as the key limiting factor in economic development. Three important conclusions were drawn from this foundation: (i) development cooperation was mainly conceived as a transfer of financial resources (in concessional conditions) from the North to the South; (ii) development cooperation was considered temporal: once the country overcome the poverty trap, aid became unnecessary; and (iii) development appeared as a direct result of the injection of resources into the poor country (the "hydraulic vision," as Deaton, 2013, called it). None of these conclusions are now defensible.

Nowadays it is admitted that market failures are ubiquitous, that there are international fields in which markets are imperfect or simply do not exist (such as in some global public goods) and, additionally, that technology and productive changes are the cause of recurrent distributive asymmetries. As a consequence, development cooperation should be understood as a required mechanism for the correction of distributive asymmetries and market failures at international level. Congruently, development cooperation should be better conceived as a permanent (not temporary) instrument for governing global interdependencies in a context of deep international inequalities.

Originally, international aid pursued two purposes: to redistribute income internationally and to incentivize economic and social changes in developing countries. For countries caught in a poverty trap, both goals could be basically coincident. However, given its nature as a decentralized system based on countries' voluntary contributions, development cooperation is clearly a sub-optimal mechanism for international redistribution (Kopczuk et al., 2005). But, well designed, it can still play a significant role as a mechanism for incentivizing changes (Kharas et al., 2011). This distinction is relevant because, while in poorer countries the distributive role of aid can be the most significant (as it is an important complement to public funds), in MICs the "catalytic" role of development cooperation acquires more relevance. This implies the need to give greater attention to the impact that international support can have in changing incentives under which agents operate, in mobilizing (and leveraging) additional resources and capacities, in alleviating restrictions and blockages to change, and in mitigating the risks and uncertainty of development investment.

However, this does not mean that the historic role of redistribution, even in MICs, should come to an end. The new ambitions set out in the SDGs mean that more resources, coming from different sources, will be required for implementing such a transformative agenda. It is true that in recent years there has been an enlargement of private financial markets, with many developing countries widening their available sources of development financing. But private capital is rather selective in its allocation and highly sensitive to contextual conditions. As a result, the enlargement of capital markets is compatible with the presence of important financial gaps for both LICs and MICs in crucial areas of any development strategy, such as those related to building sustainable infrastructure, extending social protection policies, supporting ecological transition, or strengthening the private sector. International support through official funds can fill these gaps with appropriate financial mechanisms, mobilizing additional resources with developmental purposes (concessional or not, public and private).

13.2.3 Bilateral vs. Global

International aid was mainly conceived as a bilateral policy with donors preserving their autonomy in the definition of priorities and procedures and development strategies mainly defined on a national basis. But today the range of problems shared among countries has widened, as a consequence of more intense interdependencies created by globalization. Some of these problems present the characteristics of *international public goods* (IPG)[1]: that is, goods that, once provided, no country can be prevented from enjoying and that, consequently, require some level of collective international action for their provision. The multilateral system is the most appropriate framework to articulate this response. However, there is a widely held opinion that the multilateral system, in its current form, fails to meet the right conditions to perform this task effectively. Consequently, an important role for development cooperation is strengthening the multilateral architecture and supporting those policies oriented to achieve a better provision of IPGs.

While they are different, there is a tight link between the agenda of international public goods and the development cooperation agenda (Kaul et al., 1999, 2003, Sandler 2004). A new vaccine against malaria, the fight against climate change, or the improvement of global financial stability (all of them IPGs) has more developmental impact than several aid interventions. Accordingly, appropriate financial instruments must be defined for each agenda and, when required, some trade-offs between respective priorities must be made (for example, between economic growth and environmental sustainability).

Given their resources, population, and growth, MICs play a crucial role in the IPGs agenda, not only because they are key agents for the provision of a large portion of IPGs, but also because they are among those most interested in the proper design and application of this agenda. Therefore, a function for development cooperation is to support MICs in their attempt to set appropriate international rules and governance for IPG provision.

13.2.4 Exclusive domain vs. Inclusive System

The international structure of economic and political power has seen visible changes in the last three decades. As a result of their economic progress, a small group of

[1] We prefer to use the term International Public Goods (IPGs) than the more generally used Global Public Goods (GPGs), basically because IPGs embrace not only GPGs, but also Regional Public Goods and Trans-borders Public Goods that are not global in nature.

big developing countries (mostly MICs) have acquired the status of new regional and global powers. The estimation of *polarity indices* (World Bank, 2011) confirms that developed countries have been replaced by a group of emerging economies—basically MICs—as future centers of dynamism in the international economy. Among them, China occupies a key position, but the group is expanded to include at least India, Brazil, Indonesia, Republic of Korea, Turkey, and Russia (although not all of them have a similar dynamism). As a consequence, the world has turned *more multi-polar* than before (Spence 2011; Subramanian, 2011, among others).

This process challenges the existing global governance structures and demands a more equitable distribution of voices and responsibilities among countries at the international level. The emergence of new (or not so new) providers of cooperation from the South is part of this rebalancing in the distribution of political and economic power worldwide (Mawdsley, 2012; Santander and Alonso, 2018). As a result, the development cooperation system is no longer the exclusive domain of the OECD countries: it has to involve all providers (old and new), including dual and recipient countries. This obliges us to look for a new and more inclusive governance structure for the development cooperation system, as well as new standards and rules built on a more inclusive settlement (see section 13.4).

13.3 MICs as Recipients and Providers

13.3.1 Recipients

In 2016/17, close to 52 percent of aid resources were oriented to MICs, while the remaining 48 percent were oriented to LDCs and other LICs. With minor variations, this distribution of resources has been maintained over the last 20 years (Table 13.1). Many analysts criticize this distribution of resources as an example of the regressive patterns followed by donors, at the same time that they demand more attention to the poorest countries. However, it is difficult to support this analysis with only these aggregate data. Both the number of countries considered as MIC and the relative volume of population hosted in these countries has significantly increased in the last 20 years, which affects the aggregate data of ODA. In fact, when ODA is expressed in per capita terms, the pattern of

Table 13.1 Distribution of ODA by income levels (in %)

	2000/01	2006/07	2010/11	2016/17
LDCs	35.0	39.0	49.0	44.7
Other LICs	2.9	2.3	3.8	3.6
LMICs	39.0	33.0	33.8	30.7
UMICs	23.1	25.7	13.4	20.9

Source: DAC-OECD.

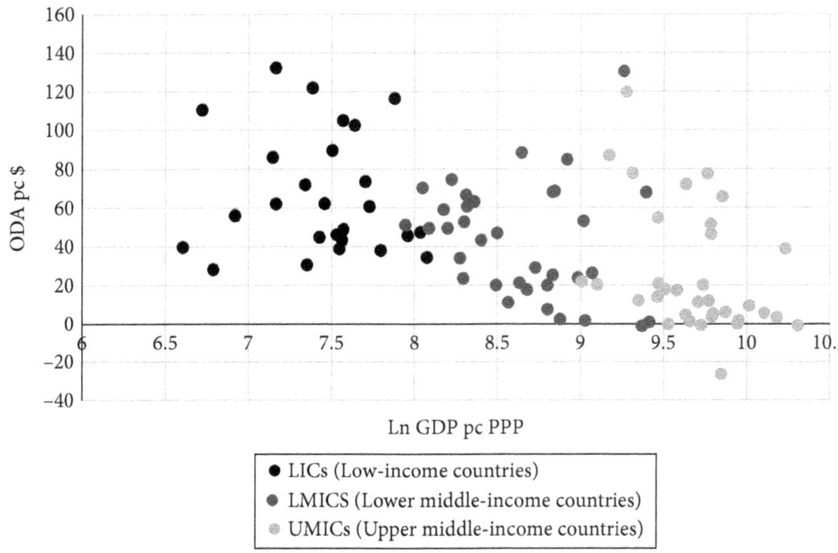

Figure 13.1 ODA per capita received and GDP per capita in PPP
Source: The World Bank.

distribution seems more progressive: in 2017, ODA per capita was US$71 in LICs, US$14 in lower middle-income countries (LMICs), and US$6 in upper middle-income countries (UMICs). This pattern is also revealed when ODA per capita is related to countries' GDP: as expected, ODA per capita decreases as GDP/capita increases (Figure 13.1). Beyond these figures, are there reasons to maintain international support to MICs?

It is generally accepted that as countries move up the income ladder their need for international financial and technical assistance, in terms of quantity and type, does evolve: concessional funds become less necessary for basic needs and countries require access to other means of support in order to face the challenges linked to higher levels of per capita income (Engen and Prizzon, 2019). As historical experience shows, these challenges are not easily overcome: many MICs have undergone—in some cases repeatedly—episodes of accelerated growth, but these have not necessarily led those economies to paths of sustainable growth over time. A first purpose of development cooperation with MICs should be to deal with these retarding factors, sometimes identified as "MIC traps."

Most of the factors responsible for episodes of MICs' slowdown concentrate around three big areas. The first area refers to the country's *governance* conditions. As countries make progress, they require increasingly complex institutions. However, advances in economic and social areas are frequently not accompanied by a parallel improvement of institutions (see Chapters 4, 5, and 6 in this volume). This situation particularly affects MICs, as they undergo the most accelerated transformations. In many cases, the problem lies not only in the weakness and limited efficiency of institutions, but also in their reduced credibility, which is fueled by the extraordinary levels of inequality and the social/regional fragmentation that is typical of some MICs.

Institutional weakness is also reflected in the fragile nature of the fiscal covenant on which the State is supported. If citizens question the legitimacy of public institutions, they are not likely to be motivated to pay taxes to finance them. Consequently, tax effort is low, tax evasion levels are high, and the financial difficulties faced by the State are recurring. This generates a vicious circle which is very difficult to escape: since public resources are low, governments supply limited public goods, thus weakening their legitimacy; at the same time, such limited institutional legitimacy causes citizens not to feel committed to supporting the State with their taxes. Therefore, strengthening the institutional framework and improving social cohesion should be one of the key work areas for international cooperation.

The second area is associated with the difficulty MICs have in sustaining a process of *productive and technological change*. As per capita income levels rise, economies have to move toward more dynamic specializations, which involves applying greater technological capabilities and more qualified human resources (see chapters 2, 3, and 6 in this volume). Reaching this goal would require a combined effort: investing in physical and human capital, promoting technological capacities, creating efficient infrastructures and enhancing a climate of fair competition in the markets. All of this should be accompanied by a careful combination of selective and temporary policies for the protection of those sectors considered key, with active support and export promotion measures. Strengthening such a complex process within a context of financial restrictions and weak institutions is not an easy task.

Environmental imperatives have set new constraints to these processes, calling for changes in existing energy and production models. In this area investment in sustainable infrastructures is crucial, being required to mobilize resources from different sources and conditions (private and public, concessional and non-concessional) (Bhattacharya et al., 2012). Development cooperation can contribute to this task using international official funds for leveraging additional resources.

A third group of problems refers to the tension between countries exposed to international financial markets and their capacity for *preserving macroeconomic stability*. MICs are characterized by their tendency to become indebted in international financial markets. However, within an environment of capital account deregulation, these markets tend to accentuate the cyclical behavior of economies, giving rise to recurring episodes of macroeconomic instability (see chapters 6, 12, and 15). With a tendency to present high debt-to-GDP ratios, securities denominated in foreign currency (and, sometimes, in limited-term bonds), and a reduced fiscal space in which to maintain counter-cyclical policies, these countries are subject to the influence of the *animal spirit* of international investors. In cases of greater tension, such instability episodes result in severe financial crises, associated with the over-accumulation of debt, bankruptcy of national banking systems, or unsustainable exchange rates (Ocampo, 2003; Ocampo and Griffith-Jones, 2007).

In order to reduce this risk, countries have to improve their capacity for mobilizing domestic resources and strengthening their national financial system. At the same time, the margin for the design of counter-cyclical macroeconomic policies has to be expanded. This involves building a sound tax system, improving economic institutions and setting rules to preserve stability throughout the cycle. Progress is also required in the correction of existing asymmetries within international financial markets, something that is far from a reality now. All these aspects can be areas for a wider approach of development cooperation.

Besides helping countries to overcome their particular development obstacles, development cooperation should encourage MICs to contribute to the global development agenda. A way to do that is through support to South–South and triangular cooperation to enable experiences and resources from a MIC to be shared with other developing countries. Along the same lines, development cooperation must support the processes of regional integration among developing countries, as a way to nurturing capacities, sharing experiences, and amplifying their voice at the international level. Some MICs play a prominent role in these processes. Finally, international support to MICs should help them be more actively involved in the provision of IPGs.

13.3.2 Providers

The OECD-DAC has defined the contents and forms of ODA registration in a precise manner, but there is no similar work by providers of SSC, which lacks internationally approved concepts and records. Some countries have made progress in proposals for measuring their cooperation (the cases of Brazil, Colombia, or Mexico being the most prominent), but these are tentative proposals. Therefore, there is a lack of reliable and comparable data referred to SSC.

Despite this, the OECD offers information on resources channeled by a large group of non-DAC countries, including those that report voluntarily (Saudi Arabia, United Arab Emirates (UAE), Kuwait, Russia, or Turkey, among others) and those on which estimates are made (such as China, India, South Africa, Qatar, Brazil, Chile, Colombia, or Mexico).[2] Considering both groups, the DAC estimates that non-DAC cooperation has risen from USD 14 billion in 2011 to close to USD 25 billion in 2017, reaching 30 billion in 2014 (Figure 13.2). Such a

[2] When countries report to the DAC, aid is expressed in net terms, but when the DAC makes estimates of non-OECD countries, aid is reported in gross terms.

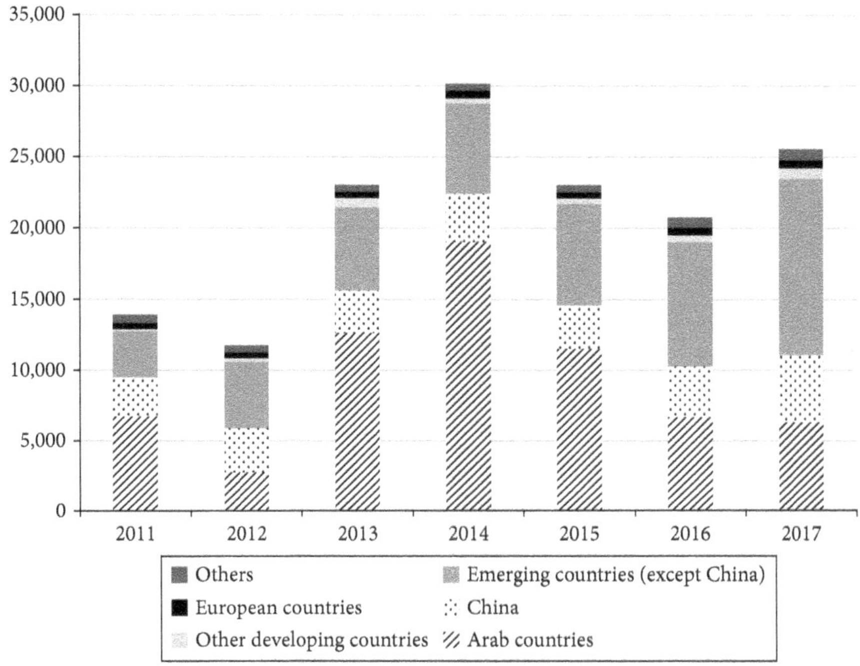

Figure 13.2 Evolution of funds disbursed by non-DAC countries in development cooperation (in billions of dollars)

Note: Arab countries: Qatar, Saudi Arabia, EAU, and Kuwait; Emerging countries: India, South Africa, Brazil, Indonesia, Turkey, and Russia; European countries: Romania, Lithuania, Bulgaria, Latvia, Estonia, Croatia, Cyprus, Malta, and Liechtenstein; Other developing countries: Mexico, Thailand, Colombia, Chile, Costa Rica, Timor-Leste, Kazakhstan, Azerbaijan.

Source: DAC-OECD.

figure would place the cooperation of these countries at around 15–20 percent of the resources mobilized by DAC members. However, the estimate is partial, both for the number of countries considered and for the type of flows recorded.[3]

Globally, SSC is mainly deployed in the technical, financial, and political fields. The first of these fields—technical cooperation—is where most of the new suppliers operate, especially those of smaller size and more limited resources. Due to their similar conditions, this type of cooperation stimulates the technical and institutional capacities of the two countries involved. In regional terms, it has been in Latin America where the technical exchange seems to have been most dynamic to date. According to SEGIB data, in the period 2006–16, almost 8,000 bilateral, triangular, and regional initiatives were registered—whether programs, projects, or actions (SEGIB, 2018, 2019). Although the picture is complex, there is

[3] The DAC registers those resources that are transferred under conditions similar to ODA, but this is limiting, since the suppliers of the South have a varied approach to cooperation.

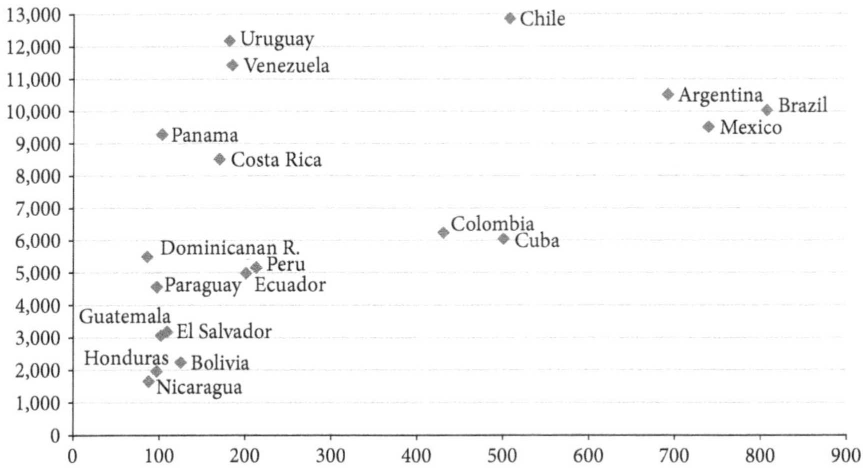

Figure 13.3 Latin American providers of South–South cooperation, 2006–2015 (annual income per capita and number of initiatives promoted)
Source: World Bank and SEGIB (2018).

a clear correlation between the level of income in the country and the number of South–South cooperation actions in which they assume a role as supplier (Figure 13.3).

A smaller set of countries (those of greater relative development) deploy financial cooperation, and a large majority do so through multilateral financial institutions, many of them regional. Among the countries that have bilateral financial cooperation instruments, China stands out, with its Development Bank of China (CDB) that has the capacity to operate both domestically and internationally. In 2016 alone, it is estimated that the CDB channeled around 280 billion dollars of investments in the country, mostly in the field of infrastructure; and, similarly, in that same year it channeled more than 12 billion dollars in investments abroad associated with the *One Belt One Road* initiative. Although with less financial muscle, another example of this type of cooperation is that of the Brazilian Development Bank (BNDES), which operates both within Brazil and internationally.

However, most of the suppliers in the South operate through multilateral financial institutions. Among them are, together with the World Bank, the system of Regional Development Banks: most notably the Inter-American Development Bank (IDB), the Asian Development Bank (AsDB), and the African Bank of Development (AfDB). Along with this, developing countries themselves have created their own multilateral financial institutions, such as the Central American Bank of Economic Integration (CABEI), the Caribbean Development Bank (CDB), the Islamic Development Bank (IsDB), or the Development Bank of Latin America, CAF. To this list of institutions have been added two other initiatives in recent years. This is the case of the New Development Bank (NBD), created by

Brazil, Russia, China, India, and South Africa, countries that bring together around 42 percent of the world's population and about one fifth of global GDP. The other major initiative is the Asian Infrastructure Investment Bank (AIIB), based in China and with a current membership of 93 countries, which began operations in January 2016.

On the other hand, also within the scope of financing, developing countries have promoted some multilateral initiatives to deal with episodes of monetary instability, such as the Chiang Mai Initiative; the BRICs Contingency Reserve Agreement; the Arab Monetary Fund; and the Latin American Reserve Fund (LARF). Although these are small funds (Chiang Mai is the largest of them), they play an important role as South–South cooperation mechanisms for the provision of monetary stability, in a context in which developing countries are highly vulnerable and distrust the IMF's ability to adapt to their requirements and needs.

Finally, there is a third dimension in which South–South cooperation has deployed in the field of policy coordination, particularly at regional and sub-regional levels. This type of cooperation is a way to stimulate policy coordination among developing countries and to build a concerted collective voice in international settings and to better enforce regional interests. Both aspects acquire special relevance in an increasingly transnational and interdependent world, in which collective action need to be articulated to respond to challenges that exceed state borders.

13.3.3 Beyond ODA

Given the kinds of problems which MICs face, development cooperation policy with MICs, instead of adopting a comprehensive approach as in LICs, should be highly selective and strategic, identifying the core issues that obstruct the path towards progress in each country. Furthermore, development cooperation should go beyond national averages, and consider sub-national perspectives in order to properly tackle internal heterogeneity and territorial inequalities. Finally, even if ODA can be part of the resources oriented to MICs, other official flows, not necessarily concessional, are important sources of financing for those development transformations that MICs require.

This approach could benefit from the transformations that the development cooperation system is currently undergoing: basically, first, a diversification in the available instruments for financing development, with an increasing presence of those oriented to mobilize private resources; and, second, an enlargement of the development agenda, including new fields previously not sufficiently considered by international aid. Both aspects are crucial for MICs.

Regarding the first aspect, there has been a strengthening of those financial institutions (both multilateral and bilateral) that support the engagement of the

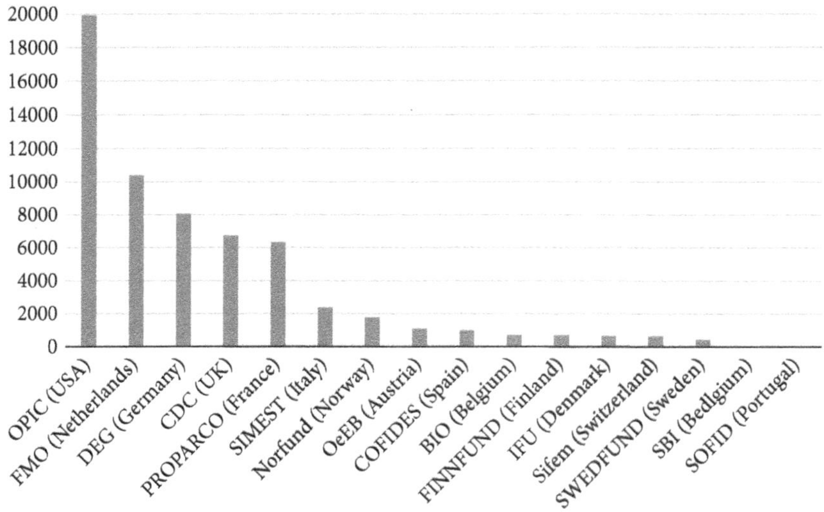

Figure 13.4 Total portfolio by DFI (million USD 2015)
Source: EDFI (2016).

private sector in development policy (Benn et al., 2017). Many multilateral financial institutions operate in this field, the most active being the International Finance Corporation and the European Bank for Reconstruction and Development. Additionally, donors have strengthened their bilateral development finance institutions (DFIs), such as CDC, Proparco, FMO, and DEG, among others. With different sizes and shareholders, these institutions have a global portfolio of USD 60 billion and channelled more than USD 11 billion in 2015, through equity investment, loans, and guarantees (Figure 13.4). However, estimates suggest that close to other USD 3 billion of private capital were directly mobilized by these operations[4] (Benn et al. 2017).

The importance acquired by these institutions is confirmed by the fact that the US has launched the new US Development Finance Corporation (DFC), consolidating the Development Credit Authority of USAID with the Overseas Private Investment Corporation (OPIC); and the EU has launched a process for reviewing its development financial architecture for development. Among the purposes of some of these initiatives is the intention to use more intensively guarantee and risk insurance facilities linked to development investment. In sum, an increasing part of the development cooperation will be associated with the financial instruments, not necessarily concessional nor computable as the ODA that multilateral and bilateral financial institutions provide.

[4] This figure seems likely to be an underestimate, as it is based on a voluntary survey.

Regarding the emergence of new fields in development finance, two seem to be of particular relevance for MICs. Firstly, the *promotion and management of sustainable infrastructure* in developing countries (Miyamoto and Chiofalo, 2015, 2016). While the role of ODA in this area is still important, other instruments of development financing seem to be more appropriate for mobilizing the magnitude of resources needed. Multilateral development banks operate in this field, as do institutions specialized in mobilizing blended resources and designing public–private partnerships.

The second field that has increased its relevance in public financing for development is related to the *environmental sustainability agenda* (Drutschinin and Ockenden, 2015; Shine and Campillo, 2016). Here international commitments have been coupled with the creation of new funds or financial facilities in areas such as climate change, water and sanitation, preserving fragile ecosystems and protecting the ozone layer, and biodiversity. Only a portion of this broad range of "environmental financing" counts as ODA, but it fits largely within the parameters of development cooperation.

13.4 New Standards and Rules

13.4.1 New Standards

Grouped within the OECD-DAC, donors have defined concepts, standards, and rules for international aid. The agreement around the minimum levels of funds concessionality and the circumstances in which tied loans were admissible became crucial standards in the 1970s definition of ODA.

Conditionality was another important issue in terms of aid standards. During the 1960s and 1970s, many donors mainly applied political conditionality to their aid, framed in the "cold war" conflict; in the 1980s and 1990s the system moved to more macroeconomic conditionality, linked to the structural adjustments plans. Now, it is broadly accepted that the ex-ante conditionality of aid is of limited effectiveness and might be even harmful, so donors have abandoned or relaxed their levels of conditionality, and any such clauses are linked more to the monitoring of achievements than to the definition of policies.

With the beginning of the new century, a new stage in the generation of aid standards was introduced. Its starting point was recognition of the necessity to increase the effectiveness of aid, improving its impact in the countries where it operates. To achieve that objective, donors accepted that it was necessary to enhance the ownership of interventions by developing countries, to reduce the transaction costs of aid via improved coordination among donors, and to provide aid with greater predictability by means of medium-term agreement frameworks between parties.

The Paris Agenda on Aid Effectiveness was the main result of this process. In 2005, in Paris, five principles for aid effectiveness were agreed: ownership of aid by recipients; alignment of aid with recipients' national policies and institutions; harmonization of donor procedures; results-based management; and mutual accountability. These principles were simplified and redefined with a more political approach in the successive conferences of Accra (2008) and Busan (2011). At this latter conference, donors adopted as main principles:

- "ownership" of aid strategies by the recipient countries;
- a focus on results/impact of interventions;
- alliances between governments and other stakeholders that are inclusive, in the face of complexity;
- transparency and accountability shared among the actors involved.

Despite the consensus generated by these agreements, the degree of compliance with them by donors has been somewhat disappointing, as some evaluations have shown (Wood et al., 2011).

Parallel to these processes, Southern suppliers have also defined the principles to which they want their development cooperation practices to adhere. In this case, there has been no governance organism like the OECD DAC, so the process has been comparatively more disorderly. However, there are some principles that are widely shared, some of them rooted in the principles nurtured by the Non-Aligned Movement. Among the most endorsed are these:

- Demand-driven cooperation: the intervention must start from an initiative promoted by the country concerned.
- Respect for national sovereignty: each country has the right to define its own development model and priorities.
- Absence of political and macroeconomic conditionality.
- Reciprocity or mutual benefit.

As with donors from the global North, it is difficult here to determine the extent to which these principles are shaping the effective practices of Southern cooperation providers.

In order to build an inclusive cooperation system, these two (or more) views (from the North and from the South) must necessarily be taken into account in an open dialogue. The approach should not necessarily start from scratch. Some of the above-mentioned standards are based on valuable experience, and supported by solid empirical studies. Having said this, the objective of this dialogue should not be to define a body of mandatory standards common to all countries. While it may be useful to recognize minimum shared standards, it is necessary for groups of countries to define particular standards (not universally shared) that they consider appropriate for their cooperation policies.

If one starts from these two considerations, it becomes clear that in certain areas the convergence seems feasible, while in other areas, the differences between North and South are not only visible, but also justified. Among the obvious shared principles, four figure most strongly: (i) ownership, which should furthermore be translated into cooperation prompted by demand; (ii) the need to align cooperation actions with a country's priorities, respecting its institutions and management procedures; (iii) the promotion of transparency and mutual accountability; and (iv) the leading role that strategic alliances must play. Accepting this, a space for consensus around these four principles can then be developed.

In some other principles, however, agreement is more difficult, because differences arise from the disparate countries' positions on the international scene. Such is the case, for example, in the contrast between the conditionality that has characterized North–South cooperation, and the respect for sovereignty and absence of conditionality claimed by South–South cooperation. Divergences are clear, which suggests the need for open debate among the parties. Another example of such discrepancy based on position in the international hierarchy is the insistence of South–South cooperation on mutual benefit as a basic objective of cooperation: while reasonable for Southern countries, this principle seems less appropriate for North–South relations, given the unequal income and capacities of the partners. Likewise, this difference justifies tied cooperation as a basis for South–South cooperation, since it entails the sharing of experiences among countries that face common problems, while tied cooperation in North–South cooperation appears to be more related to advantages associated with the donor's export capacity.

These few examples are sufficient to show that certain standards may make sense for some countries but not others. Thus, it will be important in the construction of a new system of inclusive cooperation to allow these different standards to pertain in the countries where they are relevant, while at the same time creating a set of some mutually adopted standards.

13.4.2 New Rules: Eligibility and Graduation

The OECD-DAC not only defined the requirements for resources to be computed as ODA, but it determined which countries were eligible to receive those contributions. In fact, the DAC annually publish a list of potential recipients of ODA that is based on countries' GNI per capita, in accordance with the Atlas methodology of the World Bank. When a country exceeds for a third consecutive year the threshold that defines access to the high-income group, it can no longer receive ODA. Recently, for example, Chile and Uruguay have graduated, and a similar advance may soon be experienced by Argentina, which has joined the group of high-income countries this year. Projections suggest that, over the next decade, as many as fifteen countries could graduate, indicating that this aspect will acquire increasing relevance in coming years.

The process of graduation has caused considerable discomfort among the countries affected, and this has been echoed in a large group of MICs (presumed to be the next candidates for graduation) who worry that donors will withdraw support while they still face significant structural deficits and development challenges.

In spite of such complaints, the definition of some kind of criteria for countries' eligibility seems to be reasonable when concessional resources (such as ODA) have to be distributed. These resources are scarce, which justifies their preferential dedication to the countries or regions with greater deficiencies, and to activities of high social returns but doubtful private returns. In sum, the most generous resources should go to those who need them most. In a correlative way, if eligibility rules are in effect, then graduation rules must also exist as countries overcome the problems that justified the international support. However, while eligibility can be immediately declared (once the reasons are justified), graduation should be undertaken carefully, over time. Prudence is necessary, in order to avoid setbacks in development achievements caused by the withdrawal of international support.

A more complex answer is needed when the question about eligibility refers to official resources with low or zero concessionality that are part of the new perimeter of development cooperation. Looking at the concept of sustainable development, eligibility could be questioned, since according to the 2030 Agenda all countries (rich and poor) are undergoing challenging processes of transformation in the move to sustainable development strategies. However, this option could conceivably open the door for developed countries to take the lead in cooperative action, not only as suppliers but as recipients, which would not be acceptable. Alternatively, one might argue that the very terms "cooperation for development" and "financing for development" imply that a recipient country faces structural deficiencies, or else obstacles that make its transformation particularly difficult. Indeed, it is precisely such "special" difficulties that justify international support. According to this perspective, the rules of eligibility[5] could be extended to all those mechanisms—whatever their concessionality—that usually fall within the boundaries of development cooperation. This is the option that has been adopted for registering TOSSD.[6]

If the application of eligibility and graduation criteria seems reasonable, the way in which these criteria have been defined within the OECD is clearly disputable, for many different reasons. In the first place, the criteria adopted (GNI per capita) is questionable, for at least three reasons. First, it is a variable that offers

[5] When resources are not concessional, there should not be criteria for graduation, although there criteria for eligibility should remain in terms of the definition of development for financing metrics.

[6] See http://www.oecd.org/dac/financing-sustainable-development/development-finance-standards/List-of-TOSSD-eligible-countries-alternative-methodologies.pdf

only a partial picture of a country's development achievements and deficiencies. Some crucial dimensions of development (such as democracy, institutional quality, or environmental sustainability) are not adequately reflected in the GNI. Second, GNI is shaped by the value in the market of a country's production of final goods throughout the year; it lacks any criteria of normative preference for the activities subject to valuation. Finally, per capita GNI is an average variable that says nothing about the distribution of capacities and resources in a country. This fact is especially relevant in MICs, where internal heterogeneity is very high, undermining the representativeness and meaning of average values.

Second, by choosing a single variable as a criterion and by limiting the threshold to three years, the transition period defined by the OECD is significantly shortened, and the abrupt and dichotomous nature of transition is accentuated. More generally, the graduation procedure suffers problems of efficiency, justice, and prudence: *efficiency*, because country's failures are rewarded with ODA and country's successes penalized with the withdrawal of international support; *justice*, due to the different treatment granted to countries slightly below or slightly above a certain threshold of income, which is purely arbitrary, thus accentuating distortions generated by an "inside or outside" logic; and *prudence*, because the very short transition period can frustrate progressive adaptation to change in the incentives and support received, increasing the likelihood that grave consequences may be suffered.

Definitively, the system applied by the OECD is poorly designed. The proposal to replace per capita GNI with a more complex indicator, such as HDI, seems ill-advised, not least because HDI is highly correlated with per capita GDP, meaning that the aforementioned problems of graduation would not be avoided. Furthermore, defining new categories for countries subject to graduation, would simply kick forward the problem. In a complex and heterogeneous world, rather than classify countries, we should classify problems, countries affected by these problems, and measures required to overcome them (as HPIC was defined) (Alonso et al., 2015).

An alternative procedure for eligibility and graduation is to admit that, given the multidimensionality of development, it is difficult to adequately capture the phenomenon through any synthetic indicator, however complex. As the 2030 Agenda suggests, we should admit that development unfolds on multiple dimensions, and that progress on these dimensions is not harmonious. Thus, a country may obtain achievements in one field but maintain deficiencies in many others. For example, a Pacific country such as Vanuatu can achieve progress in its income level, but remain very vulnerable to climatic threats; or a country such as Peru can improve its social prospects but require international support for its technological transformation.

The solution, therefore, is to define various dimensions of development and to identify the supporting instruments associated with each. This would be accompanied by the definition of graduation criteria that are specific to each of these dimensions. Thus, when a country reaches the threshold defined on one of the dimensions indicated, it would no longer receive the corresponding support (because it no longer needs it), but it could continue to receive support for other dimensions. This way of proceeding would dissolve the perverse "inside or outside" logic and make graduation slower and more selective (one graduates from some things, but not from others). It would also introduce an element of justice into the process, since a country would only graduate in terms of what it no longer needs.

13.5 New Governance

The changes in cooperation policy outlined in this chapter are also forcing profound changes in the governance of the system. Consolidation of a more comprehensive and coherent system of cooperation requires not only taking advantage of contributions that developing countries can make as providers of resources, but also incorporating these actors into the discussion and decision-making processes.

Nevertheless, the practical application of this approach would call for major changes in the institutional architecture through which cooperation is deployed. The DAC has thus far been the basic body of governance, responsible for defining policies and establishing consensus on development cooperation. But because it is an exclusive domain of OECD members, the DAC cannot be the response to a new and inclusive governance of the development cooperation system.

It seems necessary, therefore, to grant greater centrality to other fora in which developing countries enjoy greater voice, participation, and prominence in decision-making, and this very need has informed such new initiatives as the Development Cooperation Forum (DCF) and the so-called Global Partnership for Effective Development Cooperation (GPEDC). However, neither meets the optimal conditions to entrust to them an entire system of governance.

The DCF, created under the auspices of the UN's ECOSOC in 2007, is dedicated to monitoring trends in international development cooperation, seeking to encourage further analysis and reflection, and making recommendations in this regard. To those ends, the DCF brings together all the member states of the United Nations and forms an open space for the participation of other actors, such as civil society, the private sector, and local governments. It is, therefore, a representative and appropriate instance in which to promote discussions among the various actors, but its effectiveness in monitoring and the standardization of tasks remains minimal.

For its part, the GPEDC was created within the framework of the IV High Level Forum on Aid Effectiveness held in Busan (2011), configured as a platform that aims to strengthen the effectiveness of development cooperation policies. With the support of both the DAC and UNDP, and with a governance structure that involves countries of different income levels, GPEDC encourages dialog among the multitude of actors involved in international development cooperation. However, some developing countries regard it as a creation of the OECD, which reduces its legitimacy as an integrating forum.

Although neither of these two instances represents an optimal solution, it must be recognized that the DCF, being located within the United Nations, is better able to constitute the germ of a future body for coordination and governance of the international development cooperation system. Perhaps that future should be pursued along a dual path. On the one hand, it could take advantage of the opportunities offered by regional bodies to encourage dialogue, monitoring, and standard-setting in the field of development cooperation. As the case of the SEGIB demonstrates, in regional instances there exists a greater affinity among countries and a greater sense of belonging, which can favor more active processes of dialogue and agreement, along with more ambitious processes of learning and evaluating respective policies. On the other hand, a process of defining minimum criteria and standards on a global scale will also be necessary, and here the United Nations (through the coordinated action of its various specialized bodies, including the DCF) should play a crucial role. This double path would help to create a dense and diffuse governance structure that is regionally articulated (Alonso, 2018).

13.6 Final Considerations

In sum, limiting cooperation to fighting extreme poverty, focused on a small group of poor countries, through ODA and run by the traditional donor countries, does not seem to be a good way to meet the world's future challenges. Moreover, if that were the model, cooperation would be condemned to become increasingly irrelevant as an international policy. This tendency could be reinforced by the existence in many countries of a backdrop of growing populism, inward-looking policies, and skepticism about the advantages of multilateralism. It is worth emphasizing that, because the world is more complex, interdependent, and unpredictable than before, more international cooperation is needed now and in the future.

To be effective, development cooperation needs to be reshaped at least on three dimensions. *First*, it should modernize the way it measures impact, not just focusing on what is directly financed, but the kinds of incentives for change that it can promote. *Second*, cooperation should be able to manage the developing world's increasing diversity: it should operate with differentiated agendas and with a mixture of different instruments (sometimes beyond concessionality) in accordance with the conditions in each country; this will oblige us to deal with the trade-offs that can emerge between the objectives of enlarging the development cooperation system and preserving its focus on people and countries most in need. And *third*, the development cooperation system has to embrace all countries and actors building international collective action in favor of sustainable development. This implies promoting an open dialog around standards and mechanisms of governance for a more inclusive and democratic system.

References

Agenor, Pierre-Richard and Canuto, Otaviano (2012): "Middle-income growth traps," World Bank Policy Research Working Paper 6210, Washington, DC: The World Bank.

Aiyar, Shekhar, Duval, Romain, Puy, Damien, Wu, Yiqun, and Zhang, Longmei (2013): "Growth slowdowns and the Middle-Income Trap," IMF Working Paper 13/71, Washington, DC: IMF.

Alonso, José Antonio (ed.) (2007): *Cooperation with Middle-income Countries*, Madrid: Editorial Complutense.

Alonso, José Antonio (2018): "Development cooperation to ensure none be left behind," *Journal of Globalization and Development*, 9, no. 2.

Alonso, José Antonio, Cortez, Ana, and Klasen, Stephan (2015): "LDC and other country groupings: How useful are current approaches to classify countries in a heterogeneous developing world?" in J. A. Alonso and J. A. Ocampo (eds.), *Global Rules and Global Governance in the Post 2015 Era*, London: Bloomsbury Academy.

Benn, Julia, Sangaré, Cécile, and Hos, Tomás (2017): "Amounts mobilised from the private sector by Official Development Finance Interventions", OECD Development Cooperation Working Papers 36, Paris: OECD. https://www.oecd-ilibrary.org/docserver/8135abde-en.pdf?expires=1592584912&id=id&accname=guest&checksum=EC755AD7E9452185ADA0D1702F9836EC

Bhattacharya, Amar, Romani, Mattia, and Stern, Nicholas (2012): "Infrastructure for development: meeting the challenge," Centre for Climate Change Economic and Policy, Policy Paper, June.

Collier, Paul (2007): *The Bottom Billion. Why the Poorest Countries are Failing and What Can Be Done about it*, Oxford: Oxford University Press.

Deaton, Angus (2013): *The Great Escape*, Princeton, NJ: Princeton University Press.

Drustchinin, Anna and Ockenden, Stephanie (2015): "Financing for development in support of biodiversity and ecosystem services," OECD Development Cooperation Working Papers 23, Paris: OECD.

EDFI (2016): *Flagship Report 2016: Investing to Create Jobs, Boost Growth, and Fight Poverty*, http://www.edfi.be/news/38-edfi-flagship-report-2016.html

Engen, Lars and Prizzon, Annalisa (2019): "Exit from aid. An Analysis of country experiences", ODI Report, London: ODI.

Fallon, Peter, Hon, Vivian, Zia, Qureshi, and Ratha, Dilip (2001): "Middle-income countries: developmental challenges and growing global role," World Bank Policy Research Working Paper 2657, Washington, DC: World Bank.

Kharas, Homi, Makino, Koji, and Jung, Woojin (eds.), (2011): *Catalyzing Development. A New Vision for Aid*, Washington, DC: Brookings Institution Press.

Kaul, Inge, Grunberg, Isabelle, and Stern, Marc A. (eds.), (1999): *Global Public Goods: International Cooperation in the 21st Century*, New York: Oxford University Press.

Kaul, Inge, Conceiçao, Pedro, Le Goulven, Katell, and Mendoza, Ronald U. (eds.), (2003): *Providing Global Public Goods: Managing Globalization*, New York: Oxford University Press.

Kopczuk, Wojciech, Slemrod, Joel, and Yitzhaki, Shlomo (2005): "The limitations of decentralized world redistribution: An optimal taxation approach", *European Economic Review* 49: 1051–79.

Mawdsley, Emma (2012): *From Recipients to Donors: Emerging Powers and the Changing Development Landscape*, London: Zed Books.

Miyamoto, Kaori and Chiofalo, Emilio (2015): Official development finance for infrastructure: support by Multilateral and Bilateral Development Partners, OECD Development Cooperation Working Paper, 25

Miyamoto, Kaori and Chiofalo, Emilio (2016): "Official development finance for infrastructure: with special focus on Multilateral Development Banks," OECD Development Cooperation Working Paper, 30.

Ocampo, José Antonio (2003): *Capital-Account and Countercyclical Prudential Regulation in Developing Countries*, CEPAL, Santiago de Chile.

Ocampo, José Antonio and Stephany Griffith-Jones (2007): "A countercyclical framework for a development-friendly international financial architecture," DESA Working Paper 39, UNDESA.

Sandler, Todd (2004): *Global COLLECTIVE ACTION*, Cambridge: Cambridge University Press.

Santander, Guillermo and Alonso, José Antonio (2018): "Perceptions, identities and interests in South–South cooperation: the cases of Chile, Venezuela and Brazil," *Third World Quarterly Review* 39, no. 10: 1923–40.

SEGIB (2018): *Informe sobre la Cooperación Sur-Sur* https://www.segib.org/?document=informe-de-cooperacion-sur-sur-en-iberoamerica-2018

SEGIB (2019): Una década de cooperación Sur-Sur https://www.segib.org/una-decada-de-cooperacion-sur-sur-en-iberoamerica/

Shine, Tara and Campillo, Gisela (2016): "The role of development finance in climate action post-2015," OECD Development Cooperation Working Paper, 31.

Spence, Michael (2011): *The Next Convergence: The Future of Economic Growth in a Multispeed World*, New York:, Farrar, Straus, and Giroux.

Subramanian, Arvind (2011): *Eclipse: Living in the Shadow of China's Economic Dominance*, Washington, DC: Peterson Institute for International Economics.

Wood, Bernard, Betts, Julia; Etta, Florence; Gayfer, Julian; Kabell, Dorte, Muwanga, Naomi; Sagasti, Francisco, and Samaranayake, Mallika (2011): *Evaluation of the Implementation of the Paris Declaration. Phase II. Final Report*, Danish Institute for International Studies, http://pd-website.inforce.dk/content/pdf/PD-EN-web.pdf

World Bank (2011): *Multipolarity: The New Global Economy*, Washington, DC: The World Bank.

14
Global Value Chains, Preferential Trade, and the Middle-Income Trap

Renato Baumann

14.1 Introduction

Developing economies often face a common challenge: after a period of rapid growth they experience a slowdown in growth and productivity, falling into what has come to be known as the "middle income trap." Evidence suggests that at per capita incomes of about US$17,000 in constant international prices, the growth rate of per capita gross domestic product typically slows by an average of 3.5 percentage points (Agenor et al., 2012), apparently due to slowdowns in the rate of total factor productivity growth.

Whatever the actual reason for this outcome, the policy recommendations for dealing with such a slowdown are varied. Policies for developing economies in the 1960s and 1970s emphasized the need to overcome so-called "export pessimism" and promote exports, as a means to cope with the distortions imposed by the import substitution approach adopted by several developing economies for many years. Since the 1980s the ideas behind these policies have gone beyond the exclusive realm of merchandise trade determinants and started to incorporate paying attention to international financial aspects, as seemed to have been inevitable since the early days of globalization.

At the same time, the world started to witness an intensification of trade preferential agreements. It even became fashionable to identify the birth of a new era, when world economic (and maybe political) relations would be over-determined by a few big blocks. One outcome of this process was the intensification of regional integration initiatives. These would provide an enlarged market, allowing for gains from increasing the scale of production. It could also offer a learning opportunity for domestic producers in how to exploit external markets, and provide a "cold shower" shock to domestic producers spurring them to improve competitiveness.

The dawn of the twenty-first century would bring (at least) three new features, each with significant impact. In Europe, the convergence of Western and Eastern countries has provided the former with an additional supply of labor at lower cost,

Renato Baumann, *Global Value Chains, Preferential Trade, and the Middle-Income Trap* In: *Trapped in the Middle? Developmental Challenges for Middle-Income Countries.* Edited by: José Antonio Alonso and José Antonio Ocampo, Oxford University Press (2020). © OUP. DOI: 10.1093/oso/9780198852773.003.0014

while the creation of a common currency, adopted by several economies, contributed to reduce other costs. This has intensified productive complementarity in the continent. In North America, the consolidation of NAFTA had a similar effect, fostering the "maquiladoras" model and stimulating productive complementarity.

The third feature is the one with the biggest impact. The unmatched pace of growth by the Chinese economy, and the way its productive sector is linked to neighboring countries has become both a model and a big challenge to other developing economies. China has fostered a pattern of relationships among Asian countries, known as the "flying geese," since the 1970s and intensified this to unprecedented levels, in a modified model, via offshoring production.

Production chains in East Asia, North America, and Western Europe (in this order of relative importance, according to their performance) have imposed a new model of (mainly, but not only) industrial production. Participating in global value chains became a policy issue, even if a controversial one. Participating in value chains involves the ease of moving goods—final as well as intermediate. This means that trade policy has to facilitate such movement. The more open an economy, the bigger the chances that it might have access to production goods at low prices, and hence participate in a value chain. Market friendly trade policies—be they through multilateral reductions of tariff and non-tariff barriers or preferential trade agreements with selected economies—are an essential part of this model.

The relation between value chains and regional integration has gained momentum, partly because participation in value chains is identified as a source of competitiveness, something which is badly needed for economies facing the middle-income trap. The relationship between preferential trade and participation in value chains as a means to deal with the middle-income trap is the subject of the present chapter.

Following these introductory remarks, section 14.2 discusses the contribution of productive value chains to economic growth, identifying the different channels through which a developing economy might benefit from participating in a fragmentated productive process. The subject of section 14.3 is the role of preferential agreements, both in relation to fostering growth as well as in relation to value chains. A good deal of preferential trade agreements take place among neighboring countries, and hence have a strong regional dimension. The focus of section 14.4 is , therefore, on the ways that forming a regional preferential trade area might affect the growth of the participating economies and how these regional exercises might contribute to facilitating the participation of member countries into global value chains. In section 14.5 I propose a specific approach to identify the relationship between regional integration and global value chains, focusing on the correlation between country groups that adopt common external tariffs and indications of their participation in value chains. Section 14.6 offers some final remarks.

14.2 The Contribution of Value Chains to Economic Growth

> "Growth theory does not predict a simple relationship between trade policies and growth."
>
> "It would be informative to study the mechanisms through which trade influences growth. But data limitations greatly restrict research of this type. As a result, growth economics…has turned to the study of indirect relationship instead."

These two quotations from of Helpman (2004: 73) illustrate the difficulty of isolating the actual links implicit in the title of this section. Still, it is possible to identify some channels through which global value chains (GVCs) might be related to the growth of developing economies.

Slicing the production process is not new. It dates back (at least) to the beginning of the twentieth century, with the automobile industry adopting separate stages of production. What is (relatively) new is the fact that several stages of production take place in different countries.

Countries that have reduced production costs by accessing cheaper labor and raw materials elsewhere, and translating this into better export performance, in particular for industrial products, have signaled to potential competitors the need to try to adopt a similar approach. Such competitors are often middle-income and transition economies. They might participate in this new model via the provision of raw materials, eventually accruing further gains by becoming the assembler of parts produced in neighboring countries or—even more—by designing new products.

As Baldwin (2012: 7) aptly synthesizes, "The new 'supply' of reform came from developing nation governments seeking to industrialise by joining international supply chain….The new 'demand' for reform came from headquarter-economy firms seeking to raise the return on their firm specific know-how by combining high-tech with low wages in developing nations."

This type of production process allows countries to participate in the international market for some products when they lack the comparative advantage for doing so in isolation if, for instance, their geographical location in relation to the main markets contributes to reducing transportation costs. Furthermore, direct links with external producers should facilitate the access by domestic firms to state-of-the-art technology.

At the same time, being part of a GVC requires a good deal of specific domestic conditions. There is no "application form" for a country to become a candidate. Potential investors have to consider a specific country as a good opportunity to invest in, and this requires there to be free access to imported inputs, stable rules for the free inflow and outflow of resources, good infrastructure, qualified labor, as well as a number of other conditions.

Transnational corporations and foreign direct investment have facilitated the fragmentation of production. This has led to some ideological resistance, based on the two-pronged argument that such GVCs only contribute to foster the profitability of transnationals and that it is these companies that control the whole process.

Participating in a GVC imposes challenges at the macro level as well as a need to adapt the domestic firms' behavior, as they were often only accustomed to operating in the domestic market. Among other things, participating in a value chain involves dealing closely with foreign firms that act in accordance to different models and can involve demands for different quality and process standards, etc.

Participating in a CGV is not a universal attribute: it does not make sense for every productive sector. By definition, complementary production makes sense only for those processes that can be sliced in different stages. Hence, it does not apply for continuous processes, such as the production of steel and pulp. This is a fundamental characteristic, and a particularly important one for economies that are rich in natural resources.

As a consequence, economies such as the ones in Latin America or Africa can hardly expect to participate in GVCs to the same degree as, for example, East Asian economies. The reduced availability of natural resources in the latter has led to their emphasis on participating in the international market for manufactures, hence a higher probability of distributing the several stages of production among different countries.

This is not to say that the natural resources-rich economies cannot aim to participate in GVCs. They can, and should, make efforts in this direction, for the potential benefits it provides in terms of efficiency gains for domestic production. This is true in particular for those economies whose policy target is to diversify the composition of their export with a higher share of industrialized products.

From the perspective of the leading firms, outsourcing raises transaction costs but reduces governance risks and inefficiencies. Hence, a related topic is the need for a firm to decide whether it is better to create a productive unit in another country (offshoring) or to opt to outsource its production, in partnership with other firms operating in the domestic market.

Offshoring involves higher organizational costs than domestic sourcing due to the distance between productive units and the need to organize transactions in different environments. A productive process can involve parts of it taking place elsewhere when this implies lower costs of access to raw materials or inputs. The cost of service links between remotely located productive units must not be high, and the cost of creating a network must be small. In addition, these costs must be surpassed by the gains from access to cheaper parts and lower factor costs.

The decision to adopt a fragmented productive process therefore requires that: (a) fragmented productive blocks bring production cost savings; (b) the cost of service links connecting productive units must be not too high; (c) the cost of networking must be small (Hank and Fukunari, 2010). This means that the likelihood of fragmentation is very much dependent upon the nature of technology as well as the actual location of the productive units.

The geographical dimension tends, therefore, to gain importance. Frequent movement of technicians and managers among different productive plants, as well as transportation costs, would suggest that production stages taking place in different countries are more profitable when the distance between different plants is small.

Consequently, there is a natural tendency for sliced production to take place within limited geographical distance. This is increasingly more of a regional than a global phenomenon. It is why the usual picture of the most dynamic poles of industrial production rank, according to their export dynamism: East Asia, North America, and Western Europe. Indicators of productive complementarity among the countries in these regions are the highest. In each case,[1] it is relatively easy to identify a regional hub and the neighboring spokes, as far as industrial production is concerned. In East Asia, there is clear leadership from China, in North America the undisputed predominance of the US economy, and in Europe the differentiated role of Germany.

According to the World Bank, IDE-JETRO, OECD, UIBE, and WTO 2017 Report (henceforth GVCR 2017) the rapid productivity growth within GVCs shows that they are an efficient form of production. They have enabled developing countries in particular to move into new activities and rapidly increase their productivity.

How do developing countries benefit from participating in a value chain?

Basic sources of gain for developing countries following from their participation in GVCs are the possibility of diversifying their export bill, the potential to absorb gains from scale, and the corresponding increase in employment in the export sector. Furthermore, exporting more elaborated goods with (presumably) higher income-elasticity of demand might also provide gains from improved terms of trade.

In additon, the decision to produce offshore involves a cross-border movement of a production activity that requires a particular type of input and/or a specific kind of skilled labor. From the perspective of the developing economy, this means an inflow of capital, coupled to the transfer of some segments of production processes that are more skill-intensive than the average standard prevailing in the host country. The demand for labor becomes skewed towards higher skilled labor, thus raising the average wage.[2]

[1] For a comparison of several indicators relative to Asia and Latin America see Baumann and Ng (2012).

[2] Provided that there are transmission mechanisms within the economy, that is, the sectors participating in GVCs are not enclaves.

A precondition to participating in GVCs is to allow for the free movement of inputs and final goods. Preferential agreements are instrumental, as is a unilateral reduction of trade barriers. But this is not a sufficient condition. Participation in GVCs also demands a friendly domestic productive environment, meaning that "costs behind the border" are as binding as trade barriers, or even more so.

GVCR 2017 considers the products that have complex value chains as "contract-intensive" goods, which refers to the involvement of intense exchanges among different firms, each facing some risk of contract non-performance by others in the chain. "Domestic supply chains are an important stepping stone for improving participation in global value chains" (GVCR 2017: 73).

As far as trade policies are concerned the value chain framework implies a shift toward a broader (regional or global) policy approach, a shift from whole industries to specific tasks and business functions, a change in the assessment of competitiveness from endowments to flows stemming from transfers via GVCs, and a change of emphasis from trade barriers to behind-the-border barriers and regulatory measures.[3]

GVCR 2017 describes the process of gains stemming from GVCs as a sequencing of stages. In the host country, firms' growth increasingly becomes a function of their capabilities rather than institutional peculiarities. Initially the engagement is in sectors corresponding to static comparative advantage, such as natural resources-intense goods and light manufactures. Once countries graduate to middle-income status, firms start to integrate in GVCs with more professional services and advanced manufacturing. Institutions can help leverage GVC engagement by fostering skill-building, innovation, efficient access to capital, raising the average wage rate, etc. There is, hence, a gradual but sustainable process of positive influence stemming from the participation in GVCs that affects production in a developing economy.

Notwithstanding these presumed positive links between GVCs and developing countries growth, McKinsey (2019) shows some recent empirical indicators that call for a cautious approach.[4] Goods-producing global chains have become less trade-intensive: between 2007 and 2017 exports declined from 28 to 22 percent of gross output in goods-producing value chains. At the same time, cross-border services are growing more than 60 percent faster than trade in goods. Less than 20 percent of goods trade is based on labor-cost arbitrage. GVCs are becoming more intensive in knowledge and high-skilled labor, as well as more regionally concentrated, especially within Asia and Europe: production is increasingly being undertaken in proximity to demand.

[3] Cattaneo et al. (2013) as mentioned in GVCR 2017: 126.

[4] The study is based on 23 GVCs in both goods-producing and service industries, involving 43 countries that correspond to 96 percent of global trade, 69 percent of global output, and 68 percent of global employment.

These trends seem to favor advanced economies, given their strengths in innovation and services, and their skilled workforces. Developing countries with geographical proximity to large consumer markets may, however, benefit as production moves closer to consumers.

This type of indicator leads to a related issue: even if a developing economy tends to benefit from joining a GVC, there is no guarantee that these gains will be maximized nor sustainable over time. For instance, in chapter 3, Lee discusses the need to build and reinforce domestic capability in innovation and marketing as a necessary condition to entry into higher value-added segments and hence to assure the transition to higher income.

Participation in GVCs requires domestic reforms that might be politically sensitive. As in the case of signing preferential agreements, the objective of becoming part of a value chain can provide arguments for making viable several changes in domestic legislation and procedures that would otherwise be quite difficult to implement. What these indicators suggest is that, from the perspective of the set of developing economies, the chances of maximizing gains from participation in GVCs are not homogeneous: not only does geography matter; the role played by the degree of sophistication of domestic supply conditions is also a basic condition (Bamber et al., 2014). And even though domestic conditions are a vital component, a precondition to participating in a CGV is having an open approach to external trade. Section 14.3 discusses the role of preferential agreements in this regard.

14.3 Adding Preferential Agreements to the Policy Mix

Participating in GVCs implies the need for an open trade policy, since producers must have fluid access to imported inputs and the facility to ship the goods and services they produce. One way to provide easier access to selected markets is via preferential trade agreements (PTAs).

The number of preferential agreements signed in recent years, in parallel to the increasing importance of value-added trade—that is, production in GVCs—reaffirms the importance of identifying whether being part of a PTA increases the chances of belonging to a GVC, and if so, whether it fosters the corresponding benefits. A PTA eliminates trade barriers among its members and signals policy transparency and predictability; these are the basic conditions to attract foreign investors, that is, the cement in a productive chain. It is the mirror image of the increasing importance of regional production networks.

There are, however, a few aspects to take into account in this relationship. Estevadeordal et al. (2013) remind us that regional trade agreements are a driving force for the formation of value chains, but they also create major limitations for countries outside the block due to the rules of origin. These rules negatively affect the incentive to employ cheaper parts and materials from third countries, thus augmenting production costs, which might eventually surpass the benefits of the reduced tariffs. Furthermore, a firm wanting to participate in production networks spanning various trade agreements will find it increasingly complex to keep track of all the differences in the rules governing them.

Also, Hayakawa and Yamashita (2011) argue that PTAs may not have any actual impact on trade in parts and components since they essentially lead to tariff rates being almost negligible or significantly lower for parts and components than for final goods: margins of preference are minimal. They find that PTAs have no role in facilitating trade in parts and components when PTAs are formed, but rather increase the level of trade in parts and components 6 and 9 years after their formation.

As a consequence, PTAs play an important role in increasing the level of trade in final goods, both in the short and long run, while the positive PTA effects on trade flows in parts and components—the essence of production networks—only emerge in the long run.

At the same time, PTAs of second and higher generations comprise deep commitments, often of a WTO-plus nature, covering domestic regulations that go beyond strict trade disciplines, and these might harm the relationship with third parties, as well as reduce the degrees of freedom for policymakers to choose development policies. This would be the case, for instance, when they comprise disciplines related to investment, industrial standards, intellectual property rights, labor standards, and others.

Domestic (or regional) regulations can affect participation in value chains, to the extent that they affect costs. The basic concept of a GVC as the search for cheaper production factors and raw materials must be complemented by the vital importance of the facility to move goods—and eventually technical staff—among countries. These conditions might affect, at the micro level, the firms' decision-making process with regard to outsourcing or offshoring, hence the chances of participating in a GVC. In any case, it seems reasonable to infer that the smaller the economy the higher the probability that it will be more integrated into GVCs, because of the greater need for foreign inputs.

Berger et al. (2016) raise yet another dimension in their analysis of Vietnam: even though PTAs might stimulate the participation of developing economies in production networks, it is not clear whether "deeper" PTAs contribute to upgrading that participation or whether they merely increase activities in low value-added production stages. They find that "deep" PTAs have a direct effect on the business environment for the issues regulated in the agreements (eg, investment protection) and a potential indirect effect for related issues (eg, access to technology). That is, PTAs do not directly lead to upgrading but help set the right conditions.

Preferential trade agreements might have a regional dimension. Indeed, the more ambitious preferential agreements are often found among geographically closer countries. This is often called regionalism, and in several cases they are associated with common external trade policies. It remains, therefore, to speculate about the actual relationship between participation in value chains and membership of regional integration processes.

14.4 The Role of Regional Integration

The links between PTAs and production growth operate through the Vinerian concept of "trade creation." By reducing the barriers faced by the products of one country in accessing another country's market, the existence of preferential treatment allows for new opportunities and stimulates domestic production. Needless to say, preferential trade policies reduce one price distortion (between domestic and the partner country products) at the same time that it introduces another (between partner and third-country products).[5]

The impact of PTAs on domestic production is augmented when there are gains from the scale of production. According to Corden (1972), in this case there are not only the benefits from trade creation, but also a cost-reducing effect due to the impact on costs associated with the bigger scale of production allowed for the exploitation of an enlarged market. A basic condition for these types of production gains is, or course, that the economy that receives the benefit of the preferences in trade will only gain from this privileged situation if its initial exports are smaller than the import demand of its trade partner. It is only in this case that the preferences will stimulate an increase in exports.

There are a number of other channels through which preferential trade might foster domestic production. For instance, this will be the case when the increased imports from the partner are mostly production goods. These items can be purchased at lower prices, hence reducing production costs and therefore stimulating domestic production. Also, if the sectors with renewed exports experience technical progress, the impact on overall production is even greater.

Another transmission mechanism comprises the effects of preferential market access over the terms of trade: a positive impact might stimulate domestic production of the goods that have benefited from the process.

One further channel is the potential attraction of foreign direct investment into those sectors that benefit from the preferential treatment, with a direct impact on the rate of growth of production. Preferential trade conditions stimulate investment by reducing risk and uncertainty because of the large market now open to producers. Non-residents might also want to invest in a country with favorable market access in order to avoid being affected by trade restrictions imposed upon non-participants of the preferential agreement.

[5] See Pomfret (1997).

There can also be a positive impact on output if, by forming a customs union, each participating country receives a transfer from the rest of the union. This might imply a lump sum transfer within each country,[6] so that no individual is worse off and the government budget in each country is non-negative. As an outcome, the previous effects are not eliminated by eventual losses in the purchasing power of consumers nor by government budget disequilibrium.

Regionalism adds a number of other ways to influence output growth: it may provide a stronger "bargaining tool" for negotiations with third parties; it may be instrumental in less developed economies gaining more from donor countries and international organizations; it might be a mechanism for locking-in politically sensitive reforms; and it can be a tool to satisfy domestic political constituencies, among other effects (Ravenhill, 2017). This is not the place to discuss all the possibilities. Suffice it to mention that output growth can be affected by PTAs in several ways. So much so that there are concerns about the ideal number of preferential trade partners.[7]

There is an apparent paradox, though. Participating in GVCs requires an open approach to trade and investment. However, countries that are part of a regional integration process stimulate production at the regional level, thus penalizing external competitors. Yet PTAs might contribute to inducing country members to participate in value chains.

The Vinerian concept of regional trade creation is very much in line with the possibilities stemming from regional value chains: fostering existing activities or creating new ones for intra-regional trade is precisely the essence of promoting productive complementarity. If, additionally, production for the regional market—as is the case for the suppliers of intermediate goods—creates economies of scale, then the benefits of stimulating production on a regional basis become even more predictable (Ravenhill, 2017).

In summary, PTAs as well as participating in value chains can both be instrumental in fostering growth in developing economies, given certain conditions. Keeping those conditions in mind is fundamental in the design of policies. The related question is whether appropriation of these gains is maximized by preferential treatment to the goods from neighboring partners, that is, whether the existence of formal agreements is a necessary condition for this outcome. Section 14.5 discusses this issue more closely.

14.5 Preferential Trade Agreements and Global Value Chains

Precisely isolating the effect of preferential agreements on trade flows and—even more—on the participation in GVCs is not an easy task. Empirical works have

[6] This is the Kemp and Wan (1976) model. For a demonstration see Feenstra (2016).

[7] See the debate about the "natural partner" for integration in Krugman (1991), Summers (1991) and Bhagwati (1993).

often dealt with this issue by considering a "dummy" variable for the existence of such agreements, a procedure that does not consider the multiplicity of agreement formats. See, for instance, Johnson and Noguera (2016) and Hayakawa and Yamashita (2011).

More careful approaches, taking into account whether the existing agreement is a free trade area, a custom union, etc. also disregard the role of, say, foreign investment flows, public procurement, intellectual property rights, and others, that might influence the outcome.

The available evidence is not clear, even for a region like Asia, with a high degree of productive complementarity. For instance, UN/ESCAP (2015) reports—for the Asia-Pacific countries—a positive association between having regional integration agreements and the growing interconnected production and trade between member countries. The effects seem to be larger for intermediate than for final exports. And the impact on intra-regional exports appear to be stronger than exports to the rest of the world. Furthermore, the higher levels of trade in GVCs raise the likelihood of signing more comprehensive agreements.

Hank and Fukunari (2010) find, in contrast, that economic integration in terms of production networking or value chains has not benefited much from formal regional trade agreements. In fact, they argue, the basic weakness of the ASEAN Free Trade Area (AFTA), ASEAN Economic Community (AEC), ASEAN Investment Area (AIA), and ASEAN Framework Agreement on Services (AFAS) is that there are too many exceptions on key sectors of ASEAN economies. The standardization and harmonization of rules and regulations have been inadequate, very much like the transportation, infrastructure, and institutions to implement those trade and investment agreements.

It follows that economic integration through regional and bilateral free trade agreements can enhance regional production networking if policymakers can minimize the distortions related to regional and bilateral preferential agreements. These are results in the dynamic Asia-Pacific area. Elsewhere the outcome is even less remarkable.

For a better global view, the OECD has built a multi-country input–output database,[8] comprising information for over fifty countries. This has proved to be instrumental in identifying several aspects of trade effects that are impossible to infer from conventional trade statistics (OECD-WTO, 2012), such as a precise evaluation of bilateral trade imbalances, the qualification of market access conditions, the actual impact of trade on employment, and several others.

As it turns out, there are clear differences among regions. For instance, for several decades now South American countries have been members of at least two regional integration exercises: the Andean Community and Mercosur. In order to

[8] The database is the outcome of a joint OECD-WTO Trade in Value Added Initiative. See OECD (2013).

identify the actual and potential degree of productive complementarity, IPEA (a Brazilian Government think-tank), together with UN/ECLAC, have built a South-American Input–Output Matrix, for twelve countries, based on data for the year 2005.[9]

In their appraisal of the Matrix data Reis and Martin (2017) indicate that as far as intra-regional exports are concerned, the most important intra-regional export flows are processed food and beverages, hardly the picture associated with a regional value chain, however consistent with the region's comparative advantage in natural resources. Not surprisingly, the indications of forward linkages are very low. A first reading of these results is, therefore, that apparently the existence of formal agreements is not a sufficient condition for the creation of regional value chains.

Participation in value chains implies a significant change in the way the actual contribution of external trade is considered. The real contribution to the domestic income flow is via the actual value-added by each sector in each individual country. This has implications for the identification of net trade balances, as well as to the trade job's content, among other issues.

Despite the availability of such useful tools, isolating the effect of a policy of preferential agreements on trade flows is not an easy task. This is even more the case when the decision to adhere to (or deepen) an integration experiment takes place in tandem with the option for freer multilateral trade. It is hard to differentiate the performance in external trade flows of each of these processes.

Most countries nowadays have accumulated a significant number of preferential agreements with different partners, both with their neighbors and with third parties elsewhere. It goes beyond the purposes of the present article to measure the specific contribution (if any) of the existing signed agreements to foster the participating economies in GVCs.

A precise answer to the question of whether preferential agreements contribute to participation in value chains would require, first, a careful reading of each agreement, in order to see whether they comprise measures that might somehow affect productive decisions, as well as whether they imply different conditions for neighboring and third countries. Next, identify the relationship of those agreements with the empirical indications of participation in such chains.

Building a comparable database of bilateral preferences and—even more—going into a detailed analysis of the content of several preferential agreements—is well beyond the timing and size of the present text.

For the present purposes I depart from the very idea of a value chain, what Baldwin (2012) has called "import to export": foreign intermediates are used to producing goods and services that are subsequently exported. Presumably, the

[9] See www.ipea.gov.br/portal/index. There are only a few other regional input–output matrices. The pioneer is the one for Asia (IDE-JETRO and WTO (2011)).

technologies used for the production of output are the same for producing exports, hence one can consider the overall imports of intermediate goods as part of the process.

Based on this reasoning I propose a simple, easy to estimate approach. Custom unions shelter the domestic economy from external competition, via common external trade policy. This should allow for gains from scale to the domestic producers. At the same time, there is presumably free flow of products within the union. As an outcome, from the perspective of productive chains, two of the basic conditions are met: a larger scale of production and free movement of goods among union partners.

A custom union should, in principle, provide a more friendly environment for regional productive chains and eventually also facilitate participation in GVCs. The more intense the intra-group trade in intermediate products, the greater the chance that the country group exports might have a higher component of products fabricated in a sliced manner, as reflected in the intra-group import flows.

Participating in a value chain involves the free movement of intermediate products. The deeper the involvement with a value chain, the higher will be the ratio between intra-regional trade in intermediate inputs and total exports, as a mirror image of the sliced productive process. However, the ease with which goods move throughout the region is a necessary but not a sufficient condition for production in value chains. It is necessary that the economies involved in a given integration process have the capacity to produce or assemble the various parts into final products, in order to characterize a value chain.

In empirical terms, the question is which intermediate goods should be considered. Baumann and Ng (2012) have identified a set of 1919 Production Goods, from SITC ver. 3, at the 5-digit classification level.[10] These comprise capital goods, parts, equipments, and raw material. Since we are dealing with intra-regional trade, we can call them regional producer goods (RPG) goods. They can be traded with neighboring countries participating in a given integration exercise, as well as with the Rest of the World.

The intensity of the involvement with production in a value chain will be the ratio between the amount of intra-regional imports of these RPG products and the total value exported by the countries in the group (Total Goods: TG). The bigger this ratio, the more intense the involvement of the group of countries with chain production. The indicator (RPG/TG) can be estimated for groups of countries, in order to identify the relative intensity of participation in value chains.

The year 2000 was considered as an initial reference, to be compared with the latest data available at the time of writing in the selected database (UN/COMTRADE). For most country groups this year is 2016, but it was possible to

[10] List of items available upon request.

get 2017 data for some of the groups. For that purpose, I have considered a set of fourteen different groups of countries, with different degrees of commitment to regional integration. For each of those groups the analysis considers: (i) the size of the market (population and GDP); (ii) the existence of a common external tariff (ie, whether the group is a customs union); and (iii) the indicator described above, for the two years of reference. The joint appraisal of these variables should provide an approximate idea of the extent to which preferential agreements are decisive for the countries participating in GVCs. A brief description of these groups is presented in the Appendix.[11]

According to previous reasoning, the hypothesis that preferential agreements—mirrored by the adoption of a common external tariff, as a means to provide gains of scale and the free movement of goods at the regional level—might contribute to countries committing to productive value chains can be verified by putting together the basic data for each of the countries groups considered here.

Trade data are from UN/COMTRADE, SITC, Rev. 3. Availability of information regarding bilateral trade flows among countries is a problem in some groups.[12] Even with these shortcomings, the available data allow for a reasonable picture of these sets of countries to be drawn up. Table 14.1 summarizes the basic indicators for the several groups. Nine of the fourteen groups are customs unions, that is, they adopt a common external tariff and trade freely among the member countries. Five of the nine customs unions identified here were created after the mid-1980s, an outcome of the recent trend to foster regionalism. Coupled to the changes in production, with increasing dependency upon fragmented production processes, this indicates a parallel movement of the creation of customs unions and production in value chains, in terms of the timing of both processes.[13]

Table 14.2 shows the shares of production goods in total imports, in both regional trade and trade with third partners. According to Table 14.2, the range of situations is rather significant. As per regional trade in both years, the share of production goods varies, in the several groups, between 11 percent and 55 percent in both years, whereas, as far as trade with the rest of the world is concerned, this range is from 19 percent to 69 percent, indicating a relatively higher dependence upon non-regional sources for production goods.

[11] Country groups data are from WDI in www.worldbank.org. GDP data refer to 2017 in current value.

[12] Missing information in the UN/COMTRADE, SITC, Rev. 3 database is as follows: ASEAN—in 2000: Brunei, Laos, Myanmar; CARICOM—in 2000: Guyana, Haiti. In 2016: Bahamas, Dominica, Grenada, Guyana, Haiti, Montserrat, Trinidad and Tobago; CIS—in 2000: Uzbekistan. In 2016: Tajikistan, Turkmenistan, Uzbekistan; ECOWAS—In 2000: Guinea-Bissau, Liberia. In 2016: Côte d'Ivoire, Guinea, Guinea-Bissau, Liberia; LAIA—in 2017: Cuba, Panama, Venezuela; SACU—in 2017: Lesotho, Swaziland; UDEAC—in 2000: Angola, Chad, Congo, Democratic Republic of Congo, Equatorial Guinea, Rwanda. In 2016: Angola, Chad, Congo, Democratic Republic of Congo, Gabon.

[13] The time dimension seems to be important, according to the results obtained by Hayakawa/Yamashita (2011).

Table 14.1 Date of creation of selected country groups

Group	Common External Tariff since
ANDEAN COMMUNITY	2003
ASEAN	—
CACM	1985
CARICOM	2006
CIS	—
ECOWAS	1964
EFTA	—
EEU	2011
EUROPEAN UNION	1957
LAIA	—
MERCOSUR	1993
NAFTA	—
SACU	1910
UDEAC	1959

Source: World Bank WDI; official online pages.

Table 14.2 Relative importance of the imports of production goods

	Regional		Rest of world	
Group	(%) of total imports		(%) of total imports	
	2000	2016**	2000	2016**
ANDEAN COMMUNITY	26.2	32.8	38.8	53.4
ASEAN	38.8	47.2	49.5	66.8
CACM	35.6	36.7	48.6	48.4
CARICOM	18.1	10.7	36.2	34.7
CIS	25.9	39.9	19.1	37.3
ECOWAS	17.3	24.5	39.0	42.1
EFTA	56.1	45.4	51.1	36.4
EEU	17.6	38.9	26.8	41.4
EUROPEAN UNION	42.4	52.2	69.4	56.7
LAIA	38.1	41.6	67.6	56.8
MERCOSUR	45.4	47.3	70.8	56.7
NAFTA	30.9	50.4	19.6	49.1
SACU	38.7	18.0	53.9	16.0
UDEAC	10.4	15.0	26.8	45.4

Note: ** 2017 for EFTA, LAIA, MERCOSUR, NAFTA, and SACU.

Source: Author's own calculations.

Comparing the two periods, the share of regional production goods in total intra-regional imports was reduced between 2000 and 2016 in only three of the fourteen country groups—Caricom, EFTA, and SACU—suggesting a general increase in productive complementarity in most groups. This share is higher the bigger the GDP: the correlation coefficient for 2016 is 59.5 percent.

In terms of trade with other countries, the outcome is mixed, with seven out of the fourteen groups considered having increased the share of production goods imports: the more intense trade in production goods at the regional level has not significantly affected in general the dependence on imports of those goods from elsewhere. In Vinerian terms, there does not seem to be a "trade diversion" stemming from the more intense intra-regional trade in production goods negatively affecting imports of these products from the rest of the world.[14]

The actual correspondence between the formation of customs unions and participation in value chains remains to be discovered. As already mentioned, this relationship is considered here via the simultaneity of the existence of a common external tariff and the indicator of the share of regionally traded production goods in total exported value, for each country group. The higher the ratio of intra-regional imports of production goods to total exports in a given group, the higher the indication of value-added production in that group. Table 14.3 shows the basic information.

Forming a customs union is an attribute that does not correspond directly to the size of the participating economies, be it in terms of population (size of the domestic market) or economic activity (as indicated by their GDP). Customs unions are formed by both rich and crowded groups (such as the European Union) as well as by small economies with less people (such as SACU). Also, there is no geographic bias: there are customs unions in several continents. Furthermore, forming a customs union is not a necessary condition for the wealth of a given country group, as indicated by the GDP of NAFTA.

The figures confirm the well-known result that the degree of productive complementarity is higher than anywhere else in two groups: NAFTA and the European Union. The indicator surpasses 30 percent in both cases, and there has been a significant increase between 2000 and 2016. Of these cases, only the latter has a common external tariff, an indication that this is not a necessary condition for value-added production.

Apart from the European Union, in the remaining eight groups that form Customs Unions, it is only in CACM that the indicator barely reaches 10 percent, a rather low level. In every other group, the figure is much lower. More interesting, in three of these groups—EFTA, Mercosur, and SACU—there has actually been a reduction in the indicator between 2000 and 2016. The most remarkable

[14] An alternative reading of these figures might suggest that for those country groups with a predominance of exports of final goods, the higher share of imported inputs from the rest of the world on their total imports would indicate increased participation in a GVC: they would host the final assembly plants. A more precise evaluation, however, would require detailed analysis of the productive structure in each case, well beyond the present purposes.

Table 14.3 Basic indicators of selected country groups

Group	Population	GDP	Common External Tariff	Indicator (Imp RPG/Exp TG) (%)	
	(million)	(US$ billion)*		2000	2016**
ANDEAN COMMUNITY	110	600	Yes	2.2	2.6
ASEAN	650	2800	No	9.7	12.8
CACM	44	200	Yes	9.3	11.2
CARICOM	182	780	Yes	3.3	4.6
CIS	290	2000	No	4.8	5.4
ECOWAS	370	500	Yes	0.3	1.7
EFTA	14	1000	No	0.5	0.3
EEU	180	2000	Yes	1.9	4.1
EUROPEAN UNION	500	17000	Yes	82.7	82.4
LAIA	560	5000	No	6.4	6.1
MERCOSUR	260	2800	Yes	12.0	7.2
NAFTA	490	20000	No	37.7	45.8
SACU	65	387	Yes	5.4	1.9
UDEAC	190	260	Yes	0.2	1.0

Notes: * Current value; ** 2017 for EFTA, LAIA, MERCOSUR, NAFTA, and SACU.

Source: Author's own calculations.

fall took place in Mercosur, even though the group has adopted a common external tariff schedule since 1995. The indicator of value-added production seems to be more closely related to the level of wealth of the group (a correlation of 89 percent with GDP) than to the size of the regional market (a correlation of 49 percent with population). Clearly, the previous reasoning of gains from scale stemming from trade creation linked to the common external tariff fostering production in value chains is not sustainable.

Correlation does not imply causality and there are a number of specific explanations for the results obtained here. But the main message holds: there is a weak relationship between forming a custom union and participating in a productive network.

According to the evidence presented thus far, involvement with value chains is rather limited, from the viewpoint of most groups of countries. Competitiveness stemming from new production patterns remains a characteristic of only a few economies, and consolidating regional integration exercises is not a sufficient condition. This has significant consequences for the overall trade scenario, as well as for the set of policy prescriptions with regard to the middle-income trap.

14.6 Final Remarks

Signing preferential trade agreements and participating in value chains are two recommendations often presented to countries facing the middle-income trap. Both comprise positive and negative effects, and the links between the two policy instruments have to be better understood.

There is no shortcut leading an economy to participate in value chains. The requirements are diversified and comprise favorable conditions at the micro and the macro levels. The former means a suitable business environment, with conditions that make benefits stemming from offshoring surpass the costs. It also requires the creation or strengthening of the domestic conditions for scaling up the value-added ladder.

At the macro level one precondition—notwithstanding the high value of price stabilization, low capital cost and other elements, such as stable political and juridical environment—is to allow for the free movement of inputs and final goods. Hence, the adoption of trade barriers looks to be incompatible with value-added production. Furthermore, public policies must not impair the attraction of the relevant agents involved in this process, and this implies a friendly environment for investors and for the movement of technical staff.

As per the question of whether PTAs increase the chances to belonging to a value chain, the evidence presented here suggests that a number of customs unions fail to have significant value-added production, whereas some of the most successful examples do not adopt common tariffs. Belonging to a regional group is, therefore, not a sufficient condition for participation in a value chain.

The policy recommendation for an economy that aims to participate actively in GVCs as a means to overcome the middle-income trap comprises openness to trade and creating a business-friendly domestic environment. This might be facilitated via preferential agreements, but participation in value chains—both the initial involvement in a productive chain as well as the maximization of the gains accruing from that participation—is by and large more dependent upon domestic policies.

14.7 Acknowledgments

Opinions herein are personal and do not necessarily correspond to any institutional position. I thank Valeria Fechine for statistical support.

APPENDIX

ANDEAN COMMUNITY (1969): Bolivia, Colombia, Ecuador, Peru. Since 2003 the group has adopted a Common External Tariff, coupled to free trade for intra-regional transactions and a number of measures to facilitate customs procedures.

ASEAN—Association of Southeast Asian Nations (1967): Thailand, Philippines, Malasia, Singapore, Indonesia, Brunei Darussalam, Vietnam, Mianmar, Lao PDR, Cambodia. There is no Common External Tariff nor coordinated economic policy, but trade relations among its members are tariff free.

CACM—Central America Common Market (1960): Guatemala, Costa Rica, Nicaragua, El Salvador, Honduras. In 1985 the Convention on the Central American Tariff and Customs Regime came into force.

CARICOM—Caribbean Community (1965): Antigua and Barbuda, Bahamas, Barbados, Belize, Dominica, Granada, Guiana, Haiti, Jamaica, Montserrat, St Lucia, St Kitts & Nevis, St Vincent and the Grenadines, Suriname, Trinidad & Tobago. Since 2006 most member states apply a Common External Tariff (CET) on goods originating from non-CARICOM countries.

CIS—Commonwealth of Independent States: Azerbaijan, Armenia, Belarus, Georgia, Kazakhstan, Kyrgyzstan, Moldova, Russia, Tajikistan, Turkmenistan, Uzbekistan and Ukraine. There is no Common External Tariff.

ECOWAS—Economic Community of West African States (1964): Benin, Burkina Faso, Cabo Verde, Côte D'Ivoire, Gambia, Ghana, Guinea, Guinea-Bissau, Liberia, Mali, Niger, Nigeria, Senegal, Sierra Leone, Togo. From its very beginning it has created a customs union, with free trade among its members and a Common External Tariff.

EFTA—European Free Trade Area: Iceland, Norway, Liechtenstein, Switzerland (1960). This is an intergovernmental organization, not a customs union, hence no Common External Tariff.

EEU—Eurasian Economic Union (1995): Russia, Armenia, Belarus, Kazakhstan, Kyrgyzstan. Since 2011 it has adopted a Common External Tariff.

EU—European Union (1957): Austria, Belgium, Bulgaria, Croatia, Republic of Cyprus, Czech Republic, Denmark, Estonia, Finland, France, Germany, Greece, Hungary, Ireland, Italy, Latvia, Lithuania, Luxembourg, Malta, Netherlands, Poland, Portugal, Romania, Slovakia, Slovenia, Spain, Sweden, UK (until December 2019). This has been a customs union since its beginnings.

LAIA—Latin American Integration Association (1980): Argentina, Bolivia, Brazil, Chile, Colombia, Cuba, Ecuador, Mexico, Panama, Paraguay, Peru, Uruguay, Venezuela. There is no Common External Tariff in LAIA.

MERCOSUR—Common Market of the Southern Cone (1991): Brazil, Argentina, Paraguay, Uruguay. Has adopted a Common External Tariff since 1993.

NAFTA—North American Free Trade Area (1988): USA, Canada, Mexico. There is no common external trade policy.

SACU—South African Customs Union: South Africa, Botswana, Lesotho, Swaziland, Namibia (1910). Since its beginning it has adopted a Common External Tariff on goods imported from third parties.

UDEAC—Economic Union of Central Africa (1968): Angola, Burundi, Cameroon, Central African Republic, Chad, Republic of the Congo, Democratic Republic of the Congo, Equatorial Guinea, Gabon, Sao Tome and Príncipe, Rwanda. Since 1959 a common external tariff has applied to all imports from third countries.

References

Agénor, P. R., Canuto, O., and Jelenic, M. (2012): "Avoiding middle-income growth traps," Economic Premise 73792, #98, November, Washington, DC: The World Bank.

Baldwin, R. (2012): WTO 2.0: Global Governance of Supply Chain Trade, Center for Economic Policy Research, *Policy Insight # 64*, December.

Baldwin, R., Javier Lopez-Gonzalez (2013): Supply-chain trade: a portrait of global patterns and several testable hypotheses. *NBER Working Paper Series*, Working Paper 18957, http://www.nber.org/papers/w18957, April.

Bamber, P *et al.* (2014): "Connecting Local Producers in Developing Countries to Regional and Global Value Chains: Update", *OECD Trade Policy Papers*, # 160, OECD Publishing, Paris, http://dx.doi.org/10.1787/5jzb95f1885l-en

Baumann, R. and Ng, F. (2012): "Regional productive complementarity and competitiveness," *International Trade Journal* 26, no. 4.

Berger, A., Bruhn, D. Bender, A., Friesen, J., Kick, K., Kullmann, F., Roß, R., and Weyrauch, S. (2016): *Deep Preferential Trade Agreements and Upgrading in Global Value Chains: the Case of Vietnam*, Bonn: German Development Institute, Studies # 92.

Bhagwati, J. (1993): "Regionalism and multilateralism: an overview," in J. de Melo and A. Panagariya (eds.), *New Dimensions in Regional Integration*, Cambridge: Cambridge University Press.

Cattaneo, O., Gereffi, G., Miroudot, S., and Taglioni, D. (2103): "Joining, upgrading, and being competitive in global value chains: a strategic framework," World Bank Policy Research Working Paper No. 6406, Washington, DC: World Bank.

Corden, M. (1972): "Economies of scale and customs union theory," *Journal of Political Economy*, 80: 465–75.

Estevadeordal, A., Blyde, J., Harris, J., and Volpe, C. (2013): *Global Value Chains and Rules of Origin*, IDB, ICTSD, World Economic Forum, December.

Feenstra, R. (2016): *Advanced International Trade—Theory and Evidence* (2nd Edition), Princeton, NJ: Princeton University Press.

Hank, L. and Fukunari, K. (2010): "The internationalization of small and medium enterprises in regional and global value chains," ADBI Working Paper Series, No. 231, Tokyo: Asian Development Bank Institute (ADBI).

Hayakawa, K. and Yamashita, N. (2011): "The Role of Preferential Trade Agreements (PTAs) in Facilitating Global Production Networks," IDE Discussion Paper No. 280, February.

Helpman, E. (2004): *The Mystery of Economic Growth*, Cambridge, MA: The Belknap Press of Harvard University Press.

IDE-JETRO, WTO (2011): *Trade Patterns and Global Value Chains in East Asia: From Trade in Goods to Trade in Tasks*, Geneva: The World Trade Organization.

Johnson, R. Noguera, G. (2016): "A portrait of trade in value added over four decades," NBER Working Paper Series, Working Paper 22974, http://www.nber.org/papers/w22974, December.

Kazunobi, H., Y. Nobuaki (2011): The role of Preferential Trade Agreements (PTAs) in facilitating global production networks, IDE-JETRO, http://www.ide.go.jp, IDE Discussion Paper #280

Kemp, M. and Wan, H. Jr (1976): "An elementary proposition concerning the formation of customs union," in M. Kemp (ed.), *Three Topics in the Theory of International Trade: Distribution, Welfare and Uncertainty*, Amsterdam: North-Holland

Krugman, P. (1991):" Is bilateralism bad?," in E. Helpman and A. Razin (eds.), *International Trade and Trade Policy*, Cambridge, MA: The MIT Press.

Lim, H., F. Kimura (2010), The internationalization of small and medium enterprises in regional and global value chains, *ADBI Working Paper Series*, No. 231, http://hdl.handle.net/10419/53677

McKinsey Global Institute (2019): *Globalization in Transition: The Future of Trade and Value Chains*, January.

OECD (2013): *Industry and Globalisation—Measuring Trade in Value Added: An OECD-WTO Joint Initiative.* Paris: Organisation for Economic Co-operation and Development.

OECD-WTO (2012): "Trade in Value-Added: Concepts, Methodologies and Challenges," Joint OECD-WTO Note, March 15, 2012, available at http://www.oecd.org/sti/ind/49894138.pdf

Pomfret, R. (1997): *The Economics of Regional Trading Arrangements*, Oxford: Oxford University Press.

Ravenhill, J. (2017): "Regional Trade Agreements," in J. Ravenhill (ed.), *Global Political Economy* (5th edition), Oxford: Oxford University Press.

Reis, C. and Martin, A. (2017): "Complementaridade produtiva na América do Sul em 2005: uma análise através da matriz insumo produto regional," *Anais do X Encontro Internacional da Associação Keynesiana Brasileira*, Brasília.

Summers, L. (1991): "Regionalism and the world trading system", in Federal Reserve Bank of Kansas City (ed.), *Policy Implications of Trade and currency Zones*, Kansas City, MO, pp. 295–301.

UN/Economic and Social Commission for Asia and the Pacific (2015): *Global value chains, regional integration and sustainable development: linkages and policy implications*, E/ESCAP/71/8, Bangkok, 25–9 May.

World Bank Group, IDE-JETRO, OECD, UIBE, and World Trade Organization (2017): *Global Value Chain Development Report 2017: measuring and analyzing the impact of GVCs on economic development*, Washington, DC: World Bank.

15
Middle-Income Countries and the International Monetary System

José Antonio Ocampo

15.1 Introduction

Middle-income countries (MICs) face several problems in the international monetary and financial system. They have a dependence status in the global reserve system. Associated to this fact and to the features of finance, they face significant volatility of external financing, a fact that generates risks of macroeconomic and financial crises and constrains domestic macroeconomic policy. These risks can be contribute to the generation of a middle-income trap. The instruments that have been put in place to manage those risks, both domestically and internationally, are highly incomplete. Finally, MICs have inadequate representation in the governance of the system.

This chapter analyzes these issues. It is divided into five sections, the first of which is this introduction. Section 15.2 looks at the risks that the global reserve system generates. Section 15.3 analyzes the volatility of external financing and the domestic macroeconomic challenges it generates, and the instruments that countries can use to manage the associated risks, particularly the role of capital account regulations. Section 15.4 considers the international policy instruments: balance of payments financing and sovereign debt workouts. Finally, section 15.5 looks at the governance of the system.

In the literature on these issues, the term "emerging economies" is commonly used. Although the term has no precise definition, it is related to middle-income status, and so I will use it as synonymous of MICs throughout this chapter. The term developing economies would be used in a complementary way, to refer to low-income countries but also to most low MICs.

15.2 MICs and the Global Reserve System

The global reserve system that the world has today is the result of uncoordinated developments that evolved in the 1970s after the collapse of the gold-dollar parity

José Antonio Ocampo, *Middle-Income Countries and the International Monetary System* In: *Trapped in the Middle? Developmental Challenges for Middle-Income Countries.* Edited by: José Antonio Alonso and José Antonio Ocampo, Oxford University Press (2020). © OUP. DOI: 10.1093/oso/9780198852773.003.0015

that was a key element of the system designed at Bretton Woods. It is essentially based on the (fiduciary) dollar as the core global money, but open in principle to competitive reserve currencies. It has been complemented by sporadic issues of Special Drawing Rights (SDRs), which were introduced into the IMF Articles of Agreement in 1969, but which have remained one of the most underutilized instruments of international cooperation. The dollar is also the IMF unit of account.

This system has three basic deficiencies (Ocampo, 2017: 2). The first is the recessionary bias generated by the asymmetric burden of adjustment between deficit and surplus countries: whereas the former must adjust when financing dries up during crises, surplus countries do not face a similar pressure to correct their imbalances.

The second problem is associated with the use of a national currency as the major global currency, which is known as the Triffin dilemma (see Triffin 1961, 1968). The essential issue is that the provision of international liquidity requires that the country supplying the reserve currency runs balance of payments deficits, a fact that may eventually erode the confidence in that currency. Its major manifestation, since the collapse of the original Bretton Woods arrangement, has been the cyclical swings in the US balance of payments that are also related to variations in the real exchange rate of the US dollar.

This implies, of course, that the currency at the center of the system has an unstable value. It also implies that the system is strongly affected by US monetary policies, which are generally adopted with no regard to its international repercussions. There are obvious global implications. In the words of Padoa-Schioppa (2011: 64): "the stability requirements of the system as a whole are inconsistent with the pursuit of economic and monetary policy forged solely on the basis of domestic rationales in all monetary regimes devoid of some form of supranationality."

The third problem of the system, and one particularly relevant for MICs, is the inequity bias generated by the need of these countries to "self-insure" against strong boom–bust cycles of global finance by building up large foreign exchange reserves. Since these reserves are invested in the assets of safe industrial countries, and particularly in US government securities, reserve accumulation by these countries is nothing else than lending to rich ones at low interest rates. This is an inequity of the system.

Figure 15.1 indicates that the increase in foreign exchange reserves as a proportion of GDP in MICs started in the 1990s, following the Latin American debt crisis of the 1980s, and was particularly sharp after the series of crises in emerging economies that started in East Asia in 1997, and later spread to Russia, Latin America, and Turkey.[1] This clearly indicates that it was indeed adopted as a

[1] I use in this chapter the 2000 World Bank classification of countries according to their level of development, as it reflects much better the relative standing of different countries and regions of the world during the whole period covered in the analysis.

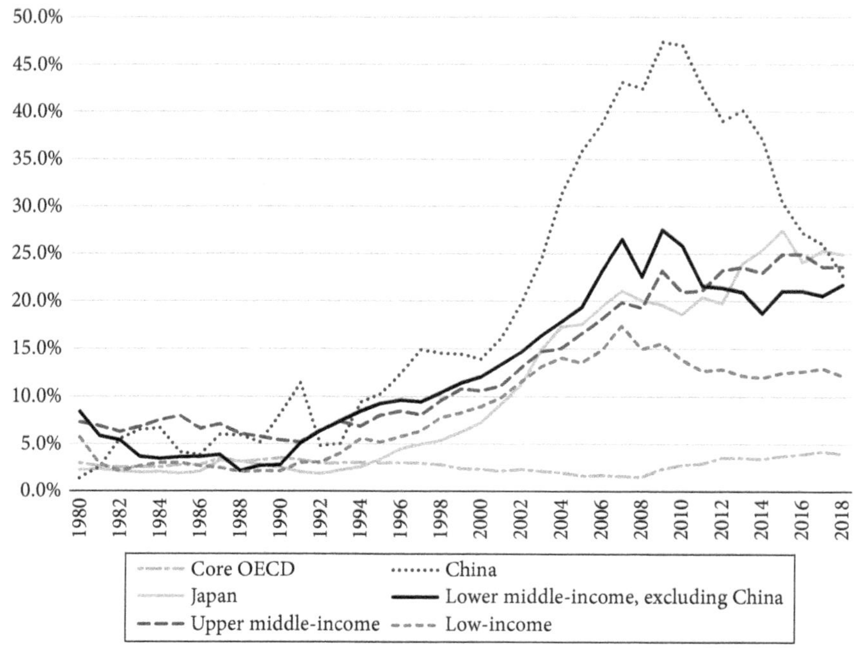

Figure 15.1 Foreign exchange reserves by level of development (% of GDP)
Source: Author's estimates based on IMF data and on World Bank classifications by level of development in 2000.

"self-insurance" policy. Among MICs, reserve accumulation in China was particularly sharp, also reflecting its rising current account surplus. The accumulation was also facilitated by the 2003–07 world financial boom, but basically ceased after the 2007–09 North Atlantic financial crisis[2]—possibly reflecting the fact that it had weaker effects on emerging economies (see section 15.3). Low-income countries also accumulated reserves, but in a weaker way. In contrast, developed countries, with the exception of Japan, kept their reserves at a low level, with a small increase after the North Atlantic crisis.

There are essentially two possible paths to reform. The first and, in a sense, inertial solution would be to let the system evolve into what it potentially already is: a multicurrency arrangement. The second would be to fully exploit the potential role of the SDRs, gradually approaching the aspirations of the 1969 reform of "making the special drawing right the principle reserve asset in the international monetary system" (Article VIII, Section 7 of the IMF Articles of Agreement). These two alternatives can be mixed, and such a combination may be politically more acceptable for the issuers of reserve currencies, particularly to the USA.

[2] I prefer this term to "global financial crisis," because although it had global effects, the crisis was concentrated in the US and Western Europe.

Although other currencies can compete with the dollar as an international means of payments and reserve assets, the competition has been relatively weak. This reflects the fact that the "network externalities" in the use of money continue to favor the US dollar, and that there is no alternative today to the market for US Treasury securities in terms of liquidity and depth. According to IMF data on the composition of allocated foreign exchange reserves, in mid-2019, 61.6 percent were held in US dollars and 20.5 percent in euro. The British pound and the Japanese yen are also used to a lesser extent, together with the Australian and Canadian dollars; as a group, these currencies represented 13.5 percent of allocated reserves.

Among emerging economies, the only one that is used to some extent is the Chinese renminbi, which has been increasing its role as a reserve currency, but represented only 2.0 percent of allocated reserves in mid-2019. This is despite the fact that China has adopted a policy of internationalization of the renminbi, which includes the creation of several swap arrangements, allowing some payments of Chinese exports to be made in that currency, and using Hong Kong and London as major centers for renminbi transactions. It is also despite the inclusion of the Chinese currency in the SDR basket in 2015.

The basic advantage of a multicurrency arrangement is, obviously, that it allows reserve holders to diversify the composition of their foreign exchange reserve assets, and thus to counteract the instability that characterizes all individual currencies under the current system—and particularly of the US dollar. But the benefits from reserve currency status would still be captured by industrial countries and gradually by China. It would not solve the recessionary bias of the current system, nor would it reduce emerging and developing countries' demand for self-insurance.

The second reform route would enhance the role of the only truly global reserve asset that the world has created: the SDRs. Under current rules, the IMF makes allocations of SDRs on the basis of a long-term need a global character, with the purpose of supplementing existing reserve assets. So far there have been three issues: the initial one, in 1970–72, for 9.3 billion SDRs; the second in 1979–81, for 12.1 billion; and a third in 2009 for 182.7 billion SDRs, which included 21.5 billion that had been approved in 1997 but had not been made effective, and a new allocation for 161.2 billion (equivalent to US$250 billion) approved by the G-20 and later by the IMF Board as part of the measures to manage the North Atlantic financial crisis.

The SDRs have represented only a small fraction of global reserves: 8.4 percent of non-gold reserves at its peak in 1972 and less than 3 percent in recent years. However, they are actively used by central banks from emerging and developing countries to pay other IMF members. As Figure 15.2 indicates, prior to the 2019 allocation, about 40 percent of allocations were used by the central banks. This proportion fell heavily with the 2009 allocation but has started to increase again

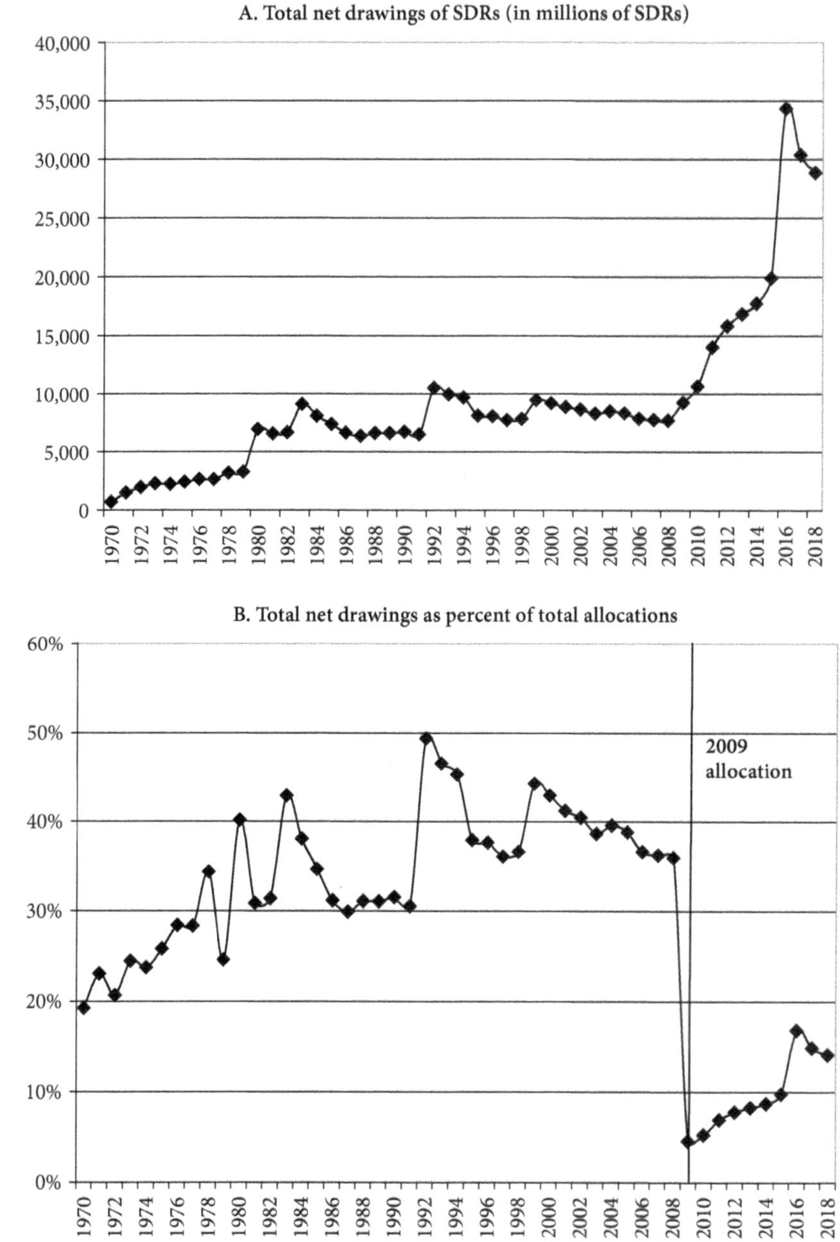

Figure 15.2 Total net drawings of SDRs (in volume and percentage)
Source: Author's estimates based on IMF data.

Table 15.1 SDR allocations by level of development (in millions of SDRs)

	Allocations (milion SDRs)			**Share in total allocations (%)**		
	1970–72	**1979–81**	**2009**	**1970–72**	**1979–81**	**2009**
High-income: OECD	6.796	7.906	108.879	73.6	65.8	59.6
United States	2.294	2.606	30.416	24.8	21.7	16.6
Japan	377	514	11.393	4.1	4.3	6.2
Others	4.125	4.786	67.070	44.7	39.8	36.7
High-income: non-OECD	17	127	3.588	0.2	1.1	2.0
Gulf countries	0	78	2.057	0.0	0.7	1.1
Excluding Gulf countries	17	49	1.531	0.2	0.4	0.8
Middle-income	1.488	2.730	54.173	16.1	22.7	29.6
China	0	237	6.753	0.0	2.0	3.7
Excluding China	1.488	2.493	47.420	16.1	20.7	26.0
Low- income	933	1.254	16.095	10.1	10.4	8.8
Total allocations	9.234	12.016	182.734	100.0	100.0	100.0

Source: Author's estimates based on IMF data and on World Bank classifications by level of development in 2000.

since then. Allocations are made according to IMF country quotas, and therefore they are much larger for high-income countries, though with a gradual decline through time (see Table 15.1). This has allowed the share of MICs to increase, while that of low-income countries has actually declined.

From the perspective of the global reserve system, a more active use of SDRs has four basic advantages. The first, and most important, would be the possibility of financing *all* IMF programs with SDRs, thus making global monetary creation similar to the way central banks create domestic money. This would follow the proposals made by the leading IMF economist Jacques Polak four decades ago (Polak, 1979). As we will see in section 15.4, this would help to consolidate the reforms of the IMF credit lines that have been introduced during the North Atlantic financial crisis, and improve the contingency facilities with the creation of a swap arrangement. It would also eliminate the dependence of IMF funding on "arrangements to borrow" and bilateral credit lines from member countries, which are not true multilateral instruments.

The best way to introduce this reform would be to treat the SDRs not used by countries as "deposits" in the IMF that could then be used by the institution to lend to countries in need. This would require, however, a change in the Articles of Agreement that created a division between the general resources and the SDR accounts, which is the basic constraint on their more active use. It would, of course, require the continuous commitment of all central banks to receiving SDRs as a means of payment, which is what gives them the character of global money.

The second advantage is the possibility of issuing SDRs during global financial crises as an instrument of international monetary policy, as was done in 2009. More broadly, SDRs could be issued more systematically, preferably in a counter-cyclical way, but guarantee at the same time that the supply of SDRs reflects the additional global demand for reserves. Most estimates indicate that average allocations for the equivalent of US$200–300 billion a year would be reasonable,[3] but even this size of allocation would only increase the share of SDRs in non-gold reserves to just over one-tenth in the 2020s, indicating that they would still largely complement other reserve assets.

The third advantage, which is particularly important for emerging and developing countries, is sharing in the seigniorage generated by issuing a global currency. It would also reduce their demand for self-insurance. Both advantages would be enhanced if there were an agreement to take into account factors additional to quota contributions to increase the share of these countries in SDR allocations—a "development link." One mechanism would be to include the demand for reserves as a criterion in SDR allocation, but a simpler solution, suggested by Williamson (2010), would be to allocate a certain proportion to emerging and developing countries (say around 80 percent), and then assigning the shares of the allocation among these countries according to IMF quotas.

The final advantage is that it would also make the international monetary system more independent of US monetary policy.

Some analysts have suggested that a reform along these lines would require an increasing demand for SDRs, which can only come from its transformation into an asset held by the private sector (Cooper, 2010; Eichengreen, 2008; Padoa-Schioppa, 2011). This could include using them to denominate private or government bonds, and as a unit of account in commercial transactions (eg, in commodity pricing). A virtual version of the SDRs could facilitate their use in private transactions, creating a global cryptocurrency that could circulate along national or regional cryptocurrencies backed by central banks. There could be intermediate solutions that would allow a partial private use of SDRs, such as allowing deposits by financial institutions in central banks (either reserve requirements or excess reserves) to be held in SDRs.

However, as the IMF staff pointed out in its report to the Board in 2018, even if "market SDRs" would be interesting, the major challenge is reinforcing the role of SDRs as a reserve asset (IMF, 2018), which could be so even if SDRs are managed mainly by central banks. The most desirable reform would involve, therefore, counter-cyclical *allocations* of SDRs that help fund counter-cyclical IMF *financing*. This would have significant advantages from the point of view of MICs.

[3] See a survey of different estimates in Erten and Ocampo (2013).

15.3 The Risks Generated by Capital Account Volatility

The IMF Articles of Agreement adopted at Bretton Woods included the commitment of countries to eventually eliminate foreign exchange regulations affecting current account transactions, but gave them full freedom to manage the capital account according to their domestic policy priorities. Following these principles, restrictions on current account transactions were dismantled—although at a rather slow pace—but capital account regulations (CARs) remained in place until relatively late.

The shift toward liberalizing capital flows started in the USA in the mid-1970s and spread to the rest of the developed world in the second half of the 1970s and was essentially completed by the early 1990s, as shown in Figure 15.3, based on the Chinn–Ito index of capital account liberalization (Chinn and Ito, 2008).[4] This coincided with an explosion of global finance, enhanced by the recycling of petrodollars after the 1973 oil shock, and was accompanied by a move toward flexible exchange rates. Capital account liberalization led, in turn, to new forms of intervention, notably swap arrangements among major developed-country central banks, and the creation of the Basel Committee on Banking Supervision in 1974 to harmonize banking regulation. As it became clear in due time, and notably during the North Atlantic crisis, financial regulation clearly lagged the explosion of global finance. One of the major reforms pushed by the G-20 after that crisis was the re-regulation of finance, coordinated by the Financial Stability Board—though with delays in implementation and backtracking in recent years, particularly by the USA.

Capital account liberalization came with a lag in the emerging and developing world. It was led by some Latin American countries in the 1970s, but experienced a reversal in the 1980s, in the face of that region's debt crisis (Figure 15.3). The liberalization process speeded up in the 1990s, led again by Latin America. Low MICs then caught up with their high middle-income partners. However, the diversity of capital account regimes in different countries meant that the average level of liberalization remained significantly below that of high-income countries. Liberalization remained limited in low-income countries. The East Asian and, more importantly, the North Atlantic crises represented new turning points, generating a stagnation and a moderate reversal of liberalization trends. Among MICs, Latin America continued to have more open account regimes than East and South Asia, the Middle East, and North Africa.

Capital account liberalization enhanced financial instability. The essential problem is that capital flows, like finance in general, are highly volatile, as underscored by the classic analyses of Kindleberger (see Kindleberger and Aliber, 2011) and Minsky (1982), and more recently by Reinhart and Rogoff (2009). Indeed,

[4] The index has a minimum value of –1.86 and a maximum value of 2.44.

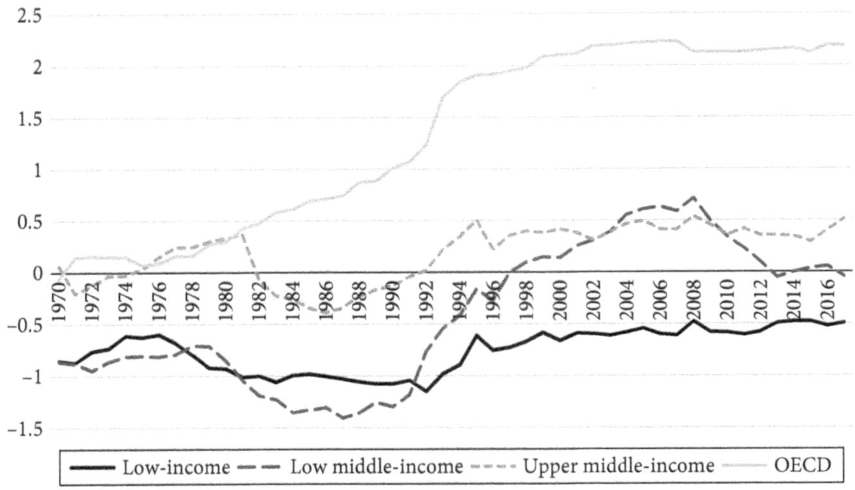

Figure 15.3 Chinn–Ito index of capital account liberalization
Source: http://web.pdx.edu/~ito/Chinn-Ito_website.htm

according to IMF (2011b: ch. 4), capital account volatility has increased over the past three decades and tends to be higher in MICs. An additional problem for these economies is that they lack the financial safety net provided by swap arrangements among central banks, which mainly benefit only developed countries.[5] What this implies is that the integration of emerging and developing countries into global financial markets is an integration into a market segmented by risk categories, in which high-risk borrowers are subject to strong procyclical swings and higher risk premiums.

The volatility of capital flows—and particularly of portfolio and debt flows—to emerging economies is shown in Figure 15.4. These countries have experienced four boom–bust cycles in external financing since the mid-1970s. The first boom took place in the second half of the 1970s, and was followed by a sharp downturn associated with the Latin American debt crisis of the 1980s. A new boom was experienced from 1991 to mid-1997, and was accompanied by a significant increase in foreign direct investment, which has remained since then as the largest and most stable form of financing. The boom in financial flows was temporarily interrupted by the Mexican crisis of December 1994, and finally ended with the series of crises in MICs that broke off in East Asia in 1997. The third boom was part of the broader global financial expansion of 2003–07 and ended up with the North American financial crisis. However, in contrast to the two previous

[5] The US Federal Reserve extended the swap credit lines to a few emerging economies (Brazil, Republic of Korea, Mexico, and Singapore) during the peak of the North Atlantic crisis, but only temporarily. There has also been a wave of swap arrangements among some emerging economies, with China as the major player.

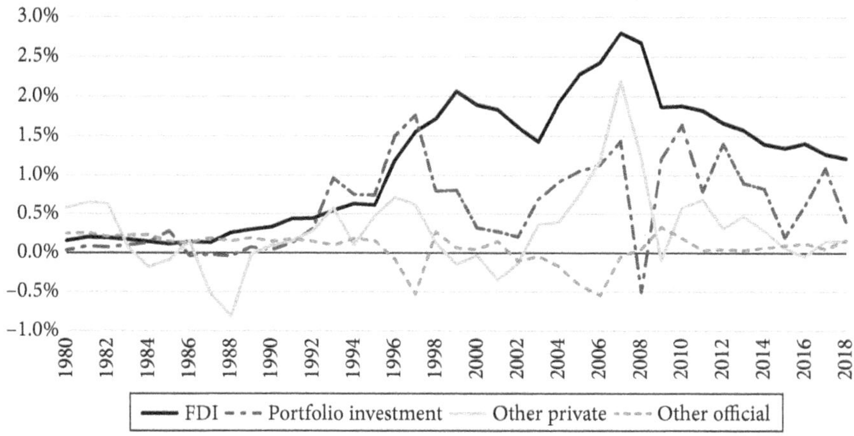

Figure 15.4 Capital flows towards emerging economies (% of GDP)
Source: Estimated from data from the Institute of Internatinal Finance.

downturns in financial flows to emerging countries, that of 2008–09 was much shorter, thanks to the strong expansion in global liquidity generated by developed countries' monetary policies, which generated, in turn, a fourth boom. There was a temporary reversal associated with changes in US monetary policies in 2013–14 and capital outflows from China in 2015 and early 2016, but the most important ones have been that of 2018–19, which generated strong shocks for some MICs, and the strong outflows of portfolio capital from emerging economies during the initial phase of the 2020 COVID-19 crisis.

These cycles have also been reflected in the evolution of the risk spreads and yields of emerging economies' bonds (Ocampo, 2017: fig. 4.3). They dramatically increased after the East Asian crisis, particularly after the Russian default of August 1998, but then rapidly declined during the 2003–07 boom. The increase in spreads during the North Atlantic crisis was also short and moderate, and was followed by a significant reduction after the crisis but also renewed volatility in 2018–20.

The heated intellectual battle over the effects of capital market liberalization in emerging and developing countries was for the most part settled by a major IMF study, published in 2003 (Prasad et al., 2003), that showed that it increases the frequency of crises and generates stronger business cycles in these economies. Procyclical capital flows have indeed been at the heart of many of the crises that these countries have experienced since the 1980s, as well as their propagation through contagion. In turn, financial crises are often followed by extended periods of slow economic growth, and may shift the growth trajectory, placing countries onto a lower GDP growth path when they start to recover.

A basic reason why these countries face these problems is that their domestic financial markets are significantly more incomplete and are plagued by variable mixes of maturity and currency mismatches in portfolios, and that their capital markets are small relative to the magnitude of the speculative pressures they face. These mismatches would cause less concern if there was an adequate development of futures markets. However, when those markets exist, they tend to have only short-term coverage and a strong procyclical performance.

Capital account volatility reduces in turn the space for counter-cyclical macroeconomic policies—a phenomenon that may be referred to as "balance of payments dominance" (Ocampo, 2016). During booms, counter-cyclical monetary policies tend to generate exchange rate appreciation, which may lead to unsustainable current account deficits; it may also lead to a deterioration in the competitiveness of tradable sectors that may have adverse effects on long-term growth. During crises, authorities may be forced to increase interest rates to avoid capital flight. If they avoid this and reduce interest rates, exchange rate depreciation may overshoot, risking a rise in domestic inflation and debt burdens for firms indebted in external markets.

Governments may also be forced to generate "credibility" during crises, which means procyclical fiscal austerity. But such policy generates economic *and* political economy pressures to also adopt equally procyclical policies during booms. This helps to explain why there is widespread evidence that fiscal accounts are highly procyclical in emerging and developing countries (Kaminsky et al., 2004). Therefore, in contrast to the notion that financial markets would have a disciplining effect, unstable external financing distorts the incentives that *all* domestic agents face throughout the business cycle, inducing procyclical behavior from both private agents and macroeconomic authorities.

Two ways to manage these procyclical pressures are the accumulation of foreign exchange reserves during booms that can be used to increase the policy space that authorities have during crises, and CARs to reduce capital flow volatility. As we saw in section 15.2, the volatility of finance and risk margins, together with the lack of adequate financial safety nets for emerging and developing countries, is what generates the need for self-insurance in the form of the large accumulation of foreign exchange reserves. However, this strategy is costly: from a country perspective, it involves accumulating an asset that has low yields (foreign exchange reserves) to compensate for private capital inflows which have higher yields/costs; if reserve accumulation is sterilized, central banks will also incur losses associated with the difference between interest receipts from the investments of reserves and the costs of the domestic instruments used for sterilization purposes.

In turn, CARs play a dual role: as a financial stability tool, and a macroeconomic policy tool. As a financial stability tool, they reduce the risk of over-indebtedness during booms, and recognize the fact that procyclical behavior and, particularly, reversibility varies significantly according to the nature of capital flows, with debt portfolio flows and short-term bank lending being particularly volatile. As a macroeconomic policy tool, they increase the space to undertake contractionary monetary policies during booms while avoiding the additional exchange rate appreciation pressures, and they can create some room for expansionary monetary policies during crises while containing capital flight and excessive exchange rate depreciation.

As Figure 15.3 indicates, major disturbances in global financial markets has generated a more skeptical view of capital account liberalization and a partial return to more intensive capital account management in several emerging and developing countries. The most frequently used are regulations on the domestic use of foreign exchange, followed by capital outflow and capital inflow restrictions, with discrimination between residents and non-residents being less common (Erten and Ocampo, 2017).

The existing literature indicates that regulations on capital inflows tend to improve their composition towards less volatile flows, and increase monetary independence, particularly the capacity to adopt contractionary monetary policies during booms without strong effects on exchange rates. In contrast, there have been more debates on their capacity to reduce the magnitude of capital inflows, and exchange rate effects are generally found to be temporary. However, when these two effects are analyzed as two dimensions of "foreign exchange pressures," CAR regulations are found to significantly reduce those pressures (Erten and Ocampo, 2017). Ostry et al. (2012) and Erten and Ocampo (2017) have also found that they reduce the recessionary effects of crises in emerging economies as well as overheating during the recovery, indicating that they have counter-cyclical effects on economic activity.

One of the most interesting global policy developments in recent years has been the renewed views on the positive role that CARs can have in the international system. This represents, in a sense, a partial return to the original Bretton Woods agreements, and stands in sharp contrast to the 1997 proposal by the IMF to include the commitment to capital account convertibility in the Articles of Agreement—a proposal that was, in any case, defeated.[6] During its 2011 Summit, the G-20 adopted a set of "coherent conclusions for the management of capital flows" (G-20, 2011), but the most important multilateral effort to rethink the role of these regulations was that undertaken by the IMF in 2011 and 2012, proposing first what it called first a "possible policy framework" (IMF, 2011a) and later an "institutional view" (IMF, 2012b). This exercise was backed by significant research by IMF staff (see, in particular, Ostry et al., 2012, and Gosh et al., 2017).

The institutional view recognized that "There is no presumption that full liberalization of capital flows is an appropriate goal for all countries at all times," and that liberalization "needs to be planned, timed and sequenced." It reinforced the view that regulations on inflows can be useful in managing the risks associated with volatile flows, but underscored that such regulations should be "targeted,

[6] A very useful review of debates in recent year is provided by Gallagher (2014).

transparent, and generally temporary." It also agreed that regulations on outflows can be useful in crisis conditions, but again should be temporary. Finally, it pointed out that regulations should avoid discrimination based on residence.

It argued, however, that "capital flow management measures"—the term the IMF used—should be employed only after other macroeconomic and domestic macro-prudential regulations have been put in place—that is, as a sort of "intervention of last resort."[7] A more ambitious policy framework should thus recognize that CARs could—and even should—be used on a permanent basis as an integral component of a counter-cyclical macroeconomic policy package, preferably based on permanent regulations that are strengthened or weakened in a counter-cyclical way. Furthermore, CAR regulations should be seen as part of a continuum of macroprudential regulations that include strictly domestic regulations (those that affect domestic assets and liabilities in the domestic currency); those that relate to the use of assets and liabilities denominated in foreign currencies in the domestic financial system; and those that regulate cross-border capital flows as such. This also implies that there should be no presumption on preference of regulation on inflows vs. outflows, or between price-based vs. quantity-based regulations; that it may be difficult to avoid discriminating between residents and non-residents; and that regulations should be modified dynamically to avoid their elusion.

Importantly, the institutional view also recognized that its own recommendations and the freedom that countries have to adopt capital account regulations under its Article of Agreements may be at odds with other international commitments, in particular trade and investment treaties that restrict the ability to regulate cross-border finance. It thus recommended that such provisions should be revised to make them consistent with the IMF's institutional view and its Articles of Agreement, and that source countries should "better internalize the spillovers from their monetary and prudential policies." It argued that the institutional view should "foster a more consistent approach to the design of policy space for CFMs under bilateral and regional agreements," including OECD rules and free trade agreements, but did not make specific proposals on how to proceed in this area.

15.4 The International Policy Instruments

15.4.1 Balance of Payments Financing

A support that MICs receive from the system is IMF financing during balance of payments crises; as I will point out at the end of this section, a few countries also benefit from regional arrangements.

Responding to the increasing importance of crises associated with the capital account, the size of IMF loans relative to the quota of individual members has

[7] This perspective was, nonetheless, more nuanced in the 2012 than in the 2011 proposal.

been increasing since the 1960s. The nature of the facilities has also changed, with the ambitious reforms adopted in 2009 as a response to the North Atlantic crisis (IMF, 2009a).[8] They have been adjusted later on to improve their novel features. The design of new credit facilities has been accompanied by debates about IMF conditionality, which were particularly heated after the crisis of emerging economies of the late twentieth century.

The 2009 reforms included the adoption of preventive or precautionary financing facilities to mitigate and hopefully avoid the contagion effects of crises. The most important is the Flexible Credit Line (FCL), which is aimed at countries with "solid fundamentals" but at risk of facing capital account problems associated with contagion, and it lacks ex-ante conditionality. Although three MICs rapidly used this credit line (Colombia, Mexico, and Poland), the fact that it has not been used by others could indicate that it is not sufficiently attractive. Its terms were improved in August 2010, when the scale of the resources was increased and the period for which it can be used was extended.

The reforms aimed at a broader set of members included the doubling of the size of other credit lines, the possibility of using the standby agreements for preventive purposes (the so-called "high-access precautionary arrangements"), and the creation in 2010 of the new Precautionary Credit Line (PCL), for countries which the IMF deems to have good policies but which do not meet the criteria of the FCL; this facility was later transformed into the Precautionary and Liquidity Line, to allow countries to use it to obtain funds of rapid disbursement for six months.

As Figure 15.5 indicates, Fund lending has clearly met its counter-cyclical objective throughout its history. It did so again during the North Atlantic crisis, but the scale of lending relative to world GDP was lower than during the Latin American debt crisis and the crises of emerging economies of the late twentieth and early twenty-first centuries. A novelty was the fact that, for the first time since the 1970s, the IMF included high-income (European) countries among its borrowers. In contrast, the demand for IMF facilities from MICs was much lower than in the past. It included preventive credit lines, that are not included in Figure 15.5 because they have not been disbursed. There has been a recent increase in the use of IMF facilities, with the 2018 Argentinean loan being the most important case.

However, these reforms have been insufficient in two ways. The first is that the resources available for IMF lending have lagged behind other global aggregates over the past three decades. This is true relative to world GDP, but even more so in relation to world trade and any financial aggregate. This is despite the fact that there has been a demand for the IMF to be more active as a source of emergency

[8] There was also a major reform of special facilities for low-income countries, but this issue will not be analyzed in this chapter.

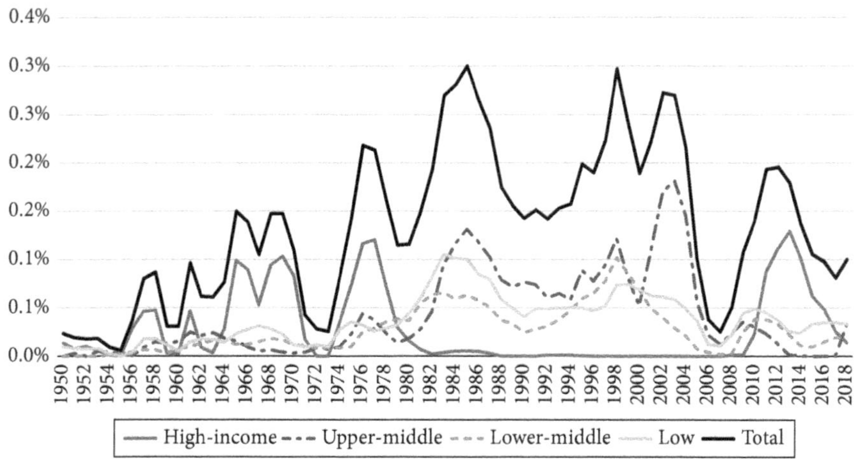

Figure 15.5 IMF lending by country categories relative to world GDP

Source: Author's estimates based on IMF data and on World Bank classifications by level of development in 2000.

financing to manage capital account shocks. Hence the importance of quota increases, but even more, as argued in section 15.3, of using SDRs as a source of resources for IMF lending. The second is the need to continue making progress in designing financing facilities that are automatic and have simpler prequalification processes. The best would be a credit facility similar to central banks' swap arrangements. This was behind the proposal by the IMF staff to create a short-term liquidity swap (IMF, 2017)—though it was not approved by the IMF Board—as well as the view of the G-20 Eminent Persons Group (2018).

Debates on IMF conditionality are as old as the Fund but their focus has changed thought time. The low-conditionality compensatory financing facility created in the 1960s and 1970s to manage exogenous external shocks essentially ceased to be used in the 1980s. In contract, the extension of conditionality beyond the strict macroeconomic realm, to include structural adjustment, became a strongly controversial issue in that decade and in the 1990s. The attack on structural adjustment features of IMF conditionality came to the forefront after the East Asian crisis.[9] The criticism had to do with the fact that they were rigid and uniform, and reflected orthodox views on economic reforms, and were excessively intrusive on domestic decision-making processes, and therefore violated the principle of "ownership" of policies by countries.

The new guidelines on conditionality approved in 2002 (IMF, 2002) introduced three basic principles: (i) member countries' ownership of policies; (ii) the

[9] The best-known criticism of IMF conditionality during the East Asian crisis is that of Stiglitz (2002).

requirement that structural conditions should be "macro-relevant" and ought to focus on the core competencies of the Fund (monetary, fiscal, and exchange rate policies, as well as financial system issues); and (iii) the need to streamline conditionality, to include only conditions that must be critical to achieve the program goals. As different evaluations indicate, this reform was effective in reducing the volume of structural conditionality and focusing it on the macro-relevant areas that are the competence of the Fund.[10] Additional reforms were introduced in March 2009, which eliminated structural performance criteria for all programs—and thus the relationship between IMF disbursements and structural conditionality—and ex-ante conditionality for the FCL.

The counter-cyclical role of IMF lending has been complemented by regional mechanisms, but this mechanism has benefited only a small number of countries. An old, small but well-functioning one is the Latin American Reserve Fund (FLAR, according to its Spanish acronym), in which eight countries participate, and which could be expanded to have broader regional coverage. The European Union mechanisms, notably the European Stability Mechanism for Eurozone members inaugurated in October 2012, has also been important, although controversial in terms of conditionality. The 2000 Chiang Mai Initiative of ASEAN + 3 (China, Japan, and the Republic of Korea) has also been important, but it has not yet been used, because access to its swap facilities beyond a certain limit (30 percent) requires an IMF program, a condition that East Asian countries regard as a stigma. It is paradoxical that the same rule has was adopted by the BRICS Contingency Arrangements when launched in 2015.

15.4.2 Sovereign Debt Workout Mechanisms

The second element of a well-structured international crisis response architecture is a system to manage debt overhangs. This is essential to avoid excessively contractionary adjustment policies during crises, and to facilitate the reentry of countries into capital markets after debt crises. This is, however, an area where international cooperation is not well developed. The only regular mechanism of this type in place is the Paris Club, which deals exclusively with official creditors. This is mixed with voluntary renegotiations with private creditors and ad hoc debt relief initiatives—the Brady Plan after the Latin American debt crises, the Highly Indebted Poor Countries Initiative (HIPCI), and its successor, the

[10] See, in particular, the 2008 evaluation of structural conditionality by the IMF's Independent Evaluation Office (IMF-IEO, 2008a), which showed advances in relation to middle-income but not to low-income countries. See also the 2011 evaluation by the Fund (IMF, 2012a) of the advance in the application of the 2009 decision on structural performance criteria and focus on core Fund competencies.

Multilateral Debt Relief Initiative (MDRI). The problem with this patchy "non-system" is that debt restructuring generally (or even always) comes too late, after over-indebtedness has had devastating effects on countries and thus on their capacity to service debts (IMF, 2014).

The lack of a multilateral framework for dealing with international debt crises involving private creditors has been a major concern for a long time. Initiatives in this area in recent decades have followed two different approaches, which are referred to as "contractual" and "statutory." The major attempt to introduce a statutory regime was the 2001–03 IMF proposals for a Sovereign Debt Restructuring Mechanism (SDRM). It failed, but led to changes in the contractual approach, in particular the spread of collective action clauses in debt contracts issued in the US market—a mechanism that was already being used in the UK. In recent years, particularly after the difficulties faced by Argentina in US courts in 2013 with its 2005 and 2010 debt restructuring, there was an additional change in the contractual approach: the agreement in 2014 by the IMF Board (IMF, 2014) to include aggregation clauses in bond issues and a new pari-passu clause, that avoids the problems of interpretation of old clauses that were subject to the judicial decisions against Argentina in the US courts, in favor of bondholders that did not participate in the debt restructurings. This decision was also backed by the major relevant private organization, the International Capital Markets Association. Eurozone bonds have also required aggregation clauses since 2013. The UN also adopted in 2015 basic principles on sovereign debt restructuring (United Nations, 2015).

What this implies is that the contractual approach and voluntary negotiations of individual countries' debt overhangs with private creditors has dominated debt restructurings. A problem with this market-oriented approach is that incentives remain in place for both debtor countries and creditors to delay restructurings. Credit default swaps may further reduce the incentive to participate in debt renegotiations and introduce a new set of actors into the process. Also, aggregation clauses do not exclude the possibility of blocking majorities in individual issues, and do not include other credits aside from bonds, particularly syndicated bank lending. Additional complications are associated with the increasing participation of international funds in the domestic debt markets of emerging economies, which has reduced the importance of the traditional division between external and internal debt, as well as the rise of the official lenders that are not members of the Paris Club (notably China).

A statutory framework is, therefore, needed, and could play a positive role in the face of the most recent tendency of emerging and developing countries' debt ratios to rise. It should operate on the basis of two basic principles: comprehensive debt restructurings, and the impartiality of the mediation and arbitration processes. The best alternative, in my view, would be to create a mechanism similar to the World Trade Organization's (WTO) dispute settlement,[11] in which there is a sequence of voluntary negotiations, mediation, and eventual arbitration with pre-established deadlines (Ocampo, 2017: ch. 5). The process could include, aside from bondholders, other creditors, including official ones. The mechanism could be created as an independent body under the UN system, but also as a system of independent mediation and arbitration in the framework of the IMF. This mechanism would be complemented with an international debt registry and a multi-stakeholder Sovereign Debt Forum, which could be organized under the umbrella of the UN Financing for Development process.

15.5 MICs and the Governance of the System

According to the analysis in the previous sections, the interests of MICs in the international monetary system relate to the design of a system that makes stronger use of SDRs, gives countries the policy space to manage capital account volatility, improves the balance of payments credit lines with more preventive tools—a global swap arrangement, in particular—and creates appropriate international mechanisms to manage debt restructuring.

Substantive reforms along these lines must be matched by the design of appropriate governance structures. There are, in this regard, three interrelated issues. The first one is the design of the apex organization of the international monetary system. The second is the design of a multi-layered architecture, with active participation of regional and sub-regional institutions. The third is the reform of "voice and participation" of emerging and developing countries in the IMF.[12]

In the first area, the major issue is the role that the G-7 and the G-20 play in international economic governance. This preference for "Gs" over representative international institutions reflects the historically revealed preference of major industrial countries for institutional mechanisms over which they can exercise direct influence, a view that some MICs that are members of the G-20 may have come to share. The basic issue is, of course, the tension between representativeness and the legitimacy associated with it, on the one hand, and power structures, on the other. Independently of the positive role that the G-20 has played in

[11] The WTO mechanism is now unfortunately discontinued, due to the refusal of the USA to agree on the nomination of Appellate Body members, which implies that that Body has less than the minimal number of members to operate since December 2019.

[12] There are other issues of governance that have been suggested by the 2009 Commission for IMF Governance Reform (IMF, 2009b) that I will not discuss here. They include the creation of a Council of Ministers envisioned by the Articles of Agreement, with effective powers to adopt the most important political decisions, thus replacing the International Monetary and Financial Committee; a clear redefinition of the relations between this Council, the Board, and Management, including reorienting the Board toward formulating strategy and monitoring policy implementation rather than the executive day-to-day functions it now exercises.

certain areas since the North Atlantic financial crisis—particularly in avoiding another Great Depression, and in strengthening global financial regulation and international cooperation in tax matters—it should be transformed into a more representative mechanism of international economic cooperation. In this regard, the best proposal on the table is that of the UN Commission of Experts on Reforms of the International Monetary and Financial System (United Nations 2009: ch. 4) to create a Global Economic Coordination Council in the framework of the UN *system*, to which the Bretton Woods Institutions (BWIs) belong, and formed on the basis of constituencies elected through weighted votes—although correcting, of course, for the problems of representation that these organizations face today, to which I will refer below. A similar proposal has been made by the Palais Royal Initiative (2011), but centered on designing an apex organization for the international monetary system.

The second governance issue is the need to develop a *dense* multi-layered global financial safety net that relies more broadly on regional and interregional institutions. Indeed, in a heterogeneous international community, the creation of *networks* of global, regional, and national institutions can provide a better system of governance than arrangements based on single global organizations. What this means is that the IMF of the future should be conceived as the apex of a *network* of regional and interregional reserve funds (Ocampo, 2006). A system such as this would be closer in design to that of the multilateral development banks, where the World Bank coexists with several regional development banks and, in some parts of the world, with several sub-regional institutions, and some interregional banks (the Islamic Development Bank and now the New Development Bank).[13] The great regional gaps that characterize the international monetary system indicate that the creation of regional monetary arrangements should be actively promoted.

The best arguments in favor of regional institutions is of a political economy character: the strong sense of ownership of these institutions by member countries. Given the incomplete nature of the existing international monetary system, these regional arrangements can also contribute in many ways to fill the gaps of the existing architecture.[14] This could include a stronger dialog on macroeconomic and financial policies, and possible monitoring and coordination of these policies. They can take different forms: payments agreements, reserve pools, emergency lending facilities, as well as swap arrangements. They can also have different degrees of multilateralization. As I have indicated, FLAR, the Chiang Mai Initiative, and the European Stability Mechanism are the three main regional frameworks in place, together with the interregional BRICS Contingency Reserve Arrangement.

[13] See, in this regard, the contributions to Ocampo (2006).

[14] See in this regard G-20 Eminent Persons Group (2018), Grabel (2017, ch. 6), McKay et al. (2011), and Ocampo (2017, ch. 6).

In relation to the third issue, the strongest statement was made by the United Nations Conference on Financing for Development that took place in Monterrey in 2002, which underscored "the need to broaden and strengthen the participation of developing countries and countries with economies in transition in international economic decision-making and norm-setting" (United Nations, 2002: para. 62). The large potential beneficiaries of such reform would be the large MICs. However, reforms have been moderate. According to the IMF's Independent Evaluation Office, the issue of emerging and developing countries' voice continues to be a major gap in the IMF, in contrast to advances in accountability over the past decade, and its traditional efficiency in terms of crisis response (IMF-IEO, 2018).[15]

In 2006 and 2008, modest agreements were adopted, which included a redistribution of the quotas and a tripling of the basic votes—those that are equally allocated to all countries, independently of their size. In 2010 a more ambitious reform was adopted, which included the doubling of quotas, a revision in the way quotas and voting power was allocated, the reduction by two of European representatives on the IMF Board, and the decision that all of its members should be elected. As Table 15.2 indicates, relative to the pre-2006 situation, the increase in the quotas (3.9 percentage points) and voting power (5.3 points) of emerging and developing countries was short of what is required. In particular, although the quota and voting power of European countries was reduced, its over-representation continued to be a fundamental problem, as is the under-representation of some

Table 15.2 Redistribution of IMF quota and votes: 2010 vs. pre-2006

	Quota (%)			Votes (%)		
	Pre-2006	**2010**	**Change**	**Pre-2006**	**2010**	**Change**
Developed countries	61.6	57.7	−3.9	60.6	55.3	-5.3
United States	17.4	17.4	0.0	17.0	16.5	-0.5
European G-10 1/	26.7	22.5	−4.2	26.3	21.5	−4.8
Other	17.5	17.8	0.3	17.3	17.3	0.0
Emerging and developing countries	38.4	42.3	3.9	39.4	44.7	5.3
China	3.0	6.4	3.4	2.9	6.1	3.1
Other winners 2/	5.8	9.7	3.9	5.7	9.3	3.6
Rest	29.6	26.2	−3.4	30.7	29.3	−1.4

Notes: 1. Belgium, France, Germany, Italy, Netherlands, Sweden, Switzerland, and the UK.
2. Brazil, India, Mexico, Turkey, and Republic of Korea.
Source: Author's estimates based on IMF data.

[15] See also the IEO's initial analysis on governance (IMF-IEO, 2008b).

emerging (particularly Asian) economies relative to their actual share in the world economy. Furthermore, the large gains by some large MICs came partly at the expense of other emerging and developing countries. So, it could only be understood as a first step of a longer-term process.

The capacity of US Congress to block this reform for five years—as it approved it only in 2015—was also a major problem, and should be a concern of the international community in the future. Even more problematic was the blocking by the USA in 2019 of a further reform, which would now have to be discussed only in the 16th General Review of Quotas, the term of which can extend until 2023. No decision has been adopted, either, to change the formula to estimate quotas, which favor small European countries.[16] The only positive step that should be formalized in 2020 is the decision to maintain the total IMF resources, though using arrangements to borrow and bilateral credit lines, which are not multilateral mechanisms. Furthermore, no steps were taken in either 2010 or recently to reduce the threshold of votes needed to approve important IMF reforms from the current 85 percent to, for example, 70–75 percent, to eliminate the veto power of the USA.

A crucial, additional reform, is guaranteeing a transparent and open process to select the heads of the BWIs based on the merit of the candidates, and *regardless of nationality*. Although the G-20 formally endorsed in 2009 the principle that the heads of all international institutions "should be appointed through an open, transparent and merit-based process" (G-20, 2009: par. 21), the election of the IMF Managing Director in 2011 and the World Bank President in 2012, their later reelections, and the election of the heads of both BWIs in 2019 continued to be effectively closed processes. So, there is a clear need to launch open processes that break with the tradition according to which the IMF is headed by a Western European and the World Bank by a US citizen.

15.6 Acknowledgment

This chapter borrows from my book on the international monetary system (Ocampo, 2017), particularly chapter 7. It updates that chapter based on the most recent debates and processes.

References

Chinn, Menzie D. and Ito, Hiro (2008): "A New Measure of Financial Openness," *Journal of Comparative Policy Analysis* 10, no. 3: 309–22.

Cooper, Richard (2010): "Does the SDRs Have a Future", available at: http://scholar.harvard.edu/cooper/publications/does-sdr-have-future

[16] The controversies relate in particular to the use of economic variability and openness indexes.

Eichengreen, Barry (2008): *Globalizing Capital: A History of the International Monetary System*, 2nd edition. Princeton, NJ: Princeton University Press.

Erten, Bilge and Ocampo, José Antonio (2013): "Building a Stable and Equitable Global Monetary Sytstem", in José Antonio Alonso, Giovanni Andrea Cornia, and Rob Vos (eds.), *Alternative Development Strategies for the Post/2015 Era*, New York: Bloomsbury, chapter 9.

Erten, Bilge and José Antonio Ocampo (2017): "Macroeconomic effects of capital account regulations", *IMF Economic Review* 65, no. 2.

G-20 (2009): "Leaders' Statement, The Pittsburgh Summit," September 24–25.

G-20 (Group of 20) (2011): "G-20 Coherent Conclusions for the Management of Capital Flows Drawing on Country Experiences", November 3–4, available at: http://www.g20.org/

G-20 Eminent Person Group on Global Financial Governance (2018): "Making the Global Financial System Work for All," October.

Gallagher, Kevin (2014): *Ruling Capital: Emerging Markets and the Reregulation of Cross-Border Finance*, Ithaca, NY: Cornell University Press.

Ghosh, Atish R., Ostry, Jonathan D., and Qureshi, Mahvash S. (2017): *Taming the Tide of Capital Flows: A Policy Guide*, Cambridge, MA: MIT Press.

Grabel, Ilene (2017): *When Things Fall Apart: Global Financial Governance and Development Finance in an Age of Productive Incoherence*, Cambridge, MA: MIT Press.

IMF (International Monetary Fund) (2002): "Guidelines on conditionality", September 25, International Monetary Fund.

IMF (2009a): "IMF implements major lending policy improvements", March 24, International Monetary Fund.

IMF (2009b): "Committee on IMF Governance Reform: Final Report," March 24, available at: http://www.imf.org/external/np/omd/2009/govref/032409.pdf International Monetary Fund.

IMF (2011a): "Recent experiences in managing capital inflows: crosscutting themes and possible policy framework", February 14, International Monetary Fund.

IMF (2011b): *World Economic Outlook*, April, International Monetary Fund.

IMF (2012a): "2011 review of conditionality. background paper 1: content and application of conditionality", June 18, International Monetary Fund.

IMF (2012b): "The liberalization and management of capital flows: an institutional view," November 14, International Monetary Fund.

IMF (2014): "Strengthening of the contractual framework to address collective action problems in sovereign debt restructurings", September 2. International Monetary Fund.

IMF (2017): "Adequacy of the global financial safety net—considerations for fund toolkit reform", IMF Policy Paper, December. International Monetary Fund.

IMF (2018): "Considerations on the role of the SDR", March 7, International Monetary Fund.

IMF-IEO (Independent Evaluation Office) (2008a): "An IEO evaluation of structural conditionality in IMF-Supported programs," International Monetary Fund.

IMF-IEO (2008b): *Governance of the IMF: An Evaluation*, Evaluation Report, Washington, DC: International Monetary Fund.

IMF-IEO (2018): *Governance of the IMF: Evaluation Update*, Washington, DC: International Monetary Fund.

Kaminsky, Graciela L., Reinhart, Carmen M., and Végh, Carlos A. (2004): "When it rains, it pours: pro-cyclical capital flows and macroeconomic policies". NBER Working Paper No. 10780, September, Cambridge, MA: National Bureau for Economic Research.

Kindleberger, Charles P. and Aliber, Robert (2011): *Manias, Panics, and Crashes: A History of Financial Crises*, 6th edition, Houndmills: Palgrave Macmillan.

Minsky, Hyman P. (1982): *Can "It" Happen Again?: Essays on Instability and Finance*. Armonk, NY: M.E. Sharpe.

Ocampo, José Antonio (ed.) (2006): *Regional Financial Cooperation*, Washington, DC: Brookings Institution Press and ECLAC.

Ocampo, José Antonio (2016): "Balance-of-payments dominance: implications for macroeconomic policy, in Mario Damill, Martin Rapetti, and Guillermo Rozenwurcel (eds.), *Macroeconomics and Development: Roberto Frenkel and the Economies of Latin America*, New York: Columbia University Press, chapter 10.

Ocampo, José Antonio (2017): *Resetting the International Monetary (Non) System*, Oxford and Helsinki: Oxford University Press.

Ostry, Jonathan D., Ghosh, Atish R., Chamon, Marcos, and Qureshi, Mahvash S. (2012): "Tools for managing financial-stability risks from capital inflows," *Journal of International Economics*, 88, no. 2: 407–21.

Padoa-Schioppa, Tomasso (2011): "The Ghost of Bancor: The economic crisis and global monetary disorder", in Jack T. Boorman and André Icard (eds.), *Reform of the International Monetary System: The Palais Royal Initiative*, New Delhi: SAGE Publications, chapter 6.

Palais Royal Initiative (2011): "Reform of the international monetary system: a cooperative approach for the 21st century," in Jack T. Boorman and André Icard (eds.), *Reform of the International Monetary System: The Palais Royal Initiative*, New Delhi: Sage Publications, chapter 2, pp. 7–26.

Polak, Jacques J. (1979): "Thoughts on an International Monetary Fund based fully on SDR", Pamphlet Series No. 28, Washington, DC: International Monetary Fund.

Prasad, Eswar S., Rogoff, Kenneth, Wei, Shang-Jin, and Rose, M. Ayhan (2003): "Effects of financial globalization on developing countries: some empirical evidence," IMF Occasional Paper, No. 220. Washington, DC: International Monetary Fund.

Reinhart, Carmen, and Rogoff, Kenneth (2009): *This Time is Different: Eight Centuries of Financial Folly*, Princeton, NJ: Princeton University Press.

Stiglitz, Joseph E. (2002): *Globalization and Its Discontents*, New York: W.W. Norton and Company.

Triffin, Robert (1961): *Gold and the Dollar Crisis* (revised edition), New Haven, CT: Yale University Press.

Triffin, Robert (1968): *Our International Monetary System: Yesterday, Today and Tomorrow*, New York: Random House.

United Nations (2002): *The Monterrey Consensus*, International Conference on Financing for Development, Monterrey, Mexico, March.

United Nations (2009): *Report of the Commission of Experts convened of the President of the UN General Assembly on Reforms of the International Monetary and Financial System* (Stiglitz Commission), New York: United Nations, , September. Available at: http://www.un.org/ga/econcrisissummit/docs/FinalReport_CoE.pdf

United Nations (2015): "Basic Principles on Sovereign Debt Restructuring", Resolution adopted by the General Assembly, A/RES/69/319, September 29.

Williamson, John (2010): "The future of the reserve system", *Journal of Globalization and Development* 1, no. o, Article 15.

Index

Note: Figures and Tables are indicated by an italic '*f*' and '*t*' respectively, following the page number.

For the benefit of digital users, indexed terms that span two pages (e.g., 52–53) may, on occasion, appear on only one of those pages.